☀ INSIGHT GUIDES

SOUTH EAST ASIA

DISCOVERY CHANNEL

APA PUBLICATIONS
Part of the Langenscheidt Publishing Group   L

INSIGHT GUIDE
SOUTHEAST asia

Editorial
Project Editor
Heidi Sopinka
Managing Editor
Scott Rutherford
Editorial Director
Brian Bell

Distribution
UK & Ireland
GeoCenter International Ltd
The Viables Centre, Harrow Way
Basingstoke, Hampshire RG22 4BJ
Fax: (44 1256) 817 988

United States
Langenscheidt Publishers, Inc.
46–35 54th Road, Maspeth, NY 11378
Fax: (1 718) 784 0640

Canada
Thomas Allen & Son Ltd
390 Steelcase Road East
Markham, Ontario L3R 1G2
Fax: (1 905) 475 6747

Australia
Universal Publishers
1 Waterloo Road
Macquarie Park, NSW 2113
Fax: (61 2) 9888 9074

New Zealand
Hema Maps New Zealand Ltd (HNZ)
Unit D, 24 Ra ORA Drive
East Tamaki, Auckland
Fax: (64 9) 273 6479

Worldwide
**Apa Publications GmbH & Co.
Verlag KG (Singapore branch)**
38 Joo Koon Road, Singapore 628990
Tel: (65) 6865 1600. Fax: (65) 6861 6438

Printing
Insight Print Services (Pte) Ltd
38 Joo Koon Road, Singapore 628990
Tel: (65) 6865 1600. Fax: (65) 6861 6438

©2004 Apa Publications GmbH & Co.
Verlag KG (Singapore branch)
All Rights Reserved
First Edition 1995
Second Edition 1999
Updated 2003 (Reprinted 2004)

CONTACTING THE EDITORS
We would appreciate it if readers
would alert us to errors or outdated
information by writing to:
**Insight Guides, P.O. Box 7910,
London SE1 1WE, England.
Fax: (44 20) 7403 0290.**
insight@apaguide.co.uk

www.insightguides.com

ABOUT THIS BOOK

This guidebook combines the interests and enthusiasms of two of the world's best-known information providers: Insight Guides, whose titles have set the standard for visual travel guides since 1970, and the Discovery Channel, the world's premier source of non-fiction television programming.

The editors of Insight Guides provide both practical advice and general understanding regarding a place's history, institutions, culture and people. Discovery Channel and its website, www.discovery.com, help millions of viewers explore the world from the comfort of their own homes and also encourage them to explore it first-hand.

In this, the second edition of *Insight Guide: Southeast Asia,* we journey to an eclectic and challenging gathering of nations and cultures: Thailand, Burma, Laos, Cambodia, Vietnam, the Philippines, Malaysia, Singapore, Indonesia and tiny Brunei. Assembling an overview of Southeast Asia was a formidable task. Fortunately, we had one great advantage: Insight Guides for each nation from which to extract insight on the many cultures, peoples and places. Our writers and photographers will help reveal it all.

◆ The Features section, with a yellow colour bar, covers the country's history and culture in lively authoritative essays written by specialists.

◆ The Places section, with a blue bar, provides full details of all the sights and areas worth seeing. The chief places of interest are coordinated by number with specially drawn maps.

◆ The Travel Tips listings section, with an orange bar and at the back of the book, offers a point of reference for information on restaurants, accommodation, travel, and all other practical aspects. Information is located quickly using the index printed on the back-cover flap, which also serves as a handy bookmark.

The contributors

This latest edition of *Insight Guide: Southeast Asia* was supervised by managing editor **Scott Rutherford**. Enlisted to distil down each existing Insight Guide for this book was Canadian **Heidi Sopinka**, an editor and writer who, when one is handy, flies helicopters. Contributing new essays for this edition were writers from Chiang Mai-based CPA, supervised by **Andrew Forbes**, and **Jim Michener**, in Vientiane.

The *Insight On* pictorial essays were researched and written by **Clare Griffiths**, an editor in Apa's London office. Sourcing the photos for the essays was the task of **Hilary Genin**, also in the London office.

European impression of Ayutthaya in the 1600s.

How to use this book

Insight Guides' proven format of informative and well-written text paired with exciting and evocative photography continues throughout this edition of *Insight Guide: Southeast Asia*. The guide is structured to convey a complete understanding of the many countries and their cultures, and to guide readers through the wide-ranging and diverse region's sights and activities.

Map Legend

—‥—	International Boundary
—‥—	National Park/Reserve
– – – –	Ferry Route
✈ ✈	Airport: International/Regional
🚌	Bus Station
P	Parking
❶	Tourist Information
✉	Post Office
✝ † ✝	Church/Ruins
†	Monastery
☾	Mosque
✡	Synagogue
🏰 🏛	Castle/Ruins
∴	Archaeological Site
∩	Cave
🗿	Statue/Monument
★	Place of Interest

The main places of interest in the **Places** chapters are coordinated by number with a full-colour map (e.g. ❶), and a symbol at the top of every right-hand page tells you where to find the map.

INSIGHT GUIDE
SOUTHEAST asia

CONTENTS

Rain forest,
Sabah, Malaysia

Travel Tips

Insight on ...

Information panels

Malaysia

Brunei

Singapore

Indonesia

Philippines

SOUTHEAST ASIA

One would be challenged to find a region with a more eclectic mix of people, culture, languages, history and lifestyles

It is not without some coincidence that the nations covered in this Insight Guide – Thailand, Burma, Vietnam, Laos, Cambodia, Malaysia, Philippines, Singapore, Indonesia and Brunei – are members of ASEAN, the Association of Southeast Asian Nations. Since its 1967 founding by Indonesia, Malaysia, Thailand, Singapore and the Philippines, ASEAN has had its ups and downs as the region's countries try to build a common identity and purpose, an admirable but impossible dream.

The withdrawal of the Western colonial powers from Southeast Asia following World War II left a power vacuum. It was clear to Southeast Asia's emerging cadre of leaders that cooperation would make their collective position stronger. But the realities behind the idea of forming an organisation were far from smooth. The climate of the 1960s was a mine field of border disputes, economic competition and differing working styles inherited from the colonial powers. An obvious obstacle was – and forever will be – the great difference in economic structures and levels of development amongst the member nations, a difference even more pronounced following the admission of Burma, Laos and Cambodia to ASEAN in the late 1990s. Consider the differences in per capita income: Singapore exceeds US$20,000, while Laos is under US$300. Expectations are going to be different, as are goals.

These Southeast Asian countries combined cover 4.5 million sq. km (1.8 million sq. miles), half the size of China and 18 times the size of Great Britain. The region's combined population of 490 million people is just over half that of India's and twice that of the United States. While the numbers are impressive, what can't be quantified and simplified is the simply awesome diversity and complexity of the region's cultures, histories, arts and people. This diversity and complexity, forgetting for the moment any political facet of decision-making, makes an ASEAN of consensus a dream.

Thailand is perhaps the best-known and most-visited Southeast Asian nation amongst Westerners. While the Thai beaches of interest have shifted over the decades, from Pattaya to Phuket to Samui, the architectural delights of Bangkok (although a civil engineer's and city planner's bad dream) and Chiang Mai, along with the diversity of the northern hill-tribe people, persist.

Until the mid 1990s, when modern hotels began punctuating the skyline, Burma's capital of Rangoon seemed a place lost in time. The people changed, but the city's momentum had long ago evaporated. To the north, Mandalay has chimed like music to the Western ear, ever since Rudyard Kipling wrote of its magic. And if Rangoon

PRECEDING PAGES: a few of Indonesia's volcanoes, Java; temple detail from Vietnam; southern village, Philippines; the holy temples of Bagan, Burma; skyline along Surawong Road, Bangkok. **LEFT:** Vietnamese violin student.

once seemed stalled in time, Bagan was and always will be frozen in time, its thousands of ancient pagodas peppering the expansive plain as testimonial to the great kings that rose and fell.

Laos and Cambodia, wedged in amongst stronger neighbours, are the region's poorest countries. Laos is increasingly opening up, and Cambodia would like to do so despite its ongoing internal problems. Laos' capital of Vientiane is indubitably Asia's most quiet and laid-back capital city, while the ancient capital of Luang Prabang to the north is not only quiet, but adorned with the best of Laos' ancient architecture. Cambodia's historical anchorage lies in Angkor, representative of the great Khmer kingdom that long ruled the region.

Vietnam has the distinction of having been a divided country for much of its modern history. Today, its economy and the people's innate entrepreneurial skills are hobbled by a stagnant leadership fearful of a brave new world of commerce and information. But the Vietnamese are an intensely resourceful people, and travellers to Hanoi, Vietnam's capital, or especially Ho Chi Minh City, the former Saigon, can't help but be impressed by the people's zeal against inertia. On the coast east of Hanoi, Ha Long Bay entrances the visitor with its otherworldly scenery. Midway between Hanoi and Ho Chi Minh, Hue is a place where the artifacts of ancient kings still hold sway over the senses.

Like Burma, Malaysia was once part of the British Empire. Unlike Burma, Malaysia has turned itself into one of the region's most important economies. Graced with a blend of colonial, Islamic and ultramodern architecture, Kuala Lumpur keeps getting higher (though it would have to outdo itself, as the world's two tallest buildings are already standing in KL) and more congested. Penang, an island off the western coast to the north of Kuala Lumpur, has long lured Westerners with its mix of cluttered Chinese alleys and white-sand beaches. Far to the east on Borneo, the states of Sabah and Sarawak are synonymous with exotic and adventurous. Wedged in between is Brunei, ruled by a sultan, the world's richest person. At the southern tip of the Malaysian peninsula is Singapore, the city-state governed like a corporation and perhaps the most efficient place on earth.

Indonesia is Southeast Asia's largest country both in size and population. It is also the world's largest Islamic nation. Jakarta is like many Asian cities, a new skyline shiny and electric, with roads below chaotic and claustrophobic. Jakarta is on Java, one of the world's most densely populated places and where some of the region's great ancient empires arose. At the eastern end of Java is Bali, increasingly modern and developed, but still intriguing with its intense self-confidence and pride in its culture and history.

The Philippines is the most unlikely of Asian nations, with nearly five centuries of Spanish and American influence – four centuries in a convent followed by 50 years in Hollywood. It's a Catholic country, an inescapable cast in Manila, where cathedrals rise to rival those of Europe. Yet in the north of Ilocos or the southern islands of the Visayas, the Western textures are well moderated by local ways. ❑

RIGHT: Sukhothai Hindu deity.

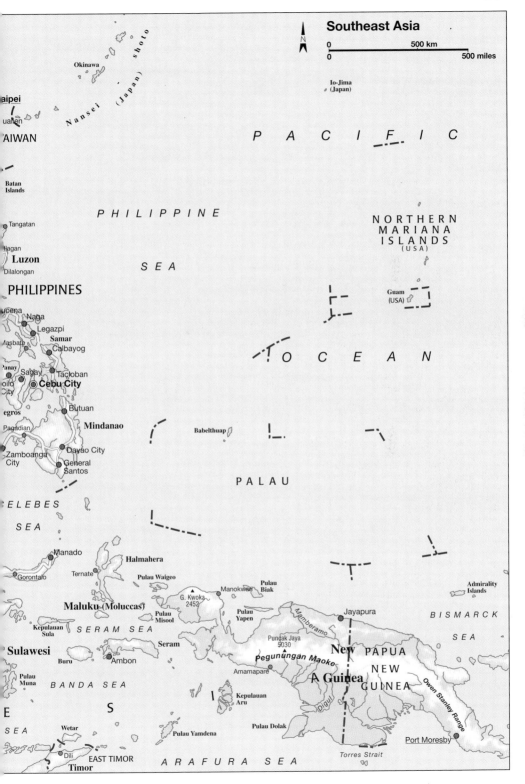

Southeast Asia

0   500 km
0   500 miles

Okinawa

Io-Jima
(Japan)

Nansei (Japan) shoto

aipei

uañen

AIWAN

P A C I F I C

Batan
Islands

P H I L I P P I N E

N O R T H E R N
M A R I A N A
I S L A N D S
(U S A)

Tangatan

Hagan

Luzon

Dilalongan

S E A

Guam
(USA)

PHILIPPINES

ucena

Naga

Legazpi

Masbate **Samar**

Calbayog

O C E A N

Panay Sagay Tacloban

ilo
City **Cebu City**

egros Butuan

Pagadian **Mindanao**

Babelthuap

P A L A U

Zamboanga
City Davao City

General
Santos

E L E B E S

S E A

Manado

Halmahera

Gorontalo Ternate

Pulau Waigeo

Pulau
Biak

Admirality
Islands

Maluku (Moluccas)

Pulau
Misool

Manokwari

G. Kwoka
2452

Pulau
Yapen

Jayapura

B I S M A R C K

Kepulauan
Sula

S E R A M S E A

Seram

Mamberamo

S E A

Sulawesi

Buru Ambon

Puncak Jaya
5030

New PAPUA

Pulau
Muna

B A N D A S E A

Amamapare

Pegunungan Maoke

A Guinea

NEW
GUINEA

Owen Stanley Range

E S

Kepulauan
Aru

Digul

Wetar

Pulau Yamdena

Pulau Dolak

Port Moresby

S E A

Dili **EAST TIMOR**

Timor

A R A F U R A S E A

Torres Strait

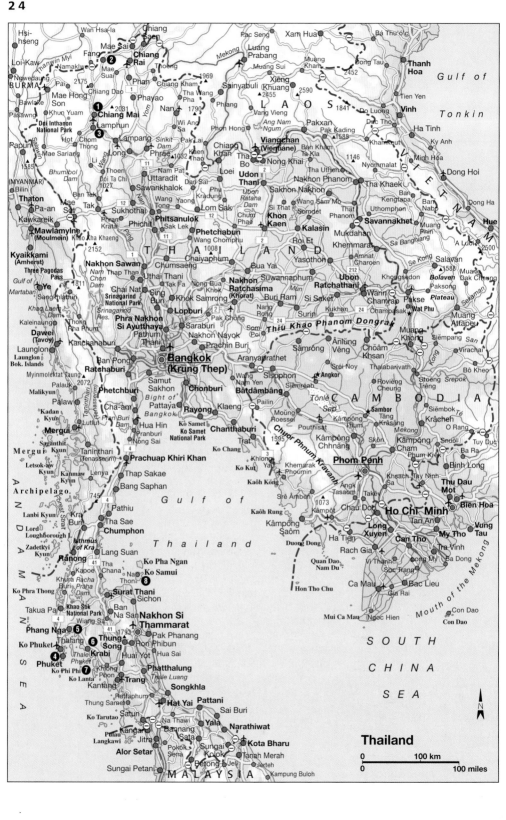

Thailand

0   100 km

0   100 miles

THAILAND

*More than any other Southeast Asian country, Thailand has
long been identified with the region's uniqueness*

L and of the Free. Land of Smiles. The former is a literal translation of the word *Thailand,* the latter a promotional slogan – and a truthful one at that. Beneath their graciousness, the Thais have a strong sense of self and a humanity without subservience. It is this pride in themselves that underlies their sense of identity and their ability to smile at the vicissitudes of life.

Thailand has a population of more than 62 million, and it is nearly the size of Central America, or of France, or twice that of England. Its capital of Bangkok (with a population, at rough estimates, of 10 million) lies on the same latitude as Madras, Khartoum, Guatemala City, Guam and Manila.

Lying inland from the apex of the Gulf of Thailand, Bangkok is the country's international gateway, and seat of government, business and the monarchy. Bangkok bears little relation to the rest of the country, a patchwork of rice fields, villages, plantations and forests whose second largest city is just a fraction – perhaps one-fiftieth – the size of Bangkok. The country is commonly divided into four regions: the Central Plains, including Bangkok, and the North, Northeast and South. Each region has its own culture and appeal. When a Thai says "I'm heading upcountry tomorrow," she or he could mean anywhere outside Bangkok's city limits.

Elevations run from sea level along the 2,600-km-long (1,600-mile) coastline to a peak of 2,600 metres (8,500 ft) in the north, a region of hills clad in teak forests and valleys carpeted in rice, fruit trees and vegetables, and bordered by Burma and Laos. The northeast is dominated by the arid Khorat Plateau, where farmers struggle to cultivate rice, tapioca, jute and other cash crops. With strong cultural affinities to neighbouring Laos and Cambodia, the region is rimmed and defined by the Mekong River. In the central plains, monsoon rains transform the landscape into a vast hydroponic basin, which nourishes a sea of rice, the country's staple and an important export.

Through this region flows the Chao Phraya River, carrying produce and people south to Bangkok, washing rich sediment down from the northern hills, and during the monsoon season, further flooding the rice fields.The south runs down a long, narrow arm of land leading to Malaysia. Rubber and palm oil plantations alternate with rice and fruit trees, an area strongly influenced by Malay culture.

Since the East discovered it a millennium ago and the West began trickling in during the 16th century, Thailand has been a powerful magnet for adventurers and entrepreneurs. An abundance of resources, a wealth of natural beauty, stunning architecture and art, and a warm, hospitable people have long proved irresistible. ❑

PRECEDING PAGES: every Thai male spends time as a Buddhist monk.

Decisive Dates

Pre-Thai civilisation

3600–250 BC: Ban Chiang culture flourishes in north-eastern Thailand.

circa 250 BC: Suvannabhumi trading with India.

4th–8th centuries AD: influence of Mon and Khmer empires spreads into Thailand.

9th–13th centuries: Khmer Empire founded at Angkor. Thai peoples migrate south from Yunnan Province of China into northern Thailand, Burma, and Laos. Lopburi becomes an important provincial capital in Khmer Empire, later tries to become independent.

Sukhothai era

1238: Khmer power wanes. Kingdom of Sukhothai founded under Intaradit.

1281: Chiang Saen kingdom founded in north.

1296: Lanna Kingdom founded at Chiang Mai. Mangrai controls much of northern Thailand and Laos.

1280–1318: Reign of Ramkamhaeng in Sukhothai. Often called Thailand's "Golden Age", the period saw the first attempts to unify the Thai people, the first use of the Thai script, and a flourishing of the arts.

1317–47: Lo Thai reigns at Sukhothai. The slow decline of the Sukhothai kingdom begins.

1438: Sukhothai is now virtually deserted; power shifts to the Kingdom of Ayutthaya, to the south and along the Chao Phraya River.

Kingdom of Ayutthaya

14th century: Area around Ayutthaya settled by representatives of the Chiang Saen kingdom.

1350: City of Ayutthaya founded by Phya U-Thong, who proclaims himself Ramathibodi I. Within a few years he controls the areas encompassed by the kingdoms of Sukhothai and the Khmer empire.

1369: Ramesuen, son of Ramathibodi, becomes king.

1390: Ramesuen captures Chiang Mai.

1393: Ramesuen captures Angkor in Cambodia.

1448–88: Reign of King Trailok, who briefly unites the Lanna (Chiang Mai) and Ayutthaya kingdoms.

1491–1529: Reign of King Ramathibodi II.

1549: First major warfare with Mon Kingdom of Pegu.

1569: Burmese capture and loot Ayutthaya.

1590: Naresuen becomes king, throws off Burmese suzerainty. Under Naresuen, Ayutthaya expands rapidly at the expense of Burmese and Khmer empires and flourishes as a major city.

1605–10: Ekatotsarot reigns, begins significant economic ties with European traders and adventurers.

1610–28: Reign of King Songtham. The British arrive and obtain land for a trading factory.

1628–55: Reign of Prasat Thong. Trading concessions expand and regular trade with China and Europe is established.

1656–88: Reign of King Narai. British influence expands. Reputation of Ayutthaya as a magnificent city and a remarkable royal court spreads in Europe.

1678: Constantine Phaulkon arrives at Narai's court and gains great influence; French presence expands.

1688: Narai dies, Phaulkon executed.

1733–58: Reign of King Boromakot. Ayutthaya enters a period of peace, and of arts and literature.

1767: Burmese King Alaungpaya captures and sacks Ayutthaya, destroying four centuries of Thai civilisation. Seven months later General Phya Tak Sin returns and expels the Burmese occupiers. He moves the capital from Ayutthaya to Thonburi, near Bangkok.

Beginning of the Chakri dynasty

1767: Phya Tak Sin crowned as King Taksin.

1779: Generals Chao Phya Chakri and his brother Chao Phya Sarasih conquer Chiang Mai, expel the Burmese from what is now Thailand and so adding most of the Khmer and Lao kingdoms to the Thai kingdom. The Emerald Buddha brought from Vientiane, Laos, to Thonburi.

1782: The now erratic Taksin is deposed and executed. Chao Phya Chakri is offered the throne, founding the Chakri dynasty and assuming the name Ramathibodi and later Rama I. Capital is moved across the river to the city that becomes known to the west as Bangkok. Under Rama I, the Siamese Kingdom consolidates and expands its strength. Rama I revives Thai art, religion, and culture.

1809–24: Reign of Rama II; best known for construction of Wat Arun and many other temples and monasteries. Rama II reopens relations with the West, suspended since the time of Narai.

1824–51: Reign of Rama III, who left as his trademark the technique of embedding Chinese porcelain fragments as decorations on temples.

1851: King Mongkut (Rama IV) ascends the throne. He is the first Thai king to understand Western culture and technology. Before becoming king he spends 27 years as a monk, studying Western science.

1868: Chulalongkorn (Rama V) ascends the throne, reigning for the next four decades. Chulalongkorn ends the custom of prostration in royal presence, abolishes slavery, and replaces corvee labour with taxation. Infrastructure, schools, military and government modernised.

1910–25: Reign of Vajiravudh (Rama VI), Oxford-educated and thoroughly Westernised.

1925–32: Reign of Prajadhipok (Rama VII). Economic pressures from Great Depression spur discontent.

End of the absolute monarchy

1932: A coup d'etat ends the absolute monarchy and ushers in a constitutional monarchy.

1939: The name of the country is officially changed from Siam to Thailand, "Land of the Free". King Ananda (Rama VIII) ascends the throne.

1942: Japan invades Thailand with the acquiescence of the military government, but a spirited if small resistance movement thrives.

1946: King Ananda is killed by a mysterious gunshot; Bhumibol Adulyadej (Rama IX) ascends the throne. The royal family becomes a symbol of national unity.

1973–91: Bloody clashes between army and demonstrating students brings down the military government; political and economic blunders brings down the resulting civilian government just 3 years later. Various military-backed and civilian governments come and go for almost 20 years.

1991: Another clash between military and civilians brings the unusual sight of the leaders of both factions kneeling in contrition before the king; as a result, the military leaves government to the civilian politicians.

1992: Thailand begins 5 years of unprecedented economic growth. The face of Bangkok changes rapidly.

1996: King Bhumibol Adulyadej celebrates 50 years on the throne, the world's longest-reigning monarch.

1997: Thailand's banking system and economy begin a free-fall as a devalued baht loses half of its value.

1998: While most other Asian economies continue to wallow in crisis, Thailand follows guidelines established by the International Monetary Fund to begin resuscitating its financial systems and economy.

1999: King Bhumibol Adulyadej celebrates his Sixth-Cycle birthday (72nd) on 5 December.

2000: Senators for the Upper House are democratically elected for the first time under a new constitution.

2001: Billionaire tycoon, Thaksin Shinawatra and his Thai Rak Thai party win the election.

2003: Shinawatra's policies strengthen the Thai economy; also comes down hard on drug trafficiking ❑

CHAKRI MONARCHY

Since 1782, a single royal dynasty – known as Chakri – has ruled over Thailand.

Rama I (Chakri)	1782–1809
Rama II (Phutthalaetia)	1809–1824
Rama III (Nangklao)	1824–1851
Rama IV (Mongkut)	1851–1868
Rama V (Chulalongkorn)	1868–1910
Rama VI (Vajiravudh)	1910–1925
Rama VII (Prajadhipok)	1925–1935
Rama VIII (Ananda)	1935–1946
Rama IX (Bhumibol)	1946–

LEFT: Ayutthayan general mounts battle elephant.
RIGHT: portrait of King Chulalongkorn, or Rama V.

PEOPLE OF THE HILLS

The tribal people of Thailand make up fewer than one in fifty of the nation's population, but their way of life continues to lure visitors

Thousands of foreigners annually trek to the tribal people's mountain villages in Thailand. The average Thai, however, views tribal people as foreigners, if not illegal aliens, and thus not entitled to the same rights as Thais. Most tribal immigration – typically from Burma or Laos – has occurred only in the past 100 years. In fact, only in the past decade have significant numbers of tribal people been granted Thai citizenship.

Thailand is home for up to 20 tribes, but there are six principal groups: Karen, Hmong, Mien, Lahu, Lisu and Akha. Living in villages at higher elevations, most hill-tribe farmers practise slash-and-burn, or swidden, agriculture. The ashes at first provide a rich fertiliser, but over the years the process depletes the soil, and unfortunately, today there's no longer much forest left to burn. Villagers used to then move their villages to a new site, but there's no place to move nowadays. With poorer soil and increasingly less of it, villagers sometimes rely on the opium poppy as a cash crop.

Karen

The 265,000 Karen form by far the largest tribe. In Thailand, they comprise two sub-groups, the Sgaw and Pwo, whose dialects are not mutually intelligible. Karens have been settled in Thailand since the 18th century and they are still (illegally) trickling in from Burma, where a Karen rebel army has been fighting the Burmese government for decades. The Karen separatist movement in Burma sometimes makes relations between Burma and Thailand edgy.

Karens were early converts to Christianity when Burma was a British colony, and some Thai Karens are Baptists or Seventh-Day Adventists. All Karens place great emphasis on monogamy, condemn premarital sex, and trace ancestry through the mother. Unlike other Thai tribes, they have long practised lowland wet-rice farming.

OPPOSITE: distinctive headdress of an Akha woman.
RIGHT: antique hill-tribe textile.

Hmong

The most recent arrivals in Thailand, Hmong are the second-largest hill tribe in the country, numbering about 80,000. The majority of them immigrated to Thailand in the 1950s and 1960s, fleeing from the long civil war in Laos. Ever on the alert for communists, the Thai military

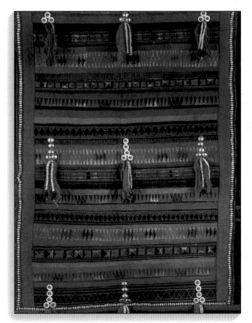

then regarded Hmong as subversives, and Hmong relations with Thai officialdom still remain complicated. Ironically, Hmong are renowned for their fierce independence and, in Laos, for anti-communism. Indeed, they were American allies during the Vietnam War.

Opium use is common, kinship is patrilineal, and polygamy is permitted. Like Thai, the Hmong language can be traced to southern China, where 4 million Hmong live today in China's Yunnan Province. Dialects and clothing identify the Hmong: Blue Hmong women wear indigo, pleated skirts and their hair in huge buns. White Hmong women wear white hemp skirts and black turbans.

Mien (Yao)

Like Hmong, most Mien (also known as Yao) probably came to Thailand from Laos, but there are also large numbers in Burma, Vietnam and China's Yunnan Province – not to mention the Laotian Mien refugee communities in San Francisco and Seattle. Many Chinese elements, such as ancestor worship and Daoism, are evident in their animistic religious beliefs. Kinship is mostly patrilineal, and polygamy is practised. The Mien

NORTHERN HOMES

With the exception of the Karen, whose range extends down to Kanchanaburi and Tak provinces, most hill tribes in Thailand live in three northern provinces: Chiang Mai, Chiang Rai and Mae Hong Son.

only slightly. The Lahu people are skilled makers of baskets and bags, and they are also famous for their hunting prowess. The Lahu dialects are of the Tibeto-Burman group.

Lisu

Lisu are easily identified by a penchant for bright colours. Lisu are good silversmiths and make jewellery for the Akha and Lahu. They are regarded by other tribal people as rather sharp business people. Animistic beliefs are combined

place great emphasis on the peaceful resolution of conflict, which is apparent in their smooth relations with Thais in general. Traditionally, Mien women can be distinguished by their black jackets and trousers, red fur-like collars and large blue or black turbans.

Lahu

Like the Karen, traditional Lahu mix animism with millennial myths, while a good proportion are also Christian. Besides the usual opium, corn and rice, Lahu have successfully cultivated chilli peppers as a cash crop. The traditional dress of the four groups – Red Lahu, Black Lahu, Yellow Lahu and Lahu Sheleh – varies

with ancestor worship. Lisu are known to cite reasons for the pre-eminence of their family, clan or village, yet, unlike other tribes, they have an organisation that extends across villages. Lisu are a sub-group of the Kachins, a large minority group in the far north of Burma. Kachin languages are Tibeto-Burman.

Akha

Akha are the hill-tribe people that most tourists want to see, drawn by the heavy ornate headdress worn by the women: silver disks festooned with old coins, beads and feathers. And unlike other tribal women, who save their finery for ceremonies, Akha wear this even while working in the fields. Animist beliefs are mixed with ancestor worship; Akha can recite their ancestry back 20 generations. Their language is Tibeto-Burman.

Other minorities

Two other groups, the Shan and Kayan, deserve mention, as their villages are frequent stops on trekking tours. However, strictly speaking, they are not Thai hill tribes.

In their settled communities, rice-growing practices and Theravada Buddhism, the Shan are very similar to Thais. Their language is similar to the northern Thai dialect, although not ferry tourists across the border to view Kayan women whose necks had been elongated by layers of heavy brass rings.

Kayan leaders had long discouraged the practice and it had virtually died out. But the tourist attraction was so great that Thai officials allowed three villages to set up west of Mae Hong Son. Many Kayan women have since donned the rings and initiated girls beginning at age five. Tours to view the "giraffe women" have been heavily promoted in Bangkok. Tourists paying to go on these tours are thus directly responsible for the return of this barbaric practice.

intelligible to central Thai speakers. Many Shans have migrated to Thailand in recent times to escape the upheavals in Burma, but Shans may have been the first Tai inhabitants of northern Thailand, in the 9th or 10th centuries. The large area of Burma bordering the northern tip of Thailand is the home of 4 million Shans and several armies battling for autonomy.

The Kayan (Padaung) are a Karennic people residing in the southern Shan areas. Until a few years ago, tours from Mae Hong Son would

LEFT: Mien resplendent in traditional clothing.
ABOVE: Hmong women are distinguished by costumes of heavy black cotton.

Cultures under threat

The cultures of Thailand's hill tribes are very much in danger of extinction. The chief culprit is not tourism: greater threats are posed by a shortage and loss of land, resettlement, lack of land rights and citizenship, illiteracy, and poor medical care. Official Thai hill-tribe policies have been shaped by the desire to discourage swidden farming and the cultivation of opium. Some of the crop-substitution programmes sponsored by the Thai government, United Nations and foreign governments have been successful, and tribal people now market coffee, tea and fruit. But such projects have not penetrated to many distant villages. ❑

THAILAND'S CUISINE

You bet it can be hot. It can also be cool. There is nothing apathetic about Thai cuisine, which most likely explains its universal appeal

Good food in Thailand is found in fascinating places, from seafood markets to floating restaurants to hawker stalls. Thais take time over their meals, talking and making an entire evening of the affair. Since dishes are typically shared by all, take several friends so that one can order and sample more dishes.

While it's true that there are very spicy regional dishes – certain southern Thai curries are notable – not all Thai food is hot and spicy. Generally, an authentic Thai meal will include at least one very spicy dish, a few that are less hot, and some that are comparatively bland, flavoured with only garlic or herbs.

A THAI APPROACH TO SWEET-TOOTH SATISFACTION

In Thailand, desserts and sweets *(khanom)* come in a bewildering variety – from light concoctions to custards, ice creams and cakes, and an entire category of confections based upon egg yolks cooked in flower-scented syrups. Bananas and coconuts grow everywhere in Thailand, and if they were to be removed from the list of ingredients available to the khanom cook, the entire edifice of Thai dessert cookery would come crashing down.

Anyone walking through a Bangkok market is bound to come across a sweets vendor selling anything from candied fruits to million-calorie custards made from coconut cream, eggs and palm sugar, generally sold in the form of three-inch squares wrapped in banana leaves. Try sampling *sangkhya maphrao awn,* a custard made from coconut cream, palm sugar and eggs,or *khao laam,* a glutinous rice mixed with coconut cream, sugar and either black beans or other goodies. *Kluay khaek* uses bananas sliced lengthwise, dipped in coconut cream and then deep-fried until crisp. Many of these sweets are amazingly inventive. You may finish off a rich pudding, for example, before realising that its tantalising flavour came from crisp-fried onions. In buying Thai sweets, picking what looks good is usually disappointment-proof. If nothing else, try a dish of *katih,* a rich and heavenly coconut ice cream.

Traditionally, rice has always been the most important dish in any Thai meal. At the start of the meal, heap some rice onto a plate and then take a spoonful or two of curry. It is considered polite to take only one curry at a time, consuming it before ladling another curry onto the rice. Thais eat with the spoon in their right hand and fork in their left, the fork used to push the food onto the spoon for transport to the mouth. Contrary to popular opinion in the west, nurtured in part by experiences in Thai restaurants abroad,

SPOON SHOCK

A surprise to some visitors is that most Thais use a spoon and fork, not the chopsticks regularly found in Thai restaurants located in Europe and North America.

kiaw wan kai, a gravy filled with chunks of chicken and tiny pea-sized eggplants. A relative, *kaeng kiaw wan neua*, has slices of beef in it. *Kaeng leuang*, a category of yellow curries, includes *kaeng karee*, an Indian-style curry that is made with chicken or beef. *Kaeng pet* is a red curry with beef or pork. A close relative is *penaeng neua*, a southern-style "dry" curry with a characteristic coconut flavour. *Kaeng som* is cooked in a hot-sour soup generally filled with pieces of either fish or shrimp.

chopsticks are not used for Thai food, but rather only for Chinese noodle dishes. Also contrary to popular belief, peanut sauce, an "indispensable" addition to nearly every dish in Thai restaurants found in Western countries, is really of Malayan and Indonesian origin and is used in Thailand only for *satay*.

Spicy and hot dishes

Kaeng means curry. The group includes the spiciest of Thai dishes and forms the core of Thai cooking. Among the green curries is *kaeng*

LEFT: styles of preparation are many, as are tastes.
ABOVE: street-cooked meal in natural packaging.

Among the fiery favourites is *tom yang kung*, a lemony broth teeming with shrimp. It is served in a metal tureen that is wrapped around a mini-furnace heated by charcoal, so that it remains piping hot throughout the meal. *Po taek* ("the fisherman's net bursts") is a cousin of *tom yang kung*, containing squid, mussels, crab and fish. *Yam* is a hot and spicy salad combining meat and vegetables. Particularly popular in northern and northeastern Thailand, it is one of the hottest dishes available.

Mild curries

Tom kha kai, a thick coconut-milk curry of chicken chunks with lemon grass, is milder than the average Thai dish. *Plaamuk tawt kratiem phrik tai* is squid fried with garlic and black pepper. When ordering, ask that the garlic *(kratiem)* be fried crispy *(krawp krawp)*. The dish is also prepared with fish. Another milder dish is *kaeng joot,* a non-spicy curry – a clear broth filled with glass noodles, minced pork and mushrooms. *Neua pat nam man hoi* is beef fried in oyster sauce garnished with chopped shallots and green vegetables.

Regional distinctions

Each of Thailand's four regions has its own cuisine. Northern and northeastern dishes are

related to Lao cooking, which is eaten with glutinous rice. Southern food is flavoured with the tastes of Malaysian cooking. Central cuisine corresponds closely to the food in Thai restaurants abroad.

Northern specialties are generally eaten with *khao niaw* or sticky rice, which is kneaded into a ball and dipped into various sauces and curries. *Sai oua* (also called *naam*) is an oily, spicy pork sausage that epitomises northern cooking. Some of the northern dishes originate from neighbouring Burma, including the egg-noodle dish *kao soy* and *kaeng hang lay,* a spicy curry which is not fiery hot. Northeastern food is simple and spicy. Like northern food, it is eaten

with sticky rice, which *Isaan* (northeastern) diners claim weighs heavily on the brain and makes one sleepy. *Som tam* is a northeastern speciality of raw shredded papaya, dried shrimp, lemon juice and chillies in a delectably spicy salad.

Heavily influenced by Malay neighbours below the southern border, southern cuisine combines Muslim tastes with Thai sensibilities. *Khao yam* is rice with *kapi* (a paste made of fermented shrimp). *Pat pet sataw* looks like a lima bean but has a slightly bitter yet pleasant flavour. This dish is cooked with shrimp or pork, together with a sprinkling of chillies. *Kanom chin,* although found throughout Thailand, is claimed to have originated in the south. Tiny bits of minced beef are stewed in a red sauce and then served atop rice noodles.

Chinese

Most lunch-time meals and dishes are derived from Chinese cuisine, and noodle dishes, a Chinese invention, have been adopted by the Thais. Those served at street-side, open-front shops come in two varieties: wet and dry. When ordering either, specify the wetness by adding the word *nam* (wet) or *haeng* (dry) to the name.

Most Thai Chinese are of Teochow descent, so the typical Thai Chinese restaurant serves Teochow dishes with a distinct Cantonese flavour. Teochow is famed for dishes such as thick shark's fin soup, goose doused in soy sauce, and roasted duck with fresh green vegetables. Fruits and teas are integral parts of every meal. Poultry, pork and seafood are essentials, as are a huge variety of fungi and mushrooms. Other Chinese cuisines are also well represented in Thailand. Shanghai food, for example, is typified by dishes that are fried in sesame or soy sauce for a long time, making them sweeter and oilier than other cuisines.

Libations

The local beer is Singha, which is quite strong and, if taken to excess, can cause a fearsome hangover. The local cane whisky is called *mekhong* and packs a wallop for the unsuspecting. Thailand has its own special coffee, made with a thick black melange of coffee, chicory and who knows what else. Ask for it black to gain the full flavour of this exotic mixture. ❑

LEFT: Thai sweets are definitive caloric lodestones.
RIGHT: Thai cuisine uses only fresh produce.

CRAFTS AND CLOTHING OF THE HILL TRIBES

Each hill tribe of Southeast Asia has its own customs, dress, language and beliefs that are reflected in their clothing and crafts.

Textiles and silver jewellery play a very important role in the ceremonial activities of hill-tribe communities. Hill-tribe women are defined by what they wear, and their choice of clothing and adornment can reveal not only what tribe they are from, but also their social status, age and even where their home town is located. However, the way of life of Thailand's hill-tribe people, for example, is changing as they are slowly assimilated into mainstream Thai society, abandoning many features of their traditional culture. This may be sad for visitors in search of traditional hill-tribe culture, but the process is inevitable and has distinct advantages for these ethnic minorities, since they can now benefit from educational opportunities and medical facilities.

Hill-tribe craft items started to be made commercially in the mid-1970s when small craft centres were set up in refugee camps. Authentic items are now rare, and expensive but good-quality modern crafts can be found in craft shops.

BRASS NECK RINGS ▷
Padaung women once wore brass rings around their arms, legs and necks; the tradition has, thankfully, diminished. Some Padaung women still make their living by posing for pictures.

◁ HMONG EMBROIDERY
Women from the Hmong hill tribe used to hand-weave cloth, but today they use ready-made fabrics for their intricately embroidered clothing. The Hmong are skilled in making indigo-dyed batik which is then embroidered with appliquéd layers of geometrically-shaped fabric to make up their skirts.

▽ LISU TEXTILES
Lisu women make distinctive clothing. In the past, the cloth was woven by hand but the Lisu now use machine-made material that they run up on sewing machines.

◁ AKHA COTTONS

Women of the Akha hill tribe spin cotton into thread with a hand spindle, then weave it on a foot-treadle loom. The cloth is dyed indigo and is then appliquéd and decorated with shells, seeds, silver or buttons and made into clothing for the family. The men make a variety of baskets and other items from wood, bamboo and rattan.

LISU CEREMONIAL WEAR ▷

On special occasions, Lisu men wear turbans and the women don large amounts of hand-crafted silver jewelry, chunky necklaces and colourful tunics with silver buttons. Men of the tribe are skilled blacksmiths. The sale of crafts means they no longer need to grow opium poppies to make a living.

▽ AKHA HEADDRESS

Married Akha women are famous for their head-dresses decorated with silver coins, which they wear all the time. Unmarried women from the tribe attach small gourds to their head-dresses.

HOW THE KAREN MAKE *IKAT*

The White Karen tribe (above) produce striped warp *ikat* textiles woven on back-strap looms. Ikat is a technique used to pattern cloth that involves the binding of the cloth with fibre or strips of material, so in places it becomes resistant to dyeing.

Before the cloth is dyed, the weft (yarns woven across the width of the fabric) or the warp (lengthwise yarns) is pulled tightly over a frame and then threads are bound tightly together singly or in bunches. The cloth is then dyed several times using different colours. As a result, complex and beautiful patterns are built up with soft, watery edges on the parts of the cloth not completely covered by the binding materials.

The dyeing process is complex, with the dominant colour of the ikat dyed first. Cotton yarns are the most suitable for making warp ikat, and the dyes used to produce these textiles are natural dyes that are easily absorbed by cotton. The most popular colours for warp ikat are indigo and red. Weft ikats use mainly yellow dyes (made from turmeric), diluted indigos and a deep crimson red extracted from the lac insect. Orange, green and purple are created by an overdyeing process.

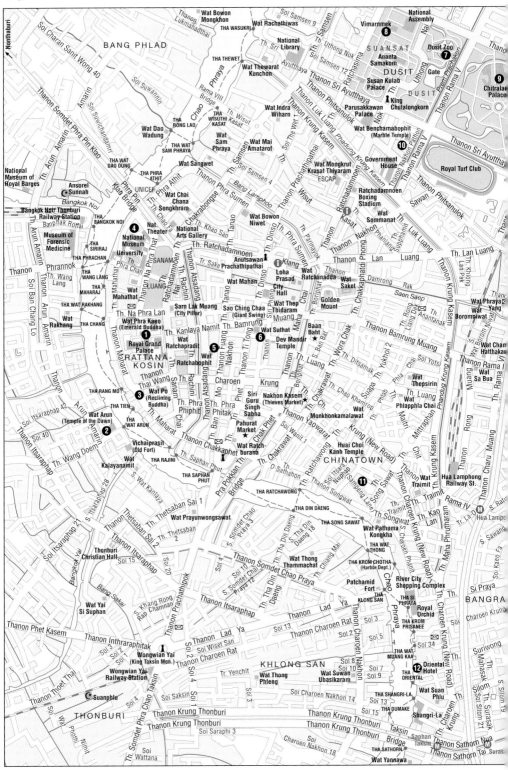

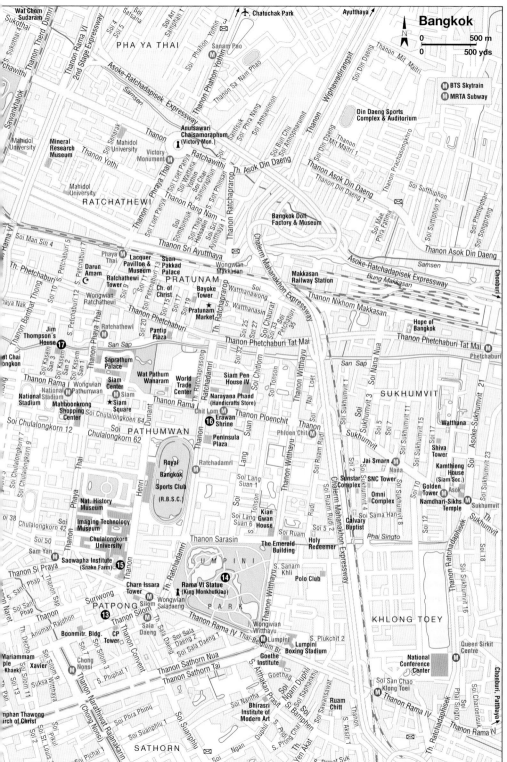

Bangkok

✈ Chatuchak Park

N

| 0 | 500 m |
| 0 | 500 yds |

Ⓜ BTS Skytrain
Ⓜ MRTA Subway

PHA YA THAI

Wat Chom Sudaram
Sanam Pao

Din Daeng Sports Complex & Auditorium

Mahidol University

Mineral Research Museum

Mahidol University

Victory Monument

Anutsawari Chaisamoraphum (Victory Mon.)

Mahidol University

RATCHATHEWI

Bangkok Doll Factory & Museum

Phaya Thai

Lacquer Pavilion & Museum

Suan Pakkad Palace

Darun Amam

Ratchathewi Tower

Wongwian Makkasan

Makkasan Railway Station

Bung Makkasan

PRATUNAM

Ch. of Christ

Bayoke Tower

Pantip Plaza

Wongwian Ratchathewi

★ Pratunam Market

Hope of Bangkok

Jim Thompson's House ⑰

Thanon Phetchaburi Tat Mai

Phetchaburi Ⓜ

Saprathum Palace

Wat Pathum Wanaram

World Trade Center

Siam Pen House IV

SUKHUMVIT

National Stadium

Siam Center

★ Siam Square

Narayana Phand (Handicrafts Store)

Shiva Tower

Mahboonkrong Shopping Center

Ⓜ Siam

Chit Lom Ⓜ

⑯ Erawan Shrine

Watthana

Kamthieng House (Siam Soc.)

PATHUMWAN

Peninsula Plaza

Jai Smarn Ⓜ Nana

SNC Tower

Golden Tower

Namdhari-Sikhs Temple

Sukhumvit

Nat. History Museum

Royal Bangkok Sports Club (R.B.S.C.)

Kian Gwan House

Omni Complex

Sunstar Complex

Imaging Technology Museum

Chulalongkorn University

Sama Han

Calvary Baptist

Phai Singto

Saowapha Institute (Snake Farm) ⑮

Holy Redeemer

The Emerald Building

LUMPINI

Sam Yan

Rama VI Statue ⑭ (King Monkhutklao)

S. Sanam Khli

Polo Club

KHLONG TOEY

Charn Issara Tower ⑬

PATPONG

PARK

Boonmitr Bldg.

CP Tower

Lumpini Boxing Stadium

National Conference Center

Queen Sirikit Centre

Chong Nonsi

Goethe Institute

Xavier

Bhirasri Institute of Modern Art

Ruam Chitt

SATHORN

BANGKOK

Map on pages 38–39

This is one of the most confounding and challenging cities in the world. Amidst its traffic-clogged roads and towering buildings are some of the most exquisite historical edifices anywhere

A t first glance, this metropolis of over 10 million people appears as a bewildering melding of new and old, and of exotic and commonplace and indeterminate, all tossed together into an expansive urban fuss. If Bangkok seems to lack order, it is because it's never had it, save for the royal core of the city, Rattanakosin, where the kings built their palaces. Bangkok begins its life on the banks of the Chao Phraya River, the "River of Kings". Although the city is some 400 years old, it became the nation's capital only in 1782, when the royal dynasty that currently rules Thailand was established.

Royal Bangkok

The southern side of Thanon Na Phra Lan is lined by the white crenellated walls of the **Grand Palace ❶** (daily 8.30am–3.30pm) complex. The only entrance and exit to the complex is in the middle. On the right are the offices of the Royal Household, to the left is the ticket booth.

The first stop within the palace grounds is **Wat Phra Kaeo** (Temple of the Emerald Buddha), a shrine for Thai Buddhists that is comparable in religious importance to Mecca or St Peter's. Passing though the gate, you will confront 6-metre-tall (20-ft) demon statues inspired by the *Ramakien*, the Thai version of the Indian epic *Ramayana*. You must walk the glittering length of the *bot* to reach its entrance. In front are scattered Chinese-style statues, which function as stand-ins for incense offerings to the Emerald Buddha inside. The 75-cm-tall (30-inch) jadeite statue is perched high on an altar near the opposite wall, clothed and enclosed in a glass case, and shielded by a towering nine-tiered umbrella.

Directly opposite the Grand Palace on the other side of the Chao Phraya River is **Wat Arun ❷**, one the river's oldest and most distinctive landmarks, dating back to the Ayutthaya period, before the Thai capital was moved south to Thonburi and later to Bangkok. The temple's 82-metre-high (270-ft) *prang*, which is featured on the 10-baht coin, is bedecked with millions of tiny pieces of Chinese porcelain donated by average Thai citizens.

Exiting from the Grand Palace, turn left on Thanon Maharat and walk south past Thanon Thai Wang, which runs into the Tha Tien river-taxi dock after passing a fresh market surrounded by early 20th-century shophouses.

Turn left (that is, east) onto Soi Chetuphon and head for the gate to **Wat Po ❸**, Bangkok's largest and oldest temple, predating the Bangkok dynasty. Its first buildings were constructed in the 16th century. Few

OPPOSITE: evening commute.
BELOW: the Emerald Buddha.

statues are more impressive than Wat Po's mammoth **Reclining Buddha**, which occupies the entirety of a long building in the northwestern corner of the extensive palace complex.

Malai, Buddhist flower offerings.

A trove of both Thai and Southeast Asian riches, the **National Museum ❹** (Wed–Sun 9am–4pm) comprises a half-dozen old and new buildings. One of oldest is at the rear of the compound, the Wang Na, dating from 1782. This vast palace once extended across to Khlong Lot and up to the Grand Palace. The name refers to the palace of the so-called second king, a deputy king of sorts. When King Chulalongkorn's heir-apparent – the second king – attempted a violent overthrow, however, Chulalongkorn abolished the office in 1887 and tore down most of the buildings. The Wang Na today is one of the remnants, serving as the National Museum and housing *khon* masks, gold and ceramic pieces, palanquins, weapons, instruments and an elephant riding-seat made from ivory.

East of the Grand Palace

At the next cross-street, Ratchabophit, turn right to visit one of the most attractive wats off the beaten tourist path. Before crossing over the canal, however, notice immediately to the north what, yes, appears to be a golden pig lording over a construction site, actually an archaeological excavation. This pig memorial was built in 1913 as a birthday present from friends to Queen Saowapha, Chulalongkorn's favourite wife, who was born in the Year of the Pig.

Across the bridge, **Wat Ratchabophit ❺** is easily recognisable by its distinctive doors, carved in relief with jaunty soldiers wearing European uniforms. Built in 1870 by Rama V (1868–1910), the design was intended to meld Western and Thai art forms. The bot's windows and entrance doors are works of art.

BELOW: the Dusit Maha Prasad, in the Grand Palace.

the first paved street in Bangkok,
ward towards it. Chinatown was f
district that, in turn, was followe
where the Oriental Hotel now s
The area has had a somewh
pursuits soon degenerated int
to opium dens and houses
(*khom khiew*). A green-ligh
while the lanterns have disa

Bangkrak and Silor

Further south and just e
district that has risen i
neighbourhood of *far*
the grand **Oriental H**
Oriental, stroll inland
touts and "copy wat
be at the less excit
Silom, which reall
Love it or hate
(actually two str
Silom has an el
the serene tem
than the rauc
there seem t

Inlaid mother-of-pearl depicts the insignias of the five royal ranks.

Continue north up Thanon Fuang Nakhon and turn right at the second corner onto Soi Suthat. Two short blocks on is **Wat Suthat ❻**. Finished during the reign of Rama III, it is noted for its enormous bot, said to be the tallest in Bangkok. The bot doors are among the wonders of Thai art. Carved to a depth of 5 cm (2 inches), they follow the Ayutthayan tradition of floral motifs, with tangled jungle vegetation hiding small animals. Immediately north of Wat Suthat is a giant red and wooden gateway. This is the 200-year-old **Giant Swing**, once the centrepiece of an annual ceremony honouring the Hindu god Shiva. A bench bearing teams of two to four standing young men was suspended from the cross-piece. When the swing was swung, the men would attempt to catch, with their teeth, a bag of gold suspended from on high.

North of the old royal city

Northward to Dusit, crossing the *khlong*, Thanon Ratchadamnoen turns into a pleasant, tree-lined boulevard that leads to an immense square with a statue of King Chulalongkorn on horseback. To the left of the square lies the spacious **Amporn Gardens**, complete with fountains, trees and an air of grandeur.

At the back of the square stands the former **National Assembly** (Parliament) building, built in 1907 by Chulalongkorn. To the east is **Dusit Zoo ❼** (daily 8am–6pm), the city's main animal park and one of the most popular places in Bangkok for family outings. A lake with boats for rent is surrounded by an aviary and enclosures containing the exotic wildlife of Asia. Behind the old National Assembly is **Vimarnmek ❽** (daily 9am–4pm), billed as the world's largest golden-teak building. As much a work of art as the treasures it holds

Map on pages 38–39

BELOW: Wat Suthat and Giant Swing.

within, Vi[...]
what was[...]
with exc[...]
Just [...]
leafy [...]
groun[...]
pose[...]
whe[...]
tur[...]

i[...]

Stained-glass window, Wat Benchamabophit.

BELOW: whol[...]
market, wes[...]
end of Chir[...]

Map on pages 38–39

TIP

For outlying trips, excellent highways now lead out of Bangkok in all directions, and what used to be a 3- or 4-hour trip can now be made in just over an hour.

OPPOSITE: garden of Jim Thompson's home. **BELOW:** lake, Lumpini Park.

At the end of Thanon Silom, just east of Patpong, is a huge and busy intersection that can take what seems a good 15 minutes to cross. To the northeast across the intersection lies respite from the relentless dust and petrol fumes of the city: **Suan Lumpini ⓮** (Lumpini Park), a tranquil and tropical oasis of greenery with boating lakes, open-air gymnasiums and outdoor cafés.

Directly west along Thanon Rama IV is the **Queen Saowapha Institute ⓯** (Mon–Fri 8.30am–4.30pm, Sat and Sun 8.30–noon), or as it is better known, the **Snake Farm**. Operated by the Thai Red Cross, its primary function is not to entertain tourists (although it does) but the serious business of producing anti-venom serum to be used on snakebite victims, of which there are many every year throughout the country. The institute, the second oldest of its kind in the world, produces serum from the king cobra, Siamese cobra, Russell's viper, Malayan pit viper and the green pit viper.

Heading north along Thanon Ratchadamri towards the intersection with Thanon Rama I, one passes two of the city's most opulent hotels, The Regent and the Grand Hyatt Erawan. At the intersection, the **Erawan Shrine ⓰** draws visitors and locals. To improve their fortunes or to pass exams, believers make offerings at a statue of a four-faced deity. Originally erected by the Erawan Hotel, now the Grand Hyatt, to counter a spate of bad luck, the shrine is redolent with incense smoke and jasmine. To repay the god for wishes granted, supplicants place floral garlands or wooden elephants at the god's feet, or hire a resident troupe to perform a traditional dance.

The intersection of Rama I and Phaya Thai is one of the best areas to shop, especially for those who like a little local colour and chaos. But there are other attractions besides shopping and eating in this area. On Khlong Maha Nag at the north end of Soi Kasemsan II is the **Jim Thompson House ⓱** (daily 9am–4.30pm). This Thai-style home is, in fact a collection of seven Thai houses acquired throughout the country and joined together by the remarkable American, who came to Thailand at the end of World War II and revived the Thai silk industry. In 1967, while on a visit to Cameron Highlands in Malaysia, Thompson mysteriously disappeared; despite an extensive search, no trace has ever been found of him. His legacy however lives in the beautiful silk sold at Jim Thompson boutiques in Bangkok.

Outside of Bangkok

The hinterland outside of Bangkok is filled with a rich variety of sights and experiences that can be visited as day-trips or overnighters from the capital. Among the highlights, 80 km (50 miles) north of Bangkok, is the old royal city of **Ayutthaya**, Thailand's capital from 1350 to 1767. The ruined city is immense, with several sites not to be missed. It was a larger and richer city than London or Paris during its time, but the golden age of Ayutthaya came to an end in 1767 when the Burmese besieged and utterly destroyed it.

If trekking in the jungle and a cool retreat is what you're after, the nearest hills to Bangkok are in the massive **Khao Yai National Park**, which sprawls across parts of four provinces northeast of the capital. Tigers and elephants call the park home. ❑

CHIANG MAI

In the northern mountains, Chiang Mai is a pleasant escape from Bangkok. It is a base from which to explore the many hill tribes and national parks that retain Thailand's more traditional textures

Map on page 24

Despite its increasingly rapid urbanisation, 700-year-old **Chiang Mai ❶** remains prized as a pleasantly cool alternative to the sticky humidity of Bangkok. Situated 300 metres (1,000 ft) above sea level in a broad valley divided by the picturesque 560-km-long (350-mile) **Mae Nam Ping**, the city reigned for seven centuries as the capital of the Lanna kingdom. In its splendid isolation, Chiang Mai developed a culture quite removed from that of the central plains to the south, with wooden temples of exquisite beauty and a host of unique crafts, including lacquerware, silverwork, wood carvings, ceramics and umbrella-making. Although the hospitality of both the hill tribes and the northern Thais is sometimes strained by the sheer numbers of visitors, the northern people remain more gracious than in many other cities.

Origins

Chiang Mai's story actually begins further north, in the town of Chiang Rai. Its founder and king, Mangrai, ruled a sizable empire that ran as far north as Chiang Saen, on the Mekong River. He founded Chiang Rai in 1281. But when the Mongol ruler Kublai Khan sacked the Burmese kingdom of Bagan in 1287, Mangrai feared that his realm might be threatened and so formed an alliance with the rulers of Sukhothai, then Siam's capital. With his southern boundaries secure, Mangrai captured the old Mon kingdom at Lamphun. To centralise his rule, he established a new base in the Ping River Valley in 1296. This new capital he named Chiang Mai, or New City.

The location was chosen by the auspicious sighting of white deer along with a white mouse with a family of five, all at the same time, or so the story has it. Rather than building on the banks of the Ping, which often floods, he built his city – with the help of 90,000 labourers – half a kilometre to the west, surrounding it with stout brick walls.

Less than a century after Chiang Mai's founding, however, Ayutthaya replaced Sukhothai as the capital of Siam. This new kingdom had its own expansionist dreams and ambitions, including designs on its neighbour to the north. For the next 400 years, there was fierce competition and sometimes open warfare. In the 16th century, Ayutthaya crushed an invasion by Chiang Mai, and Chiang Mai's power waned. To compound its troubles, the region was invaded in the early 1700s by the same Burmese enemy who were laying siege to Ayutthaya.

Although the Burmese were finally defeated, the people of Chiang Mai were so exhausted and discouraged by the constant conflict that they abandoned

OPPOSITE: northern hill-side farming.
BELOW: modern Chiang Mai.

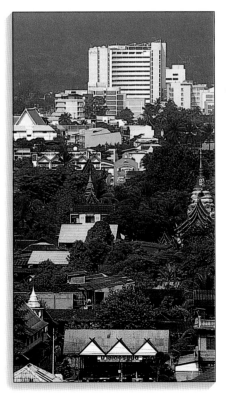

TIP

Be careful on the streets on 13 April, and for several days thereafter. Songkran, the traditional Thai new year, is when people sprinkle water on friends to bless them. In Chiang Mai, especially, it rapidly degenerates into a deluge. Tourists and strangers are not excluded.

BELOW: Wat Chiang Man, first temple built by Mangrai.

the city. It remained deserted until 1796, when the Burmese army was defeated; new nobles began restoring the city to its former prominence. It continued to enjoy autonomy from Bangkok until the railway brought meddling central government administrators. In 1932, following the death of the last king of Chiang Mai, the north was finally fully incorporated into the Thai nation.

Old Chiang Mai

The commercial centres of downtown are along Thanon Tapae, with numerous hotels, shops and guest houses. Hotels have also sprung up along Thanon Huai Kaeo, which leads out to Doi Suthep.

The city's history begins with **Wat Chiang Man**, which translates as "power of the city". It was the first *wat* to be built by Mangrai, who resided there during the construction of the city in 1296. Located in the northeast part of the old walled city, it is the oldest of Chiang Mai's 300-plus temples. Two ancient, venerated Buddha images are kept in the abbot's quarters and can be seen on request. The first image, Phra Sae Tang Tamani, is a small 10-cm-high (4-inch) crystal Buddha image taken by Mangrai to Chiang Mai from Lamphun, where it had reputedly resided for 600 years. Apart from a short sojourn in Ayutthaya, the image has remained in Chiang Mai ever since. On Songkran in April it is paraded through the streets. The second image, a stone Phra Sila Buddha in bas-relief, is believed to have originated in India around the 8th century. Both statues are said to possess the power to bring rain and to protect the city from fire.

The only other important structure in Wat Chiang Man is Chang Lom, a 15th-century square *chedi* buttressed by rows of stucco elephants.

Imperiously positioned at the head of the city's principal thoroughfare is **Wat**

Phra Singh, which is noted for three monuments: a library, chedi and the Viharn Lai Kham. The former, a magnificent Lanna-style wooden library on the right side of the compound, is raised on a high base decorated with lovely stucco angels. Behind the main viharn, built in 1925, is a beautiful wooden *bot,* and behind this, a chedi built by King Pha Yu in 1345 to hold the ashes of his father. Wat Phra Singh's most beautiful building is the small Phra Viharn Lai Kham, to the left of the bot. Built rather late in the Lanna period, in 1811, the wooden building's front wall is decorated in gold flowers on a red lacquer ground. Intricately carved wooden window frames accent the doors.

The interior walls of the Viharn Lai Kham are decorated with murals commissioned by Chao Thammalangka, who ruled over Chiang Mai between 1813 and 1821. Although focusing on the Buddhist stories of Prince Sang Thong (on the north wall) and the Tale of the Heavenly Phoenix (south wall), they also record in fascinating detail aspects of early 19th-century Lanna society and exhibit clear indications of persisting Burmese cultural influence.

Calamity is associated with **Wat Chedi Luang**, built in 1401 to the east of Wat Phra Singh. A century and a half later, a violent earthquake shook its then 90-metre-high (295-ft) pagoda, reducing its height to 42 metres (140 ft). It was never completely rebuilt, although it has been impressively restored. Even in its damaged state, the colossal monument is majestic. For 84 years the Emerald Buddha, now in Bangkok, was housed here before being moved to Vientiane. King Mangrai was reportedly killed nearby by an untimely bolt of lightning.

Close to the wat's entrance stands an ancient and tall gum tree. When it falls, says a legend, so will the city. As if serving as counterbalance, the *lak muang,* or city boundary stone in which the spirit of the city is said to reside, stands near

Map on page 24

BELOW LEFT: Wat Suan Dok.
BELOW RIGHT: northern children

its base. The viharn of **Wat Pan Tao**, adjacent to Wat Chedi Luang, formerly a palace, is a masterpiece of wooden construction. Its doorway is crowned by a beautiful Lanna peacock framed by golden *naga*, or mythical serpents.

Located one kilometre northwest of the city walls, **Wat Jet Yod** was completed by King Trailokaraja in 1455. As its name "Seven Spires" suggests, it is a replica of the Mahabodhi Temple in India's Bodhgaya, where Buddha gained enlightenment while spending seven weeks in its gardens. The beautiful stucco angels that decorate its walls are said to bear faces of Trailokaraja's own family. Although similar to a temple in Burma's then-capital of Bagan, it did not stop the Burmese from severely damaging it during their invasion of 1566.

Outside Chiang Mai

A steep series of hairpin curves rises up the flanks of **Doi Suthep** – 15 km (9 miles) northwest of the city – to Chiang Mai's best-loved temple, **Wat Doi Suthep**. The site was selected in the mid-1300s by an elephant that was turned loose with a Buddha relic strapped to its back; where it stopped, it was believed, a temple should be built. It not only climbed the slopes of Doi Suthep to this site, it dropped dead here.

The ascending road passes the entrance to the **Huai Kaeo Falls**, where a minibus goes to the top. The scenery en route is spectacular, with the road winding its way to a large car park beneath Wat Doi Suthep. Seven-headed naga undulate down the balustrade of a 290-step stairway that leads from the parking lot to the temple. For the weary, a funicular makes the same ascent for a few baht. Below from the wat, Chiang Mai is spread at one's feet.

From the upper terrace, a few more steps lead through the courtyard of the

Chiang Mai is known for its fine umbrellas.

BELOW: Songkran festival in Chiang Mai.

temple itself. In the late afternoon light, there are few sights more stunning than that which greet one at the final step. Emerging from cloisters decorated with murals depicting scenes from the Buddha's life, one's eyes rise to the summit of a 24-metre-high (80-ft) gilded chedi, partially shaded by gilded bronze parasols. The chedi is surrounded by an iron fence with pickets culminating in praying *thevada*, or angels. Appearing in the east and west ends of the compound are two viharn. At dawn, the eastern one shelters chanting nuns in white robes. At sunset, the one on the west holds orange-robed monks chanting their prayers.

From the parking area of Wat Doi Suthep, a road ascends a further 5 km (3 miles) to **Phuping Palace**, the winter residence of the royal family. Constructed in 1972 and situated at 1,300 metres (4,265 ft), the palace has audience halls, guest houses, dining rooms, kitchens and official suites. It also serves as headquarters for royal agricultural and medical projects carried on among hill tribes and in villages. When the royal family is absent, the public may stroll (Fri–Sun, and holidays) through well tended gardens.

Map on page 24

Commercialised hill tribes

From the palace entrance, the road continues through pine forests to the commercialised Hmong hill-tribe village of **Doi Pui**. The village has been on the tourist track for some time, but improvements over the past decade have brought material benefits to its inhabitants, including a paved street lined with souvenir stands. It is possible to wander by the houses to glimpse how the people live.

At one time subsistence farmers, the tribespeople have learned that visitors come bearing gifts, and aiming a camera automatically triggers a hand extended for a donation. Hmong are itinerant farmers here, as they are in Burma and

BELOW: northern Akha woman feeding cattle.

Map
on page
24

TIP

Chiang Mai is best
visited during winter,
late November through
early February, when it
is abloom with an
astounding variety of
beautiful flowers.
Numerous resorts in
Mae Sa Valley carpet
the hillsides with
flower gardens, and
in February is the
Flower Festival.

*Buddha image in a
niche at Wat Kukut,
Lamphun.*

Laos. They once depended upon opium cultivation for their livelihoods; despite government efforts to steer them towards more socially acceptable crops, many still cultivate patches deep in the hills. An interesting insight into opium farming is provided by Doi Pui's **Opium Museum**, which describes in detail the process of cultivation and harvest. For those who lack the time to go deeper into the northern hills, this Hmong village offers a tainted example of hill-tribe life, though one doubts it retains much of its original personality.

Once an agricultural region, the **Mae Sa Valley** cultivates a new money-earner – tourism. Waterfalls, working elephant camps, butterfly farms, orchid nurseries and a charming private museum called **Mae Sa House Collection** (with prehistoric artifacts and Sukhothai ceramics, among many things) vie for the visitor's attention. The valley also has quiet resorts along its river.

North of Chiang Mai

To reach the northern town of **Fang ❷**, take Route 107 north from Chiang Mai (beginning at Chang Puak Gate) towards Chiang Dao. The road passes through rice fields and small villages, then begins to climb past Mae Taeng into the Mae Ping Gorge, which forms the southern end of the Chiang Dao Valley. Ahead, on the left as one follows the river's right bank through scenic countryside, is the massive outline of Chiang Dao mountain.

At the 56-kilometre marker is the **Chiang Dao Elephant Camp** (daily 8am–5pm), on the bank of the Mae Nam Ping. Twice daily, a line of elephants walk into the Ping to be bathed by *mahout* for the amusement of tourists, who reward the baby elephants with bananas. The elephants then move to a dusty arena to demonstrate how to make huge logs seem like toothpicks, picking them up or dragging them with great ease across the teak-shaded open space.

About 60 km (40 miles) from Chiang Mai on Route 107, a dirt road branches left and goes to **Doi Chiang Dao**, which at 2,186 metres (7,175 ft) is Thailand's third-highest peak. A jeep or a trail bike is needed to negotiate this 9-km track, which leads to the Hmong village of Pakkia up the mountain. Entry to the sanctuary is restricted and permission must be obtained from the wildlife headquarters near Wat Pa Bong at the foot of the mountain.

Further north, Route 107 enters the town of **Chiang Dao**, located 70 km (45 miles) from Chiang Mai. Chiang Dao is a quiet, wooden town supplying surrounding villages, but its cafes and general stores are interesting. At the far end of town, a simple road leads off to the left for 5 km (3 miles) to some caves. Guides with lanterns lead visitors deep into high caverns with Buddha statues. In a deeper section is a large, reclining limestone Buddha.

South to Lamphun

The road south from Chiang Mai is one of the most beautiful in northern Thailand. **Lamphun ❸** itself dates back from the mid-6th century and is famed for two old *wat*, attractive women, and young and prolific *lamyai* fruit trees.

To gain the best perspective on Lamphun's **Wat Prathat Haripunchai**, enter through its riverside gate, where large statues of mythical lions guard its portals. Inside the large compound, monks study in a large Buddhist school set amidst monuments and buildings, which date as far back as the late 9th century. A kilometre west of Lamphun's old moat stands **Wat Kukut**, dating from the 8th century. (It's also known as Wat Chama Devi.) The temple has a superb pair of unusual chedi. Erected in the early 1200s, the larger chedi consists of five tiers, each of which contains three niches. Each niche holds a Buddha statue.

South of Lamphun, beyond Pasang, is the hill-top pilgrimage centre of **Wat Phrabat Tak Pha**, said to protect a footprint of the Buddha. ❑

Thailand's Gems: Crystal Power

Thais have turned a national passion for gems and jewellery into one of the country's largest export industries. Rubies, sapphires and jade are among the best bargains, while gold, silver and diamond products, finished by master craftsmen, are also popular buys.

Rubies, the name given to red, gem-quality corundum stones, vary in shade from pinkish or purplish to the brownish-red found in Thailand, depending upon the stone's chromium and iron content. A really fine ruby can appear to glow like hot coal. Since prehistoric times, rubies have been associated with a range of spiritual and supernatural beliefs. The Burmese thought rubies conferred invulnerability, and that they could foretell danger by loss of colour or brilliance. Most of the rubies in Thailand traditionally originated from the Chanthaburi region, and from the Pailin area of Cambodia, which together account for around two-thirds of the world's supply of rubies. A small number come from Vietnam and parts of Africa.

Thailand's ruby mines were known in early times, with the first known reference coming from a Chinese traveller, Ma Huan, in AD 1408. Now they are close to depletion. At Bo Rai, once the king of Thai ruby-mining towns, abandoned equipment litters the landscape. Where there used to be hundreds of traders, just a few remain. Supplies from the Cambodian side of the border have become sporadic. Rubies from the remote Mogok and Mong Hsu mines in upper Burma, where primitive, back-breaking extraction methods still apply, are relatively rare and highly sought-after for the international market when they get to Thailand.

An important distinction is made between prime-quality unheated stones, most of which come from Mogok, and less valuable heat-treated samples, originating primarily in Mong Hsu. The latter tend to look like bad garnet before treatment, after which they turn into bright-red gems.

Sapphires, also composed of corundum, come in different colours, from the highly-prized rich-blue to orange, green, yellow, pink and colourless varieties. Sapphire was traditionally believed by Buddhists to produce a desire for prayer, to help ward off negative energies, and to promote calm. Thailand's sapphires now come mainly from Sri Lanka, Australia and Africa. Locally mined sapphires in Kanchanaburi and Phrae, and Cambodian stones from the Pailin area, are increasingly limited in number and quality.

In recent years, Thailand has also become a major centre for processing diamonds, catering to a large foreign as well as thriving domestic jewellery.

Shopping for gems and jewellery in Thailand is easy and rewarding, so long as one sticks to reputable stores. (If in doubt, contact the local Tourism Authority of Thailand office for authorised gem and jewellery establishments.) Many scams involving gullible tourists have been reported. They often take the form of an individual with a "special offer", backed up by a convincing story. A polite but firm refusal will deflect the scam. ❏

RIGHT: blue sapphire in hand.

THE SOUTHERN ISLANDS

Significant numbers of travellers come to Thailand for its seductive southern islands – Phuket, Samui, Phi Phi. Whether they want to be pampered or find rustic ambience, the islands can satisfy

Map on pages 24, 57

Thailand's south, a long arm of land sometimes likened to an elephant's trunk, contains 14 provinces and is rich in stunning scenery. In many ways the south is a world far removed from the rest of the country, especially in the deep south near Malaysia. A different climate, religion and type of farming make it unique among Thailand's regions. Groves of rubber trees are more common than fields of rice, and the gilded dome of a Muslim mosque becomes a more familiar sight than the sloping orange roof of a Buddhist temple. For many years, access to the south's secluded areas, especially the islands, was a major undertaking. While access to the south is easy these days, there is still a sense of adventure and remoteness to one's travels here.

Phuket

The undeniable physical beauty of **Phuket ❹** is even greater than its exquisite beaches. This beauty stems from its picturesque villages, coconut groves, and rubber plantations as much as its patchwork of wild flowers presented against a backdrop of forested hills. For centuries Phuket was a backwater. The long road south from Bangkok to reach it, the lack of a bridge across the causeway, bad roads on the island itself, and a seeming lack of interest in developing it for recreation meant that it languished in relative isolation for decades despite natural resources of tin, rubber and coconut.

OPPOSITE: southern island fishing, Phang Nga Bay.

Today, the road from Phang Nga on the mainland crosses the 600-metre (2,000-ft) Thaothep Kasaetri Bridge to Phuket, an island about the same size as Singapore. The sojourn to Phuket town, 30 km (20 miles) south, soon reaches the heart of the island. The crossroads at **Ban Tha Rua ❹** to Surin Beach and Khao Phra Taeo National Park is dominated by two bronze statues of female warriors, swords in hands. The pair are sisters: Chan and Muk. In 1785 they led an army of villagers to repel Burmese invaders on Phuket.

Unlike many Thai provincial centres, the town of **Phuket ❸** on the island's southeast coast has a rich identity of its own. The charm of Phuket's old buildings is complemented by the many Chinese shrines that accent the city with bright splashes of colour. Of note is the brightly painted **Jui Tui Temple** and its smaller companion **Put Jaw** next door, which sit just past the market on Thanon Ranong. Like many similar Chinese shrines elsewhere in Asia, their central altars are dedicated to Kuan Yin (Quanyin), the goddess of mercy. Jui Tui is the starting point for the five days of colourful and bizarre parades that mark the annual Phuket Vegetarian Festival in October.

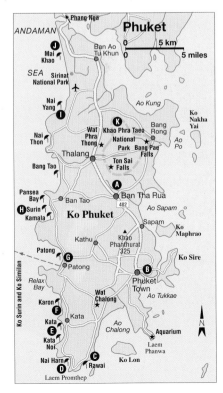

In 1786, Capt. Light sought to secure Phuket for England. Thai claims and England's desire for a more strategic island to guard the Straits of Malacca led Light to drop the plan and found Penang, which became England's primary colony on the Malay peninsula until the founding of Singapore in 1819.

Southeast along the coast is **Rawai ⊙**, whose foreshore is a mass of rocks that lies exposed during low tide, when clam hunters venture out, turning over the stones in search of dinner. Rawai holds one of the island's handful of *chao lay*, or sea gypsy, villages. The sea gypsies were once nomadic fishing families, roaming from island to island. They are skilled fishermen both above and below the water. From a young age, they learn to dive to great depths in search of lobsters, prawns, and crabs, staying below for up to 3 minutes. However, diminishing stocks and environmental and tourism concerns have robbed the sea gypsies of traditional fishing grounds.

Phuket's glory, however, lies in its many beautiful beaches, and it has a wealth of them. From Rawai the coastal road continues over the north–south ridge of hills, offering great views for 45 km (28 miles) as far as Ko Phi Phi. Continue south around Prom Thep to **Nai Harn ⊙**, one of the island's prettiest beaches. Further north, the more picturesque bays of **Kata Noi** and **Kata ⊙** have a more intimate feel due to their smaller size. There is fine snorkelling at the southern end of Kata Noi beach. Relax Bay, with its single hotel, Le Meridien Phuket, offers some snorkelling along its northwestern rocks. **Karon Beach ⊙** is a long quiet strip of sand backed by hotels and restaurants at its top, middle and bottom, with empty plots of former rice paddy in between. Both Karon and Kata are much less frenetic than Patong, but with a growing choice of hotel, dining and watersport facilities.

The most developed beach is **Patong ⊙**, due west of Phuket town on the opposite side of the island and north of Karon. In the early 1970s, Patong was little more than a huge banana plantation wedged between the mountains and a wide crescent of sand. The plantation is now a tourist city-by-the-sea, with

BELOW: offering at a Chinese temple, town of Phuket.

multi-storey condominiums and hotels rising above night markets, seafood emporiums, beer bars, discos, and tour shops. Dive shops offer trips into the bay or west to the **Similan Islands National Marine Reserve,** considered one of the best diving areas in Asia, with crystal-clear water and ample marine life.

Some 3 km (2 miles) north of Patong, quiet **Kamala Bay** retains charm around its Islamic hamlets with their well-kept gardens against a backdrop of forested hills rising to over 500 metres (1,600 ft). The tranquillity won't last. At the northern end of Kamala, a giant Disney-like theme park rises.

The attractive coastal road north to **Surin Beach ◐** passes mouthwateringly compact **Singh Beach**, its sandy cape hedged by verdant headlands. Larger Surin Beach with its dappled seafood shacks soon gives way to idyllic **Pansea Bay** dominated by two proprietary resorts, the Chedi and the Amanpuri. The long beach at **Bang Tao** is dominated by the immense Laguna Phuket, which shelters five large resorts.

Nai Yang Beach ◑, just south of the airport, is now under the jurisdiction of **Sirinat National Park**. There are a few Spartan bungalows for rent in the national park. With a good map it is possible to drive along Phuket's scenic west coast from Nai Yang to the island's southern tip, Prom Thep.

North of Nai Yang is Phuket's longest beach, **Mai Khao ◒**. The beach, 9 km (5½ miles) long, is relatively undeveloped, a haven for beachcombers and the giant sea turtles that come ashore from December through February to lay their eggs. If needing wilderness, green forest can be experienced on hikes through **Khao Phra Taeo National Park ◓**. Wild bears and cats still live there, all of them keen to avoid human contact. The park is fringed by two pretty waterfalls: Ton Sai on the west, and Bang Bae on the east.

Map on page 57

Rua hang yao, *the Thai long-tail boat.*

BELOW: Kata Noi.

Phang Nga and Krabi

The town of **Phang Nga ❺** is revealed as a lovely, peaceful township left behind in Thailand's development surge. The main objective of any first-time trip here, however, should be to the geological wonderland of **Phang Nga Bay**.

Just before the mouth of Phang Nga River, the boat approaches the base of **Khao Kien** mountain, where a cavern contains primitive paintings depicting human and animal forms. Such cave daubings are quite common in the limestone caves in the area. They were painted by primitive people around 2,000 years ago. The floors of many caves in Phang Nga and Krabi are still scattered with the discarded sea shells of prehistoric people. Tide fluctuations have compromised archaeological evidence. Forty thousand years ago, it was possible to walk to Phi Phi. Five thousand years ago, sea levels were higher than at present.

Ko Ping Kan is perhaps the most spectacular of Phang Nga's islands. Behind the beach, the mountain seems to have split in two, the halves leaning against each other. Locals say they are two lovers. This area was the setting of part of a James Bond movie, *The Man with the Golden Gun*.

About 50 km (30 miles) south of Phang Nga, **Thanboke Koranee National Park**, near Krabi, is one of the most beautiful in Thailand. The town of **Krabi ❻** itself is a small but bustling service centre built opposite mangrove swamps along the Krabi River.

From town, Krabi River mangroves can be explored by renting a long-tail boat, first stopping off to visit the huge cavern inside the Kanab Nam twin peaks, which the flank the river. Traditionally, the leaves, bark, fruit and mosses of the surrounding mangroves provided folk cures for the alleviation of lumbago, kidney stones and menstrual pains. The trees also provided a source of

TIP

From Krabi, visitors can catch long-tail boats sailing out to Railae Beach, with larger ones leaving daily for Ko Phi Phi, and for Ko Lanta from November to May.

BELOW: one of Phang Nga's many caves, and rocky retreat near Krabi.

weak alcohol and leaves for wrapping tobacco. Two rare bird species inhabit the mangroves: the mangrove pitta and the brown-winged kingfisher.

Map on page 24

Ko Phi Phi

Turquoise waves caress a beach so dazzlingly white, it is almost painful to the eye. The water is so crystalline, colourful fishing boats seem suspended in mid-air. With palm-fringed beaches and lofty limestone mountains as a backdrop, **Ko Phi Phi ❼** arguably surpasses Phuket as one of the most beautiful islands in Asia. Phi Phi lies equidistant, about 45 km (30 miles), from both Phuket and Krabi. The island is in fact two islands: the smaller **Phi Phi Ley**, a craggy limestone monolith similar to the other shrub-covered peaks of Phang Nga Bay, and **Phi Phi Don**, a national park with an epicentre of anarchic tourism development. Should the diving bug bite, Phi Phi Island has several dive shops where visitors can earn their open water scuba certification.

Popularity, however, has brought pollution and floating garbage to the Phi Phi islands, and one wonders how long it is before they are no longer the idyllic retreats sought by many.

Ko Samui and Ko Pha Ngan

Nowadays, about three million tourists descend upon **Ko Samui ❽** every year. There are luxury hotels, fancy restaurants, a modern airport, easy transport, a few absolutely chaotic and stressful commercial strips, and the full panoply of water sports and other diversions.

In addition to all the outlets for water sports, in the interior are several waterfalls descending from the heights of **Khao Phlu**, the island's highest point at 635 metres (2,080 ft). Sprinkled elsewhere around the island are a go-kart track, snake farm, butterfly aviary and lots of snooker parlours. The numerous signs for "monkey shows" are opportunities to see pig-tailed macaques engaged in their usual jobs on coconut farms. They twist coconuts from the tree tops, then retrieve and deposit them in burlap bags.

Aside from attendance at the Catholic Church or immigration office, there's no reason to linger among the drab cement blocks of Samui's biggest town, the western port of **Na Thon**. Ferries to Ko Pha Ngan and Anthong National Marine Park depart from Na Thon.

Long ago, the original beachcombers and today's tasteful hotels were drawn by a 6-km (4-mile) swathe of soft, silky sand at **Chaweng**, on the eastern coast. The sand at its half-sized southern neighbour, **Lamai**, is slightly lower grade. South of Lamai, the smaller beaches of **Ban Hua Thanon** and **Ban Bangkao** are nothing to write home about, but the coral reef is healthy near the former and the latter is a charming Muslim village. From either, make a day trip inland and swim at the two-tiered waterfall at **Na Muang**. On the western side of the island, **Ban Taling Ngam** offers a couple of rather deluxe resort retreats.

Almost the entire northern coast of Ko Samui is occupied by three lovely bays. For panorama, head along the north shore to **Maenam**. The sand is coarser than that of the east, but the 4-km stretch is little

BELOW: beach on Ko Samui.

Map on page 24

TIP

Song thaew – small pickup trucks converted to taxis – serve Ko Samui. Cheap and fast, they rarely refuse a fare and will load up until passengers are hanging from the tailgate and roof.

RIGHT: beach on Ko Phi Phi.
BELOW: Big Buddha.

developed. East of Maenam, **Bo Phut** is much narrower, but relatively protected, whichever way the wind blows. Popular with French and Italian families, it's a short walk from the cute little fishing village of Ban Bo Phut. As for **Bangrak** (better known as **Big Buddha Beach**), it's a mystery why anyone stays here unless they enjoy the din from the adjacent road or the jets roaring overhead. Or perhaps it's the view of the indisputably large Buddha statue and its complement of especially garish souvenir shops. Quieter **Choeng Mon**, on the island's northeastern spur, has decent sand and water, and is within quick access of Chaweng's commercial facilities.

Last but not least, located 30 km (20 miles) west of Ko Samui, are the attractions of 41 brilliant isles comprising **Ang Thong National Marine Park**. Daylong package trips voyage to Ko Wua Talab, park headquarters, and Ko Mae Ko. But these tours allow little time to investigate any more than a viewpoint and a cave on Wua Talab, and the clear, pea-green saltwater lake on Mae Ko. On both, the designated swimming spots have negligible coral and fish. For the more adventurous, it is possible to rent a tent on Ko Wua Talab and enjoy the serenity of the islands after the tour boats have gone.

Ko Pha Ngan

If Ko Samui is increasingly the island of package tours and brief vacations, its neighbour 15 km (9 miles) to the north, **Ko Pha Ngan**, is a refuge for backpackers on leisurely world tours and Europeans lazing away winter-long holidays. From the cacophonous southern port town of **Thong Sala**, a ferry port for Ko Samui and Ko Tao (except for e-mail and mountainbike rentals, there's little call to hang around Thong Sala), there is a newly-paved 10-km (6-mile)

stretch that runs due north to the village of **Cha Loak Lam**, a favourite stopover on the north coast for trawlers. East of Cha Loak Lam, the justly prized beach of the moment is **Hat Khuat** (Bottle Beach), which can only be reached by sea. Probably the quickest way to get there is from Ban Cha Loak.

Continuing eastward and down the coast, one could well enjoyably argue the merits of **Hat Sadet** (with a waterfall and jumbo rocks bearing the graffiti of Thai royalty) or **Thong Nai Pan**, with wonderful cliff viewpoints, a double-barrelled bay and a coral reef. Eventually you will reach the pretty southern cove of **Hat Tien**, which offers an additional choice of beaches on either side. Pick one and drop anchor.

Just 10 minutes away by long-tail boat is **Hat Rin**, better known internationally than Pha Ngan itself due to its monthly all-night "full-moon" party. The biggest bashes of the year take place in December and January, when leading British DJs fly in with cutting-edge sounds and hordes of young clubbers. There's even a thrice-daily boat connection between Hat Rin and Samui. Nonetheless, the roller-coaster road joining Hat Rin and Thong Sala is now paved and has further opened up the intervening villages and so-so beaches of **Ban Tai** and **Ban Khai**.

An easy stroll up a hill from Ban Tai is **Wat Khao Tham**, where Australian and American teachers run 10- to 20-day Buddhist meditation courses here. ❏

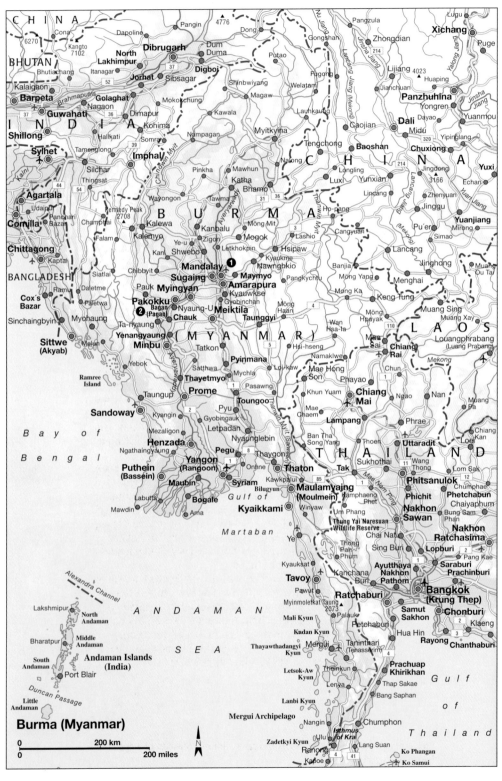

Burma (Myanmar)

BURMA

Visiting Burma has always been a magical experience

but now there is also an ethical dimension

Travellers contemplating a trip to Burma will be aware that it is regarded by a large section of the global community as a pariah because of the human rights abuses of the Burmese people by the ruling military junta. The burning question is this: does visiting Burma endorse the current regime or, in a small way, reduce the country's isolation from the outside world and constrain the junta's actions? Both views have convincing advocates, and informed travellers must make up their own minds.

The essence of Burma lies in its atmosphere, its varied scents and colour, its ambience recalling past ages. That eternal beauty will remain after today's political repression has become part of history, and we hope that keeping this section of the book up to date may play a part in ensuring that the country and its deeply religious and dignified people will not be forgotten or ignored.

Today, even the country's name is contentious. In 1989, the Burmese authorities implemented a series of name changes replacing colonial names with equivalents closer to actual Burmese usage. The most important change was to the name of the country, officially changed from the "Union of Burma" to the "Union of Myanmar". The same is true with "Rangoon", which became "Yangon", a name given to the city as far back as 1755 by Alaungpaya when he captured and renamed the city of Dagon. The river Irrawaddy is now the Ayeyarwady, the Sittang changed to Sittoung, the Chindwin to Chindwinn, and the Salween to Thanlwin.

Of the cities, Pegu became Bago, Pagan changed to Bagan, Tavoy to Dawei, Prome to Pyay, Moulmein to Mawlamyaing, Maymyo to Pyin-U-Lwin, Magwe to Magway, Bassein to Pathein, Mergui to Myeik, and Sandoway to Thandwe. Tenasserim is now Tanintharyi and Arakan has become Rakhaing. Burmans are now called Bamar, the Karen are called Kayin, and the Arakanese are called Rakhaing. In this book we use the new names, with the old names in parentheses in the first reference of each chapter.

The name of the country, however, will remain Burma and that of the language Burmese, since this is derived from the internationally accepted term "Tibeto-Burman". We have made a distinction between the Bamar (Burman) people, the country's majority ethnic group, and the Burmese, a term that represents all the peoples of Burma. Indigenous terms used are from the Burmese language, except for Pali language words in religious contexts. ❑

PRECEDING PAGES: fishing on Inle Lake, in central Burma; Shwedagon Pagoda in the northern part of Yangon.

Decisive Dates

The early empire
3000–5000 BC: Anyaathian culture flourishes in northern Burma.
circa 500 BC: The Pyus enter the upper part of the Ayeyarwady (Irrawaddy) River basin.
3rd century BC: Mons settle in the Sittoung Valley.
AD 832: Pyu state of Sri Ksetra founded. Conquest of Pyt capital of Halin by Tai-Shans of Nan-Chao.
9th century AD: The Mramma people, known as the Bramars, come from the China-Tibet border area, overrun the Kyaukse plain and establish themselves as a

major power in the rice-cultivation region. From Bagan, they control trade routes between China and India.

The Burman dynasties
1057 AD: Anawrahta founds first Burman empire.
1084-1113: Golden Age of Bagan. Under Kyanzittha, the golden age of pagoda-building begins.
1287: Mongol invasion of Bagan leads to fall of first Burman empire. Mons establish state at Martaban.
1364: Inwa founded as capital of a Shan-Bamara dynasty in northern Burma.
1369: Mon capital transferred to Bago.
1385–1425: War between the Mons and Shans.
1519: Portuguese establish trade station, Martaban.
1531: Second Burman Empire established.

1600–13: Portuguese, de Brito, rules at Thanlyin.
1635: Burma capital is moved to Inwa. British, French and Dutch develop trade with Burma.
1752: Mons conquer Inwa, ending the Second Burmese Empire.
1755: Alaungpaya founds new dynasty and Third Burmese Empire at Shwebo.
1767: Burmese conquer Thai capital of Ayutthaya.
1785: Rakhine is conquered by King Bodawapaya.

Colonial period to World War II
1824–1826: First Anglo-Burman war; under Treaty of Yandabo, Britain gains the regions around Rakhine and Tanintharyi.
1852: Second Anglo-Burman war; Britain annexes Yangon and Southern Burma.
1861: King Mindon (1853–78) transfers his court to the new city of Mandalay.
1886: Britain annexes all of Burma.
1886–95: Burmese wage guerrilla warfare against British in northern Burma.
1937: Burma is separated from India.
1939: Communist Party of Burma (CPB) is founded.
1941: Japanese military enters Burma.
1942–45: Most of Burma under Japanese occupation.
1943: Declaration of Burma's independence under the Japanese military.
1945: Burma National Army starts anti-Japanese uprising. Allies reconquer all of Burma.
1947: Aung San-Attlee agreement is signed. Panglong agreement is signed. Constituent assembly elections are held. Aung San and six other members of interim government are assassinated. Constituent assembly adopts new Burmese constitution. Nu-Attlee agreement concluded.

Independence
1948: Burma regains independence as Union of Burma and leaves British Commonwealth. CPB goes underground and civil war begins.
1949: Kayin rebellion breaks out.
1951: First parliamentary elections in post-independence Burma are held.
1956: Second parliamentary elections.
1958: Ruling party splits into two factions. A caretaker government, headed by General Ne Win, assumes office.
1960: Border agreement and treaty of friendship and non-aggression concluded between Burma and People's Republic of China. U Nu's Pyidaungsu Party wins in parliamentary elections.
1961: Union Parliament makes Buddhism the official state religion.

Military rule

1962: Military coup brings to power the Revolutionary Council (RC) of General Ne Win, who declares the "Burmese Way of Socialism". Burma Socialist Programme Party (BSPP) founded.

1963: Peace talks between the RC and various rebel organisations and groups are held in Yangon.

1964: All legal political parties and organisations except BSPP are banned. Nationalisation of all export trade and commodity distribution is implemented.

1967: Anti-Chinese riots in Yangon.

1969: Former Prime Minister U Nu founds Parliamentary Democracy Party to fight RC from abroad.

1971: First BSPP Congress is held and the Twenty-Year Plan (1974–94) announced. Ne Win's state visit to China marks normalisation of official relations.

1974: New constitution becomes effective, creating the Socialist Republic of the Union of Burma.

1979: Burma withdraws from Non-Aligned Movement.

1980: A congregation of Buddhist monks convenes in Yangon to set out ways to "purify, disseminate and perpetuate" Buddhist teaching. U Ne Win announces his retirement from Presidency. U San Yu replaces him.

Revolution and military reaction

1987: UN General Assembly approves Least Developed Nation status for Burma.

1988: Major demonstrations at Yangon University campuses. On 26 July, Brigadier-General Sein Lwin elected as BSPP's new chairman and chairman of state council (President of the State). On 3 August, martial law is declared in Yangon. Five days later general strike and demonstrations in Yangon; the army kills many demonstrators. Dr Maung Maung replaces Sein Lwin on 12 August. The largest demonstration in Yangon occurs on 28 August and martial law is lifted there. U Nu sets up League for Democracy and Peace.

SLORC takes power

September 1988: U Nu proclaims "parallel government" with himself as Prime Minister. On 18 September, the military takes power in a coup. State Law and Order Restoration Council (SLORC), headed by General Saw Maung, is formed. Aung Gyi, Tin U and Daw Aung San Suu Kyi found National League for Democracy (NLD). BSPP is now the National Unity Party (NUP).

1989: Rebellious Wa troops capture CPB's headquarters at Panghsang, ending Communist insurgency. The English name of Burma is changed to Myanmar.

LEFT: the only portrait of King Mindon, founder of Mandalay. **RIGHT:** General Ne Win, head of the Revolutionary Council in 1963.

1990: "Multi-party democracy" general elections held. NLD gains over 80 percent of seats, but the SLORC retains power and continues its repression of NLD.

1991: Daw Aung San Suu Kyi is awarded Nobel Peace Prize while under house arrest.

1992: UN Human Rights Commission condemns Burma for serious rights violations. General Saw Maung resigns and is succeeded by General Than Shwe (Vice-Chairman of SLORC), who becomes new Prime Minister. Burma is readmitted to Non-Aligned Movement. Two decades of martial law and curfew end.

1993: The largest rebel group, Kachin Independence Organisation (KIO), signs a cease-fire agreement with the government, ending a 30-year war in the north. Fol-

lowed by agreements with 14 other insurgent groups.

1995: In July, Aung San Suu Kyi is freed from 6 years of house arrest. SLORC secretary Lieutenant General Khin Nyant offers that when a new constitution is finished, they will return power to a civilian government.

1998: Burma is admitted to the Association of Southeast Asian Nations (ASEAN).

2000: ASEAN Economic Ministers' summit is held in Yangon amid continuing human rights violations and unrest.

2001: Significant talks stall when the authorities fail to meet Aung San Suu Kyi's demands on political prisoners and movement restrictions on NLD leaders.

2002: The UN helps secure Aung San Su Kyi's release from house arrest. General Ne Win, accused of plotting to overthrow the military, dies after a long illness. ❑

THE BURMESE

The population of Burma is unquestionably a collection of diverse people,
its origins found in the cultures of ancient China and Thailand

The old name Union of Burma implied that the nation was and is a federation of many peoples. But it is an uneasy federation. "Burma Proper", as it was called by the British and chief settlement area of the Bamar (Burman) majority, is encircled by separate minority states of the Chin, Kachin, Shan, Kayin or Karen, Kayah (Red Karen), Mons and Rakhines (Arakanese). Through the centuries, there have been mistrust, antagonism, and frequent wars among the various groups, and the situation is no different today.

The current administrative divisions were built into Burma's 1948 constitution, which was based on a model devised by the British. During the colonial era, the British, on their favoured principle of "divide and rule", made a distinction between Burma Proper and "Outer Burma", the latter comprising the settlement areas of the ethnic minorities. Burma Proper was placed under the direct rule of British India, but the minorities were left with much greater autonomy under indirect rule. At this time, nearly 250 separate languages and dialects were spoken.

While the Bamars were denied a place in the colonial army, the various minorities were heavily depended upon by the British for their fighting skills. The racial enmity between the Bamars and the minorities festered just beneath the surface until independence was granted in 1948. Since that time, a succession of violent domestic confrontations has played havoc with the nation's hopes of internal peace.

No less than 67 separate indigenous racial groups have been identified in Burma, not including the various Indians, Chinese and Europeans who make the country their home.

Traces of prehistoric people

Long before ancestors of the modern Burmese moved from central Asia and Tibet, prehistoric people inhabited the area that is now known as Burma. These aborigines eventually moved on toward what is today Indonesia. No trace of them is found in the present-day population of Burma. The Andaman Sea islanders in the Bay of Bengal and the Semang of the Malay Peninsula might be direct descendants.

In historic times, three separate migrations were important in Burma's development.

First to arrive were the Mon-Khmer people from the arid, wind-swept plains of Central Asia, and it is not difficult to imagine their motivation. Anyone who has seen the mountains of golden rice piled high at harvest time will understand why the first Mon-Khmer kingdom was called Suvannabhumi, or the Golden Land.

Then came the Tibeto-Burmans, who pushed the Mon-Khmer people further to the south and east, away from the middle reaches of the Ayeyarwady (Irrawaddy) River. First the Pyus, then the Bamars moved down the valleys of the Ayeyarwady and Sittoung (Sittang) rivers,

LEFT: monk in the mountains of northern Burma.
RIGHT: old photo of Naga, an animistic people from the mountainous Sagaing Division.

establishing their magnificent empires at Sri Ksetra and Bagan (Pagan).

Between the 12th and 14th centuries, the Tais (known today in Burma as Shans), a Sino-Tibetan race, began moving south from Yunnan down the river valleys. When they tried to force the Bamars out of the Ayeyarwady Valley, centuries of warfare followed.

Bamars and Mons

As the majority racial group and the predominant landholder, as well as the group holding the reins of the present government, the Bamars bear the brunt of much interracial hostility.

The Buddhist Mons live mainly around the cities of Mawlamyine (Moulmein) and Bago. Before the Bamars came, they were the most powerful group in Burma. In 1995, after decades of armed resistance, they signed a cease-fire agreement with the Burmese army. Today, the Mons – who number just over 1 million – are largely assimilated in the mainstream Burmese culture, although they continue to use their own language and have retained their own sanctioned state within the Burmese union.

Padaung and Wa

Among the smaller minority groups belonging to the Mon-Khmer language family are the Padaung and the Wa. Both groups have gained a certain fame – or notoriety – that far exceeds their meagre numbers.

There are only about 7,000 Padaungs, all of whom live in the vicinity of Loikaw, capital of Kayah State. Their "giraffe women" were publicised by various ethnographers of the 19th and 20th centuries. Despite the illusion, the women's necks have not been elongated at all – their collarbones and ribs have been pushed down. But the result is essentially the same: the rings become a permanent necessity as no muscles develop where they support the head. If the rings are cut off, as they were in the past as a punishment for adultery, the head is unsupported and suffocation can follow.

The Wa are the notorious frontier inhabitants of Burma's northeast. About 300,000 Wa live in remote habitats on both sides of the border with China. Until the 1940s, there was little known about them, except that they were head-hunters who offered human skulls as sacrifices to their gods. Most of the Burmese Wa live in the east of the vast Shan State.

Shan

Shan. Siam. Assam. All three geographical names have the same root meaning, an indication of the widespread migration and settlement area of this race. The word means "free people", a theme that might have been the guiding force behind their medieval move down the alluvial plain of the majestic Chao Phraya River.

Most of Burma's 4 million Shans are Buddhists who make their homes in valleys and on high plains. Living at an average altitude of 1,000 metres (3,280 ft) above sea level, the Shans are Burma's leading producers of fruit, vegetables and flowers and, over the centuries, they have developed sophisticated irrigation systems in the river valleys.

After the Shan State, the Shans' next largest concentration is in Kachin State, but they can also be found throughout much of Burma.

Kayin, Red Karen and Kachins

The Kayin people belong linguistically to the Tibeto-Burman-speaking majority of Burma. There are presently 3 million members of this race living in Burma. Although they have their own separate administrative division – the Karen (Kawthule) State – only about one-third of the Kayin population lives there.

The Kayahs, or Red Karen, have the smallest state in Burma in terms of area as well as population. Virtually all members of this ethnic group – about 75,000 – reside here. The Kayahs are primarily hill people, making their living by dry cultivation of rice, millet and vegetables.

Kachin State is a real hotch-potch of hill tribes. Throughout this large, mountainous district in the far north, Jinghpaws (Kachins), Shans and Bamars share space with Maru, Lashi, Azi, Lisu, Rawang, Tailon, Taikamti, Tailay, Kadu and

a tourist destination, since both sides of the border are inhabited by some of the most colourful people in Southeast Asia.

Rakhaing and Chin

The Rakhaing (Arakanese), who are also known as Rakhine, inhabit Rakhaing State and constitute about 4 percent of the total population. Although closely related to the Bamar, the latter have had their hands full dealing with this coastal race over the two centuries since

> **ETHNIC MEDLEY**
>
> "In no other area are the races so diverse, or the languages and dialects so numerous…"
>
> C.M. Enriquez
> *Races of Burma* (1933)

Kanang villagers without any recognisable settlement pattern. The label Kachin is sometimes indiscriminately applied to all inhabitants of this state. In fact, the only true Kachins are the Jinghpaw people. Traditionally hilltop dwellers, their lifestyle and social structure are distinctly different from those of the Shans. Animism and sorcery are a part of daily life.

After decades of fighting the government, cross-border trade with China has developed tremendously. The region has great potential as

Rakhaing was annexed by King Bodawpaya.

The Rakhaing are about 75 percent Buddhist and 25 percent Muslim, with the two groups having little to do with each other.

With its exposure to monsoons, Rakhaing gets far more rain and has higher humidity. The entire transportation system is therefore dependent on boats, and cultivated land is always situated close to navigable waters.

The Chin, and related Naga people, make up about 2 percent of Burma's population. They live in the far northwest, spilling over the border into India and Bangladesh. Most Chin are animists who practise slash-and-burn agriculture to grow dry rice. ❑

LEFT: an elderly Kachin woman savours a puff on a local cheroot. **ABOVE:** *thanaka*-bark makeup is a traditional sun-block for Burmese women.

BUDDHA, JAMBUDIPA AND THE 37 NAT

Religion is a defining element in Burmese life. Buddhism permeates the everyday lives of Burma's people, placing great emphasis on individual achievement

It has often been said that Burma is the most profoundly Buddhist country in the world. That may well be true. But the brand of Buddhism practiced in this isolated land is unique on the face of the globe.

particularly that of the Brahmans. According to the Burmese, the European-Asian continent is called Jambudipa. It is the southern of four islands situated at the cardinal points surrounding Mount Meru, the centre of the world.

Burmese Buddhism, theoretically, is Theravada or Hinayana Buddhism, that sect of Buddhism adhering most closely to the Buddha's teaching, and which is the dominant form of Buddhism that is found throughout much of Southeast Asia. It was preceded in Burma, however, by the animistic beliefs of the hill tribes and by the Hindu-Brahmanism of early traders, which has had a profound effect on the cosmological concept of the people.

Burmese cosmology

Strictly speaking, Burmese cosmology is Buddhist cosmology, but it has been shaped by millennia of influences from other cultures,

This southern island is the only place where future Buddhas can be born. This is because Jambudipa is a place of misery compared to the other abodes of this universe.

There are, in fact, 31 planes of existence on, above, and below Mount Meru. They can be divided into three main groups: the 11 planes of *Kama-Loka*, the realm of the sensuous world; the 16 planes of *Rupa-Loka*, the realm of subtle material matter; and finally, the four planes of *Arupa-Loka*, the realm of formlessness.

ABOVE: a monk rests between periods of meditation in a monastery. **RIGHT:** many popular tattoos represent animistic deities.

King Anawrahta, founder of the First Burmese Empire, devoted his attention to simplifying spiritual beliefs. When he introduced Theravada Buddhism into Upper Burma as the national religion, he was unable to eliminate the animistic beliefs of his people. Despite radical measures, 36 of the countless *nat* survived in the people's daily activities. For the Burmese, these 36 nat serve nearly the same purpose as the saints of the Catholic Church. In both cases they are called upon in times of need. So Anawrahta introduced a 37th figure – Thagyamin – and made him king of the nat. He thereafter tolerated the popular worship of these 37 nat, once it had been established that they were also followers of the Buddha's teachings.

Beatitudes of Buddhism

Theravada Buddhism is recognised as the principal religion of about 80 percent of all Burmese people. While there are significant numbers of Hindus, Muslims, Christians and primitive animists (especially among the northern hill tribes), it is safe to say that over 99 percent of the Bamars (Burmans), Mons, Shans and Palaungs are Theravadins.

The division between the Theravada and Mahayana styles, while developing for some

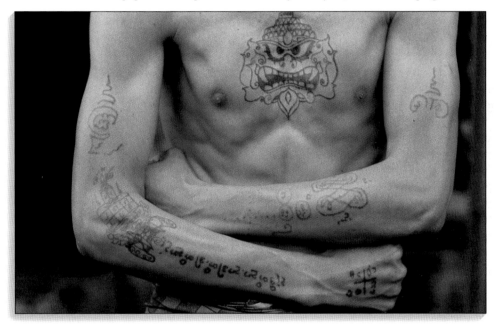

THREE JEWELS, FOUR NOBLE TRUTHS, AND THE EIGHT-FOLD PATH

As there is no true form of worship in the Theravada style of Buddhism, the only true ritual to which both monks and laity submit themselves is the recitation – three times a day – of the "Three Jewels," or the *Triratna*: "I take refuge in the Buddha. I take refuge in the Dhamma. I take refuge in the Sangha."

The formula of the "Three Jewels" offers solace and security. These are needed for strength, if one understands the "Four Noble Truths" expounded upon by Gautama Buddha in his first sermon:

- Life always has in it the element of suffering
- The cause of suffering is desire

- In order to end the suffering, give up desire and give up attachment
- The way to this goal is the Noble Eight-fold Path

The Noble Eight-fold Path consists of right views, right intent, right speech, right conduct, right means of livelihood, right endeavour, right mindfulness, and right meditation. This "path" is normally divided into three areas: views and intent are matters of wisdom; speech, conduct or action, and livelihood are matters of morality; and endeavour, mindfulness, and meditation are matters resulting from true mental discipline.

time, actually occurred in 235 BC when King Ashoka convened the Third Buddhist Synod at Pataliputra, India. The Buddhist elders (Theravada means "the way of the elders") held tight to their literal interpretation of the Buddha's teaching. They were opposed by a group which sought to understand the personality of the historical Buddha, and its relationship to one's salvation. Theravada Buddhism is actually a more conservative, more orthodox, form of the Buddhist thought.

The latter group became known as the Mahayana school. It established itself in Tibet, Nepal, China, Korea, Mongolia, Japan and

Vietnam, where its further development varied greatly from region to region. The Theravada school, meanwhile, has thrived in Sri Lanka, Burma, Thailand, Laos and Cambodia.

No soul

The Buddha denied the existence of a soul. There is no permanence, he explained, for that which one perceives to be "self". Rather, one's essence is forever changing. The idea of rebirth, therefore, is a complicated philosophical question within the structure of Buddhism. When a Buddhist (or any person, for that matter) is reincarnated, it is neither the person nor the soul which is actually reborn. Rather, it is the sum of

one's *karma*, the balance of good and evil deeds. One is reborn as a result of prior existence. A popular metaphor used to explain this transition is that of a candle. Were a person to light one candle from the flame of another, then extinguish the first, it could not be said that the new flame was the same as the previous one. Rather, in fact, its existence would be due to that of the previous flame.

The Noble Eight-fold Path, therefore, does not lead to salvation in the Judeo-Christian sense. By pursuing matters of wisdom, morality and mental discipline, one can hope to make the transition into *nirvana*, which can perhaps best be defined as extinction of suffering, cessation of desire. It is not heaven, nor is it annihilation. It is simply a quality of existence.

The monk

There are no priests in Theravada Buddhism. But the faithful still need a model to follow on the path to salvation. This model is provided by the colourfully clad Southeast Asian monks. In Burma, there are about 800,000 monks. Most of these are students and novices who put on the monk's robe only temporarily; nearly all male Burmese devote a period – from a few weeks to several years – in their lifetime to the monkhood. There are three fundamental rules to which the monk must subscribe. First, the renunciation of all possessions, except eight items: three robes, a razor for shaving, a needle for sewing, a strainer (to ensure that no living thing is swallowed), a belt, and an alms bowl. Second, a vow to injure no living thing and to offend no one. Finally, the vow of complete sexual celibacy. The monk must make his livelihood by seeking alms, setting out two hours before dawn and going door to door. The food received is the monk's only meal of the day.

A young Burmese begins his novitiate at around the age of nine. For the majority of Burmese, the novitiate does not last long. Most have left the monkhood before their 20th birthday. Those who are fully ordained have all hair shaved from their bodies. They devote their lives to meditation, the study of the Pali scriptures, and the instruction of the laity. ❑

LEFT: the head-shaving part of a young Burmese boy's *shin-pyu*, the initiation as a novice into the order of monks. **RIGHT:** Rangoon monks pause during their daily alms-collection rounds.

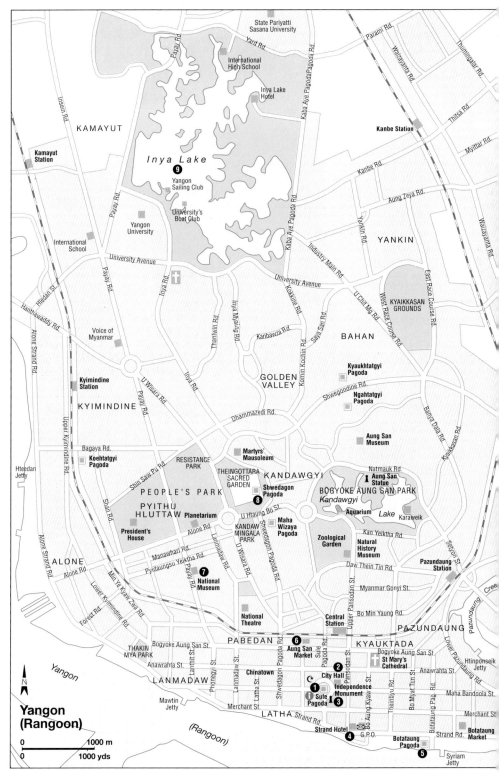

Yangon (Rangoon)

YANGON (RANGOON)

Map on page 80

Kipling had ogled, Theroux has prophesied. Burma's capital of Yangon, or Rangoon, continues to evoke lyricism from those who venture among its streets of "dispossessed princes"

It's been more than 100 years since Kipling sailed up the Yangon River to the Burmese capital of Yangon (Rangoon), and now, as then, the glistening golden stupa of the Shwedagon Pagoda continues to dominate Yangon's landscape and image as perhaps few other structures do in any other major city of Southeast Asia. The massive pagoda not only is a remarkable architectural achievement, it is also the perfect symbol of a country in which Buddhism pervades every aspect of life. Indeed, it is hard to imagine a more stunning sight than watching the first rays of dawn bounce off the brilliant gold-plated pagoda and reflect in the serene waters of the nearby lake.

But while the Shwedagon Pagoda may dominate Yangon from its post of Singuttara Hill north of the city centre, it is far from the whole show. If you look beyond the ageing British colonial architecture of most of Yangon's buildings, you will find an oddly cosmopolitan city of 19th-century charm, with quiet, tree-lined avenues and a people that are known to be gracious and fun-loving. Even though the city centre around Sule Pagoda is sprouting high-rise buildings, the facelift that is being conducted by the present government has changed little of the appearance of the city, preserving some of the city centre with a bit of the ambience present when the British left in 1948.

BELOW: girl with *thanaka* bark paste on her face.

Water on three sides

A burgeoning city of 5 million people (the population has more than quarupled in three decades), Yangon is surrounded on three sides by water. The Hlaing or Yangon River flows from the Bago (Pegu) Yoma down Yangon's west and south flanks, then continues another 30 kilometres (20 mi) to the Gulf of Martaban. To the east of the city is Pazundaung Creek, a tributary of the Hlaing.

To the north are the foothills of the Bago Yoma. It is here that one finds the Shwedagon (*see page 86*) and the charming lakes artificially created by the British, now the centres of residential districts.

We first hear of "Dagon, the town with the Golden Pagoda" from European travellers in the 16th century. An English merchant, Ralph Fitch, in 1586 described Shwedagon as "the fairest place, as I suppose, that is in the world." But it was the nearby town of Syriam, across the Bago and Hlaing rivers from Dagon, that was the most important European trading colony and Burma's main port well into the 18th century.

King Alaungpaya essentially founded Yangon and started it on its modern path in 1755 when he captured the village of Dagon from the Mon people. He called the settlement Yangon, or "End of Strife", which the British then converted into Rangoon, a

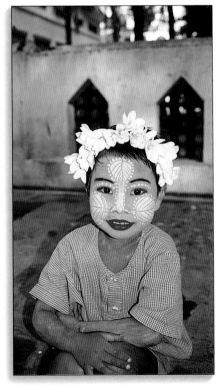

name that was carried for over 150 years. With the destruction of Syriam the following year, Yangon assumed its commercial functions. After the British conquered the town in 1824 during the First Anglo-Burmese War, its importance as a trade port flourished. But fire devastated the town in 1841. Then, 11 years later, it was again almost completely destroyed in the Second Anglo-Burmese War.

Exploring Yangon

In the downtown area, amidst the mildewing grey brick government offices erected by the British colonialists, and the gleaming high-rise hotels built by Singaporean investors, is the city's commercial centre, its markets and cinemas. And it is here, especially in the markets, that the true colours of Yangon's diverse population can be seen.

If the Shwedagon is the soul of Yangon, then surely the **Sule Pagoda ❶** is its heart. For centuries it has been the focus of much of the social and religious activity of the city. The British anchored the pagoda as the centre of the urban area when they structured their Victorian street-grid system around it in the mid-19th century. Today, the 48-metre (157-ft) pagoda remains among the taller structures in the city centre, and although the street names have been changed to Burmese from English, the thoroughfares in the central city still intersect at right angles with geometrical symmetry.

The origins of the Sule Pagoda are bound up in the mythical pre-history of Burma. Perhaps the most credible tale is that of two monks who were sent from India as missionaries to Thaton around 230 BC. After some hesitation, the king of Thaton gave them permission to construct a shrine at the foot of Singuttara Hill. In it the monks preserved a hair of the Buddha that they had carried from

TIP

As with all pagodas, visitors to Sule Pagoda should stroll around in a clockwise direction. Sule Pagoda's eight sides are dedicated to the days, planets and animals of the eight cardinal points.

BELOW: colonial architecture, and father and daughter on way to worship.

Map on page 80

India. The octagonal structure of Sule Pagoda, which is consistent up to the bell and inverted bowl, clearly indicates its Brahman-Buddhist heritage. During the first centuries of the Christian era, when the influence of Indian merchants and settlers was especially strong, astrology blended with *nat* worship and Buddhist doctrine to create the unique Burmese brand of Buddhism. Even today, Sule Pagoda, whose name and shape document this religious development, is a magnetic centre for astrologers and fortune-tellers.

Colonial remnants

On the northeast corner of Sule Pagoda Road and Maha Bandoola Street, facing Sule Pagoda, is the **Yangon City Hall ❷**. Built by the British, it is a massive stone structure worth a glance for its colonial architecture with a Burmese touch. Note especially the traditional Burmese peacock seal high over the entrance.

On the southeast corner of the intersection is **Maha Bandoola Park**, named after a Burmese general of the First Anglo-Burmese War. In the centre of the park is the **Independence Monument ❸**, a 46-metre (150-ft) obelisk surrounded by five smaller 9-metre (30-ft) pillars. The monument represents Burma's five former semi-autonomous states – Shan, Kachin, Kayin (Karen), Kayah and Chin – in union with their larger Bamar (Burman) brothers.

On Strand Road is the famous **Strand Hotel ❹**. By stopping over for the night or even just for a meal, a visitor might turn nostalgic over the British colonial era. Before its substantial and expensive renovation in the mid 1990s, most of the formerly mosquito-infested rooms were cooled by electric paddle fans and serviced by dribbling water pipes. Indian waiters, however, still hover

A cheerful hat pedlar in Yangon.

BELOW: Yangon street in colonial days.

attentively over every table and every guest in the high-ceilinged restaurant, which now carries a real menu. Since the Beverly Hills-class facelift, rooms are no longer as reasonably priced as they were during the 1980s. Nevertheless, it's worth stepping into the teak-furnished lounge for a cup of tea or bottle of cool beer.

Heading east on Strand Road for several blocks, you'll come to the **Botataung Pagoda ❺**. It is said that when eight Indian monks carried some relics of the Buddha here more than 2,000 years ago, 1,000 military officers *(botataung)* formed a guard of honour at the place where the rebuilt pagoda stands today. One of the pagoda's treasures, locked away, is a tooth of the Buddha, which Alaungsithu, a king of Bagan, tried unsuccessfully to acquire from Nan-chao (now China's Yunnan province) in 1115. China gave the relic to Burma in 1960.

At the end of Botataung Pagoda Road is the **Syriam Jetty**. Persons intent on making the 45-minute ferry trip across the river to Syriam should be warned, however, that the Syriam ferry leaves not from this jetty, but from the Htin-bonseik Jetty on Pazundaung Creek, some distance east on Monkey Point Road (the eastern extension of Strand Road), then north. On the way you'll pass near the lively **Botataung Market** on the left and a teak mill on the right. Though the ferry crossing is a fascinating experience, there is, for the less adventurous, the Thanlyin bridge across the Bago River that connects Yangon with Syriam and shortens the travelling time considerably.

West and north of the Sule Pagoda is Yangon's market district. Largest of Yangon's markets and a must for every visitor is the **Bogyoke Aung San Market ❻** (formerly the Scott Market). At the corner of Sule Pagoda Road and Bogyoke Aung San Street, next to the red-brick Railway Administration

BELOW: Water Festival, Yangon.

Building with its Moorish arches (one day to be converted into a first-class hotel), you can find under one roof all the consumer goods a Burmese family could possibly need or want. From spices to bicycles, local artefacts to Japanese stereo systems, everything is available here. Before World War II, a large majority of the inhabitants of Yangon were Indian or Chinese. To the south of the Bogyoke Market, off Shwedagon Pagoda Road, are the open-air markets – especially noted for the delicious Chinese soup sold at many of its stalls – and the Thein Gyi Zei, or Indian market. The oft-described "1000 Scents of the Orient" dominate this wholesale fruit-and-vegetable market: red chillies and cinnamon bark, mangosteen and durian, dried fish and seafoods.

The **National Museum** ❼ (Mon–Fri 10am–3pm) is in a neighbourhood filled with foreign missions. The showpiece of the museum is the Lion's Throne, upon which King Thibaw once sat in his hall of audience at Mandalay Palace. Taken from Mandalay in 1886 after the Third Anglo-Burmese War, the throne and 52 other pieces of royal regalia were carried off by the British. Some items were left behind in the Indian Museum in Calcutta; others were kept in the Victoria and Albert Museum in London. They were returned to Burma as a gesture of goodwill in 1964 after Ne Win's state visit to Britain. The throne, made of wood, is 8 metres (27 ft) high and is inlaid with gold and lacquer work. It is a particularly striking example of the Burmese art of wood carving. Among the other Mandalay Regalia, as they are known, are gem-studded arms, swords, jewellery and serving dishes. Also in the archaeological section of the museum are artefacts from Burma's early history in Beikthano, Sri Ksetra and Bagan (Pagan). There is an 18th-century bronze cannon, a crocodile-shaped harp and many other items.

Map
on page
80

The government has prohibited selling betel nuts on the streets with hopes of getting rid of the red stains that still mark many lower sections of the house walls.

BELOW: women sweeping outside Shwedagon Pagoda to gain merit.

Map on page 80

"'There's the old Shway Dagon,' said my companion.... The golden dome said, 'This is Burma, and it will be quite unlike any land you know about.'"

– RUDYARD KIPLING

Letters from the East,
1889

OPPOSITE: part of Shwedagon, 1900.
BELOW: Shwedagon Pagoda.

Shwedagon Pagoda

It has been said there is more gold on the **Shwedagon Pagoda** ❽ (daily 4am–9pm) than in the vaults of the Bank of England. The bell-shaped stupa, soaring nearly 100 metres (330 ft) above its setting on Singuttara Hill, is plated with 8,688 solid-gold slabs. The tip of the stupa is set with 5,448 diamonds and 2,317 rubies, sapphires and topaz. A huge emerald sits in the middle to catch the first and last rays of the sun. All of this is mounted upon a 10-metre-high (33 ft) umbrella (*hti*), built upon seven gold-plated bars and decorated with 1,500 gold and silver bells. The central stupa is surrounded by more than 100 other buildings, including smaller stupas, pavilions and administrative halls.

According to legend, inside the stupa are eight enshrined hairs of Gautama Buddha, as well as relics of three previous Buddhas. While the origins of the pagoda are shrouded in legend, it was definitely well established when Bagan dominated Burma in the 11th century. Queen Shinsawbu, who ruled in the 15th century, is revered today for giving the pagoda its present shape and form. She established the terraces and walls around the stupa, and gave her weight in gold to be beaten into gold leaf and used to plate the stupa. This act has been repeated by many rulers in the course of the pagoda's history.

Much of the pagoda's history is recounted in its bells. For example, a bell weighing 30 tons was plundered in the early 1600s by a Portuguese mercenary intent upon melting it into cannons. As he attempted to ferry the bell across the river, it fell into the water and was never recovered. In the early 1800s, the British tried the same thing, with the same result, though the bell was recovered.

Standing before the stupa (*see photograph, pages 66-67*) is humbling. With a circumference at platform level of 433 metres (1,420 ft), its octagonal base is ringed with 64 smaller stupas. Northwest of the main stupa is the Maha Gandha Bell, cast of bronze in 1779 and which the British unsuccessfully tried to carry off. It weighs 23 tons and has a diameter of nearly 2 metres (6½ feet). Behind in the northwest corner of the compound are two Bodhi trees, adorned with flowers and small flags.

The eight enshrined hairs, which Gautama Buddha, close to achieving enlightenment in Bodhgaya, India, plucked from his own head, had an arduous journey to Burma. Half of them were lost to misfortune. When the Burmese king opened the casket containing the hairs, all eight were in place, emitting a brilliant, heavenly light that rose high above the trees. The blind could see, the lame could walk. The earth quaked, and a shower of precious stones rained down.

Northern Yangon

Continuing northeast through the winding residential streets north of the Shwedagon, past the "Rangoon Modern" stucco houses built for Westerners during the colonial era, you'll reach the huge and artificial **Inya Lake** ❾. On the southern shore are the Yangon Arts and Sciences University, with over 10,000 students, and the Myanmar Sailing Club, which sponsors races on the lake. Perhaps the best known structure on the lake is the Inya Lake Hotel, built by the Soviet Union in the early 1960s. ❑

MANDALAY

The city of Mandalay, made famous in Rudyard Kipling's verse,
is not only the religious and cultural centre of upper Burma,
it is also the economic hub for the entire region

Map on page 68

Mandalay

The capital of Upper Burma is a young city at just one and a half centuries or so. Nostalgia for Burma's last royal capital, enchantment with the myriad of pagodas dotting all corners of the region's landscape, and the warmth and vitality of the indigenous people weave a strong spell around the visitor that seems impossible to escape.

Mandalay ❶, 620 km (400 miles) north of Rangoon, is only 80 metres (260 ft) above sea level. Sprawling across the dry plains of the upper Ayeyarwady (Irrawaddy) River rice-growing district, Mandalay has a population of around 700,000 people. Scenic beauty and historical tragedy are inextricably meshed in this city. There is the indestructible Mandalay Hill with its kilometre-long covered stairways and remarkable pagodas, and below it are the ruins of the Royal Palace, King Mindon's "Golden City" of ancient prophecy. In the middle of the city is Zegyo Market, centre of trade for all the people of Upper Burma who can be seen there in their colourful national costumes. Skilled artisans and craftsmen are found here, working their age-old wonders with gold and silver, marble and chisel, thread and loom. The sluggish Ayeyarwady flows by with its bustling wharves and flotilla of rice-laden boats.

Mandalay was founded in 1857 by King Mindon to coincide with an ancient Buddhist prophecy. The "Golden City" was formally completed in 1859, and Mindon then shifted his government and an estimated 150,000 people from nearby Amarapura in 1861, dismantling most of the previous palace and taking it with him to to help create the new capital.

The dream of Mandalay was short-lived, however. In November 1885, King Thibaw handed the town over to the British army and went into exile with his queen. Mandalay soon became just another outpost of British colonialism, albeit one crowned by richly furnished palace buildings, which by now had been renamed Fort Dufferin.

The palace structures were almost universally built of teak, and this was their demise. In March 1945, British troops shelled the stronghold, at the time defended by a handful of Japanese and Burmese soldiers. By the time the siege had ended, the interior of the Golden City was in ashes. All that remained intact before part of the palace was reconstructed were the walls and the moat.

Centre of the world

Mindon had built his **Royal Palace** on the model of Brahman-Buddhist cosmology to represent the centre of the world, the fabled Mount Meru. The palace formed a perfect square, with the outer walls facing the four cardinal directions, and the 12 gates, three

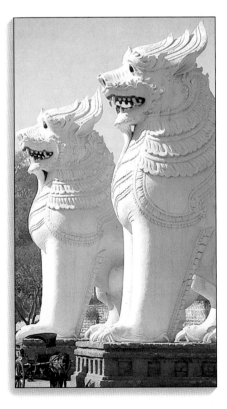

LEFT: rain-soaked rice paddies, central Burma.
BELOW: *chinthes* of Mandalay Hill.

Mandalay's founder, King Mindon.

on each side, are marked with the signs of the zodiac. In the exact centre of the palace was the throne room, called the Lion's Room. The Royal Palace with the Lion's Room and the *pyathat* have been rebuilt.

These days the renovated palace shares the grounds of **Mandalay Fort** (Mon–Fri 8am–6pm) with the army. The grounds and a museum on Mandalay's history are open to the public. A little to the west is a scale model of the ancient palace created by archaeologists. The model indicates the location of all main and secondary buildings within the old palace walls, and it gives a good idea of the "centre of the world" concept. King Mindon's mausoleum is also in the palace grounds.

Mandalay Hill

You might start a visit to Mandalay by climbing famous **Mandalay Hill**, which rises 240 metres (790 ft) above the surrounding countryside. The slopes of Mandalay Hill are clothed in covered stairways, which contain small temples at regular intervals. There are 1,729 steps to the top, but the walk is not particularly difficult. About halfway up the hill, you'll encounter the first large temple, said to contain three bones of the Buddha.

About two-thirds of the way to the top of the hill stands a gold-plated statue of the Shweyattaw Buddha. His outstretched hand points to the place where the Royal Palace was built. This stance is unique; in all other Buddha images anywhere else in the world, Gautama is in one of the *mudra* positions. The statue was erected before King Mindon laid the first stone of his Golden City and symbolises Gautama Buddha's prophecy.

BELOW: a bronze *dvarapala.*

On the way up the steps, there is also a statue of a woman kneeling in front of the Buddha, offering to him her two severed breasts. According to legend, Sanda Moke Khit was an ogress, but she was so impressed by the Buddha's teachings that she decided to devote the rest of her life to following the Enlightened One. As a sign of humility, she cut off her breasts. The Buddha smiled as he accepted the gift, and the ogress's brother asked why he did so. He replied that Sanda Moke Khit had collected so many merits that in a future life she would be reborn as Min Done (Mindon), king of Mandalay.

At the base of Mandalay Hill's southeast stairway, surrounded by a high wall, is Mindon's **Kuthodaw Pagoda**. Its central structure, the 30-metre (100-ft) high Maha Lawka Marazein Pagoda, was erected in 1857 and modelled on the Shwezigon Pagoda in Nyaung U, near Bagan (Pagan). Sometimes called the "world's largest book", it was created by a team of 2,400 monks who required almost six months to recite the text. The canons were recorded on the marble slabs by devoted Buddhist scholars, and the letters were originally veneered with gold leaf.

Close to the Kuthodaw are other important pagodas and monasteries. Not far from the south staircase is the **Kyauk-tawgyi Pagoda**. Begun in 1853, the original plan was to model this after the Ananda Temple at Bagan, but the 1866 revolt hampered this and other projects. The building was eventually completed in 1878. The main point of interest here is a huge Buddha figure carved out of a single block of marble from the Sagyin quarry. This undertaking was of ancient Egyptian proportions: 10,000 men required 13 days to transport the rock from the Ayeyarwady River to the pagoda site. The statue was finally dedicated in 1865, with 20 figures on each side of the image representing the Buddha's 80 disciples. A painting of King Mindon is also contained within the pagoda.

The **Sandamuni Pagoda** was built on the site where King Mindon had his provisional palace during construction of the Mandalay Palace. There are two monasteries located south of the Kuthodaw Pagoda, not far to the east of the palace moat. The **Shwe Nandaw Kyaung**, at one time part of the royal palace, is the only building from Mindon's Golden City that has survived the ravages of the 19th century.

Beside the Shwe Nandaw lie the remains of the **Atumashi Kyaung**, which means Incomparable Monastery. Before it burned down in 1890, taking with it four sets of *Tipitaka* in teak boxes, this was a building of extraordinary splendour and grace.

Maha Muni Pagoda

The most important religious structure in Mandalay is the **Maha Muni (Great Sage) Pagoda**. It is also called the Rakhaing (Arakan) Pagoda or Payagyi Pagoda. Located about 3 km (2 miles) south of the city centre on the road to Amarapura, this pagoda was built in 1784 by King Bodawpaya and was reconstructed after a fire a century later.

The Maha Muni Buddha figure is almost 4 metres (13 ft) high and is coated with layers of gold leaf several centimetres thick. Except during the rainy season, when the Buddha's body is cloaked with robes, you can watch the Buddhist

Map on page 68

An important trading city on the crossroads of India and China, Mandalay is the centre of Burmese Buddhism and also of Bamar nationalism.

BELOW: Kuthodaw Pagoda.

Map on page 68

faithful pasting on the thin gold leaf. Only six of the Khmer bronzes have survived the centuries – two *dvarapala* (warriors or temple guardians), three lions, and a three-headed elephant. They are kept in a small building in the Maha Muni Pagoda courtyard. Streets with covered stalls lead up to the Maha Muni Pagoda from all directions, providing the bazaar atmosphere for which Burma was once famous amongst foreigners.

There are four other Buddhist buildings in the vicinity of downtown Mandalay that are definitely worth visiting. Fortunately, the city's grid street plan makes them easy to find.

The makers of oiled bamboo paper live on 37th Road. This kind of paper, which is placed between layers of gold leaf, is produced by a remarkable 3-year process of soaking, beating flat and drying of bamboo.

Heading north from the Maha Muni Pagoda, one first encounters the **Shwe In Bin Kyaung**. This monastery, situated to the south of 35th Road, contains very fine 13th-century woodcarvings. At 31st Road and 85th Street stands the **Setkyathiha Pagoda**, rebuilt after being badly damaged in World War II.

Proceeding northward leads to the **Eindawya Pagoda** at 27th Road and 89th Street. The pagoda houses a Buddha figure made of chalcedony (a form of quartz), carried to Burma in 1839 from Bodhgaya, the place in India where Gautama achieved Buddhahood. The pagoda was built in early 1847 by King Pagan Min. Today it has been covered with gold leaf. The oldest pagoda in the city is the **Shwekyimyint Pagoda**, on 24th Road between 82nd and 83rd streets. Erected in 1167 by Prince Minshinsaw, the exiled son of King Alaungsithu of Bagan, it houses a Buddha image consecrated by the prince himself.

A couple of blocks from the Shwe Kyi Myint, at 24th Road and West Moat Road, are the **National Museum and Library** (Wed–Sun 10am–4pm). The museum collection extends across many eras of Burmese history. One of its most interesting pictures shows King Thibaw and Queen Supyalat on the eve of their exile. The library is widely noted for its assemblage of important Buddhist documents.

Market centre of the north...

In 1890, Rudyard Kipling penned the famous verse:
"On the road to
  Mandalay
Where the flyin'
  fishes play
An' the dawn comes
  up like thunder
outer China 'crost
  the Bay!"
Kipling had never been to Mandalay. If he had been, he might have noticed the complete absence of flying fishes.

For the Chins of the west, the Kachins of the north, and the Shans of the east, Mandalay is the primary market for goods. And the **Zegyo Market**, located on the west side of the city centre, on 84th Street between 26th and 28th roads, is Mandalay's most important bazaar. The Italian Count Caldrari, first secretary of the Mandalay municipal government, had the Zegyo Market laid out around the Diamond Jubilee Clock, which had been erected in honour of Queen Victoria's 60-year reign. Rebuilt as a new concrete structure, the market still offers visitors a fine opportunity to see Burma's ethnic minorities in their national costumes, and at the same time gives an insight to daily Burmese life.

Part of Mandalay's enchantment comes from its location beside the Ayeyarwady River. At the western end of A Road, which follows the railroad tracks north of the Shwe In Bin Kyaung, one finds the jetties where the ships that ply the "Road to Mandalay" are docked.

...and craftsmen of the south

In the southern part of Mandalay, especially in the precincts of the Maha Muni Pagoda, are the artists' and craftsmen's quarters. Here you can watch as Burmese men, using the same skills and methods as their forefathers, pursue their trade in religious sculpture – Buddha images in all positions, Buddha footprints, lotus-blossom pedestals, or even the occasional Virgin Mary, a reminder of earlier missionary days.

OPPOSITE: the fabled Maha Muni.

In the area around Mandalay, visitors should make it a point to see other artisans – the silk and cotton weavers of Amarapura; the silversmiths of Ywataung; and the bronze and brass workers from Kyi Thun Kyat. ❑

BAGAN

One of Asia's most venerable wonders and home of the temple of omniscience, Bagan is an ancient and deserted city full of awe-inspiring pagodas

Map on page 68

In many respects **Bagan** ❷ has changed very little in the past century. It remains the way Sir James Scott saw it, as "Burma's deserted capital on the Irrawaddy, thickly studded with pagodas of all sizes and shapes". It was – and still is – a veritable elephants' graveyard of medieval Burmese culture. There is nowhere, perhaps, a sight so striking as the view across the plain of Bagan (also, Pagan), one ancient red-brick pagoda after another rising above the flat land on the dusty eastern shore of greatest river in Burma.

Between the time of Anawrahta's conquest of Thaton in 1057 and the overrun of Bagan by Kublai Khan's forces in 1287, some 13,000 temples, pagodas, *kyaung* and other religious structures were built on this vast plain. After seven long centuries, just over 2,000 of these remain standing.

There has been a settlement in the region of Bagan since early in the 2nd century AD, when Thamuddarit, a Pyu king, led his followers here. The walls of the city were erected by King Pyinbya in 849, but it was left to King Anawrahta, 42nd ruler of the Bagan dynasty, to usher in the city's age of glory, and to his successor, King Kyanzittha, to perpetuate that glory.

The economic centre of the Bagan plain today is at **Nyaung U**, about 5 km (3 miles) to the north of the walled village of Bagan. There are a few important monuments in the immediate vicinity of Nyaung U, notably the Shwezigon Pagoda, and there are others a few kilometres to the south of Bagan village near Myinkaba. The picturesque Bagan village, once situated around the main temples, was relocated in a controversial military operation in 1990 to clear the principal temple quarter of local habitations. **New Bagan**, as it is called, has now been reconstructed some 8 km (5 miles) south of its original site, close to the village of Thiripyitsaya.

Bagan monuments

Many travellers begin their exploration of the ancient ruins at the **Ananda Temple**, just to the east of the old city wall. This impressive whitewashed edifice dominates the view as one approaches Bagan from the north. Considered the masterpiece of Mon architecture, it was completed in 1091. When the great temple was completed, Kyanzittha is said to have been so awe-struck by its unique style that he personally executed the architect by Brahman ritual to assure that the temple could not be duplicated, thereby sealing its permanence and importance. At present, some of the statues in the temple are actually copies because the originals were destroyed by temple thieves.

The desecration of temples has been, in fact, a serious problem in Bagan. As far back as mid-16th century, Thohanbwa, Shan King of Innwa (Ava), gave

LEFT: one of Bagan's pagodas.
BELOW: Ananda Temple.

impetus to the temple robbers when he said, "Burma pagodas have nothing to do with religion. They are simply treasure chambers." It was Thohanbwa, in fact, who ordered many of the Bagan pagodas to be plundered in order to fill his own treasure chambers.

The most important time of year at the Ananda Temple is January, when an exuberant festival is held to raise money for the upkeep of the temple. This is a joyous spectacle, and the corridors and vestibules of the temple, normally lined with small stalls, are especially lively.

Temple of omniscience

The centre of Bagan is dominated by the **Thatbyinnyu Temple**, about 500 metres (1,550 ft) to the southwest of the Ananda. Known as the "temple of omniscience", it is the tallest building in Bagan at 61 metres (201 ft). The construction of this temple introduced the idea of placing a smaller "hollow" cube on top of a larger Bamar-style structure, whereas the previous Mon-style temples were of one storey. The centre of the lower cube is solid, serving as a foundation for the upper temple, which houses an eastward-looking Buddha figure.

A short distance north of the Thatbyinnyu is the **Thandawgya**, a huge seated Buddha figure. Six metres (19½ ft) tall, it was erected by Narathihapate in 1284. The Buddha's hands are in the *bhumisparsa* mudra, signifying the moment of enlightenment.

Close to the bank of the Ayeyarwady River is the 12th-century **Gawdawpalin Temple**, built by King Narapatisithu in Bamar style to resemble the Thatbyinnyu Temple. This impressive building suffered more than any other monument in the 1975 earthquake. Just south of the temple is a museum

BELOW: Thatbyinnyu Temple and Tally Pagoda.

Map on page 68

containing displays of Bagan's varied architecture, iconography and religious history. Along the museum verandas are stones collected from the region, bearing inscriptions in various languages – Burmese, Mon, Pyu, Pali, Tamil, Thai and Chinese.

The oldest of the Bamar-style temples, the **Shwegugyi Temple** is a short distance up the road toward Nyaung U. King Alaungsithu had it built in 1131, and it took just seven months to raise, according to the temple history inscribed on two stone slabs within.

Atonement for patricide

Despite his brief tenure as king, Narathu is remembered as the founder of Bagan's largest shrine, the **Dhammayangyi Temple**. Deeply concerned about his *karma* for future lives after having murdered his father, Narathu built the Dhammayangyi to atone for his misdeeds. Today, it is the best-preserved temple in Bagan, with a layout similar to that of the Ananda Temple but lacking the delicate, harmonious touch of its prototype, perhaps reflecting the black cloud that hung over central Burma during Narathu's reign. The Dhammayangyi Temple is over a kilometre (⅔ mile) to the southeast of the city walls towards Minnanthu.

About halfway between the temple and the walled Bagan centre are the **Shwesandaw Pagoda** and the **Shinbinthalyaung**, which houses a reclining Buddha. One of only three religious structures Anawrahta built in Bagan, the Shwesandaw was erected in 1057 upon his victorious return from Thaton. Its stupa enshrines some hairs of the Buddha sent to Anawrahta by the king of Bago. The long, flat building within the walls of the Shwesandaw enclosure contains the Shinbinthalyaung Reclining Buddha, over 18 metres (60 ft) in

It is said that Narathu oversaw the construction of Dhammayangyi Temple himself, having stone masons executed if a needle could be pushed between the bricks.

BELOW: monks receiving their daily meal.

Shwesandaw Pagoda.

length. Created in the 11th century, this Buddha lies with its head facing south to denote a sleeping Buddha (only a dying Buddha's head would point north).

The last Bamar-style temple built in Bagan, the **Htilominlo Temple**, is about 1.5 km (1 mile) northeast of Bagan proper on the road to Nyaung U. King Nantaungmya had this building constructed in 1211 at the place where he was chosen to be king. The Htilominlo Temple is 46 metres (150 ft) high and 43 metres (140 ft) on a side at its base. Four Buddha figures placed on the ground and four more figures on the first floor face the cardinal points. Some of the old murals can still be discerned, as can a number of the friezes. Several old horoscopes, painted to protect the building from damage, can be found on the walls.

Entering Bagan from Nyaung U, the road passes through the **Sarabha Gateway**, the only section of King Pyinbya's 9th-century city wall that is still standing and that has recently been reconstructed. Although the rest of the wall consists of overgrown hillocks strewn with rubble, Bagan's guardian spirits – the Mahagiri *nat* – have their prayer niches in this eastern gateway. The two *nat*, Nga Tin De (Mr Handsome) and his sister Shwemyethna (Golden Face), are called Lords of the Great Mountain because it is believed they made their home on sacred Mount Popa. After Thagyamin, king of the *nat*, they are the most important spirit beings in Burma.

One of the few secular buildings in Bagan that has been preserved over the centuries is the **Pitakat Taik**, King Anawrahta's library. The library is near the Shwegugyi Temple. Across the main road is the **Mahabodhi Temple**. This temple is an exact replica of a structure of the same name in India's Bihar State, built in AD 500 at the site where the Buddha achieved enlightenment. The pyramid-like shape of the temple tower is a kind that was highly favoured during India's Gupta period, and it is quite different from the standard bell-shaped monuments in the rest of Burma.

BELOW: Mahagiri *nat*, "Golden Face".

Of warships and monks

A short distance north of Bagan's Mahabodhi is the **Pebinkyaung Pagoda**, most notable for its conical Singhalese-style stupa. The stupa contains relics mounted on top of the bell-shaped main structure in a square-based relic chamber. The construction of this pagoda in the 12th century confirms that close ties existed between Burma and Sri Lanka, a result of the concern shown by King Anawrahta for the propagation of Theravada Buddhism.

A few steps from the Pebingyaung on the banks of the Ayeyarwady is the **Bupaya Pagoda**. According to tradition, the pagoda was built by the third king of Bagan, Pyusawti (AD 162–243). As the original Bagan Pagoda, this edifice became the basic model for all pagodas built after it. It has a bulbous shape, similar in some ways to the Tibetan *chorte,* and it is built on rows of crenellated walls overlooking the river. Because of the way it stands out on the banks, it is used as a navigation aid by boats. On the pagoda grounds, beneath a pavilion with a nine-gabled roof, is an altar to Mondaing, *nat* of storms.

The **Mimalaung Kyaung Temple**, near the old city's south gate, was erected in 1174. The small, square temple is characterised by multiple roofs and a tall spiral pagoda that stands on a 4-metre (13-ft) high plinth intended to protect it from destruction by fire and floods. The temple's creator, Narapatisithu, is noted in Bagan's history for the manner in which he acceded to the throne in 1173. His brother, King Naratheinka, had stolen his wife and made her queen while Narapatisithu was on a foreign campaign. The wronged sibling returned to Bagan with 80 of his most trusted men, murdered his brother and ensconced himself on the throne. His wife, Veluvati, was spared and remained queen.

Just to the east of this temple is the **Pahtothamya Temple**, which according to tradition dates from before Anawrahta's reign. King Taungthugyi (931–964), also known as Nyaung U Sawrahan, is said to have built the temple to look like those at Thaton. No temple ruins have ever been unearthed at Thaton to allow comparison, however, and the architectural style of this temple has been proven to be that of the 11th century.

To the east is the **Nathlaung Kyaung Temple**, a perfect example of the religious tolerance that prevailed in Bagan during the so-called Era of the Temple Builders. It is thought to have been constructed by Taungthugyi in 931 – more than a century before Theravada Buddhism was introduced from Thaton – and was dedicated to the Hindu god Vishnu. Immediately to the north, the **Ngakywenadaung Pagoda** is much like the Pahtothamya Temple attributed to King Taungthugyi in the 10th century. A bulbous structure on a circular base, it stands 13 metres (43 ft) high.

A short distance south of walled Bagan is the **Mingalazedi Pagoda**, the last of the great stupas erected during the Era of the Temple Builders. Six years in construction, it represents the pinnacle of Bamar pagoda architecture. The terraces are adorned with large terracotta tiles depicting scenes from the *Jataka*.

Map on page 68

BELOW: Bagan's temples with balloons overhead.

Map on page 68

TIP

Those travelling during the second week of the Burmese month of *Nadaw* (November/December) can witness Buddhist pilgrims converging for the festival at Shwezigon Pagoda.

RIGHT: young monks.
BELOW: guardian *nat* of the arts.

To Nyaung U and beyond

About 1.5 km (1 mile) down the road from Bagan proper, towards the regional centre of Nyaung U and almost directly opposite the Htilominlo Temple, lies the **Upali Thein**, or Hall of Ordination. Named after the monk Upali, it was erected in the first half of the 13th century. The Upali Thein was renovated during the reign of the Konbaung dynasty in the late 1700s; during the renovation, its walls and ceilings were decorated with beautiful frescoes representing the 28 previous Buddhas, as well as scenes from the life of Gautama. Sadly, the plaster came off the walls during the 1975 earthquake, and most of the fresco work was destroyed.

Near the village of Wetkyi-in are the **Gubyauknge Temple**, notable for the fine stucco work on its exterior walls, and the **Wetkyi-in Gubyaukgyi Temple**, a short distance further east. The Kubyaukgyi dates from the early 13th century, and it has a pyramidal spire very similar to that of the Mahabodhi. Inside are some of Bagan's finest frescoes of the *Jataka* tales.

A short distance west of Nyaung U village is the **Kyanzittha Cave**, a cave temple that served as monks' lodgings. Although its name points to Kyanzittha as its creator, it probably dates from Anawrahta's reign. The long, dark corridors are embellished with frescoes from the 11th, 12th and 13th centuries; some of the later paintings even depict the Mongols who occupied Bagan after 1287.

The **Shwezigon Pagoda**, a short walk north of the cave temple, is the prototype for all Burmese stupas built after the rule of Anawrahta. It was built as the most important reliquary shrine in Bagan, a centre of prayer and reflection for the new Theravada faith that Anawrahta was establishing in Bagan.

Cave temples

There are several cave temples to the east of Nyaung U. Just one kilometre (⅔ mile) to the southeast of the town are the caves at **Thamiwhet** and **Hmyathat**, formed by the excavation of hillsides during the 12th and 13th centuries. Their purpose was to give monks a cool place to live and meditate, a refuge from the scorching heat of central Burma.

About 3 km (2 miles) upstream from Nyaung U, standing on the ledge of a cliff overlooking the Ayeyarwady, is the **Kyaukgu Temple**. The structure could be described as an ideal cave temple – the manner in which it is built into the hill-side gives the impression that a small stupa stands on top of the temple, when it actually rests on a pillar. The Kyaukgu's ground floor dates from the 11th century.

Minnanthu temples

The village of Minnanthu is located about 5 km (3 miles) southeast of Bagan proper. There is a large number of temple ruins in the vicinity, but few of major significance. One of the largest is the **Sulamani Temple**, not in Minnanthu itself but about halfway between the village and Bagan. Immediately to the north of the Minnanthu village is the **Lemyethna Temple**, built by Naratheinhka's minister-in-chief, remembering a poem written by his predecessor and namesake, Ananthathurya. ❏

LAOS AND CAMBODIA

Long forgotten by the travellers of the world, both Laos and Cambodia are slowly emerging as challenging adventures

Together, Laos and Cambodia form the little-known hinterland of Indochina. In the colonial period they were considered backwaters by the French, who concentrated on exploiting the resources of Vietnam – the third and dominant country in French Indochina. During the long years of warfare that followed independence they were once again considered backwaters, and this view of them continued, though they were hardly forgotten by the military strategists of both sides. Communist Vietnam used the Ho Chi Minh trail through Laos to re-supply its forces in the south, while the United States waged a viciously destructive "Secret War" against the North Vietnamese Army and its Lao allies, the Pathet Lao.

Meanwhile sleepy Cambodia was similarly sucked into the quagmire. Used as a base sanctuary by the Vietnamese Communists, it was secretly – and illegally – carpet-bombed by the US Air Force. The consequences of Communist victory in 1975 were far more terrible for the Cambodians, "liberated" by the auto-genocidal Khmer Rouge, than for the Lao people. Nevertheless, for almost the next two decades, both countries experienced impoverishment and isolation from the outside world.

Nowadays all this is changing fast. Both Laos and Cambodia have opened their doors to the international community and, in particular, to overseas visitors. The governments in both Vientiane and Phnom Penh see tourism and its related industries as a way to accelerate national development and assure a more prosperous future.

There are other good reasons for linking Laos and Cambodia. Each carries the scars of the Indochina Wars, and there are areas in both countries that must remain off limits to travellers until mines and other detritus of past battles have been cleared. Both have a long tradition of Indic culture as well as being culturally related through Theravada Buddhism and long years of interaction with neighbouring Thailand. Each is startlingly beautiful, populated by generous and friendly people, and both have benefited from the French culinary tradition – as Cambodia's King Sihanouk once put it: "I am an anti-colonialist, but if one must be colonised it is better to be colonised by gourmets."

Today Laos and Cambodia are free, independent members of ASEAN and stand on the verge of development and prosperity as the 21st century unfolds. There has never been a better time to visit them. ❑

PRECEDING PAGES: That Luang, Vientiane; a traditional dancer's hands.

Decisive Dates

A great kingdom rises and falls

2000 BC–AD 500: development of an early pottery and bronze culture, based on wet rice cultivation and associated with the Ban Chiang culture, in the central Mekong Valley.

AD 802: Jayavarman II claims independence from Javanese control and sows the initial seeds of the Khmer/Angkor empire by declaring himself the first *davaraja*, or god-king.

1050: Khmer empire is weakened by internal fights.

1131–50: Suryavarman II reigns over the Khmer

empire and builds Angkor Wat. The Khmer empire is strengthened and now includes most of Thailand, Laos, and southern Vietnam.

1200s: Khmer empire is in decline.

1279: the Sukhothai kingdom in Siam is founded by Ramkamhaeng; parts of Laos, including Vientiane, come under Sukhothai control for a short time.

1349: Fa Ngum begins coalescing townships into the Lan Xang kingdom, establishing his capital at Xiengdong Xiengthong (Luang Prabang).

1353–73: reign of Fa Ngum over the Lan Xang empire.

1373–1547: successors of Fa Ngum continue to rule Lan Xang, fighting wars against Burma and Siam.

1431: Angkor is abandoned, and Cambodia becomes part of the Sukhothai kingdom.

1574–78: Lan Xang is subsumed by Burma.

1633–90: reign of King Souligna Vongsa, a high point and "golden era" in Laotian culture.

1690–1713: succession struggles for the throne of the Lan Xang empire. In 1713, the Lan Xang empire is divided into smaller kingdoms of Luang Prabang, Vientiane, and Champasak.

1778: Siam takes control of Luang Prabang, Vientiane, and Champasak.

France introduces itself

1867–87: a French expedition up the Mekong River reaches Luang Prabang. Siam must now deal with France, which already controls Vietnam.

1890: French colonial rule of Laos begins; a treaty is concluded in 1893 between France and Siam that acknowledges French control over Mekong territory.

1930: France officially designates Laos as a French colony. Communist Party of Indochina is founded.

1940–45: all Lao territories west of the Mekong are given to Thailand; Laos is occupied by Japan in 1945. Lao Issara (Free Lao) guerrillas take control of Vientiane and establish a provisional government.

1946: King Sisavang Vong is deposed and France reoccupies Laos. Sisavang Vong declared king-in-exile by Lao Issara government, exiled in Thailand.

1947: Laos becomes a constitutional monarchy. Elections are held for the National Assembly. Prince Souvannarath forms the government of Kingdom of Laos.

1949: Laos is granted limited self-government within the French Union. The Lao Issara government, in exile, is dissolved, but some members join the Pathet Lao.

1950: United States and Britain recognise Laos and Cambodia as part of the French Union. The Pathet Lao form a "resistance government".

Independence from France

1953: Laos and Cambodia gain independence from France, but France retains control of military affairs.

1954: Geneva Conference on Indochina establishes armistice in Cambodia, Laos and Vietnam.

1955: Laos is admitted to the United Nations.

1956: Pathet Lao set up the Lao Patriotic Front (LPF).

1957: first Lao coalition government is formed under Prince Souvanna Phouma.

1959: northern Laos erupts in fighting with communist insurgency, with possible North Vietnamese involvement. Lao King Sisavang Vong dies; Savang Vatthana takes the throne and rules until 1975.

1960: a provisional government is formed in Laos after an army coup attempt. A coup d'état topples the rightist government; a counter-coup group led by the army declares martial law. Phoumi Nosavan captures

Vientiane, and the Soviets begin an airlift to Pathet Lao troops. Prince Norodom Sihanouk is elected head of state in Cambodia.

1961–62: heavy fighting breaks out between Soviet- and Western-backed factions in Laos. Another Geneva Conference on Laos establishes a peace amongst the various factions. A second coalition government is formed, but civil war resumes.

1964: North Vietnamese troops expand the Ho Chi Minh Trail through Lao territory. The Lao coalition government collapses.

1968: fighting intensifies between Pathet Lao and the Royal Lao Army.

1970: Cambodian Prince Sihanouk is deposed in a right-wing coup led by Lt-Gen. Lon Nol, who aligns himself with the U.S. Sihanouk forms a Cambodian government in exile, supported by the Khmer Rouge.

1972: Lao People's Party changes its name to Lao People's Revolutionary Party, which it retains today.

1973: the Laotian government and Pathet Lao sign the Vientiane Agreement that establishes ceasefire.

1974: a third coalition government in Laos takes office by royal decree.

Communist victories

1975: the collapse of Cambodia and Vietnam to the communists. Fighting begins anew in Laos, and top rightist ministers and generals escape to Thailand. The LPLA "liberates" provincial capitals, and a "Revolutionary Administration" takes control in Vientiane. The third provisional government collapses, and King Savang Vatthana abdicates. The Lao People's Democratic Republic (LPDR) is proclaimed, and Souphanouvong becomes its first president, staying in power until 1991. Forces – mostly Khmer Rouge – loyal to Cambodia Prince Sihanouk take Phnom Penh. Cambodia is renamed Democratic Kampuchea, and "Year Zero" begins, led by Pol Pot. Millions die in Khmer Rouge "social engineering".

1977: a treaty of friendship and cooperation between Laos and Vietnam is signed.

1978: Vietnam invades Cambodia, taking Phnom Penh at the beginning of 1979. The Khmer Rouge regroup in the countryside.

1988: first Lao elections since 1975 are held at the district and provincial levels.

1989: national elections in Laos are held for delegates to the first Supreme People's Assembly. The last Vietnamese troops leave Laos. In Cambodia, Vietnamese forces withdraw. The nation's name is changed back to

Cambodia; fighting continues between anti-government forces, nominally led by exiled Prince Sihanouk, and the Phnom Penh government.

Steady Laos, chaotic Cambodia

1991: Souphanouvong retires as president of Laos. A new constitution is adopted; Kaysone Phomvihan becomes president. A UN accord brings an unsteady peace to Cambodia; Sihanouk returns to the country.

1992: In Laos, Kaysone dies and is replaced as president by Nouhak Phomsavan.

1993: UN-sponsored elections result in a coalition government with two prime ministers: Hun Sen and Prince Ranariddh. They fail to get along.

1994: the Friendship Bridge between Thailand and Laos opens.

1995: Prince Souphanouvong dies, ending the last direct link between the monarchy started by Fa Ngum and the government in Laos.

1997: fighting between factions erupts in Phnom Penh; co-prime minister Prince Ranariddh leaves Cambodia for exile. Pol Pot is denounced by the Khmer Rouge and sentenced to house arrest. Laos joins ASEAN, the Association of Southeast Asian Nations.

1998: Ranariddh returns to Cambodia. Pol Pot dies in the jungle. Elections leave Hun Sen in power.

1999: Cambodia joins ASEAN. Laos moves closer to Thailand as Vietnamese influence diminishes.

2003: Gradual transition to market economy continues. ❏

OPPOSITE: royal urn, at Wat Xieng Thong, Luang Prabang. **ABOVE:** upper gallery of Angkor Wat.

PEOPLE OF THE MEKONG

Nestled as they are amidst various cultures, some often more powerful, it is no surprise that Laos and, to a lesser degree, Cambodia are comprised of many peoples

Some political scientists say Laos is an unnatural nation. There is an element of truth in this view: there are dozens of ethnic groups dotting the country, and ethnic culture is highly segmented and extremely complex in Laos. Still, travellers will find the Lao, of whatever persuasion, most accommodating and friendly.

It might be said that charm and friendliness is Laos' most exportable commodity. One former expat, Judy Rantala, a retired social worker who lived in Laos during the mid-1970s, expressed this sentiment best in her book, *Laos*: "In my admittedly short visit I found among the Lao people what endeared me to them years ago and in fact is validated by everyone I know who has ever lived in Laos: the people continue to be peace-loving, non-confrontational, generous and friendly. They have a capacity to adapt and to avoid becoming bitter or disillusioned or discouraged. Their buoyant sense of humour and sense of self-worth are as strong as I remember. I hope they can – I hope they will – preserve the freshness of spirit which makes this often overlooked small country a treasure-pot of human dignity and grace."

Over 75 percent of the population of Laos are subsistence farmers. Most villages are far from roads or other transportation links, and less than 20 percent of its 5 million people live in towns or cities. Laos is one of the world's poorest countries, with a per-capita income of less than US$300 annually. The population density is quite low for Asia: around 20 people per square kilometre.

There are over 60 ethnic peoples in Laos, divided into three major groupings: Lao Soung, the upland Lao of the mountainous regions and comprising less than 20 percent of the population; Lao Theung, about a quarter of Laos' population and living on the slopes of mountains; and Lao Loum, the lowlanders and the politically dominant and most numerous group, with over half of the population. The Lao Loum originally derived from southern China and are ethnic cousins of Thais in northeastern Thailand. Today they dominate the fertile plains of the Mekong River basin. The Lao Theung, of Mon-Khmer heritage, were nomadic people and today practise slash-and-burn agriculture.

The Lao Soung are newcomers to Laos, arriving from China and Burma in the 1700s and inhabiting the high mountain regions. Hmong and Mien (Yao) hill tribes, also found in northern Thailand, are Lao Soung.

Cambodia's population of 11 million is dominated by Khmer – nearly 90 percent of the country's people – with substantial numbers of Vietnamese and Chinese, along with small numbers of ethnic minority groups, the largest of which are the Cham, a Muslim people. Other groups include Lao, Shan and Thai. Historically, the Khmer culture has been considerably influenced by the once great kingdoms centred in Java and India.

LEFT: young girl offers alms to monks.
RIGHT: harvesting the rice.

Village life

The village is the most important economic and political unit. Among some tribes there are well defined territories claimed by the village. Generally, these are associations to safeguard the village's farming, fishing and hunting rights, rather than political units.

Traditional houses are made of natural jungle products. Bamboo is the most popular building material, split for studs and rafters, or plaited for walls and roofs. Where bamboo is unavailable or impractical, thatch or other available varieties of wood may be utilised. Houses are generally on stilts, with the floor of the house

local beliefs about evil spirits. Just as many of the villages erect protective devices against malevolent spirits, so do individuals. Since evil spirits are thought to be able to approach the village from only one direction, the house may be built with doors and windows on the opposite side of the house, so that the spirits will not be able to enter. In addition to this style of house construction, many tribal houses employ additional means to ward off evil spirits or to appease them in case it has not been sufficiently frightened. A structure typical of many animistic villages is that of the spirit house. The village spirit house may be dedicated to the

above the ground. Raising the house on stilts not only provides protection from wild animals and the moist ground during the rainy season, but also creates a space below the house for storage, animal pens, children's play, or as a shady area out of the hot sun.

Some of the Montagnards in south Laos and northeast Cambodia utilise longhouses up to 100 metres in length. These provide living quarters for a number of families – more than a hundred people may live in a single longhouse. Normally the inhabitants of the individual longhouses are related, and so are members of an extended patrilineal or matrilineal family.

Most houses are erected in harmony with

spirit of the village, or there may be numerous spirit houses erected by individual households of the village. The latter are usually quite small, from just a few inches to perhaps a metre in length and width. Regardless of the size, these houses have great significance.

Another ritualistic feature of some tribal villages is the sacrifice pole. While individual sacrifices of chickens and pigs to the spirits require only small temporary sacrificial poles, water-buffalo sacrifices require a larger pole or post. The heavy sacrificial post may be located in the centre of the village, near the village burial grounds or in some other prominent place. These poles may be simple or elaborate.

Social structures

Because of the religious influence of sorcerers, they also exercise both political and economic authority. Their positions as religious leaders and communicators with the supernatural world make them members of the community elite, possessing an aura of influence and importance exceeding that of most religious figures in Western civilisation.

Family structure will vary greatly from tribe to tribe. In some tribes, parents choose marriage partners for their chil-

determined by whether the family is patrilineal (after the father's family) or matrilineal (after the mother's family). Customs pertaining to divorce vary widely between tribes. However, in spite of the many differences, the family plays a central role in tribal life throughout the two countries.

Except for some limited wet-rice farming, the major means of farming among the tribespeople is the slash-and-burn method, or swidden farming, in which bushes, vines and trees in a chosen area are cut down,

> ### LAO LINGUISTICS
>
> Lao contains 28 vowels, 33 consonants, and 6 tones. Also spoken in parts of Thailand and Cambodia, Lao has borrowed from the Indian Sanskrit and Pali.

dren based upon alliances or economic factors. Others allow the male to choose his own bride with the encouragement and support of the clan. A few tribes are so structured that the girl or her mother makes the choice of groom. Some tribes require dowries of the husband, others dowries of the wife, while some have none at all. Marriages usually require an intermediary, as a buffer when dowry bargaining becomes serious.

When children are born, their names will be

allowed to dry, and then burned. Crops such as mountain rice, millet, corn, pumpkin, squash, and manioc are planted. After the fields have been used for one to three years, they are abandoned and new fields slashed and burned. Harvesting is shared by men and women, with children joining in as soon as they are old enough. Children are also responsible for looking after cattle and buffalo, and for the caring of younger siblings. Those too feeble or old for heavy labour perform lighter tasks, like making bows and arrows or baskets. Because crafts primarily serve the practical needs of daily life, most tribes have not developed residual arts and crafts. ❏

LEFT: young hill-tribe boy, and fishing on the Mekong River, Vientiane. **ABOVE:** irrigating the field, and retaining the traditional dance through practice.

ARCHITECTURE

While the domestic architecture of Laos and Cambodia is typically practical and simple, structures of religious and royal importance are amongst the world's finest

As is the case in most of Southeast Asia, the buildings of Laos and Cambodia were traditionally built of wood, generally in plentiful supply throughout the region. As such, relatively few truly venerable structures remain standing in their original form. Notable exceptions include, of course, the stone temples of Angkor and similar buildings erected under royal patronage.

Many of the area's temples have been frequently reconstructed over the centuries, permitting some observations regarding local styles and construction methods. Inevitably, any brief look at the architecture of these two countries centres on buildings of religious or royal significance. Domestic architecture is on the whole simple and practical, though often borrowing forms and certain adornments from temple structures.

In Laos, the main architectural influences are obviously Buddhist and Thai. Just as in neighbouring Thailand, certain regional variations are distinguishable.

The predominant styles are conveniently referred to as Vientiane and Luang Prabang. While the former shares several features with central Thai styles, the latter is akin to styles found in northern Thailand. A third style, referred to as Xieng Khuang, after the central province of the same name, is now sadly less in evidence, as the province was so heavily bombed during the CIA secret war from 1968 to 1975. A few examples remain in Luang Prabang, however.

Temple architecture

The basic layout of a Lao temple follows the pattern of Theravada *wat* throughout Southeast Asia. The most important structure is the *ubosot*, known in Lao as the *sim*. This is the building where new monks are ordained.

Subsidiary structures include the *viharn,* where Buddha images are housed, a *haw trai,* or scripture library, and various *thaat,* or stupas. The larger of these *thaat* are said to contain relics of the Buddha; smaller ones – *thaat*

kaduk, or bone stupas – contain ashes of the long deceased.

It is perhaps the *thaat* which most distinguishes a truly Lao temple. The archetypal shape is that of That Luang in Vientiane, a four-cornered pillar curving in and then out before tapering away at the top. Stupas of other shapes

generally indicate Thai or Khmer influence. The principal exception, and a genuine oddity, is the hemispherical That Mak Mo, or Watermelon Stupa, in Luang Prabang.

It is in the *sim* that regional differences are most identifiable. The typical Vientiane-style sim is a tall rectangular brick building of narrow aspect covered in stucco. The roof is sharply sloped and high-peaked, generally with an odd number of tiers and supported by tall, thick pillars at the front and rear. The whole is raised on a high, multi-level pediment with a veranda at front, and sometimes at the back. In some cases, a terrace runs all the way around, after the Bangkok fashion. A staircase leads up to the veranda, often guarded by carved *naga* or *nyak* (mythical giants). The edges of the roof, in common with other styles of Lao temple, normally have a fringe of carved repeating flame motifs, with large hooks, known as *jao faa*, pointing to the sky at the corners. The main doors are usually of heavy carved wood. Often, shading the front veranda, high up, is an intricately carved wooden panel depicting mythical creatures against a background of intertwined foliage, testament to the skill of local artisans.

WAT'S ITS MEANING?

As in Thailand, the Lao *wat (vat)* defies accurate translation, although one might call it a temple or monastery. Still, these words don't do the *wat* justice.

Perhaps the most splendid example of the style is Wat Xieng Thong, which also has magnificently carved shutters, showing scenes from the local variant of the Indian epic classic *Ramayana, Pha Lak Pha Lam.*

The most distinctive feature of the few remaining Xieng Khuang-style temples is the single-tiered roof, unusual in Lao temples. Like that of a Luang Prabang-style *sim*, the roof sweeps low, but for structural reasons the cantilevered roof supports are far more prominent, giving the

A Luang Prabang-style sim has a far more modest plinth. Like its northern Thai counterparts, the layered roofs slope more gently and often come almost to the ground. The supporting pillars vary in height to support the various roof layers, and are normally slightly tapered towards the top, as they were traditionally made from stout tree trunks.

Much of the elegant yet subdued sparkle of Luang Prabang comes from the gold leaf that so often adorns the local temple doors and walls.

LEFT: the distinctive *thaat* of Vientiane's That Luang, representative of Lao temple stupa.
ABOVE: Wat Xieng Thong, Luang Prabang.

building a pentagonal shape when viewed from the front. The pediment, stepped after the Vientiane-style but usually not so high, is curved, lending the whole a touch of grace.

Limited principally to the difficult-to-access province of Sainyabuli, there is a fourth style of Buddhist temple in Laos, that of the Thai Lu, an ethnic minority from Yunnan's Sipsongpanna. These temples are rather squat in appearance, with low whitewashed walls and small windows. The roof is of two or three tiers, the lower of which slopes towards the front and back as well as the sides. Steps leading up to the main doors often have thick-set *naga* balustrades. The *thaat* of such temples are generally octagonal, gilded and, especially at festival times, bedecked in swaths of Thai Lu fabric, replete with beads and pieces of foil. These temples are very different from the Lao norm.

Colonial influences

The coming of the French in the late 19th century led to some distinctively colonial-style architecture in the main cities of the country, principally Luang Prabang and Vientiane. Many of these buildings were torn down or left to crumble after Lao independence, yet some fine examples still remain along the wide boulevards of Vientiane. Most are solid brick structures

with shuttered windows and tiled roofs, reminiscent of French provincial buildings. Particularly noteworthy is the restored Bibliothèque Nationale opposite Nam Phu fountain.

Grander examples include the Presidential Palace in Vientiane, and the former Royal Palace in Luang Prabang, now a museum. The latter exhibits a pleasing blend of French style and Lao motif. The former, for obvious reasons, is not open to the public, and its splendour can only be glanced from behind the guarded gates.

Lao architecture under the Communists tended towards dull functionalism. Many of the buildings of this era can still be seen, particu-

larly at some of the major road intersections in Vientiane's city centre. These buildings, at their worst, can inspire a sense of jaded, weary depression on the most serenely tropical evening. Wander southeast along the river from the Lane Xang Hotel – until recently Vientiane's premiere hotel, and itself hardly a vision of elegance – and glance to the left at the dull, grey, egg-carton school to see why socialism was such a misfit, and failure, in the country.

Happily, in recent years there has been increasingly more freedom and inventiveness in Lao building design. Traditional Lao forms have been rediscovered and blended with the functional into original and pleasing structures.

Cambodian architecture

Unlike Laos, Cambodia hasn't yet been in a position to make present-day architecture a high-priority issue. For the time being, the story of Cambodian architecture reaches its apogee in the Angkor period between the 9th and 13th centuries. More recent buildings of interest include the Royal Palace in Phnom Penh, together with some French colonial structures in that city.

Several centuries before Jayavarman II (802–850) proclaimed himself *devaraja,* or "god-king", Cambodia and southern Vietnam, known to the Chinese successively as Funan then Chenla, were highly Indianised states as a result of trade with South Asia. Architectural relics from Chenla, some of which can still be seen in present-day Cambodia, are typically square, sometimes octagonal, brick towers standing on stepped pedestals, showing distinct Indian influence and also more local invention.

From the beginning, Angkorean art and architecture were inspired by Chenla temples, and indirectly by Hinduism. Buildings were erected in honour of Shiva and, less often, Vishnu. The temples represent Mount Meru, home of the gods of Indian mythology. The central tower, a blunt tower, is the peak of the mountain, which is surrounded by walls representing the earth, and moats or lakes symbolising the oceans.

In many Angkor complexes, the latter cleverly and conveniently served a practical purpose as part of the complex irrigation and water supply system. ❏

LEFT: colonial architecture, now a restaurant in Vientiane. **RIGHT:** detail of temple door.

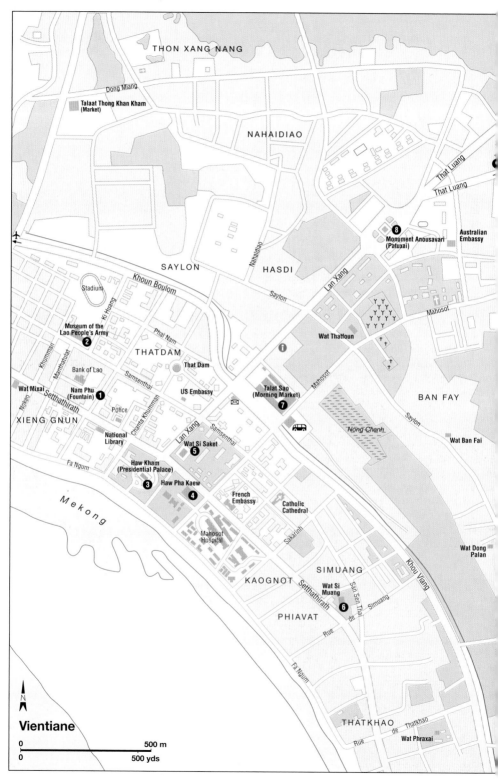

THON XANG NANG

Dong Miang

Talaat Thong Khan Kham (Market)

NAHAIDIAO

That Luang
That Luang

Monument Anousavari (Patuxai) ❽

Australian Embassy

SAYLON

HASDI

Khoun Boulom

Stadium

Sayton

Lan Xang

Mahosot

Museum of the Lao People's Army ❷

Ki Huang

Phai Nam

Wat Thatfoun

THATDAM

That Dam

Bank of Lao

Samsenthai

US Embassy

Mahosot

Talat Sao (Morning Market) ❼

BAN FAY

Wat Mixai

Nam Phu (Fountain) ❶

Setthathirath

Police

Nokeo

Chanta Khumman

Lan Xang

Samsenthai

Saylon

Nong Chanh

Wat Ban Fai

XIENG GNUN

Khumman

Mantthatiat

National Library

Wat Si Saket ❺

Fa Ngum

Haw Kham (Presidential Palace)

❸ Haw Pha Kaew ❹

French Embassy

Catholic Cathedral

Wat Dong Palan

Mekong

Mahosot Hospital

Sakarinh

SIMUANG

Khou Viang

KAOGNOT

Setthathirath

Wat Si Muang

San Sen Thai

de

Simuang

PHIAVAT

❻

Rue

Fa Ngum

N

Vientiane

THATKHAO

Thatkhao

de

Rue

Wat Phraxai

0 _____ 500 m
0 _____ 500 yds

VIENTIANE

Long closed to tourism after the Pathet Lao takeover,
the capital of Laos is now open for business. Exceedingly low-rise
and low-key, Vientiane is compact enough to negotiate on foot

L ethargic and crescent-shaped, Vientiane reclines on the left bank of the Mekong River. It is about midway between the Chinese and Cambodian borders with Laos, and about midway between Hanoi and Bangkok. Thus, it is not without foreign influences. It is a city that is not quite a city, at least by the frantic standards of other Asian capitals. Traffic is light, and one can even safely cross the main boulevards on foot without fear of death.

In the mid 1500s, Vientiane was the fortified capital of the Lan Xang kingdom, ruled by Setthathirat. Within the city were a palace and two *wat*, or temples: That Luang and Wat Phra Kaeo, which at the time was the home for the venerable Emerald Buddha, originally from the Chiang Rai area and now in Bangkok within a wat of the same name. The royal city was called the City of Sandalwood, or Vieng Chan, a name still used today.

The Emerald Buddha remained in Vientiane for over two centuries, until 1778, when the Thai army, led by Gen. Chakri, who would later become the first king in the still-ruling Chakri dynasty, retrieved it and returned the diminutive jade statue to Thai possession. In the early 1800s, Vientiane was sacked by the Siamese again; most of the city was completely destroyed.

With a population of half a million, Vientiane is home today to a little over 10 percent of the country's population. It is a manageable city for the most part, walkable in the downtown districts, and cheap transport to outlying sights such as That Luang is easy to find. Bicycles are completely useful and appropriate, and cheap to rent. The city's architecture is modestly eclectic and low-rise, reflecting both French colonial and generically modern influences.

Central Vientiane

As Vientiane has no central plaza for orientation, locals and visitors alike often use **Nam Phu ❶**, a water-fountain circle on Thanon Setthathirath, as a reference, as it is strategically placed among an assortment of travel agencies, airline offices, bakeries, restaurants, *tuk-tuk* (taxi) stands, guest houses and hotels. Less than a decade ago, hardly any of these commercial establishments existed, as the ruling Pathet Lao had closed the country to tourism in 1975, indirectly preserving the Laotian capital in a time warp.

To the north of Nam Phu, on Thanon Samsenthai, one of two main east–west arteries in the city, is the **Museum of the Lao People's Army ❷** (Mon–Fri 8am–1pm and 2–4pm, Sat 8–11.30am). Built in 1925, this elegant structure was once the French governor's resident, and was used by the Lao government as an administrative building before being converted into a

Map on page 118

BELOW: mailbox in Vientiane.

museum in 1985. The permanent exhibition provides a selective history of Laos' struggle for independence, leaving out major details like the heavy Vietnamese involvement in the "revolution". But it is filled with interesting artefacts from the war, particularly the weapons, clothing and supplies of key revolutionary figures. Just north is the **National Stadium**, and to the east is the **Lao Plaza Hotel**, one of the grandest hotels in Vientiane or anywhere else in Laos, for that matter.

Just a couple of minutes' walk south of Nam Phu is the **Mekong River**, one of those classically mighty rivers that lures travellers like moths to light. A dike parallels the Mekong for several kilometres, and almost all of it is walkable. A small road, Quai Fa Ngum, parallels both river and dike. The dike is actually the old town wall, and its purpose was twofold: a line of defence from ill-intentioned outsiders and protection from rising waters of the Mekong. Recent excavations along the river's banks have revealed ancient artefacts, especially pottery.

The perspective from the path on the dike along the river is a century old. Little has changed if one squints hard enough, but the part of Quai Fa Ngum near the central downtown area is lined by renovated buildings, and between the road and river are numerous but simple outdoor cafes on stilts, popular meeting places for both locals and foreigners. The river itself, especially when it is low, is a time capsule – naked children swim, grandmothers spin silk under houses, women on verandas suckle babies, husbands sip *lao-lao* and talk. Across the river is Thailand.

BELOW: view of downtown from Pratuxai.

East of Nam Phu is the **Presidential Palace** ❸ (Haw Kham), once the royal palace and today closed to the public. Adjacent is **Haw Pha Kaew** ❹, the royal temple of King Setthathirat, who built it in 1565 to house the Emerald Buddha.

Destroyed by the Thais in 1827, the wat was rebuilt after World War II. The wat contains a gilded throne, Khmer Buddhist stelae and bronze frog drums belonging to the royal family.

Map on page 118

On the northern side of Thanon Setthathirath is **Wat Si Saket** ❺, dating from 1818. Established as a monastery, the wat is perhaps the only structure that was not destroyed by the Thais in 1827. The interior walls surrounding its central *sim* are filled with small niches containing more than 2,000 miniature silver and ceramic Buddha images, most of them dating from the 16th to 19th centuries.

Further east is **Wat Si Muang** ❻, the most active temple in Vientiane because it houses the village pillar, or *lak muang*, the cornerstone that houses the city's protective deity. When the temple was dedicated, a pit was dug and, so the legend goes, a virgin was sacrificed at its bottom when the pillar was dropped in, a harbinger of good luck to the capital's citizens.

Beginning at the Presidential Palace, a major boulevard, Lan Xang, heads northeast past **Talat Sao** ❼ (daily 6am–6pm), the morning market and probably the country's best, to the rather overwhelming **Monument Anousavari** ❽, officially known as **Patuxai** (Victory Gate). Finished in 1969 in memory of those killed in war prior to the Communist takeover of Laos, it offers the best non-bird's-eye view of the capital.

Patuxai, also known as Monument Anousavari.

Past Pratuxai and on high ground 3 km (2 miles) from downtown sits stately 16th-century **That Luang** ❾ (Tues–Sun 8–11.30am and 2–4.30pm). Herein lies a relic of the Buddha, a breastbone. Like the downtown temples, That Luang has been rebuilt several times. Representing a miniature Mount Meru, the mythical peak, and some 45 metres (150 ft) tall, it is painted gold and dazzles eyes year-round. Flanked on two sides by smaller temples, it sees scant monkish

BELOW: Buddhist ceremony in That Luang.

Map on page 118

TIP

Up close, That Luang may not meet every traveller's expectations of a sacred monument. It seems to be constructed of painted concrete. Still, it is highly revered.

RIGHT: boat on the Mekong. **BELOW:** herbs in bottles.

activity except on holidays, especially during the annual That Luang festival. Then watch out. Everybody shows up from miles around. The whole hilltop assumes a carnival air, and festivities begin with vendors selling tickets to see a two-headed water buffalo and end two weeks later with a fireworks display second to none in all Laos. Yet people do visit That Luang year-round. Women seeking merit on their journey to Nirvana bring flowers and balls of rice to its ancient gates at dawn. Art students take up position under nearby flame trees to sketch it. Lao and foreigners alike visit its stark if spacious interior. But when it is festival time, those wanting a good position in That Luang's interior show up before sunrise. The remainder sit on straw mats, the crowd extending out several hundred metres. To be Lao is to be devout, and also to be lucky – monks sell lottery tickets immediately outside That Luang's main entrance on festival days.

Wax-paper castles adorned with fake money are carried on poles atop shoulders into the complex the day before the main festival day. These castles are made by families from all over town seeking to gain merit. That evening, people holding candles circle the temple three times in an age-old tradition. The next day is a solemn one as the patriarch speaks. Then everyone wanders away, and temple life returns to pastoral normality.

Beyond Vientiane

There is plenty to do in a day using Vientiane as a hub. The most exotic day-trip, perhaps, is to **Phu Khao Khuai** (Water Buffalo Mountain), a pine-forested plateau surrounded by 2,000-metre (5,500 ft) peaks. Here, nature rules. Butterflies, big as an open hand, dart and hover among blossoms hidden in high grass everywhere. One of the country's National Biodiversity Conservation Areas, it

is said to be full of local wildlife, including elephants, black bears, tigers and clouded leopards. The second most exotic day-trip is to the waterfall at **Tad Leuk**.

The trek through the sea-of-a-forest to the waterfall west of Thabok requires a rugged vehicle, but the horizontal and vertical zig-zagging course from Thabok to the waterfall is well marked. The falls are almost as big as the famous Kong Phapheng Falls in Champassak province. Tad Luek remains as pristine as the day the Lao spirits got together in revelry and made it. The banks of the Nam Leuk leading to and from Tad Leuk are camouflaged by jungle and make it impossible to do much hiking. But perhaps this adds to Tad Leuk's charm and enchantment – one can sit in the cool shade for hours.

Another splendid day-trip is to **Ban Thalet** and the lake at **Nam Ngum**. The dam creating the lake provides electrical power to much of Laos, and Laos exports significant amounts to neighbouring Thailand. Small restaurants overlook the blue-green water, and the setting is almost European due to so many alpine-like peaks surrounding the lake. Nam Ngum itself is dotted with picturesque islands, one or two of which offer guesthouses. To the north of the lake is **Vang Vieng**, noted for its scenery of limestone formations, especially caves, and waterfalls. Hmong and Mien (Yao) people inhabit the area, and the caves are part of their mythology. ❑

LUANG PRABANG

The temples and culture of Luang Prabang, capital of Laos and seat of the monarchy until the 16th century, have been so well preserved that the city is now a World Heritage Site

Map on page 106

F or centuries prior to its founding, the area around **Luang Prabang ❶** played host to various Thai-Lao principalities in the valleys of the Mekong, Khan, Ou and Xeuang rivers. It was in 1353, though, that King Fa Ngum consolidated the first Lao kingdom, Lan Xang (One Million Elephants), on the site of present-day Luang Prabang. The city was known as Xawa, possibly a local form of Java, but it was renamed Meuang Xieng Thong (Gold City District). A little later, King Fa Ngum received the gift of a Sinhalese Buddha image called Pha Bang from the Khmer sovereign, from which the city's modern name derives.

In 1545, King Phothisarat moved the capital of the Lan Xang kingdom to Vientiane, but Luang Prabang remained the royal heart of the kingdom. After the collapse of Lan Xang in 1694, an independent kingdom was established in Luang Prabang, which co-existed with kingdoms based in Vientiane and Champasak further south. At various times forced to pay tribute to the Thais, the Vietnamese, and most recently the French, kings ruled Luang Prabang until the monarchy was officially dissolved by the Pathet Lao in 1975. The last king and queen were imprisoned in a cave in the northeast of the country, where it is thought they perished some time in the 1980s. An official statement on this has never been issued.

Luang Prabang's royal legacy, although a story of decline, combines with its splendid natural setting at the confluence of the Mekong and Khan rivers to create one of the most intriguing and magical cities in Asia. The city is crowded with old temples and dominated by the 100-metre-high (330 ft) rocky outcrop, Phu Si. In 1995, Luang Prabang was added to UNESCO's World Heritage List.

Palace and temples

In the centre of Luang Prabang, between Phu Si and the Mekong, is the **Royal Palace Museum** (Haw Kham; Mon– Fri 8.30am–10.30am), which offers an insight into the history of the region. The palace was constructed early in the 20th century (commencing in 1904) as the residence of King Sisavang Vong, in a pleasing mix of classical Lao and French styles, cruciform in layout, and mounted on a multi-tiered platform.

In a room at the front of the building is the museum's prize piece, the famed Pha Bang Buddha image. The 83-cm-tall (33-inch) image, in the *mudra* attitude of Abhayamudra, or "dispelling fear", is almost pure gold and weighs around 50 kg (110 lb). Legend holds that the image originated in Sri Lanka in the first century AD, before being presented to the Khmers and later to King Fa Ngum. The image was twice seized by the Siamese in 1779 and 1827 before

LEFT: Buddha image, Wat Chieng Thong. **BELOW:** royal palace.

finally being restored to Laos by Thailand's King Mongkut in 1867. In the same room are several beautifully embroidered silk screens and impressive engraved elephant tusks. The rest of the museum houses a fairly substantial collection of regalia, portraits, diplomatic gifts and art treasures. Interesting are the varied friezes, murals and mosaics throughout.

Across the road to the west of the Royal Palace is **Wat Mai Suwanna-phumaham** (Mon–Fri 8.30–10.30am). Dating from the early 19th century, this temple was for some time the residence of the Sangkhalat, the Supreme Patriarch of Buddhism in Laos. The *sim*, or ordination hall, is wooden, with a five-tiered roof in classic Luang Prabang style. The main attraction here is the stunningly gilded walls of the front veranda, the designs of which recount scenes from the *Ramayana*, the ancient Indian epic, and from the story of the Buddha's penultimate incarnation. For the first half of the 20th century, the Pha Bang was housed here, and it is still put on display here during the Lao New Year celebrations. Within the temple compounds are two long boats, in their own shelter, that play their part, too, at New Year.

On the other side of Thanon Phothisarat rises Phu Si, a sheer rock with wooded sides. At the foot is the derelict **Wat Paa Huak**, which despite its abandonment contains very well-preserved 19th-century murals showing Mekong scenes. From this temple, 328 steps wind up Phu Si to **Wat Chom Si** on the summit, which has an impressive gilded stupa in classical Lao form. The summit also offers fine views of Luang Prabang and surrounding mountains.

The path continues down the other side of Phu Si, past an anti-aircraft gun to **Wat Tham Phu Si**, a cave shrine housing a Buddha image of wide girth in the style known locally as Pha Kachai. Close by the main road is **Wat Pha Phut-**

BELOW: overlooking Luang Prabang and river.

Map
on page
106

thabaat, a temple containing a 3-metre-long (10-ft) Buddha footprint and originally constructed in the late 14th century. There is another Buddha footprint temple, **Wat Pha Baat Tai**, behind Talat Sao, the fresh produce market in the southern part of town. This wat is more modern and decidedly garish, and it shows distinct Vietnamese Buddhist influence. It is a fine place from where to watch the Mekong slip by.

Heading north along Thanon Phothisarat, from the foot of Phu Si towards the confluence of the Nam Khan and the Mekong, takes one past a string of glittering temples, interspersed with evocative colonial buildings. **Wat Paa Phai** (Bamboo Forest Temple) on the left is noteworthy for its century-old fresco and carved wooden facade depicting secular Lao scenes. Further along the street, also on the left, is **Wat Saen** (One Hundred Thousand Temple), the name of which refers to the value of the donation with which it was constructed. This temple is noticeably different in style from most others in Luang Prabang, and the trained temple-eye will immediately identify it as heavily Thai-influenced. The *sim*, built in 1718, has been restored twice in the 20th century.

The most renowned temple

Close to the tip of the peninsula, on the banks of the Mekong and reminding the visitor of the importance of river transport in Laos, is Luang Prabang's most renowned temple, **Wat Xieng Thong** (Golden City Monastery; Mon–Fri 8.30–10.30am). This temple, which epitomises in its low sweeping roofs the classic Luang Prabang style of temple architecture, was built in 1560 by King Sai Setthathirat and was patronised by the monarchy right up until 1975. Inside the *sim*, the eight thick supporting pillars, richly stencilled in gold, guide the eye to the

BELOW: carving windows.

serene golden Buddha images at the rear, and upwards to the roof that is covered in *dhamma* wheels. On the outside of the *sim*, at the back, is an elaborate mosaic of the tree of life set against a deep red background. Throughout, the combination of splendid gold and deep red lend this temple a captivatingly regal atmosphere.

Adjacent to the *sim* is a smaller building, dubbed by the French **La Chapelle Rouge** or Red Chapel, containing a unique reclining Buddha figure. What makes the image so unusual are the Lao proportions, especially the robe curling outwards at the ankles, and the graceful position of the hand supporting the head. This figure was displayed at the Paris exhibition in 1931, but happily it returned to Luang Prabang in 1964 after several decades in Vientiane. The Red Chapel itself is exquisitely decorated. On the outside of the rear wall is a mosaic showing rural Lao village life, executed in the 1950s to celebrate two and a half millennia since the Buddha's attainment of *nirvana*. Also in the Xieng Thong compound are various monk's quarters, reliquary stupas and a boat shelter. Close to the east gate is a building housing the royal funeral carriage.

Another temple of note – one cannot get away from the fact that Luang Prabang is primarily a city of temples – is **Wat Wisunalat** (Mon–Fri 8.30–10.30am), also known as **Wat Vixoun**. Built by King Wisunalat in 1513, this is the oldest temple in the city still in use. The *sim*, rebuilt in 1898 under the inspiration of the original wooden structure destroyed by fire in 1887, is unique in style, with a front roof sloping down over the terrace. Sketches by Louis Delaporte of the original building exist from the 1860s, confirming what a later visitor wrote: "Wat Wisunalat is shaped like a boat, the same shape that orientals give to their coffins. The wooden walls are sculpted with extreme refinement and delicacy."

Although the wood has gone, the builders who performed the restoration

Temple mural detail.

BELOW: Wat Wisunalat.

attempted to capture the shapes of the original wood in the stucco work. Inside is an impressive collection of Buddhist sculpture. In the temple grounds is the That Pathum, or Lotus Stupa, which is affectionately referred to as That Mak Mo, or Watermelon Stupa. It is just as distinctive as the temple itself. The stupa is over 30 metres (100 ft) high and was constructed in 1504, at which time it was filled with small, precious Buddha images. Many of these were stolen by marauders from Yunnan, in China, in the 19th century, but the rest are now safely on display in the Royal Palace museum.

Next to Wat Wisunalat is the peaceful **Wat Aham**, formerly – before Wat Mai took the honour – the residence of the Supreme Patriarch of Buddhism in Laos. The temple's red facade combines with striking green yak temple guardians and mildewed stupas to provide an atmosphere of extreme tranquillity. The temple rarely has many visitors, other than those quietly making offerings at an important shrine at the base of the two large, old pipal trees.

Beyond Luang Prabang

In fact, the city possesses far more notable temples than are indicated here. A few kilometres to the southeast of town is a forest retreat, **Wat Paa Phone Phao**, with a three-storey pagoda replete with an external terrace near the top that affords excellent views of the surrounding country side. The chedi is a popular destination for locals and visitors alike.

Across the river from the centre of the city, in Xieng Maen District, are no less than four more temples set in beautiful surroundings, one of which, **Wat Tham Xieng Maen**, is situated in a 100-metre-deep (300-ft) cave. This is generally kept locked, but the keys are held at nearby Wat Long Khun, the former retreat

Map on page 106

BELOW: Hmong new year celebrations.

Map on page 106

of kings awaiting coronation. A small donation is requested for having someone open up the cave temple. Boats transport people across the river to this side from a jetty behind the Royal Palace.

A short distance to the east of the city, about 4 km (2½ miles) beyond the airport, is the Thai Lü village of **Ban Phanom**, renowned as a silk- and cotton-weaving village. On weekends, a small market is set up for those interested in seeing the full range of fabrics produced. However, villagers are willing – sometimes too willing – to show off their goods at any time. All weaving is done by hand on traditional looms, a fascinating process to watch.

In the vicinity, a few kilometres along the river, is the **Tomb of Henri Mouhot**, the French explorer who took the credit for "discovering" Angkor Wat in 1860. He died of malaria in Luang Prabang in 1861, although his tomb was abandoned and not discovered till 1990.

A two-hour, 25-km (15-mile) journey by long-tail boat upriver from Luang Prabang is the confluence of the Mekong and the Nam Ou. Opposite the mouth of the Nam Ou, in the side of a limestone cliff, are the **Pak Ou Caves**. Legend maintains that King Sai Setthathirat discovered these two caves in the 16th century, and they have been venerated ever since. Both are full of Buddha images, some of considerable age. The lower of the two caves, **Tham Ting**, is easily accessible from the river. The upper cave, **Tham Phum**, is reached by a staircase and is much deeper, requiring a torch for full exploration. There is a pleasant shelter between the two caves, an ideal spot for a picnic lunch.

RIGHT: taking aim with a slingshot. **BELOW:** bicycles on the move.

On the way to Pak Ou, boats will stop by request at **Ban Xang Hai**, the jar-maker village and named after the village's former main industry. Archaeologists digging around the village have unearthed jars dating back more than 2,000 years. Today, jars abound, but they are made elsewhere, and the village devotes itself to producing *lao-lao*, the local moonshine rice-wine. Opposite, at **Ban Thin Hong** and close to Pak Ou village, recent excavations have uncovered even older artefacts – tools, pottery and fabrics – around 8,000 years old. The site hasn't yet been properly developed.

Trails and waterfalls

There are several waterfalls in the vicinity of Luang Prabang that can make for attractive half-day or day excursions, perhaps combined with stops in some of the villages along the way. About 30 km (20 miles) south of town are the multi-tiered falls of **Kuang Si**, replete with interesting limestone formations and crystal-clear pools. Food vendors keep most of the local visitors at the lower level of the falls, which can be very crowded on holidays. There is a second pool and waterfall up a trail to the left of the lower cascade that makes for good swimming, and it is generally quieter. The trail continues to the top of the falls, though after rain it can be hazardously slippy.

The falls at **Taat Sae**, also south of town, are closer to the city, and hence more crowded at weekends, although they are often deserted in the week. The falls here have more pools and shorter drops. They can be reached by boat from the delightful village of Ban Aen on the Nam Khan river. ❏

ANGKOR

The cities and palaces of ancient Europe were diminutive in both size and detail compared with those of Angkor. Still, until a century ago, the ruins of Angkor were hidden by the overgrowth of jungle

Maps on pages 106, 134

R evealed to the West only by its fortuitous "discovery" in 1860, **Angkor** ❷ was the capital of a powerful kingdom whose rulers boasted in their inscriptions that it had "for its moat the Ocean, and for its boundaries China, the Suksma Kamrata [apparently western tribal names], and the territory of Champa [southern Vietnam]". This Khmer state arose on the foundations of other pre-Angkorian, "Indianised" Cambodian states, referred to in old Chinese records as Funan and Chenla. The Angkor period is conventionally considered to have begun in AD 802 with the reign of King Jayavarman II, lasting until 1431, when the capital was abandoned.

The Khmer kings and others of the ruling classes left many inscriptions, hundreds of which have been found and interpreted. These have granted us some insight into royal, religious and administrative questions, and permitted the occasional glimpse into other levels of life as well. The sophisticated and immensely alluring sculpture of the Khmer, which in some large temple bas reliefs can measure hundreds of metres, also provides us with a most revealing archive about this ancient people and their way of life. Art and architecture changed in style over the long period of the existence of the cities in the Angkor region, and fairly sophisticated dating is now possible. Much of the art is, of course, regally oriented, dream-like in its splendour and other worldliness. But the overwhelming impact of the Khmer is best summed up by Angkor Wat, the world's largest religious structure, covering some 80 hectares (200 acres), or by the splendid royal temple called the Bayon. On its towers, the serenely smiling face of the god-king as the Bodhisattva Avalokiteshvara is represented on a gigantic scale.

Khmer architecture

Not unlike the ancient Egyptians, the Khmers are quintessentially identified by their fabulous architecture. Just as Egypt is instantly associated with pyramids and temples, so the Khmer are recognised by the truly staggering achievement of their splendid temples. Some are Buddhist, and others are Hindu, dedicated to their kings and the cult of the *devarajas*, or god-kings. The Khmers aspired to represent no less than the Hindu universe in miniature, centred on the mythical Mount Meru, the main tower of the edifices, with the sanctuary facing east and surrounded by the continents. The outer ocean is represented by the moat, often usefully linking into the city's extensive hydraulic system. Simpler, earlier temples evolved into the later classical form, with five peaks for the central "mountain" and outer courts and towers.

Bas relief depicting apsara, or divine dancers.

Khmer architectural efforts culminated in Angkor Wat, but the Angkor area altogether includes well over a hundred temples. The latest NASA surveys, in 1998, revealed that there is much more to find, including a temple northwest of Angkor. It is said to be as big as a football stadium and to date from before the ninth century, and is thus very important for the study of Angkor's origins.

Surrounding the temples was once a city of wooden structures, including everything from royal palaces carved in fantastic detail, down to the most temporary market shelter. All this has vanished, except on the bas reliefs, leaving the temples isolated from their original setting and amidst the ever encroaching jungle.

OPPOSITE: Angkor Wat at twilight.

The tremendous efforts involved in erecting these structures depended on a strong state machinery administering an extensive human-power resource. An elaborate hydraulic system had to be maintained, with a network of canals and dikes serving the reservoirs. A break-down of the delicate balance of resources, food supplies and administration doubtless eventually caused the collapse of the system. But while it was maintained, the Khmer architects, craftsmen and builders, under the command of the kings who ordered their labours, were able to produce structures that are recognised world masterpieces.

Historical outline

The Angkor period commenced with the reign of Jayavarman II (AD 802–850), who established himself in the region at various centres, building temples at Mount Kulen, 40 km (25 miles) northeast of Angkor, and also at Roluos, situated to the southeast of Angkor. Jayavarman's monarchy evoked the concept of the *chakravatin*, the universal monarch, and the *devaraja*, or god-king. The royal temple was regarded as Shiva's dwelling place, the holy mountain.

Internal struggles consumed the eras of several rulers until Suryavarman II took the throne in 1113, reigning until 1150. It was he who built Angkor Wat. In his time, the Khmer frontiers remained extended, embracing a substantial area of what is now Thailand. Suryavarman's religious inclinations favoured Vishnu, as represented at Angkor Wat.

In 1177, a Cham invasion – perhaps sparked by Khmer raids into Cham territory – caused widespread destruction at Angkor, until repelled by Jayavarman VII, the last of the great Khmer kings. Jayavarman fought to regain the ravaged city of Angkor Thom, and then freed the rest of the empire after killing

TIP

When visiting Angkor Wat, stay on the well used paths, as there are mines on some outlying tracks.

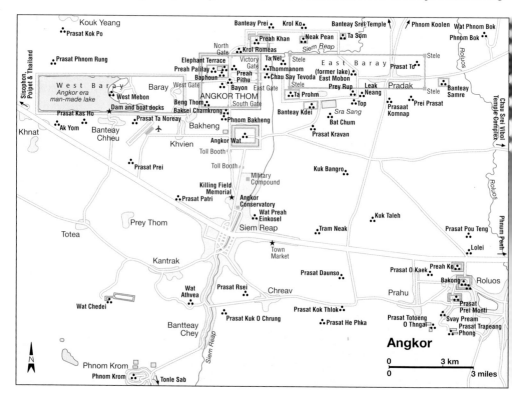

the king of the Cham. Jayavarman was a Mahayana Buddhist, perhaps in reaction to the discredit that the Cham defeat had brought to the divine incarnations of Shiva or Vishnu who had ruled the Khmer so long. His reign saw tremendous building activity in the area. This was the swansong of the Khmer monarchy. In 1431, weakened and unable to maintain themselves in the face of the strong monarchy established at Ayutthaya in Thailand (which had already captured Angkor once in 1389), the kings of Angkor are supposed to have retreated to a new capital at Phnom Penh. Alternatively, it has been proposed that another line of kings installed themselves near Phnom Penh, and that some sort of monarchy continued at Angkor. But slowly Angkor became a ghost city, some of it taken over by the jungle, some parts occupied by monks.

Angkor Wat

Seven kilometres (4 mi) north of **Siem Reap**, the nearest town and where most of the hotels are located, the moated temple of **Angkor Wat** occupies an area of almost 2 square kilometres (500 acres). It was built by King Suryavarman II as a microcosmic representation of the celestial world. Every aspect of the structure possesses meaning on a religious and metaphorical level. The king was identified as the god Vishnu, the deity honoured here, and Angkor Wat seems to have been both a royal temple and a mausoleum.

The temple is immensely imposing, the world of the gods seemingly floating on the waters of the 190-metre-long (625-ft) moat. The pillared galleries and towers bestow an impressive breadth, height, and mass, while the incredibly lavish carvings and bas reliefs fill every corner with information about the heavenly world. As a construction project alone, the effort involved is awe-inspiring.

A stone causeway approaches the temple, or *wat*, from the west, and an earthen one from the east. Within the moat, the temple "island" is walled, with four gates; the western gate is the main entrance. The triple-towered porch measures 235 metres (770 ft) in width, and is elaborately decorated, with the figures of the divine dancing girls, the *apsaras*, prominent.

A massive statue of Vishnu stands to the south, holding the deity's various attributes in its eight arms. From the porch, an avenue nearly 500 metres (1,600 ft) long, flanked by *naga* serpents, leads past two so-called library buildings and two pools to another walled area, the central temple approached by a staircase from a cruciform terrace. Inside this inner area, around the temple and completely enclosing it, is a gallery or cloister accessible from doorways on either side of an entrance pavilion. The cloister houses the tremendous series of bas reliefs 2 metres (6½ ft) high, for which Angkor is so famous. The carved reliefs represent stories from the *Ramayana*, the Indian epic account of Rama's search for his wife, Sita, snatched away by a demon king of Lanka, and the great battle described in the *Mahabharata*. There are also scenes of the king and his court, and a magnificent depiction of a military parade, the different contingents and their leaders named in accompanying inscriptions. Finally, scenes of heaven and hell shown what the good can expect *(apsaras)*, and the bad (various tortures).

Map on page 134

Apsaras reflected the perfect image of female beauty. Heaven was their abode, and they lived mainly to have sex with heroes and even holy men.

BELOW: bas relief at a gate to Angkor.

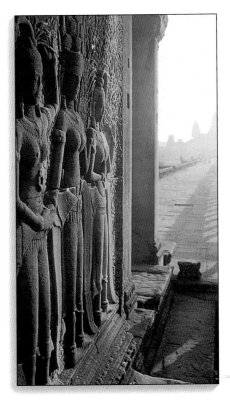

Map on page 134

Angkor Thom was much larger than the whole of ancient Rome, and it was surrounded by a moat 100 metres wide and over 10 km (6 miles) long.

OPPOSITE: stone image, Bayon.
BELOW: temple detail.

Within this gallery, at a higher level, is another gallery with stone-mullioned windows, linked to the outer gallery by a cruciform cloister and the flanking galleries. Here in the "Gallery of a Thousand Buddhas" were once kept the images that pious Cambodians had dedicated to the temple. Finally, inside the second gallery with its four corner towers, presumably shrines, lies the main temple, the golden mountain of Jambudvipa, the abode of the gods. Raised high on a stepped platform, accessible by staircases, another gallery with four corner towers encloses the central great tower, to which it is also linked by four axial galleries. A great statue of Vishnu, representing the king, was enshrined here, the focus of this huge effort.

Angkor Thom and the Bayon

The inner royal city of Angkor, **Angkor Thom**, already occupied by such monuments as the Phimeanakas and the Baphuon, was restored after the Cham invasion by Jayavarman VII. The huge quadrangle, 3 km (2 miles) on each side, is delineated by a broad moat and defended by a wall 8 metres (26 ft) high, with gates sculpted with mythical figures and huge faces.

The temple in the centre of Angkor Thom, called the **Bayon**, makes an extraordinary impression with its numerous towers sculpted with over 200 large faces of King Jayavarman VII as Boddhisattva Avalokiteshvara. Directly north of the Bayon, facing the town's central square, is **Elephant Terrace**, sculpted with a frieze of elephants. This 350-metre-long (1,150-ft) monument may have had some relation to the royal apartments.

The Bayon temple, not dedicated to one deity but more like a national pantheon to all the Khmer deities, is constructed on three levels. With the plethora of towers, set rather close together, the temple gives a rather crowded impression. The first enclosure is surrounded by a magnificent set of bas reliefs, 1,200 metres (4,000 ft) of them, depicting battles by sea and land with the Chams, royal scenes and processions, and other tableaux, with a good deal of information about local life and fauna as well. The carving is incredibly detailed. The second level also has bas reliefs, now much damaged. The third level represents the world mountain, with shrines for the Buddha, Shiva, Vishnu and others.

The temples of the Roluos group, built at the former capital, Hariharalaya, are interesting as precursors to the greater monuments of Angkor. **Preah Ko**, dedicated by King Indravarman in AD 880 to his ancestors, is characterised by six towers built of brick on a stone terrace guarded by lion figures. The remains of some of the elaborate stucco work that would once have covered the brickwork illustrates the fine level to which this technique had been brought.

Bakong was also built by Indravarman as his state temple, dedicated to Shiva. It is a representation of Meru as a five-tiered pyramid platform surrounded by towers constructed of brick with stone plinths, doorways and lintels. Some stucco work survives. The pyramid, topped with a tower and with smaller shrines standing on the level below, rises within an enclosure, surrounded by a moat representing the ocean. ❑

ANCIENT ARTEFACTS OF SOUTHEAST ASIA

Southeast Asia's ancient culture drew its inspiration from diverse religious and artistic influences, leaving the world one of its richest inheritances

The ancient artefacts found in Southeast Asia reveal a wealth of information about the history, traditions, social organisations and religious beliefs of the region. Since early times, the cultural traditions of the region have blended with those of India and China as traders from these countries came to exploit the rich supply of gold and spices. The gradual infusion of the powerful Hindu-Buddhist cultural traditions of India through *vaisyas* (Indian merchants) and *brahmanas* (religious men) resulted in the so-called "Indianisation" of Southeast Asia. This process only took place in areas that had direct contact with India; northern Vietnam, for example, was under Chinese influence and was not affected. This is not to say that the artistic culture of the Indianised kingdoms was not innovative and extraordinary. Indian themes and designs only provided a base for the indigenous people to develop their artistic styles, and it is their genius that is reflected in the artefacts and superlative architecture created at that time.

THE SOUTHEAST ASIAN INNOVATION DEBATE

Bronzeware dating from 3600 BC found in Ban Chiang, in northeast Thailand, has revealed that bronze technology was probably transferred from Thailand to China, not the other way round. This find is significant to the on-going argument that the region was a centre of innovation rather than merely a receptacle of outside influences.

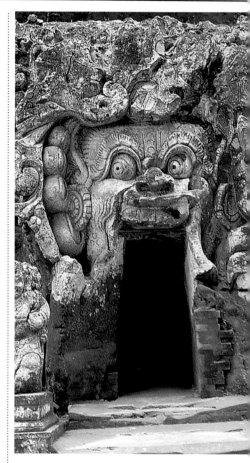

△ **ELEPHANT CAVES, BALI**
Goa Gajah, the Elephant Caves, date back to the 11th century. The sculpted face of the cave has links to Tantric Buddhism or perhaps Bhairavite Siwaism.

▷ **THUNDER-DRUM**
A 7th-century bronze thunder-drum made in Vietnam by the Dong Son. Thunder-drums produce a huge volume of sound and were used to bring on the monsoon thunder.

◁ **BUDDHIST INFLUENCES**
By the end of the 15th century, Theravaha Buddhism was the dominan religion across much of Southeast Asia's mainland.

△ **EARLY CLASSIC JAVANESE**
This beautiful 9th-century *bodhisattva* (goddess) at Candi Sari, Java, shows a strong Indian influence.

▽ **PREHISTORIC THAILAND**
Some of the pottery unearthed at Ban Chiang, Thailand, is believed to be 4,500 to 5,700 years old.

△ **EAST JAVANESE PERIOD**
A *candi* depicted in the reliefs of Candi Panataran Java, the most important *candi* of the East Javanese Period (11th–15th century).

▽ **HINDU CARVINGS**
The Hindu god Indra mounts his elephant, Erawan, in a relief at Myohaung's Htukkan-thein Pagoda, in Burma.

△ **CHAMPA KINGDOM**
These stone dancers in Da Nang, Vietnam, were carved by the Cham, creators of some of the finest Vietnamese art.

THE PLUNDERING OF BOROBUDUR

Borobudur is one of the most impressive monuments ever created by people. It was built around AD 800 when the Sailendra dynasty of central Java was at the height of its artistic and military power, taking 75 years to complete. It probably fell into neglect by about AD 1000. It was completely overgrown and suffering from earthquake damage when it was rediscovered in 1814 by a military engineer serving under Thomas Stamford Raffles.

In the years that followed, Borobudur was uncovered to the elements and to people, enduring almost a century of decay, plunder and abuse, during which thousands of stones were "borrowed" by people living nearby. Scores of priceless sculptures ended up as garden decorations in the homes of the rich and powerful. Typical of the attitude of Dutch officials at the time was the presentation, in 1896, of eight cart-loads of Borobudur souvenirs to visiting King Chulalongkorn of Thailand, including 30 relief panels and five Buddha statues. Many of these and other irreplaceable works of Indo-Javanese art ended up in private collections, residing now in private museums worldwide, a process replicated region-wide.

Vietnam

0   100 km

0   100 miles

VIETNAM

Vietnamese remind travellers that Vietnam is a nation, not a war. It's a nation with a heritage as rich as any

In the early 1400s, the Chinese invaded Vietnam, one of many such invasions over the centuries. The Chinese were soundly defeated by the Vietnamese. Le Loi, emperor of Vietnam, might have had the Chinese prisoners killed. He chose otherwise. Le Loi apologised to the Chinese court for defeating its army, made peace with China, and provided the defeated Chinese troops with horses and ships for their return north. Le Loi knew that, although momentarily defeated, China would never disappear.

Indeed, the presence of its leviathan neighbour to the north has, perhaps more than anything else, sculpted the nature of the Vietnamese mind. Centuries of fending off China's invasions, while at the same time not making China too angry, has given Vietnamese a pragmatism, a patience, and a solid sense of national identity. Vietnamese are highly educated and literate (over 90 percent), and they have an open desire to learn from others, and to admit mistakes.

About the size of Germany or Arizona, Vietnam challenges the best of travellers. After decades of war, and with an economy that was subsequently throttled, the country's infrastructure – or lack of it – can test the most hardened traveller's patience. But Vietnam is truly one of those destinations where the inconveniences pale beside the remarkable, and where the beauty of its 78 million people and culture seduce all.

Northern Vietnam is anchored by Hanoi, an ancient city established nearly 1,000 years ago. This political capital clings to the rhetoric of a socialist system while at the same time embracing a government-controlled capitalism. The dilapidated villas and façades of the French colonial era give the city an ambience not found elsewhere in Asia.

Southward, following the historical movement of the Viet people, the traveller finds a chain of coastal provinces washed by the South China Sea. In the old imperial city of Hue, an overwhelming sense of the past pervades its older streets. The antiquities don't end here. In the lands of the ancient kingdom of Champa are decaying sanctuaries, temples and towers that testify to the conquest by the Viet people from the north.

Then there is Ho Chi Minh City. Often still called Saigon, it is reviving its long-time image as a proverbial hustling and bustling city of people on the make and on the go. Where Hanoi is quiet, Ho Chi Minh City screams. Where Hue has a subtle and refined beauty, Ho Chi Minh City grabs by the lapels and shakes. If Hanoi is a city of earth tones, Ho Chi Minh City is neon, all lit up in gaudy lights. ❏

PRECEDING PAGES: river boat on the Mekong; descendants of Hue's royal family.

Decisive Dates

Beginnings

2879 BC: Legendary founding of the Van Lang Kingdom by the first Hung king.

2879–258 BC: Hung dynasty.

1800–1400 BC: Phung Nguyen culture, the Early Bronze Age.

200 BC–AD 938: Chinese rule.

210 BC: Kingdom of Au Lac established. Chinese general Chao Tuo founds Nan Yueh (Nam Viet).

AD 39: Trung sisters lead a rebellion against Chinese.

AD 43: Trung sisters' rebellion is crushed by the

Chinese general Ma Yuan, and subsequently, the Viet people are placed under direct Chinese administration for the first time.

542–544: Ly Bi leads uprising against China's Liang dynasty to create independent kingdom of Van Xuan.

939–967: Ngo dynasty.

968–980: Dinh dynasty.

970–975: Dinh Bo Linh gains Chinese recognition of Nam Viet's independence by establishing a triputary relationship with China's Song dynasty.

980–1009: Tien Le dynasty.

1009–1225: Ly dynasty.

1225–1400: Tran dynasty.

1400–1428: Ho dynasty.

1428–1776: Le dynasty.

Division and reunification

16th century: Decadence of Le dynasty leads to the country's division into two rival principalities.

1543: Descendants of the Le dynasty occupy the country's southern capital after a series of fierce battles. The southern court is founded near Thanh Hoa.

1592: The death of Mac dynasty's last king, Mac Mau Hop, ends the war.

1672: Lord Trinh consents to partition the country at the Linh River.

early 1770s: Struggle between French and Chinese factions begin with the court.

1776–92: Tay Son Uprising.

1792–1883: Nguyen dynasty.

1861: French forces capture Saigon. The French defeat the Vietnamese army and gain control of Gia Dinh and surrounding provinces. Six years later, the entire southern part of the country is annexed as a French colony.

1862: Treaty of Saigon cedes three southern provinces to the French.

1893: Emperor Ham Nghi and Phan Dinh Phung organise a royalist movement and stage an unsuccessful uprising at Ha Tinh.

1904: Japanese military victory over Russia convinces the Vietnamese that Western military power is no longer invincible.

1907: Eastward Movement is established by Phan Boi Chau and Cuong De. French authorities discover the scheme and negotiate with Japan to extradite all Vietnamese students.

1919: Ngyuen Ai Quoc (later known as Ho Chi Minh) attempts to present a programme for Vietnamese rights and sovereignty at the Versailles Peace conference but is turned away.

1921: Ho Chi Minh joins French Communist Party as founder member.

1923: Ho Chi Minh goes to Moscow to be trained as an agent of the Communist International.

1930: Ho Chi Minh successfully rallies several Communist groups and becomes the founder of the Indochinese Communist Party.

World War II and after

1939: World War II begins.

1942–43: Ho Chi Minh imprisoned in China.

1943: Ho Chi Minh is released and recognised as the chief of the Viet Minh.

1945: Japan overthrows French colonial rule and renders Vietnam "independent" but under Japanese "protection". The Japanese surrender to the Allies some months later. The Viet Minh commences the August Revolution, gaining effective control over much of Vietnam. In September Ho Chi Minh declares Vietnam's independence in Hanoi.

1946: Ho Chi Minh visits Paris during negotiations with France; hostilities begin following violation of agreements.

1951: Ho merges Viet Minh with the Lien Viet and announces the formation of the Workers Party (Lao Dong), a disguise for the Communist Party that had officially disbanded, but was still active.

North-South divide

1954: Geneva accord divides Vietnam at the 17th parallel. South Vietnam is led by Prime Minister Ngo Dinh Diem, and North Vietnam under the Communist Ho Chi Minh.

1955: Diem refuses to hold general elections. Start of Second Indochina War. Direct United States aid to South Vietnam begins.

1959: Group 559 established to infiltrate South Vietnam via the Ho Chi Minh Trail.

1960: National Liberation Front of South Vietnam (NLF) is formed. During the 1960s, the southern Communist movement – the Viet Cong – grows stronger.

1962: United States military personnel in Vietnam total about 3,200.

1963: Ngo Dinh Diem, president of South Vietnam, is overthrown and assassinated.

1965: United States begin bombing military targets in North Vietnam. First United States ground combat troops land in Vietnam at Danang.

1968: My Lai massacre. Tet Offensive includes a raid on the American embassy that stunned and embarrassed the United States.

1969: Ho Chi Minh dies without seeing his efforts completed. Peace negotiations drag on in Paris between 1968 and 1973.

1973: Paris Peace Agreement aims to put an end to hostilities. The last United States troops depart from Vietnam in March.

1975: In April, North Vietnamese troops enter Saigon. The South Vietnamese government surrenders.

A unified Vietnam

1976: Vietnam is officially reunified.

1977: Vietnam is admitted to the United Nations.

1978: Vietnam signs friendship treaty with the Soviet Union. The invasion of Cambodia by Vietnamese troops and the subsequent so-called "Chinese lesson" augurs a new cycle of war.

1979: Vietnamese forces begin invasion of Cambodia.

LEFT: traditional theme of simple pleasures.
RIGHT: the legendary Ho Chi Minh in the 1950s.

The Cambodian government of Pol Pot is overthrown when Phnom Penh falls to Vietnamese forces.

1979: China retaliates by invading Vietnam. After less than 3 months, Chinese forces withdraw.

1982: Fifth National Party Congress.

Economic shifts

1986: Sixth Party Congress. Programme of socio-economic renovation called *doi moi* is launched.

1987: Law on Foreign Investment is passed.

1988: New contract system is implemented to encourage Vietnamese farmers to cultivate their land. Rice production experiences an immediate upsurge.

1989: Vietnamese troops leave Cambodia.

1990: Vietnam adopts a new course in foreign affairs, and peace talks in China take place. Diplomatic relations established with the European Union.

1991: China relations normalised.

1994: Trade embargo lifted by the United States.

1995: Diplomatic ties are restored with the US, and a US embassy opens in Hanoi. Vietnam is admitted to the Association of Southeast Asian Nations (ASEAN).

1997: Reforms initiated in 1996 stall. Foreign investors leave because of corruption and bureaucracy.

2000: Bill Clinton visits Vietnam as a follow-up to the conclusion of a trade agreement with the US.

2001: Continuing economic stagnation.

2003: Economy shows signs of life as new laws to attract foreign investment are introduced. ❑

THE VIETNAMESE

Like much of Southeast Asia's population, the people of Vietnam are of diverse backgrounds, giving the country a colourful heritage that enchants today

Who are the people of Vietnam? Although most of the population of 78 million lists as its ethnicity Kinh, the accepted term for the native race, in reality most Vietnamese have evolved from a mixture of races and ethnicities over thousands of years. That mixture is quite naturally the result of repeated invasions from outside Vietnam, particularly from China, and continual migrations within Vietnam, commonly from north to south.

In Vietnam today, the Viet, or Kinh, in fact form the majority of the people, representing about 90 percent of the population. But there are also dozens of distinct minority groups, including the Cham and Khmer of the south, two groups whose own kingdoms were long ago vanquished by invading Vietnamese from the north.

The Vietnamese

Studies of folk songs from the hill region of northern Vietnam and from the coastal area in the northern part of central Vietnam affirm that the Vietnamese originated in the north's Red River Delta. These agricultural, fishing and hunting people were probably animistic.

Their traditional forms of dress, although unique to the region of Indochina, is found in certain Oceanic islands.

Throughout monsoon Asia, which includes northern Vietnam, a shared culture existed from a very early era, as evidenced by its tools, vocabulary and certain essential rites and traditions, such as the blackening of teeth, water festivals, bronze drums, kites, tattooing, betel nut and *cajeput*, pole houses, cock-fighting and mulberry cultivation. Remains of five races have been found in Vietnam: Melanesians, Indonesians, Negritos, Australoids and Mongoloids. The most predominant of these were the Indonesians and Mongoloids.

Studies on the origins of the Vietnamese show that the people who settled on the

Indochinese peninsula and its bordering regions came from several places: China, the high plateaus of Central Asia, and islands in the South Pacific. Thus, Vietnam can be considered a proverbial melting pot into which major Asiatic and Oceanic migrations converged. Two major Viet emigrations from the coastal

and southern provinces of the Chinese empire added to this population. The first occurred during the 5th century BC, at the fall of the Viet kingdom of the lower Yangtze River valley, and the second, during the 3rd century BC, when the Au, or Au Tay, from Guangxi, invaded northern Vietnam.

Ethnic minorities

More than 50 ethnic minorities inhabit the mountainous regions that cover almost two-thirds of Vietnam. (In the 1990s, a small tribe of fewer than 100 members was found in a northern province, a tribe distinct from previously identified ethnic groups.) Of Vietnam's 1 mil-

---

LEFT: elderly woman at northern market.
RIGHT: the young Duy Tan, emperor of Annam.

lion Chinese, only 3,000 have kept their Chinese nationality, while the rest, referred to as Hoas, have adopted Vietnamese nationality.

The ethnic minorities living in the mountainous regions in central and southern Vietnam form another important group. Called Montagnards by the French, these tribes include Muong, Ra De, Jarai, Banhar and Sedang living in the high plateaus of the west. Totalling around 700,000 people, they have always opposed foreign influence and only recently have begun to integrate into the national life.

The Cham and Khmer number around 400,000. The Chams inhabit the Phan Rang and

Phan Thiet regions, while Khmer are found in the Mekong Delta. The Chams possessed a brilliant culture that lasted for more than a thousand years. It's vestiges can still be seen in the ruins of the Poh Nagar temple and the shrines and Buddhist monasteries at Dong Duong, and in the large scale irrigation systems, temples and towers of central Vietnam.

Today, some Cham preserve their customs, language and script with a religion that is a modified form of Hinduism. Others are Muslim.

In the north

The highlands and midland regions of northern Vietnam are home to many ethnic minorities

and diverse tribes, including the Tay, who number just under a million and are found in village groups in the provinces of Cao Bang, Lang Son, Bac Thai, Quang Ninh, Ha Giang, and Tuyen Quang, and in the Dien Bien Phu region.

The villages, or *ban*, of the Tay are located in valleys near flowing water, where they build their traditional houses, usually on stilts. They cultivate rice, soybeans, cinnamon, tea, tobacco, cotton, indigo, fruit trees and bamboo on the mountainsides above the village. The influence of Viet culture is evident in their dialect and customs, which distinguish them from the other Tay-Tai speaking groups.

The Nung, in many aspects similar to the Tay, share the same language, culture and customs, and often live together in the same villages, where they are referred to as Tay Nung. Numbering about 340,000, they live in Cao Bang and Lang Son provinces.

There are about 76,000 Tai living along the Red River, in the northwest of Vietnam, often together with other ethnic minorities. Their bamboo or wooden stilt houses are constructed in two distinctly different styles. The Black Tai build homes shaped like tortoise shells, while the White Tai construct dwellings of a rectangular form.

The San Chi, numbering more than 77,000, live in village groups mainly in Ha Giang, Tuyen Quang and Bac Thai provinces, but they are also found in certain regions of Lao Cai, Yen Bai, Vinh Phu, Ha Bac and Quang Ninh provinces. They are of the Tay-Tai language group and arrived from China at the beginning of the 19th century. The Giai, also of the Tay-Tai language group, number about 30,000 and emigrated from China about 200 years ago. Their villages are often built very close to those of the Tay, Nung and Tai.

The Lao number about 7,000 and belong to the Tay-Tai language group. They are actually closer to the Tai minority then their Laotian namesakes across the border. Their homes are built on stilts in the form of a tortoise shell, like those of the Black Tai. Their traditional costume also resembles that of the Tai.

The Lu belong to the Tay-Tai language group. They number around 3,000 and are found in the Phong Tho and Sin Ho districts of Lai Chad Province, in well arranged villages of 40 to 60 dwellings. They arrived from China and occupied the Dien Bien Phu area as part of the Bach Y settlement in the first century AD.

The Hmong, who number more than 400,000, are found in villages known as *giao* throughout the highlands of eleven provinces. Due to their wars with the feudal Chinese, they emigrated to Vietnam from the southern Chinese kingdom of Bach Viet at the end of the 18th and beginning of the 19th centuries. Once they reached Vietnam, they settled in northwestern provinces. As skilled artisans, the Hmong produce a variety of items, including handwoven indigo-dyed

the slash-and-burn method. This form of agriculture has become less sustainable as population density increases.

The Dao are extremely skilled artisans. They make their own paper, used primarily for writing family genealogies, official documents and religious books. The women plant cotton, which they weave, dye with indigo, and embroider.

Central highlands

The Jarai, or Gia Rai, are located in the provinces of Gia Lai, Kon Tum, and Dak Lak,

cloth, paper, silver jewellery, leather goods, baskets, and embroidery. The Hmong have no written language. Their legends, songs, folklore and proverbs have been passed down from one generation to the next through the spoken word.

The Dao first arrived from China in the 18th century. Belonging to the Hmong-Dao language group, the Dao number about 35,000 and are found in the middle and lower regions of Thanh Hoa Province, living in large villages or small isolated hamlets, cultivating rice using

LEFT: portrait of a Muong woman.
ABOVE: Dao woman with her children, and a 19th-century photograph of Meo tribeswomen.

and in the north of Phu Khanh. They belong to the Malay-Polynesian language group and arrived in the Tay Nguyen Highlands from the coast a little less than 2,000 years ago. They live a sedentary lifestyle in villages known as *ploi*, or sometimes *bon*. Jarai villages, with at least 50 homes, are built around a central *nga rong*, or communal house.

The community of the Jarai ethnic group is composed of small matriarchal families, with each family an economically-independent unit within the entire village. A council of elders, with a chief as head, directs village matters. The chief is responsible for all the village's communal activities. ❑

LITERATURE

Literature and poetry are long-honoured traditions of the Vietnamese,
who find in both an aesthetic and historical foundation to their character

Writers and poets have always occupied a place of high esteem in Vietnamese society. A seemingly endless wealth of oral storytelling traditions, consisting of myths, songs, legends, folk and fairy tales, constitutes Vietnam's most ancient literature. Later, as the society developed, there were scholars, Bud-

literature, which introduced new ways of expressing ideas – and reflected rising nationalist feelings in Vietnam.

During the 20th-century wars for Vietnamese independence from outside powers, northern writers confined themselves mainly to stories meant to unify the people and to inspire the

dhist monks, kings and court ministers – many of whom were also talented writers and poets – who wrote down their thoughts and related epics using adopted Chinese characters *(chu nho)*. This literature was greatly influenced by Confucianism and Buddhism.

Even more poems and literary works were undertaken with the advent of *chu nom*, a complicated script based on chu nho. However, the Vietnamese found the romanised alphabet, introduced by foreign missionaries, to be a more accessible means of communicating than the foreboding need to use thousands of different ideograms. Indeed, Vietnamese literary prose and poetry were influenced by European

population during difficult times. Communist Party cadres strictly controlled publishing after the end of the Vietnam War in 1975, and even today, government censors must approve writings before their publication.

The publication in the early 1990s of *The Sorrow of War*, by a Vietnam War veteran from the North under the pseudonym of Bao Ninh, was the first war novel to confront the gruesome realities of war and the psychological effects upon surviving soldiers. Another writer, Duong Thu Huong, has had her works translated, and her writing includes thinly veiled criticism of government and party officials. For a time, she was imprisoned for crimes against the state.

Today, writers with reputations for criticism are presumed to be under close surveillance. Despite the appearance of a new period of openness, Party leaders have warned at gatherings of writers that they must focus on ideas that are of a benefit to the nation. An improved economy and increased contact with the outside world have meant that interest in literature, always intense in Vietnam, has declined somewhat. Still, for a poor nation, literacy is high at over 90 percent – it's common for people to read for leisure.

> **POETIC CULTIVATION**
>
> Vietnamese follow the declaration by Confucius that "personal cultivation begins with poetry, is made firm by the rule of decorum and is perfected by music."

ment, attitude or mood. The subtleties and nuances are sophisticated and aesthetic.

Vietnamese poetry falls into two major categories: *ca dao*, a popular folk song, oral in origin but collected and transcribed in written form; and *tho van*, literary poetry written by kings, scholars, Buddhist monks, mandarins, Daoist recluses, dissidents, feminists, revolutionaries – even the die-hard Marxists. Poetry has become such an important medium that present-day political slogans must be written in verse to be effective.

Poetry

Above all else, poetry dominates the Vietnamese arts. The language of Vietnam is a natural tool for poetry, as each of its syllables can be pronounced in six tones to convey six meanings. By combining these tones and modulating certain words, a sentence turns into a verse and plain speech becomes a song.

Another group of words made up of repeated syllables can cast a discreet shade on the meaning, conjuring up a particular colour, move-

---

LEFT: Bao Ninh, author of *The Sorrow of War*.
ABOVE: those who passed the official exams became men of letters and members of officialdom.

The Tale of Kieu

Nearly every Vietnamese reads and remembers a few chapters of a 3,254-verse story published 200 years ago called *The Tale of Kieu*. Pupils begin studying it in the sixth grade.

Kieu was written by one of Vietnam's most esteemed forefathers, Nguyen Du, and is now considered the cultural bible and window to the soul of the Vietnamese people. One may wonder how *Kieu* came to occupy its special position in Vietnamese literature. Why is the complex tale of a woman's personal misfortunes regarded by a whole people as the perfect expression of their essential nature, of their national soul? After all, the protagonist Kieu is a prostitute. "This shows," explains a Hanoi writer and critic, "how important the simple people are to Vietnamese. Our most important literary figure is not a king, not a warrior, not a hero, but a simple prostitute."

Regardless of age, gender, geography or ideology, to the Vietnamese the epic of Kieu is the heart and mind of their nation.

Born in the village of Nghi Xuan, in northern Vietnam's Ha Tinh Province, Nguyen Du came from an old aristocratic family of mandarins and scholars. His father was prime minister in the Thang Long (now Hanoi) court of Emperor Le. He grew up in a country, under the nominal rule

of the Le dynasty, torn by civil war. After Gia Long, a descendant of the southern Nguyen warlords, defeated the Tay Son brothers and was declared emperor, Nguyen Du became an official of several northern provinces, distinguishing himself as an honest and able administrator. In 1806, at the age of 41, he was summoned to the capital of Hue to serve as high chancellor.

Having reunited Vietnam, Gia Long faced the problem of national security, foremost of which meant establishing diplomatic relations with China. All Vietnamese envoys to China were chosen from the cream of Vietnamese *literati*, as it was by intellectual, rather than military, might that Vietnam sought to impress

China. So Nguyen Du, already recognised as a great poet, was a natural choice to be emissary. After five years in China, he returned and devoted most of his time to literary pursuits until his death at the age of 53 in 1820.

A literary school founded in 1979 to train writers was named after Nguyen Du, over the objections of government officials who preferred to name the school after a war hero.

What makes *The Tale of Kieu* as relevant today as it was two centuries ago is Nguyen Du's ability and courage to lay bare the whole spectrum of society. The vices and virtues, ugliness and beauty, nobility and trickery, all entangled in a seemingly hopeless tragic comedy, reflect the true face of Vietnam. The prostitute Kieu also personifies the inherent contradiction faced by the Vietnamese.

"Within the span of a hundred years of human existence, what a bitter struggle is waged between talent and fate", lament the opening lines. And, in the conclusion, Nguyen Du writes, "When one is endowed with talent, do not rely upon it".

The perplexing paradox

Deep in their hearts and behind their gracious modesty, the Vietnamese know they are not lacking in talent, *tai*. At the same time, they do not understand why this tai, which has helped them win their independence against formidable foreign invasions and enabled them to develop a respectable culture and civilisation, has failed to bring them lasting peace and enduring prosperity. Unable to solve this paradox, most believe they are *oan*, a word meaning wronged and which appears throughout *Kieu*.

Even Vietnamese who fled the country after the war ended in the 1970s turn to the tales of Kieu for comfort, especially in the cultural isolation of a new land and language. Huynh Sanh Thong, a Vietnamese scholar at Yale University who translated *Kieu* into English, wrote in his introduction that immigrants "know most of its lines by heart, and when they recite them out loud, they speak their mother tongue at its finest. To the extent that the poem implies something at the very core of the Vietnamese experience, it addresses them intimately as victims, as refugees, as survivors." ❑

LEFT: the Temple of Literature in Hanoi.
RIGHT: page of Latin-Annamese text.

Language

In the Vietnamese language, the word for natural disaster is *thien tai,* from Chinese. The word for cheese is *pho mat,* from the French *fromage.* There are also sounds and words from English and Russian. Thousands of words in the contemporary Vietnamese language – as much as 80 percent of the language – comes from Chinese, a reflection of the centuries of non-too-harmonious relations between Vietnam and its massive neighbour to the north, including the influence of Chinese literature.

There is a touch of French, with words that entered the lexicon first during the colonial period of the 18th and 19th centuries, and well into the 20th century. A dab of English was left by the Americans during the Vietnam War, and subsequent years of fraternisation with the former Soviet Union introduced Russian. In fact, expressions and nomenclature indicating 20th-century technology and ideas are often expressed with French, English and Russian words. The newest foreign linguistic invasion – that of consumerism – is represented by Japanese. The word most commonly used to refer to a two-wheeled motorised vehicle, for example, is *honda.*

Variations: Distinct dialects within Vietnam reveal strong regional identities, as well. Often northerners and southerners confess they cannot understand each other. Foreigners might need two translators, one to translate the foreign language into Vietnamese, another to translate the Vietnamese into another dialect. Some letters of the alphabet are pronounced differently, and the vocabularies of northerners and southerners contain distinct words. Even the syntax is different. In addition to Vietnamese, the country's many ethnic minorities speak their own distinct languages and dialects. In the Mekong Delta, for example, so many people speak the Khmer of Cambodia that local television has a Khmer-language broadcast.

Yet the country does share one language, a blend of several languages – ancient and modern – that has evolved through Vietnam's contact with other cultures. Its roots, while still debated, come from a mixture of Mon-Khmer, Thai and Muong.

Written Vietnamese: Chinese influence during the first centuries of Vietnam's history led to the extensive use of Chinese characters known as *chu nho,* which replaced an ancient written script of Indian origin, preserved and used today only by the Muong minority.

After independence in the 10th century, scholars realised the necessity and advantages of developing a separate written Vietnamese language. Several tentative attempts were made to modify the characters of Chinese, but it was a 13th-century poet, Nguyen Thuyen, who managed to incorporate the previous efforts into a distinct, but very complicated script known as *chu nom.*

Although standardised for popular literature, chu nom never received official recognition, and most Vietnamese writers continued using the more complicated Chinese calligraphy.

Today, however, Vietnam has a romanised alphabet, thanks to a French Jesuit missionary, Alexan-

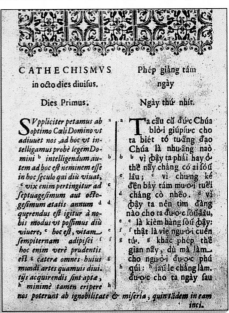

dre de Rhodes, who developed a script called *quoc ngu* in 1651.

Quoc ngu was, at first, used only by Catholic church and the colonial administration, gaining widespread popularity only in the early part of the 20th century. The study of quoc ngu became compulsory in secondary schools in 1906, and two years later, the royal court in Hue ordered a new curriculum, entirely in quoc ngu. It became the national written language in 1919.

Now, only scholars use the traditional calligraphic chu nom to decipher ancient carvings and writings. And during holidays, such as the lunar new year (Tet), people buy scrolls written in Chinese characters for their homes. ❑

A FEAST OF FRUITS

There is a sizeable range of fruits in Southeast Asia, many of which may be unfamiliar. As well as bananas and pineapples, there are brilliantly coloured and strangely shaped fruits for the adventurous

In Asia, people love food, and during the afternoon they snack on an incredible variety of fruits. For visitors who are in need of a boost, fruit can be a great source of refreshment and energy. Traditional fruit sellers have glass-fronted carts stacked with blocks of ice and pealed pieces of seasonal fruits. Choose a selection of what you want to eat and the vendor will pop it into a bag for you along with a toothpick for spearing the slices. Some fruits, like pineapple, are eaten with a little salt and ground chilli, a twist of which is supplied separately. Don't be afraid of this combination – the natural sweetness of the pineapple is enhanced by this bitter condiment, surprisingly enough.

One of the best ways to cool down is to drink a delicious fruit juice. Another favourite drink is fruit juice blended with ice, what Westerners might call a fruit "smoothie". You can have syrup mixed in to sweeten your juice or salt added (as the Thais like it) to bring out the flavour of the fruit.

CONTROVERSIAL DURIAN

People either love or hate durian. Ask any visitor to those Southeast Asian countries where durians are popular (nearly all) to recall the first time they came across it and they will describe, in detail, its "perfume". To most foreigners the durian's odour is repugnant, but for the Asian the fruit commands the utmost respect, even if most hotels prohibit them in hotel rooms. (Signs are often posted near elevators.)

According to devotees, the rewards of eating durian far outweigh any objections to its smell. The only way to enter the great durian debate is to try it for yourself. If you can't face eating the fruit *au naturel* there is durian cake, ice-cream and chewing gum.

◁ **JACKFRUIT**
The ripe, rich yellow sections of the jackfruit are waxy-textured and semi-sweet. When green they are used in curries, and the flowers and young shoots are eaten in salads.

RAMBUTAN ▷
The hairy rambutan (*rambut* means hair in Malay) is a close relative of the lychee, and its translucent, sweet flesh has a similar taste. There is a technique to squeezing it open to avoid squirting yourself with its juices.

▽ **STAR FRUIT**
This sweet, yellow fruit is native to India. It has a thin waxy skin with a crisp texture and sweet-tart juice. It can be found in fruit salads or can be candied and eaten as a confection. The unripe fruit is bright green and is sometimes added to dishes that require an acidic taste.

△ CUSTARD APPLE
The custard apple looks like a small, light green hand-grenade and can be pulled apart by hand. The pulp is soft, often mushy, very sweet and very tasty. It is best to eat it with a spoon.

▽ MANGOSTEEN
Thais believe durian requires the cool, refreshing sweet taste of the mangosteen as a chaser. See if you can guess how many sections your mangosteen has before you break it open.

DURIAN
he most expensive of Asian
uits has mushy flesh that
stes good with sticky rice and
conut milk. Ignore the smell
d you will be rewarded.

PANESE PEAR ▷
his crunchy and slightly
y fruit is usually eaten
w. Its semi-sweet flavour
n be enhanced by dipping it
to slightly salted water.

THAILAND'S GROWING CONCERN

Farming and fishing have always been at the centre of Thai life. Despite rapid industrialisation, this is still the case. Thailand is self-sufficient in food, and agribusiness is an important pillar of the Thai economy, claiming nearly a quarter of GDP and making Thailand the main net food exporter in Asia. Thailand is the world's leading exporter of canned pineapple and has big overseas markets in canned logans and rambutans.

Fruit production is expected to increase as available land and labour resources dwindle and farmers switch from producing staple crops, such as rice and cassava, to cash crops like soya beans, fruits, sugar cane and rubber. Large fruit farmers are starting to process their products before they reach the consumer, and many are now applying for loans to invest in equipment to dry and freeze their produce. Although some of this produce will be sold to Thailand's neighbours, much of it will end up in the snack food departments of Japanese supermarkets – Japanese businesses have already set up factories in Thailand to process fruits, vegetables and nuts for their home market.

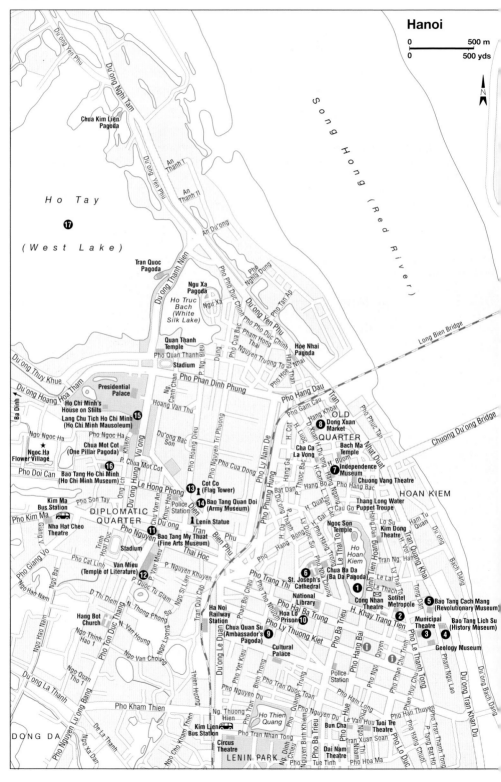

Hanoi

0 — 500 m
0 — 500 yds

N

Song Hong (Red River)

Ho Tay
(West Lake)

⑰

Chua Kim Lien Pagoda

Du'ong Yen Phu
Du'ong Nghi Tam
Du'ong Yen Phu

An Thanh I
An Thanh II
An Du'ong
Du'ong Thanh Nien

Tran Quoc Pagoda

Ngu Xa Pagoda
Ho Truc Bach (White Silk Lake)
Ngu Xa

Pho Nghia Dung
Pho Pho Duc Chinh
Pho Pho Duc Chinh
Pho Pham Hong Thai
Cua Dong Pho Nguyen Truong To
Du'ong Yen Phu
Pho Tan Ap

Quan Thanh Temple
Pho Quan Thanh
Stadium
Pho Bieu
Dung

Hoe Nhai Pagoda
Pho Hoe Nhai
Pho Hang Than

Long Bien Bridge

Du'ong Thuy Khue
Du'ong Hoang Hoa Tham

Ba Dinh
Pho Phan Dinh Phung
Pho Hang Dau
Pho Gam Cau
Hang Khoai

Presidential Palace
Hoang Van Thu
Ng. Cam Chan

Ho Chi Minh's House on Stilts
Lang Chu Tich Ho Chi Minh (Ho Chi Minh Mausoleum) ⑮

Ngo Ngoc Ha
Pho Ngoc Ha
Du'ong Bac Son

Chua Mot Cot (One Pillar Pagoda)
P. Chua Mot Cot
Pho Hoang Dieu
Pho Nguyen Tri Phuong
Pho Cua Dong
Pho Ly Nam De

Ngoc Ha Flower Village ★

Bao Tang Ho Chi Minh (Ho Chi Minh Museum) ⑯
Pho Doi Can

Le Hong Phong
Du'ong Hung
Ong Ich Khiem
Pho Son Tay

Cot Co (Flag Tower) ⑬
Bao Tang Quan Doi (Army Museum) ⑭

OLD QUARTER
Dong Xuan Market ⑧

H. Cot
D. Xuan Dau
Hang Ga
H. Buom
Hang Bo
Cau Go

Bach Ma Temple
Cha Ca La Vong
Independence Museum ⑦
Chuong Vang Theatre

HOAN KIEM

Thang Long Water Puppet Troupe

Kim Ma Bus Station
DIPLOMATIC QUARTER
Pho Nguyen Thai Hoc
Pho Kim Ma
Giang Vo
Du'ong Van An
Police Station
Tran Phu
Du'ong Thai Hoc
Phu Bien Phu
Thai Hoc

Nha Hat Cheo Theatre
Stadium
Pho Cat Linh
Van Mieu (Temple of Literature) ⑫
P. Van Mieu
P. Nguyen Khuyen
P. Quoc Tu Giam

Lenin Statue ⑪
Bao Tang My Thuat (Fine Arts Museum)

Ngoc Son Temple
Ho Hoan Kiem
Kim Dong Theatre

Tran Ng.
Hang Dao
Lo Su
Ham Tu Quan
Tran Quang Khai
Bach Dang

Pho Giang Vo
Ngo Bai
Pho Giang Vo
Ngo Hao Nam

Hang Bot Church
Ngo Thinh Hao 1
Ngo Van Chuong

D. Thi Diem
N. Thong Phong
Su. Van Hanh
Ngo Si Lien
Tran Quy Cap

P. Ton Duc Thang
N. Van Huong
Ngo Luong

Ha Noi Railway Station
Du'ong Le Duan
Thien Huong

Ho Thien Quang
Ng. Thuong Hien

Chua Ba Da (Ba Da Pagoda) ①
Pho Trang Thi
St. Joseph's Cathedral ⑥
National Library
Hoa Lo Prison ⑩
Chua Quan Su (Ambassador's Pagoda) ⑨
Cultural Palace

Pho Quang Trung
Pho Hai Ba Trung
Pho Ly Thuong Kiet
Pho Tran Quoc Toan
Pho Nguyen Du
Pho Tran Nhan Tong

Cong Nhan Theatre ②
Sotitel Metropole
Municipal Theatre ③

Pho Ngo Quyen
Pho Ba Trieu
Pho Hang Bai
Pho Le Thai To
Pho Hang Trong
Pho Hang Khay

Bao Tang Cach Mang (Revolutionary Museum) ⑤
Bao Tang Lich Su (History Museum) ④
Geology Museum

Dinh Tien
Ngo Huyen
Le Thach
Le Lai
Le Thai To

Pho Ham Long
Police Station
Le Van Huu
Pho Han Thuyen

Pho Ngo
Pho Phan Chu Trinh
Pho Le Phung Tong
Pham Ngu Lao
Du'ong Tran Khan Du
Du'ong Bach Dang

Pho Kham Thien
Kim Lien Bus Station
Pho Tran Nhan Tong

Bun Cha
Tuoi Tre Theatre
Dai Nam Theatre

Circus Theatre
LENIN PARK
Tue Tinh
Pho Lo Duc
Pho Hoa Ma

DONG DA
Pho Nguyen Luong Bang
De La Thanh
Ngo Xa Dan
Ng. Cho Kham
Thien

Chuong Du'ong Bridge
Nhat Tan
Pho Phuc Tan

HANOI

Vietnam's capital city may not be the country's most dynamic city – Ho Chi Minh City leads by far – but Hanoi retains an ambience in architecture and layout that recalls the earlier French years

Map on page 158

Today, with a population of about 3 million, Hanoi extends more than 2,000 sq. km (800 sq. miles) in size. The city centre has evolved little since 1955, leaving Hanoi's original character very much intact, preserved in its traditional pagodas and temples, colonial architecture, tree-lined streets and lakes. The soul of this ancient Thang Long city rests in the old town centre, which dates from the 15th century.

The city centre comprises four districts: Hoan Kiem (Restored Sword), Hai Ba Trung (Two Trung Sisters), Dong Da (where King Quang Trung defeated the Manchu invasion in 1789) and Ba Dinh. It also incorporates 11 recently integrated suburban districts (*quan*). In the northwest, the city is bordered by Ho Tay, or West Lake. West of Hanoi, hills extend up to the 1,200-metre (4,000-ft) summit of Mt Ba, 65 km (40 miles) from the city.

Hanoi is accessible from the north by three bridges: Long Bien, Chuong Duong, and the newest, Thang Long, a modern span changing into a four-lane highway to Noi Bai Airport. The 1,682-metre-long (5,520-ft) **Long Bien Bridge** was built by the French and opened in 1902 by Governor-General Doumer, after whom it was originally named. It suffered some damage from American bombing during the Vietnam War, but it was continually repaired. Until 1983, all northbound road and rail traffic passed over it. These days, it is reserved for cyclists, pedestrians and trains.

BELOW: Government Guest House.

In the centre of Hanoi

In the very heart of the old town of Hanoi lies **Ho Hoan Kiem ❶**, or Lake of the Restored Sword. Legend has it that in the 15th century, King Le Thai To was given a magic sword by a tortoise that lived in the lake. He used the sword to drive the Chinese from the country, but later the tortoise is said to have snatched the sword from his hand and disappeared into the lake. Near the middle of the lake is a small, 18th-century tower, Thap Rua, or Tortoise Tower.

Across from the park is the **State Guest House**, a compound with a hotel in the back and an ornate French colonial building, painted yellow with green trim, in front. It was once the palace of the French governor of Tonkin. Today, Vietnamese officials meet visiting foreign dignitaries here.

The unofficial hub for foreign business people is **Sofitel Metropole ❷**, which dates back to French colonial times. Not far from the Metropole is one of Hanoi's landmarks, the **Municipal Theatre ❸** (Nha Hat Lon), commonly called the Opera House.

Behind the Municipal Theatre, the **Bao Tang Lich Su ❹** (History Museum; Tues–Sun 8am–4pm) occu-

Legends are woven into Hanoi's history. In 1010, according to one legend, King Ly Thai To founded the city after seeing an auspicious golden dragon rise from the area. He named the city Thang Long, or Ascending Dragon.

pies the old archeological research institution of l'Ecole Française d'Extrème Orient. The History Museum opened in 1910, was rebuilt in 1926, and reopened in 1932. Exhibits displayed here cover every era of Vietnam's fascinating and complex history. Near the History Museum, the **Bao Tang Cach Mang** ❺ (Revolutionary Museum; Tues–Sun 8am–4pm, Sat 8–11.30am) on Tong Dan Street documents the struggles of the Vietnamese people from ancient times up until 1975.

From the north side of Hoan Kiem Lake, many streets lead to Hanoi's Old Quarter and, on Nha Chung Street, the oldest church in the city, **St Joseph's Cathedral** ❻ (the Vietnamese call it the "big church"), consecrated on Christmas night in 1886. A narrow passageway next to 5 Nha Tho, the street facing the cathedral, leads to the **Chua Ba Da**. This charming pagoda was built in the 15th century after the discovery of a stone statue of a woman during the construction of the Thang Long citadel. The statue, which was thought to have magical powers, disappeared and has since been replaced by a wooden replica.

On Ly Quoc Su Street, to the right of the cathedral, is the small **Chua Ly Trieu Quoc Su**, also known as Chua Kong, the Pagoda of Confucius. It contains some attractive wooden statues and an old bonze, who is said to have lived there for over 60 years without ever leaving the building. The Bach Ma Temple on Hang Buom Street is dedicated to the deity Bach Ma. Originally built during the 9th century, it was reconstructed in the 18th and 19th centuries.

In a small house on Hang Ngang Street is the **Independence Museum** ❼ (admission fee). Here, Ho Chi Minh wrote Vietnam's declaration of independence, which borrows considerably from America's own declaration, and it was where communist revolutionaries met in secret.

BELOW: art shop, and ticket seller at the Fine Arts Museum.

The area around the busy **Dong Xuan Market** in the northern part of the so-called Old Quarter is an interesting place to explore. The market is a good place to find cheap clothing and kitchenware, and in the surrounding streets farmers squat on the pavement selling their produce to passers-by.

Southwest of Ho Hoan Kiem, several blocks away on Quan Su Street, is the **Chua Quan Su ❾ (Ambassadors' Pagoda)**. In the 17th century, the site was a house used to accommodate visiting foreign ambassadors and envoys from other Buddhist countries. Two blocks away was the infamous **Hoa Lo Prison ❿**, called the Hanoi Hilton by American POWs incarcerated within. Although the prison has been largely demolished to make way for a hotel and office tower, the main gate and front portion have been preserved as a museum. Across the street from the prison is the Hanoi People's Court. To the south of the prison and the Quan Su pagoda there is a small and lovely lake, Ho Thien Quang, where visitors can rent paddle boats. Across the street is an entrance to Lenin Park, and to the right, Hanoi's circus.

The old French Quarter

West from the centre of town is the old French quarter, or what is now the diplomatic area of Hanoi. Here, the old villas house foreign embassies and government offices on quiet, tree-lined streets. The **Bao Tang My Thuat ⓫** (Fine Arts Museum; Tues–Sun 8am–4pm), on Nguyen Thai Hoc Street, features an extensive collection of artefacts. Exhibits cover some of Vietnam's ethnic minorities and history. On display are beautiful wooden statues of Buddha dating from the 17th century, Dong Son bronze drums, and other Vietnamese art, both ancient and contemporary.

Map on page 158

TIP

Keep an eye out at the Dong Xuan Market for caviar, French wine, champagne and Russian vodka, as they are surprisingly cheap in Hanoi and definitely the genuine article.

BELOW: street flower vendor.

Map on page 158

Nearby, across the street, is the **Van Mieu** ⓬ (Temple of Literature). Built in 1070 under the reign of King Ly Thai Tong, the temple is dedicated to Confucius. In 1076, the temple was adjoined by the Quoc Tu Giam, School of the Elite of the Nation, Vietnam's first national university. The large temple enclosure is divided into five walled courtyards. After passing through the Van Mieu gate and the first two courtyards, one arrives at the Khue Van Cac (Pleiade Pavilion), where the men of letters used to recite their poems. Through the Dai Thanh Mon (Great Wall Gate), an open courtyard surrounds a large central pool known as the Thien Quang Tinh (Well of Heavenly Clarity).

To the north nearby, on Dien Bien Phu Street, is one of the symbols of Hanoi, **Cot Co** ⓭, the flag tower. Built in 1812 under the Nguyen dynasty as part of the Hanoi citadel, the hexagonal 60-metre (200-ft) tower is more or less all that remains of the citadel, which was destroyed at the end of the 19th century. Next to it, **Bao Tang Quan Doi** ⓮ (Army Museum; daily 8.30am–4.30pm) chronicles Vietnam's battles for independence and unification against the French and American patrons of the former South Vietnam. Across the street is a small, triangular-shaped park with a statue of Lenin.

Further down Dien Bien Phu looms the imposing and impressive structure of **Lang Chu Tich Ho Chi Minh** ⓯ (Ho Chi Minh Mausoleum; Tues–Thurs, Sat and Sun 7.30–11am), in Ba Dinh Square. Ho's embalmed corpse lies in a glass casket in this monumental tomb – contrary to his wish to be cremated. It was from this square that Ho Chi Minh read his declaration of independence speech on 2 September 1945. Nearby is the unique **Chua Mot Cot** (One Pillar Pagoda). Built in 1049 under the Ly dynasty, this beautiful wooden pagoda rests on a single stone pillar rising out of a lotus pool. The small Dien Huu Pagoda shares this lovely setting.

Mausoleum of Ho Chi Minh.

Behind the park with the pagodas is the modern **Bao Tang Ho Chi Minh** ⓰ (Ho Chi Minh Museum; Tues–Sun 8am–4pm). A massive concrete structure, the museum has some rather bizarre exhibits, but it presents a thorough history of Ho's life.

Ho Tay, lake of mists

From Ba Dinh Square, where the National Assembly building is located across from the mausoleum, and where there is a war memorial, head north toward **Ho Tay** ⓱ (West Lake), formerly known as the Lake of Mists.

This lake, the largest in Hanoi, lies in an ancient bed of the Red River. In the 17th century, the pagoda was transferred to its present site on the tiny peninsula of the Ho Tay and renamed Tran Quoc Pagoda (Defence of the Country). Separated from the lake by Thanh Nien Street is **Ho Truc Bach** (White Silk Lake). This was the ancient site of Lord Trinh's summer palace, which became a harem where he detained his wayward concubines. This lake derives its name from the fine white silk the concubines were forced to weave for the princesses of ancient Vietnam. Villas, hotels and restaurants have now sprung up around the lake.

Nearby, the ornate temple of **Den Quan Thanh** beside the lake was originally built during the Ly dynasty (1010–1225). It houses a huge bronze bell and an enormous, four-ton bronze statue of Tran Vu, guardian deity of the north, to whom the temple is dedicated.

Southwest of the city, in Dong Da district, is the **Go Dong Da** (Mound of the Multitudes) on Tay Son Street. According to one legend, Go Dong Da was formed by the bodies of Chinese soldiers killed after Quang Trung's victory. Very little remains of the temple that was built on the site so long ago, but dozens of steps lead to the top of the mound. Beyond the mound is a large statue of Quang Trung, built in the Social Realist style that long dominated public art in Vietnam. ❑

OPPOSITE: a Vietnamese dinner.

HAI PHONG AND HUE

Map
on page
144

Along Vietnam's Pacific coast are some of Southeast Asia's most spectacular cultural and geographical wonders, including Hai Phong, mystical Ha Long Bay, and the ancient city of Hue

Heading east from Hanoi eventually leads to white-sand beaches washed by the South China Sea. Bien Dong, as the South China Sea is called in Vietnamese, is a focus of contention between Vietnam and China, as both claim rights to the sea and to the islands offshore, which sit atop potentially rich oil reserves. Before reaching the coast, the road passes through the relatively flat province of Hai Hung, famous for its beautiful orchards. Fruit from Hai Hung, especially longan and lychee, is reputedly the best in northern Vietnam, supplying the royal court in earlier times.

In Hung Dao commune, the **Den Kiep Bac**, 60 km (40 miles) from Hanoi, dates from the 13th century. The temple is dedicated to the national hero Tran Hung Dao, who vanquished the Mongols in the 13th century and was made a saint by the people. His army encamped here in the Kiep Bac Valley. His statue – plus those of his two daughters, Gen. Pham Ngu Lao, and the genies of the Northern Star and Southern Cross – are venerated in this temple.

Nearby, **Chua Con Son** is the home of another national hero, Nguyen Trai (1380–1442), who helped King Le Loi chase out the Ming invaders and free the country from Chinese domination at the beginning of the 15th century. At the foot of the hill, the well maintained **Hung Pagoda** contains statues of Nguyen Trai, his maternal grandfather and the three superior bonzes who founded the Truc Lam Buddhist sect.

OPPOSITE: Ha Long Bay sunset. **BELOW:** collecting salt.

Hai Phong

The road between Hanoi and **Hai Phong ❶**, Vietnam's third-largest city and the north's most important port, is jammed with the clutter of an economic boom. Hai Phong itself occupies the right bank of the busy Cam River, 120 km (75 miles) from Hanoi in the northeast of the Bac Bo delta. The city, built in 1888, is crossed by 16 rivers.

The most famous of these is the Bach Dang River, where in AD 938 the national hero Ngo Quyen defeated the large southern Chinese Han fleet. The Song-dynasty invaders suffered a bitter defeat here in 981 and the Mongols suffered the same fate in 1288. The first of the French warships arrived in Hai Phong in 1872; the last units of the French expeditionary forces left the same way in 1955. The port of Hai Phong, inland from the eastern sea, constitutes an important gateway for Vietnam's foreign trade.

Like every city in Vietnam, Hai Phong has its temples. The pagoda of **Du Hang** in the south of the city was built three centuries ago, but restored often since. It is dedicated to Le Chan, the valiant woman warrior who aided the Trung sisters in the uprising against

the Chinese in AD 39. The Hang Kenh *dinh*, or communal house, off Nguyen Cong Tru, houses a surprising 500 wooden sculptures representing the themes of everyday life.

The communal house in Cung Chuc village, in Vinh Bao district, is worth visiting for its unique architecture, and for its clay statues. The traditional entertainment staged here during local traditional festivals includes water puppetry and water-buffalo fights.

The Elephant Mount, near Hai Phong, offers the pagoda of **Long Hoa** and vestiges of a citadel fortress dating from the 16th century. Halfway up the mountain, the Chi Lai communal house has been converted into a museum, where neolithic bronze artifacts are displayed. Caves within the mountain served as guerrilla base camps against the French in the 20th century.

From Hai Phong, travellers can also visit the village of **Bao Ha**, which has earned a reputation for its high-quality wood-carving ever since it was founded by the master craftsman Nguyen Cong Hue, in the late 17th century. After his death, his students carved his likeness and built a temple in his honour. One of his most famous statues can be seen in the **Ba Xa Temple** at Bao Ha. Most of the work produced by the village craftsmen is of a religious nature, although they also turn out a variety of carved animals.

From Hai Phong, ferries travel to Ha Long Bay, stopping along the way at the Cat Ba archipelago, 80 km (50 miles) from the coast. Its 366 islets and islands cover some 20,000 hectares (50,000 acres). The area is known for its beautiful beaches and interesting grottoes. The largest island, **Cat Ba**, occupies 190 sq. km (75 sq. miles), and its landscape features forested hills, coastal mangroves and waterfalls.

TIP

The fish market in the port of Hai Phong is worth a visit early in the morning, when the fishermen are arriving with their catches, often with some unusual sea products.

BELOW: picture perfect Halong Bay.

Boats from Hai Phong also leave for the island of **Cat Hai** and **Do Son**, a peninsula east of the city and where palm-fringed sandy beaches set against pine-forested hills stretch far out into the clear waters of the **Vinh Bac Bo** (**Tonkin Gulf**). Vietnam's only casino (but not its first – there was a raucous gambling den in Saigon before President Ngo Dinh Diem outlawed it in the 1950s) sits alone on the cliffs of Do Son. The casino is open to foreigners only.

Map on page 144

Vinh Ha Long

No trip to northern Vietnam would be complete without a trip to Quang Ninh Province. This province shares a common border with China in the north, and harbours one of the wonders of the world with probably the most stunning scenery in Vietnam: **Vinh Ha Long ❷** (**Ha Long Bay**).

The bay's tranquil beauty encompasses 4,000 sq. km (1,500 sq. miles), dotted with well over 1,600 limestone islands and islets, many of them without names. Bizarre rock sculptures jutting dramatically from the sea and numerous grottoes have created an enchanted, timeless world. The sails of the junks and sampans gliding on the bay add further to the beauty of the scene. Ha Long Bay appeared in the French film *Indochine*, and is a UNESCO World Heritage Site.

The most spectacular of all the bay's grottoes is the beautiful cave of **Hang Dau Go**, with its stalactites and stalagmites resembling beasts, birds and human forms. It was christened the Grotte des Merveilles (Wonder Grotto) by the first French tourists who visited it in the late 19th century.

A boat trip from **Hong Gai** on the bay includes stops at some of the grottoes, including the Bo Nau (Pelican) cave, the 2-km-long Hang Hanh tunnel, and the Trinh Nu (Virgin) cave. Boat trips can also be arranged from **Bai Chay**.

The name Ha Long means the Landing Dragon, evoking an ancient dragon that, in the mists of time, is said to have descended in the bay.

BELOW: waiting for boats, Ha Long Bay.

Ha Long Bay has been the setting of many historic battles against invasions from the north. It is believed that the sharp bamboo stakes that General Tran Hung Dao planted in the Bach Dang River to destroy Kublai Khan's fleet were stored in caves here.

Hue, city of kings

The ancient imperial city of the Nguyen kings, **Hue** ❸ is located 12 km (7 miles) from the coast, midway between Hanoi and Ho Chi Minh City on a narrow stretch of land in Thua Thien Hue Province, which borders Laos in the west. The first noble to reach Hue was Lord Nguyen Hoang (1524–1613), in the spring of 1601. He found a particularly good location to build a capital and erected the Phu Xuan Citadel.

Chinese motif, 17th-century building.

Nguyen Hoang also built the **Chua Thien Mu** (Celestial Lady Pagoda), which remains intact on the left bank of the Perfume River, said to be named after a type of fragrant plant that grows near its origins. The seven tiers of the temple's octagonal tower each represent a different reincarnation of Buddha. The main temple, Dai Hung, is in an attractive garden of ornamental shrubs and trees.

Nguyen Hoang was the first in an uninterrupted succession of 10 feudal lords to rule over the area of Hue until 1802. That year, after quelling the Tay Son uprising, the 10th Nguyen lord proclaimed himself Emperor Gia Long and founded the Nguyen dynasty, which would last for 143 years, until 1945. But just 33 years into dynasty's reign, the French invaded Hue. A quick succession of emperors graced the throne. The anti-French demonstrations and strikes of the colonial era were followed by the Japanese occupation in 1945 and the abdication of Bao Dai, the last of the Nguyen emperors, in August of the same year.

BELOW: guardian at Thien Mu Pagoda, and part of Thien Mu Pagoda.

The relative peace that reigned after 1954, when Hue became part of South Vietnam following the country's division into two parts, was shattered under Ngo Dinh Diem's regime. Repressive anti-Buddhist propaganda sparked off a series of demonstrations and protest suicides by Buddhist monks in 1963.

Map on page 144

Always an important cultural, intellectual and historical city, Hue remains one of Vietnam's main attractions. The charm of this timeless old city lies not only in its historical and architectural value, but also in the natural beauty of its location along the banks of the Perfume River.

The **Imperial City** (Dai Noi; daily 7am–5.30pm) of Hue is made up of three walled enclosures. The Hoang Thanh (Yellow Enclosure) and the Tu Cam Thanh (Forbidden Purple City) are enclosed within the Kinh Thanh (exterior enclosure). Stone, bricks and earth were used to build the exterior wall, which measured 8 metres (26 ft) high and 20 metres (65 ft) thick, built during the reign of Emperor Gia Long. The Yellow Enclosure is the middle wall enclosing the imperial city and its palaces, temples and flower gardens. Through the Ngo Mon, a gate, walk across the Golden Water Bridge, which at one time was reserved for the emperor. It leads to the **Dien Thai Hoa** (Palace of Supreme Peace), the most important palace in the imperial city.

In front of the temple, completely undamaged, stands the magnificent **Hien Lam Cac** (Pavilion of Splendour), with the nine dynastic urns lined up before it. The **Dien Tho** palace, built by emperor Gia Long in 1804, served as the Queen Mother's residence. **Tu Cam Thanh** (The Forbidden Purple City) was reserved solely for the emperor and the royal family. The main building in the enclosure is the **Can Thanh** (Palace of Celestial Perfection).

Another world lies beyond the walls of the citadel, which is surrounded in the

The urns in the Pavilion of Splendour, cast in 1822 during Minh Mang's reign, are decorated with motifs of the sun, moon, clouds, birds, animals, dragons, mountains, rivers, and historic events. Hundreds of artisans from all over Vietnam were involved.

BELOW: river view from Thien Mu.

Map on page 144

TIP

Minh Mang's tomb can be reached by hiring a small motorboat from any of the local owners opposite the Perfume River Hotel. Alternatively, take a car to Ban Viet village. From there, hire a boat across the Perfume River.

RIGHT: tomb of Tu Duc.
BELOW: entrance to Khai Dinh's tomb.

south and east by Hue's commercial area. This is confined mainly to the area around the arched Trang Tien Bridge, which spans the Perfume River, and the Gia Hoi Bridge. Both bridges lend their names to the areas surrounding them. Located in Phu Cat, with its mainly Chinese and Minh Huong (Vietnamese-Chinese) population, is the lively **Dong Ba Market**, which has been around since the beginning of the 20th century.

Near the Forbidden Purple City, the **Museum of Royal Fine Arts** (daily 7.30am–4pm), built in 1845 under Emperor Thieu Tri, houses treasures bequeathed by the royal family and nobility. Across the street, the **Hue Provincial Museum** (daily 7am–5pm) was opened in 1975 and houses one of the finer collections related to the Vietnam War. Missiles, tanks and other weaponry guard the courtyard.

Royal tombs and pagodas

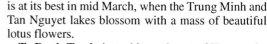

Unlike the other dynasties, the Nguyen dynasty did not bury its members in their native village, Gia Mieu, in Thanh Hoa Province. Instead, their imperial tombs lie scattered on the hillsides on either side of the Perfumed River, to the west of Hue. Although the dynasty had 13 kings, only seven of them reigned until their deaths. And only they are laid to rest in this valley of kings. Behind and on either side of the temple are the houses built for the king's concubines, servants and soldiers who guarded the royal tomb. The emperor's body is laid in a concealed place *(bao thanh)*, enclosed by high walls behind securely locked bronze doors.

Minh Mang's Tomb is located where the Ta Trach and Huu Trach tributaries of the Perfume River meet. Its construction was begun a year before his death, in 1840, and was finished by his successor Thieu Tri in 1843. The setting is at its best in mid March, when the Trung Minh and Tan Nguyet lakes blossom with a mass of beautiful lotus flowers.

Tu Duc's Tomb, just a bit southwest of Hue, can be reached by a very pleasant cycle ride through pine forests and lush hills. The mausoleum construction, begun in 1864, took three years to complete.

Thieu Tri's Tomb is located nearby. Thieu Tri, Minh Mang's son, was the third Nguyen emperor and reigned from 1841 to 1847. His tomb was built between 1947 and 1948, and in the same elegant architectural style as his father's, but on a much smaller scale.

Khai Dinh's Tomb is completely different from any of the other Nguyen tombs. If anything, it resembles a European castle, its architecture a blend of the oriental and occidental. A grandiose dragon staircase leads up to the first courtyard, from where further stairs lead to a courtyard lined with stone statues of elephants, horses, civil and military mandarins.

Gia Long's Tomb, 16 km (10 miles) from Hue on a hillside, is somewhat inaccessible by road. However, a more pleasant way to reach the tomb is by boat. The tomb, began in 1814, was completed a year after the emperor's death in 1820. Despite incurring damage during the Vietnam War, the wild beauty of the site, with its mountain backdrop of Thien Tho, makes the effort to get there well worthwhile. ❑

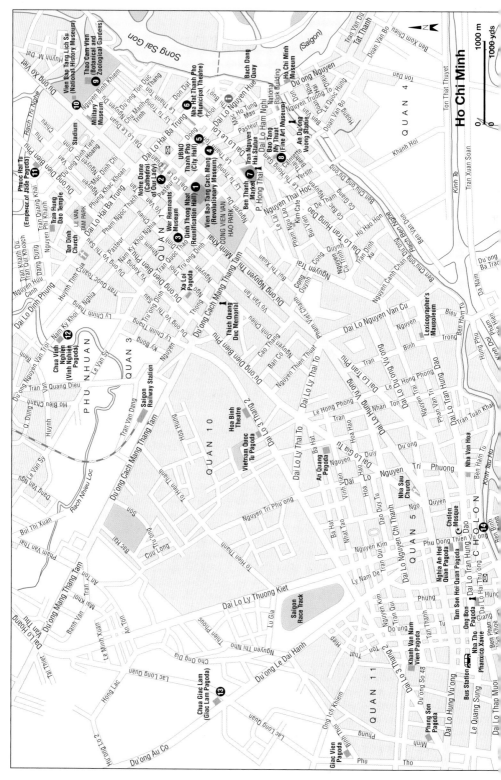

Ho Chi Minh

0 — 1000 m
0 — 1000 yds

HO CHI MINH CITY

Once known as Saigon – and still called so by many residents – and once the capital of the former South Vietnam, this southern city is the entrepreneurial centre of Vietnam today

Map on page 172

Built on the site of an ancient Khmer city, **Ho Chi Minh City** was a thinly populated area of forests, swamps and lakes until the 17th century. By the end of the 18th century, the area had become an important trading centre within the region. Different theories expound on the origins of the name "Saigon" – what Ho Chi Minh City was called before the Communists changed the official name of the city. The name Saigon is still used by many people, even in official or public capacities. The river coursing through the city remains the Saigon River, for example, and the state-owned tour company is Saigon Tourism. Some say the name derives from the former name Sai Con, a transcription of the Khmer words *prei kor* (kapok-tree forest), or *prei nokor* (the forest of the kingdom), in reference to the Cambodian viceroy's residence, which was located in the region of present-day Cholon.

In the 19th century, southern Vietnam continued to prosper. In 1859, the French captured Saigon and it became the capital of the French colony of Cochinchina a couple of years later. The French filled in the ancient canals, drained marshlands, built roads, laid out streets and quarters, and planted trees. The city developed rapidly, acquiring something of the character of a French provincial town, served by two steam-powered trams.

After the division of the country in 1954 into North Vietnam and South Vietnam, Saigon became the capital of the Republic of South Vietnam, until it fell to the Communists in April of 1975. The revolutionary authorities renamed it Ho Chi Minh City, after the founder of the modern Vietnamese state. Ho Chi Minh was, of course, anathema to supporters of the southern regime that lost the war. To many of its 5 million inhabitants, the city remains Saigon.

The modern city

Today, 80 km (50 miles) inland from the coast, Vietnam's largest city and river port sprawls across an area of 2,000 sq. km (760 sq. miles) on the banks of the Saigon River. The French presence still remains in this southern city, lingering not only in the minds of the older generation but physically in the legacy of colonial architecture, and in the long, tree-lined avenues, streets and highways they left behind.

Prominently located in the city's District *(Quan)* 1 is a building that symbolises, to the Communists, the decadence of the Saigon regime. The former Presidential Palace of South Vietnam is now called **Dinh Thong Nhat ❶** (Reunification Hall; daily 7.30am–4pm), and it is open to the public as a museum. Surrounded by extensive gardens, this large and modern edifice rests on the site of the former

BELOW: city street.

Interior of the former Presidential Palace, now known as Reunification Hall.

BELOW: Communist tank entering the Presidential Palace in 1975.

French governor's residence, the Norodom Palace, which dated back to 1868. After the Geneva Agreement put an end to French occupation, the new president of South Vietnam, Ngo Dinh Diem, installed himself in the palace.

In 1963, the palace was bombed by a South Vietnamese air force officer and a new building known as the Independence Palace was erected to replace the damaged structure. The present building was designed by Ngo Viet Thu, a Paris-trained Vietnamese architect, and completed in 1966.

The left wing of the palace was damaged by another renegade South Vietnamese pilot in early 1975, and before the month was out, on 30 April, tanks from the Communist forces crashed through the palace's front wrought-iron gates and overthrew the South Vietnamese government.

Today, the former palace can be visited as a museum, with everything left much as it was in April 1975 when South Vietnam ceased to exist. The ground floor includes the banquet room, the state chamber (from where the South Vietnamese government surrendered), and the cabinet room, which was used for the daily military briefings during the period leading up to the overthrow of the South Vietnamese government. In back of the palace is Cong Vien Van Hao Park, a nice and shady green spot. In front, Le Duan is bordered by a large park shaded with trees, where street vendors from the countryside gather to sell their wares. On one side, near Thai Van Lung Street, men who fought for the former regime gather most mornings, perhaps still plotting for a way to leave Vietnam.

Further down Le Duan is the **Cathedral of Notre Dame ❷**, with two bell towers, standing in the square across from the post office. Construction of this cathedral began in 1877, and it was consecrated in 1880. A statue of the Virgin Mary stands in front of the cathedral, looking down Dong Khoi Street.

The former War Crimes Exhibition, now the **War Remnants Museum ❸** (Nha Trung Bay Toi Ac Tranh; daily 7.30am–4.45pm) occupies the former U.S. Information Agency building on Vo Van Tan Street, near Reunification Hall. Among items on display here are American tanks, infantry weapons, photographs of war atrocities committed by the Americans, and the original French guillotine brought to Vietnam in the 20th century, which saw a lot of use during the colonial period. Graphic pictures of deformed children illustrate the effects of chemical defoliants such as Agent Orange. Although a visit here is likely to be distressing, it is a sobering reminder of the human cost of war and is a must-see for many visitors.

The **Vien Bao Tang Cach Mang ❹** (Museum of the Revolution; Tues–Sun 8am–4.30pm), one block east from Reunification Hall on Ly Tu Trong Street, is found in a white neoclassical structure once known as Gia Long Palace. The walls of the former ballrooms of this colonial edifice are now hung with pictures of the war, and there are displays of the flat-bottomed boats in which Viet Cong soldiers hid guns.

A network of reinforced concrete bunkers stretching all the way to the Reunification Hall lies beneath the building. Within this underground network were living areas and a meeting hall. It was here that President Diem and his brother hid in the early 1960s just before they fled to a church in Cholon, where they were captured and subsequently shot.

If Reunification Hall is a symbol of the former South Vietnam regime, then the UBND **Thanh Pho ❺** (City Hall), at the top of Nguyen Hue Street, is the symbol of the French colonial era. It was finished in 1908 after almost 16 years of ferment over its style and situation. Its ornate facade and equally ornate inte-

Map on page 172

BELOW: Notre Dame, and city hall.

rior, complete with crystal chandeliers and wall-size murals, is now the head-quarters of the Ho Chi Minh City People's Committee. Illuminated at night, the building is a lure for insect-hungry geckos.

Across the street, near the **Rex Hotel**, there is a plaza with a statue of Ho Chi Minh in his role as favourite uncle to all children. The plaza is crowded on weekend nights with young people, parents with children, and hustlers trying to sell souvenirs or cyclo rides to tourists.

Nguyen Hue is being developed into a broad boulevard lined with fancy hotels and upscale restaurants. This area of town buzzes with energy, especially at night. At the corner of Le Loi, there is another plaza with a fountain that is crowded with a carnival-like atmosphere into the evenings. Near the end of Le Loi is the **Nha Hat Thanh Pho ❻** (Municipal Theatre), which faces Dong Khoi Street between the Caravelle and the Continental hotels. The theatre was originally built in 1899 for opera, but was used as the fortress headquarters of the South Vietnam National Assembly. These days, it serves its original purpose, and every week, a different program is on show there – anything from traditional Vietnamese theatre to acrobatics, gymnastics and disco music.

At the junction of Ham Nghi, Le Loi and Tran Hung Dao boulevards, in the centre of town, is the busy **Ben Thanh Market ❼**. The market covers over 11,000 sq. metres (120,000 sq. ft) and was opened in 1914. Here is an amazing collection of produce, meat, foods, CD players, televisions, cameras, calculators, refrigerators, fans, jeans and leather bags, all imported. At the back of the market, small food stalls serve a wide variety of local dishes and snacks. Not far from the Ben Thanh Market, down Duc Chinh Street, is the **Bao Tang My Thuat ❽** (Fine Art Museum; Tues–Sun 7.30am–4.30pm), housed in a grand

TIP

The Art Museum displays what can be described as war art, such as a lacquer painting depicting guerrillas in the jungle and a bronze statue of a man collecting rice for the war.

BELOW: best baguettes outside of France, and rainy season in the city.

Map on page 172

colonial-era building. Displays include ancient and contemporary Vietnamese art, porcelain and sculpture.

The **Mariamman Hindu Temple**, three blocks from the Ben Thanh Market and on Truong Dinh Street, was built at the end of the 19th century and caters to the city's small population of Hindu Tamils.

At the end of Le Duan, **Thao Cam Vien** ❾ (Botanical and Zoological Gardens) provides a welcome alternative to the noisy chaos of the streets and constitutes the most peaceful place in Ho Chi Minh City. The attractive gardens were established in 1864 by two Frenchmen – one a botanist, the other a veterinarian – as one of the first projects the French embarked upon after they established their new colony. The zoological section, somewhat run-down, houses rather dejected-looking birds, tigers, elephants, crocodiles and other indigenous species in cages built during the colonial era.

Vien Bao Tang Lich Su ❿ (National History Museum; Tues–Sun 9am–4.30pm), located just within the entrance of the botanical gardens, was built by the French in 1927. It documents the evolution of Vietnam's various cultures, from the Dong Son Bronze Age civilisation through to the Funan civilisation, the Chams and the Khmers. Among its exhibits are many stone and bronze relics, stelae, bronze drums, Cham art and ceramics, and a display of the traditional costumes of ethnic minorities. Behind the building, on the third floor, is a research library with an interesting and quite extensive collection of books from the French era. Just opposite the museum is the Den Hung, a temple dedicated to the ancestors of Hung Vuong, founding king of Vietnam.

The small Sino-Vietnamese **Phuoc Hai Tu** ⓫ (Emperor of Jade Pagoda), at 73 Mai Thi Luu, dates from the early 1890s. It was built by Cantonese Buddhists

BELOW: National History Museum.

Map on page 172

and is one of the city's most colourful pagodas. The elaborately-robed and Daoist Jade Emperor surveys the main sanctuary. Just to his right is the triple-headed, 18-armed statue of Phat Mau Chau De, mother of the Buddhas of the Middle, North, East, West and South. A door off to the left of the Jade Emperor's chamber leads to the Hall of Ten Hells, where carved wooden panels portray, in no uncertain detail, the fate that awaits those sentenced to the diverse torments found in the 10 regions of hell.

The more recent Buddhist **Chua Vinh Nghien** ⑫ on Nam Ky Khoi Nghia, District 3, is the newest and largest of the pagodas in the city. Built with aid from the Japanese Friendship Association, this Japanese-style pagoda was begun in 1964 and finished in 1973. The temple's screen and large bell were made in Japan. The bell, a gift from Japanese Buddhists, was presented during the Vietnam War as the embodiment of a prayer for an early end to the conflict. The large three-storey funeral tower behind the main temple holds ceramic burial urns containing the ashes of the dead.

The **Chua Giac Lam** ⑬, on the western outskirts of the city and thought to be the oldest pagoda in the city, dates from the end of the 17th century. Carved wooden pillars within the main building bear gilded inscriptions in old Vietnamese *nom* characters, which have also been used on the red tablets that record the biographies of the monks of previous generations, whose portraits adorn the left wall. The pagoda houses many beautifully carved jackwood statues.

RIGHT: fountain of Reunification Hall, and Le Duan Boulevard.
BELOW: dockside, Saigon River.

Cholon

Ho Chi Minh City's Chinatown, **Cholon** ⑭, was formerly a separate city, but it is now in the Ho Chi Minh City's District 5, thanks to the outward growth of the suburbs. Cholon remains a thriving commercial centre in its own right. With a population of around half a million Hoas – Vietnamese of Chinese origin – Cholon has come a long way since 1864, when it was home to just 6,000 Chinese, mostly shopkeepers or traders, 200 Indians and 40,000 Vietnamese. Today, countless small family businesses operate in this noisy and bustling Chinatown.

Two interesting temples can be visited on Nguyen Trai Street, near Cholon. At number 710 is the richly-decorated **Chua Pho Mieu**, or **Thien Hau Temple** (Heavenly Lady, or Tin Hau), more commonly known as Chua Ba (Women's Pagoda). This Chinese temple, dedicated to the Goddess Protector of Sailors, was built by Cantonese Buddhists at the end of the 18th century. The temple is frequented mainly by women, who bring their offerings to the altar of the Heavenly Lady. Among the other altars is one dedicated to the protection of women and newborn babies, and yet another to sterile women or mothers who have no sons.

The smaller **Chua Ha Chuong**, at number 802, contains several wooden sculptures and statues, including a statue of the god of happiness and an altar for sterile women.

A large and elegant mosque, built in 1935, on Dong Du Street serves the city's Islamic community. Only a handful of Indian Muslims remain, since most fled the country after 1975. ❑

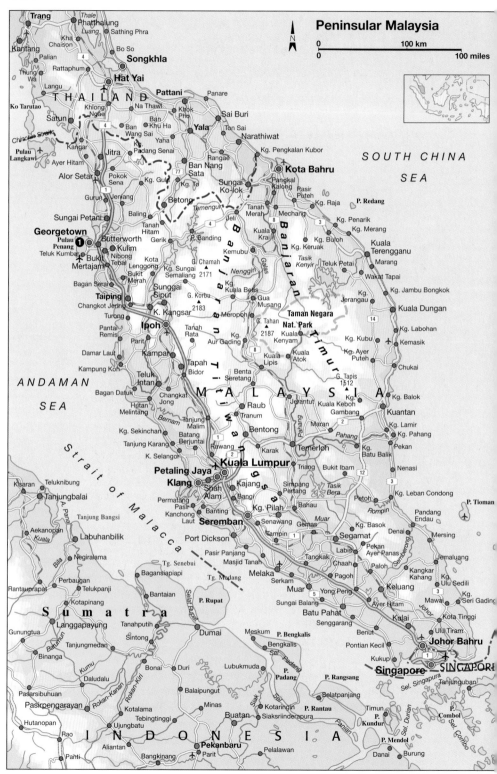

Peninsular Malaysia

0   100 km
0   100 miles

SOUTH CHINA SEA

THAILAND

ANDAMAN SEA

MALAYSIA

Strait of Malacca

Sumatra

INDONESIA

SINGAPORE

MALAYSIA

Once the anchor of the British Empire in Southeast Asia,
Malaysia has an especially independent identity

O ver the centuries, Malaysia has been open to millions of visitors from all over the globe, and its people have changed, absorbed and adapted customs and traditions from far-flung countries to suit the Malaysian way of life. Travel brochures romantically depict Malaysia's way of life as a land of beaches with coconut palms and sands as fine as flour, lost idyllic islands and amazing coral reefs.

On the other hand, the pages of Somerset Maugham's short stories paint vivid mental pictures of colonial bungalows set in the heart of a rubber plantation, with tea served on the verandah by a young Malay boy, while the Indian *punkah wallah* moves the fan into action to keep the *orang putih* (white man) cool in the heat of the tropics. Another portrayal of Malaysia lies between the covers of naturalist Alfred Russell Wallace's *Malay Archipelago*, allowing us to imagine ancient jungles screaming with monkeys, brimming with butterflies, and hiding legendary animals such as the most intelligent of primates (next to humans), the orang-utan.

Situated in the middle of Southeast Asia, with a land area of 342,000 sq. km (132,000 sq. miles), Malaysia is about the size of Japan, but with only a fraction of the population – about 22 million compared to Japan's 125 million. Peninsular Malaysia accounts for 40 percent of the land area and 86 percent of the population. The East Malaysian states of Sabah and Sarawak are separated from the peninsula by 640 km (400 miles) of the South China Sea, but each of the 13 states has a charm and character of its own. Malay and indigenous tribes make up over half the population, while Chinese, Indians and others also come under the broad spectrum that is covered by the term "Malaysian".

Since independence in 1957, Malaysia has faced a series of economic and political pitfalls and triumphs. Perhaps the biggest achievement is a complete transformation of the Malaysian economy from almost total dependence on raw commodities, such as rubber and tin, to a broad manufacturing base.

Kuala Lumpur possesses the world's tallest buildings and orderly traffic snarls to rival Manhattan's. But beneath this modernity are Chinese shophouses and a palpable colonial residue. The island of Penang, once the British Empire's most important Southeast Asian outpost, is a bit complicated to define easily, for its sandy beaches and cluttered, old-feeling urban centre don't fit in the same descriptive breath. And Sarawak and Sabah, on the island of Borneo, which Malaysia shares with Indonesia, are breathtaking in both their biological diversity and grandeur and in the wreckless way many of the natural resources, especially wood, have been exploited. ❑

PRECEDING PAGES: spinning tops on the peninsular east coast; Kuala Lumpur.

Decisive Dates

The early centuries

38,000 BC: Remains of people found in Sarawak, on Borneo, date back 400 centuries.

2500 BC: Proto-Malays spread south from Yunnan area in China.

300 BC: Earliest signs of Bronze and Iron Age cultures in Malaysia.

200 BC: Start of trading contacts with India and China.

100 BC–AD 200: Emergence of trading kingdoms in the Isthmus of Kra.

AD 500–800: Development of local trading polities

with Hindu-Buddhist orientation on Bujang Valley and in northern Perak.

1290: First Muslim states begin to develop in northern Sumatra.

The rise of Malacca

1400: Foundation of Malacca.

1403–10: Malacca comes under protection of imperial China.

1409: Emperor of China sends Admiral Zheng Ho to Malacca to proclaim it a city and kingdom.

1445: Malacca becomes a sultanate.

1450: Expansion of Malaccan "empire".

1509: The first Portuguese arrive at Malacca.

1511: Malacca falls to the Portuguese.

1511–1699: Empire of Johor under the Malacca line.

1528: Sultan Muzaffar Syah establishes the Perak Kingdom.

1641: The Dutch take Malacca from the Portuguese; start of Dutch dominance in area.

1699: Assassination of Sultan Mahmud of Johor at Kota Tinggi.

1699–1819: Empire of Johor, mostly at Riau, under Bendahara line.

1699–1784: Period of Menangkabu-Bugis struggle for domination of the Straits of Malacca.

1722: First ruler of Trengannu Kingdom installed.

1784: Death of Raja Haji at Malacca; Dutch break Bugis power in area.

1786: British occupy Penang.

1812: Death of Sultan Mahmud Syah, last ruler of united Johor-Riau kingdom.

Colonial Malaya

1819: British occupy Singapore.

1824: Anglo-Dutch Treaty; Malacca is peacefully ceded to the British.

1826: British treaty with Bangkok limits the spread of Thai influence on the Malay Peninsula.

1831–32: The Naning War.

1840s: The importance of tin increases, bringing an influx of Chinese tin miners to the western coast.

1841: James Brooke established as Rajah of Sarawak.

1846: British annex the island of Labuan.

1858–68: Civil war in Pahang.

1866: Start of Selangor civil war.

1874: Start of British intervention and control in Perak, Selangor and Sungei Ujung.

1875–76: The Perak War.

1881: British North Borneo Chartered Company establishes a centre in North Borneo (what is present-day Sabah).

1891–95: Pahang Rebellion.

1895–1905: Mat Salleh Rebellion. The introduction of new taxes had earlier created general discontent, and Mat Salleh gathers many supporters in his revolt against the North Borneo Company. (Today, he is still regarded as one of Sabah's most famous heroes.)

1896: Treaty of Federation – the Federated Malay States (FMS) are created.

1909: Treaty of Bangkok transfers four northern Malay states from Thai to British control.

1914: Johor brought under British control.

1914–18: World War I.

1920–41: British adopt decentralisation policy in FMS; early signs of a Malay nationalism opposing British rule begin to surface.

Malaya, Merdeka, Malaysia

1941–45: Japanese conquest and occupation.

1945: British reoccupy Malaysia.

1946: Malayan Union Scheme introduced and anti-Malayan Union Movement; formation of UMNO; formation of MIC; Sarawak and British North Borneo become Crown colonies.

1948: Malayan Union Scheme abandoned; Federation of Malaya inaugurated. State of emergency declared by government.

1954: Large numbers of Communist guerrillas are killed. Many more surrender in 1958, and the few remaining guerrillas retreat deep into the jungle.

1955: With the Communists largely eliminated, Malayans begin to clamour for independence.

1956: Tunku leads a delegation to London to negotiate for independence.

1957: Malaya becomes independent, and the Union Jack is lowered for the last time.

1960: The state of emergency ends.

Post-independence

1960: Formation of the Association of Southeast Asia (ASA) with the Philippines and Thailand.

1961: Tunku proposes a political association – called Malaysia – that would include Malaya, Singapore, North Borneo, Sarawak and Brunei.

1963: Creation of Malaysia.

1963–66: Confrontation with Indonesia, which intensifies its "Crush Malaysia" campaign. In 1966, Soekarno is ousted from power in Indonesia; the new Indonesian government, led by Soeharto, is not keen to continue the confrontation, and a peace agreement brings the conflict to an end. The Philippines drops its claim on Sabah and recognises Malaysia.

1965: Singapore leaves Federation and becomes an independent nation.

1969: Riots in the wake of the general elections on 13 May are the result of simmering racial tension between Malays and Chinese. Violent outbreaks, mainly in Kuala Lumpur, kill hundreds of people and destroy a considerable amount of property.

1970: Start of the New Economic Policy (NEP), established to encourage a fairer distribution of wealth among the races.

1981: Malaysia's fourth prime minister, Dato' Seri Dr Mahathir Mohamad, takes office.

1983: Constitutional crisis involving the position of Malaysia's hereditary rulers.

LEFT: Sultan Abu Bakar of Johor.

RIGHT: Dato' Seri Dr Mahathir Mohamad, Malaysia's Prime Minister for two decades.

1987: UMNO racked by power struggle between Mahathir Mohamad and Tengku Razaleigh Hamzah; Mahathir administration detains prominent opposition politicians, trade unionists, educators and church/community leaders.

1988: Deregistration of UMNO; formation of UMNO *Baru* (New UMNO) by Mahathir Mohamad.

1989: Communist Party of Malaysia abandons its 41-year armed struggle to overthrow the government.

1990: General elections – the ruling coalition retains its two-third majority in Parliament.

1990s: The national car project, Proton, leads an effort towards high-tech industries, part of the effort to transform Malaysia into fully developed nation.

1996: Malaysia launches its first satellite.

1997: After the opening of the world's tallest pair of buildings, the Petronas Towers, economic and political downturn ensue. Verbal scuffles break out with Singapore. The ringgit plummets and Mahathir makes accusations of foreign conspiracies.

1998: Kuala Lumpur is the first Asian city to host the Commonwealth Games. The arrest of deputy prime minister Anwar Ibrahim provokes a political crisis.

1999: Mahathir is re-elected with a comfortable majority, although the Islamic Party (PAS) gains ground. Anwar Ibrahim is jailed on charges of corruption.

2001: Poor US economy stymies Malaysia's growth.

2003: Mahathir retires and Abdullah Ahmad Badawi is appointed as the new Prime Minister. ❏

THE MALAYSIANS

Islam, colonialism and the Orang Asli provide the threads for the multi-ethnic and interwoven culture of the Malaysian people, not all of who are Malay

The traveller in Malaysia will encounter warm and engaging people, their lifestyles embedded with rich yet culturally diverse traditions. First there are the Orang Asli, the indigenous people of Malaysia who have managed to retain some of their centuries-old roots. Those who followed, the Malays, built upon traditions of the soil and ocean, but embraced influences from elsewhere as well. And because of its rich resources and strategic location, Malaysia attracted still others, including Indians, Chinese, and Europeans.

Orang Asli

The Malay term *orang asli* means "original people" and covers three more or less distinct groups and a score or more of separate tribes. Orang Asli has become a convenient term for explaining those groups of people who do not belong to the three predominant races found on peninsular Malaysia. Of the estimated 90,000 Orang Asli, 60 percent are jungle dwellers, while the other 40 percent are coastal peoples, many of them dependent upon fishing.

The Negritos mostly inhabit the northeast and northwest, and are the only truly nomadic tribes of the Orang Asli. Practising little or no cultivation, the Negrito tribes pride themselves on their mobility, and possessions are thought only to be a hindrance to their lifestyle.

The Senoi are thought to have common ancestors with the hill tribes of northern Cambodia and Vietnam, arriving in present-day Malaysia between 6,000 and 8,000 years ago.

The last group of Orang Asli were the latest group to arrive, no earlier than 4,000 years ago. Many of this group have a distinct resemblance to the Malays, not surprising as modern Malays have a common ancestry with many of them.

Malays

The Malays, long linked to the land, are known as *Bumiputra*, or Sons of the Soil. Although the rift between the farm and the city generally

LEFT: Muslim girls. RIGHT: Orang Asli family.

widens as years go by, it does not threaten the strong unity the Malays derive from a common faith. The laws of Islam immediately set a Malay apart from non-Malay Malaysians. With ample food and a warm climate, life in the more isolated villages remained the same for centuries. Today, little has changed, for the most

part, as the Malay *kampung* remain peaceful enclaves where the simplicity of an uncluttered life is still cherished.

Intermarriage between races is uncommon, though Muslim foreigners are accepted, keeping the Malay-Muslim cultural identity distinctly separate. In the home of the Malay family, traditional customs are observed daily. The village mosque wakes up several times a day to call the faithful to prayer, often interrupting evening television programmes that are now an everyday part of kampung family life.

Muslims in Malaysia are subject to enforceable religious laws, such as that a Muslim woman can't be alone with a non-related male.

Indians

Indians began visiting Malaysia 2,000 years ago following rumours of fortune in a land their ancestors knew as Suvarnadvipa, the fabled "golden peninsula". Tamil blood even flows through the royal lineage dating back to 13th-century Melaka (Malacca), where the first sultanate grew up. But it was not until the 19th century that Indians arrived and stayed in large numbers, employed mainly as rubber tappers or other plantation labourers. Most came from southern India, and approximately 80 percent were Tamil and Hindu, with smaller numbers of Sikh, Bengali, Keralan, Telugu and Parsi.

Malaysian Indians still maintain strong home ties with their former villages, sometimes even taking wives in India and bringing them back to live in Malaysia.

The greatest cultural influence was brought over by the southern Indians, leaving a rich and colourful stamp on Malaysian life: bright silk saris, Tamil movies, the indomitable prevalence of the Hindu faith, and banana-leaf curries have added further diversity to Malaysian culture.

Chinese

The Chinese population makes up over a third of the country's total, yet its presence in and control of major industries such as rubber, tin and import and export companies would seem to make the numbers far greater.

Mainland China remains important to the Chinese, but until recently, Malaysian Chinese were forbidden by the Malaysian government to return to mainland China for fear of Communist intrusions. But the older generations regularly sent financial help to relatives in China, while others saved their money to return and die on their home soil.

The Chinese in Malaysia are defined by their history of hardship and pioneering, as well as the three important Chinese ethical threads: Confucianism, Daoism and Buddhism. Even if

converted to Islam or Christianity, this background is deeply rooted. Consequently, many of traditional Chinese festivals and rites are regularly and openly celebrated in Malaysia.

Peranakans

The colourful Peranakan culture was first established when Chinese trade missions established a port in Malacca in the early 1400s. Intercultural relationships and marriages were naturally forged between traders and local Malay women, as well as between Malacca's sultans and the Chinese Ming-dynasty emperors. Subsequent generations of Chinese-Malays were known as Straits Chinese, or Peranakans, which in Malay means "born here". When the Dutch colonists moved out in the early 1800s, more Chinese immigrants moved in, thus diluting Malay blood in the Peranakans, so that later generations were almost completely Chinese.

Eurasians

When the sultanate of Malacca fell to Portuguese invaders in 1511, the new rulers sought to establish control by encouraging Portuguese soldiers to marry local women. As can be expected, a strong Eurasian

People of Borneo

The two easternmost states of Sabah and Sarawak, situated in the northern part of the island of Borneo, which Malaysia shares with Indonesia, have the most diverse racial groups of all Malaysia. Most of them are of Mongoloid extract and moved here some time ago from Kalimantan (Indonesian Borneo). They generally live in the interior along jungle rivers, although some also live near the coastal regions, while others with some formal education have found

> ### LONGHOUSE STAYS
>
> Most tribes, especially the Iban, are extremely hospitable and guests are welcomed with a glass of strong *tuak* (rice wine) before being offered a bed.

community grew up with loyalty to Portugal through its ties of blood and the Catholic religion. Eurasians are proudly protective of their unique cuisine, and often continue to speak Cristao, a medieval dialect once spoken in southwestern Portugal, but now used only in parts of Malaysia which have long-entrenched Eurasian populations.

In neighbouring Singapore to the south, both Eurasians and Peranakans make up part of the population, Eurasians in smaller numbers.

LEFT: Indian newsstand vendors are common in urban areas; Peranakan culture in Malacca.
ABOVE: Dayak woman, Sarawak.

work in towns, commercial centres and in industries throughout Malaysia.

The majority of the indigenous tribes have traditions and ways of living in common, but each group has some unique belief or activity that sets it apart from the rest. Most of the rural peoples of Sabah and Sarawak live in longhouses, large buildings that house the entire community under one roof, and may contain up to 60 families or more.

Borneo was once known for its headhunters. However, in the head-hunting days, taking the heads of one's enemies only occurred when the community was suffering some plague. Today head-hunting is outlawed. ❏

NATURAL HISTORY

More than two-thirds of peninsular and Bornean Malaysia is jungle. The green
cover begins at the edge of the sea and climbs to the highest point of land

The rain forests in this region are the oldest in the world, making those in Africa and South America seem adolescent in comparison. While creeping ice ages were swelling and shrinking across the northern hemisphere, the Malaysian jungles had lain undisturbed for an estimated 130 million years. Some of the

in Malaysia is the elegant hibiscus, the country's national flower. The world's largest flower, the *Rafflesia*, is unique to Southeast Asia. The entire plant of Rafflesia consists of just the flowerhead, which can measure up to 1 metre (3 ft) across and weigh up to 9 kilograms (20 lbs). A parasite, it sucks food from the roots

most unique and diverse species of animal and plant life evolved here, and some of the most primitive and remote tribes still inhabit this jungle world, living much like their ancestors did a thousand years ago.

The Malaysian jungles, on the peninsula and in particular on Malaysian Borneo, have generated much scientific interest and continue to do so. The diversity in flora and fauna is truly staggering. In Malaysia, for example, there are over 15,000 species of flowering plants, including 2,000 trees, 200 palms and 3,000 species of orchids, the most exotic of flowers, as well as beautiful highland roses rivalling their English counterparts. The most prominent flower

of the *Cissus liana*, a tree, and starts life as a red bulb. The Rafflesia grows in size and finally bursts open, revealing its pink, red and white interior. The Rafflesia's intensely smelly glory (to attract pollinating insects) lasts only a week, after which it shrivels up into the moist jungle earth from where it was born.

Another world's first is the towering *tualang* tree, tallest of all tropical trees. It can reach up to 80 metres (260 ft) in height and more than 3 metres (10 ft) in girth. The famous pitcher plants can be seen everywhere on the slopes of Mount Kinabalu in the state of Sabah, on Borneo, their honeyed jaws stretched open waiting for a careless insect to drop in.

Malaysia's jungles also hold thousands of species from the animal kingdom, many of which are unique to the region, while others were introduced from elsewhere in Asia.

Almost 300 species of mammals live here, including tigers, elephants, sleek civit cats *(musang)*, rhinoceros (though sadly, their numbers are greatly diminishing), black-and-white tapirs, leopards, honey bears, and two kinds of deer – the *sambar* and the barking deer *(kijang)*, with its dog-like call. Malaysia is

RUBBER GAMBLE

What stands out in Malaysia is the rubber tree. Now taking up more than three-quarters of all the developed land, this plant was originally viewed with great scepticism by the coffee planters.

Whether venturing into the jungle or not, you will be sure to see anywhere in Malaysia some of the 736 species of birds, and quite a few of the 150,000 species of insects. Of the over 1,000 species of butterfly in Malaysia, the king of them is the Rajah Brooke's birdwing – the national butterfly – with its emerald markings on jet-black wings. There are over a hundred more other breathtakingly vivid butterflies, as well as magnificent moths. They are best seen at butterfly farms found throughout the

also home to the region's tiny mousedeer (which is not technically a deer at all), wild forest cattle *(seladang)*, the scaly anteater *(pangolin)*, the badger-like *binturong* with its prehensile tail, and many kinds of gibbons and monkeys, including the quaint and slow loris with its sad eyes and lethargic manner. Borneo is also the home of the extraordinary orangutan ("forest man" in Malay), treated like another tribe by the jungle peoples, and the proboscis monkey, the male of the species parading its pendulous nose.

LEFT: strangling fig provides sculptural form. **ABOVE:** a familiar sight in Malaysia – working the rice fields.

country, especially in insect-abundant Cameron Highlands.

Along the coastline, there are extensive areas of mud swamps and mangroves. Behind the mangroves are the lowland dipterocarp forests, which extend up to an altitude of 600 metres (2,000 ft). Trees grow to majestic heights of 80 metres (262 ft) or more, with the first branches 20 metres (65 ft) above ground. This is called the triple canopy forest. Commercially, this region is the most important; from here comes timber, Malaysia's main natural export. Recently, efforts have been made to control timber exploitation so that Malaysia's jungle will assure the industry a green future.

The next level of forest is mostly oak and chestnut, and above 1,500 metres (5,000 ft), it becomes a kind of never-never land with elfin forests consisting of small gnarled trees, 3 to 5 metres (10–16 ft) high, covered with folds of hanging mosses and lichen. The highland forests, for the most part, are left untouched and unlogged as catchment areas, ensuring the fertility of the soil.

With conservation gaining importance in Malaysia, the government has set aside tracts of land as national parks or game reserves where strict hunting laws are enforced. This state of affairs has come a long way from the days

when animals were killed, not just for food, but also for their skins, horns or feathers.

Agricultural lands

As far as the eye can see, the lush green vegetation of the tropics smothers the landscape. Yet, contrary to its looks, Malaysia is not suited to agriculture.

Unlike the Nile River Basin or the Ganges Valley, where seasonal rains flooding the land bring new fertile soil, the torrential downpours in Malaysia wash away the thin but valuable topsoil. In many places, only red mud remains. Erosion is one of Malaysia's oldest problems. Geologists believe that the Malay peninsula and

Borneo were once a single rugged land mass, joined together and running the entire length of the Indonesian and Malayan archipelago. For millennia, sun, wind, and torrential rains reduced the mountains to hillocks and outcrops. Precious soils were washed into the sea, and fingers of land became cut off by subsidence and erosion. This meticulous work of nature continues today.

Still, despite the shifting landscape and annual monsoon rain, Malaysia's early settlers were basically food growers. As far back as AD 500, crops such as sugar cane, bananas, pepper and coconuts were grown for export, while rice was introduced to these lands over 1,000 years ago. Traditionally, both men and women were involved in the cultivation of this crop – the staple food and prime source of income for the rural Malay. The tempo of *kampung* life has quickened with the introduction of double cropping, using hybrids of rice that reap a second crop each year.

Tides upon the sea

Almost completely surrounded by water, Malaysia was where the regional monsoons met, and where the tides of the Indian Ocean and the South China Sea flowed together into the Strait of Malacca. Seafaring merchants, explorers, adventurers and pirates, seeking the wealth of the Malayan and Indonesian archipelago, stopped along these coasts to wait for the winds to change in their favour. Malaysia was the halfway point to this interchange, linking China to India and India to the Moluccas.

Piracy on the high seas was a widespread, lucrative and once-honourable profession, attracting merchants, noblemen, tribes-people and fishermen alike. For centuries, sailors trembled at the thought of passing unarmed through Malaysian waters at night. (It's still a problem.)

Much of the coast is surrounded by coral reefs of vivid colours, and creatures both beautiful and curious find their home here. The east coast has found profitable possibilities for its long stretches of beach and coral islands, as tourists, eager for sunshine and palm-fringed coral sands, flock to the coconut-sheltered beach huts and developed holiday resorts all along the coast. ❑

LEFT: a butterfly rests on a hibiscus.
RIGHT: orang-utan hanging on in the jungle.

SOUTHEAST ASIAN WILDLIFE

Southeast Asia is home to spectacular endemic animals, ranging from bizarre-looking hornbills to Komodo dragons and the huge Atlas moth

Southeast Asia's wildlife form part of the Indo-Malayan realm, a zoological and geographical zone comprising most of tropical Asia. Several animal species are unique to Southeast Asia, and in some cases entire sub-families and even orders are confined to this area. Distinct species include leaf monkeys, gibbons and flying lemurs. Only one family of bird is restricted to this realm, the leaf birds and ioras.

The region has rich reptilian and amphibian fauna, with many species of lizards (including geckos and the Komodo dragon, the world's largest lizard), colourful and numerous poisonous snakes, crocodiles, and turtles. Marine life is abundant and thrives in the region's rich coral reefs. Birds include colourful kingfishers, the maleo (an exotic megapode that buries its eggs in communal mounds), magnificent argus pheasants, and emerald ground-dwelling pittas.

ENDANGERED SPECIES

The rate of species loss – plants and animals – is probably greater today than in any other time in human history. Humans pose the greatest threat to endangered species through the destruction of habitat, hunting and poaching, and the illegal trade in live animals on the endangered list. Visitors should avoid buying gifts made from animal products.

◁ **ASIAN TIGER**
Only 5,000 to 7,500 tigers exist today. In the past 50 years the Bali and Javan sub-species of tiger have become extinct, largely through hunting.

△ **BANGTENG BULL**
The mainly nocturnal Banteng is one of two species of regional wild cattle. Today, it can be found in the Baluran National Park in Java.

▽ ATLAS MOTH

The night-flying, richly patterned, dark-brown Atlas moth may span as much as 25cm (14 in) and is one of the largest moth species in the world.

▽ MANTIS

Not an exotic plant, but an exotic insect, the flower mantis uses its camouflage to fool predators and to catch prey.

THE VANISHING ORANG-UTAN

Wild orang-utans once ranged in much of Southeast Asia, but today they are found only in Borneo and Sumatra. The present population is estimated to be less than 30,000 – half that of a decade ago. Habitat destruction by logging and cash-cropping is the greatest threat to their survival. It is estimated that 80 percent of the forest in Indonesia may be logged by 2010. The international trade in orang-utans has declined, but demand for orang-utans as pets continues, particularly in Indonesia. It is estimated that five to six animals (often mothers) die for every orang-utan – often an infant – that is traded. The death of adult females increases the risk of extinction.

▽ JAVAN RHINO

The Javan Rhinoceros is the world's rarest large mammal. Fifty animals can be found on the Ujung Kulon peninsula in western Java.

△ ASIAN ELEPHANT

Since 1990, the population of the Asian elephant has declined by 97 percent. Today there are less than 30,000 elephants in Asia.

▽ GREEN TURTLE

Adult green turtles weigh up to 180kg (400lb). Females lay about 80 eggs in the sand. The eggs take about 50 days to incubate.

▷ WRINKLED HORNBILL

The rare wrinkled hornbill is found in coastal and lowland forests. It has a bark, often of two notes, and flies in small flocks.

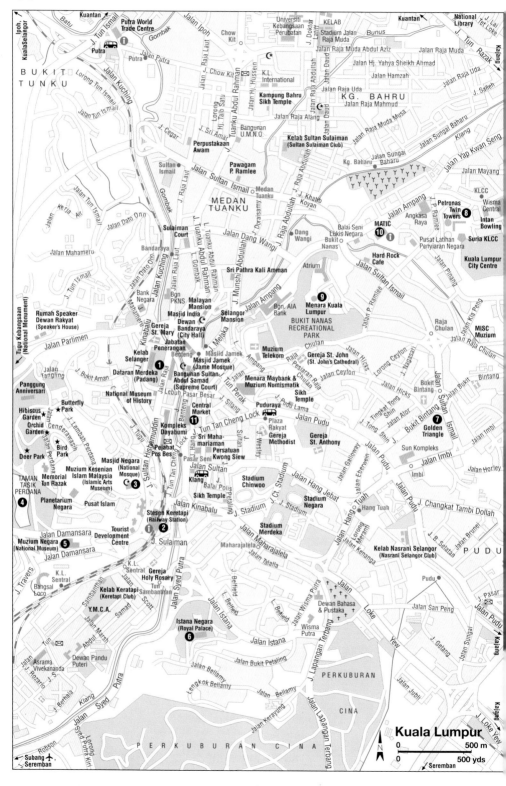

Kuala Lumpur

N

0   500 m

0   500 yds

KUALA LUMPUR

Map on page 198

A mining outpost just a century ago and now the capital of Malaysia with a population of 1½ million, Kuala Lumpur is certainly a big city – and it has the world's two tallest buildings

Kuala Lumpur

To the newcomer, Kuala Lumpur – or "KL" as it is popularly known – is a fascinating mixture of old and new, increasingly so with the completion of the world's tallest buildings in downtown KL, in 1997. Mosques of Moorish design, elaborate Chinese temples and crowded shophouses, Hindu temples with towering gates, and Indian restaurants and regal remnants of the shipshape British order – all set the colourful scene of multi-ethnic activity.

A century and a half ago, Kuala Lumpur was a precise representation of what its name means in Malay: "muddy river mouth". At that time, a group of tin prospectors, financed by the local Malay chief, journeyed upriver to the confluence of the less-than-crystal-clear waters of the Klang and Gombak rivers. Today, it is the seat of government for Malaysia, with its own administration headed by a minister of cabinet rank. Over the past decade, the skyline of the city has changed beyond all recognition as new high-rise buildings continue their upward thrust.

City centre

If you cross the Gombak and Klang rivers, you will come to the old city centre for British colonial rule, with its Moorish administrative buildings that are still important today. The Old City Hall and a British colonial club face **Dataran Merdeka**, or the **Padang ❶**. Casting its shadow on the Padang is the imposing **Bangunan Sultan Abdul Samad**. Once the core of colonial KL, this building was the colonial secretariat headquarters. It now houses the **Supreme Court**. It was the first building to be built in a North Indian-cum-Moorish style, a trend brought to Malaysia by two architects, A.C. Norman and A.B. Hubbock. Both men had spent some time in India, and they deemed that an architectural style featuring Moorish, Indian and Arabic motifs would best suit a predominantly Muslim country, apparently ignoring the fact that the Malays already had a very highly developed and practical building style of their own.

Until the opening of the National Mosque after independence, the **Masjid Jamek** (Jamek Mosque) was the principal Muslim centre for prayer in the city. There are other buildings in the area around the Padang built in Moorish style, and which have influenced more recent edifices since.

Along the same side of the river but further down from the Padang – connected to the Central Market and central business district by a pedestrian bridge – is the towering, white **Kompleks Dayabumi**. Below this complex are shops and restaurants, and the equally

BELOW: Petronas Towers, the world's tallest buildings.

Meticulously designed to meet Victorian standards, the construction of the KL Railway Station was actually held up because the design failed to meet British specifications that the station roof must support one metre of snow.

impressive **Pejabat Pos Besar** (General Post Office). Beyond these modern buildings on Jalan Sultan Hashamuddin lies the **Stesen Keretapi ❷** (Railway Station). To arrive by rail in Kuala Lumpur is a fantastic experience, as turrets, spires, minarets and Arabic arches greet the eye in every direction. Inside, the design is that of many large Victorian railway stations in England. Within the railway station is a post office, a selection of restaurants, and a hotel. The wonderfully old-fashioned **Heritage Station Hotel** underwent renovation in recent years, although it still retains an air of faded grandeur. Opposite the station is the Malaya Railway Administration Building, with the same Moorish design.

Up the road from this Victorian enclave is the **Masjid Negara ❸** (Sat–Thurs 9am–6pm; Fri 3–6pm), the national mosque. Completed in 1965, the jagged 18-point-star roof and the 70-metre-tall (240 ft) minaret catch the eye. The 18 points of the star represent the 13 states of Malaysia and the five pillars of Islam. Its Grand Hall – busiest on Fridays – can accommodate 8,000 worshippers. On the roof are 48 smaller domes, their design and number inspired by the great mosque in Mecca. The mosque is an impressive building with cool marbled halls, long galleries, and reflecting pools outside in the courtyard. The minaret rises from the centre of one of these pools. The mosque is set within 5 hectares (13 acres) of fine gardens.

The best-known and most popular of KL's parks is **Taman Tasik Perdana ❹** or the Lake Gardens (Mon–Sat 10am–6pm; Sun 8am–6pm), comprising 92 hectares (240 acres) of undulating green with magnificent trees and flowering plants. Popular with visitors and locals alike, they are especially busy at weekends. You'll see joggers puff their way past picnickers, hand-holding lovers and old Chinese folk going through their *tai chi* routines.

BELOW: the Sultan Abdul Samad Building houses the Supreme Court.

Map on page 198

For a taste of wildlife, the **Bird Park** and **Butterfly Park** (daily 9am–5pm) house local and foreign species in forested enclosures. The **Planetarium** sits in a carefully thought-out garden. It has a 36-cm (14-inch) telescope, a theatre, and the Arianne IV space engine used to launch Malaysia's first satellite, the Measat I. Other attractions in the gardens include an orchid garden and deer park. Within and around the park are several interesting buildings.

On a smaller hill but in an imposing position stands the **National Monument** (Tugu Kebangsaan), erected to commemorate those who died in the struggle against the Communist insurgency in the 1950s. At the edge of the gardens, on an incline on Jalan Damansara and facing Jalan Travers, is the **Musium Negara** ❺ (National Museum; daily 9am–6pm). The museum was initially built on the site of the old Selangor museum, which was destroyed during World War II. The rebuilt museum was opened in 1963.

Prisons, palaces, towers and mansions

In the southern part of Kuala Lumpur is the **Istana Negara** ❻ (National Palace), the official residence of the king. The palace was the town house of a wealthy Chinese *towkay* and was sold and converted into a palace for the sultans of Selangor in 1926, and is now for the king, a position that is rotated amongst the regional sultans. Beyond the National Palace and further south along Jalan Lepangan Terbang is a small road, Jalan Kerayong, that climbs a steep hill. Follow it to find yourself near the Chinese cemeteries, with a commanding view over the city. On this hill stands the largest and newest Buddhist temple in KL, completed in 1985: the **Tien Hau Temple**. It was built by several Chinese multi-millionaires who, it is said, each donated one pillar. It is known that the cost of the temple was phenomenal, but the exact figure remains a secret.

The fulcrum of modern consumer life in Malaysia is the intersection of Jalan Sultan Ismail and Jalan Bukit Bintang, an area of expensive shops, high-class restaurants, and international hotels and sophisticated nightlife. It is often called the **Golden Triangle** ❼. You will find a number of large shopping malls in this area: Sungai Wang Plaza and the adjacent Bukit Bintang Plaza offer more than 500 shops, including some of the best bookstores in KL; Imbi Plaza concentrates on computers and software; KL Plaza has fashion accessory shops and electronic outlets; flashy green Lot 10 has European designer boutiques and Isetan.

The city's newest landmark is currently the world's tallest building, or, rather, pair of buildings: the **Petronas Twin Towers** ❽, two identical towers that are linked midway up by a skybridge. The towers reach a numerically auspicious 88 storeys above the traffic-congested streets and make up part of a larger development called the **Kuala Lumpur City Centre** (KLCC) which includes the huge Suria KLCC shopping mall, an excellent concert hall and the sprawling KLCC Park.

Visitors can ascend to the towers' skybridge on the 42nd floor, but for a higher view try the **Menara Kuala Lumpur** ❾ (daily 10am–10pm), a 421-metre (1,380-ft) telecom-and-tourism tower built in 1995, and one of the highest such structures in the world.

At the National Palace, yellow is the colour for royalty, and only kings may walk on the welcoming yellow carpet, while politicians and visiting dignitaries tread on the red one.

BELOW: National Monument.

Map on page 198

Historic Jalan Ampang presents a very different aspect of urban architecture – a row of old tin miners' mansions that have been well preserved despite the tropical weather. The tin empire gave mine-owners the money to build lavish mansions, and these were generally built along Jalan Ampang itself. The best preserved of these mansions is Dewan Tunku Abdul Rahman, built in 1935 by a wealthy Chinese tin mogul and rubber planter named Eu Tong Sen. In the late 1980s it was refurbished and commissioned as the **Malaysian Tourist Centre ❿** (MTC; open daily 24 hours).

Chinatown and other districts

Chinatown lies within the boundaries of Jalan Sultan, Jalan Bandar (now known as Jalan Tun HS Lee, once the old High Street) and along Jalan Petaling. The area is bustling with good eateries and exotic oddities, including jewellers and goldsmiths, casket and basket makers, dry-goods shops, pet shops, optical houses, and herbalists. Near here is the **Central Market ⓫**. A former fruit-and-vegetable market, this Art Deco showpiece was saved from demolition by conservation-minded architects, who eventually won an award for their restoration and renovation efforts. It is currently a favourite hangout for KL's youth.

Central Market has it all, from key-chains and batik scarves, to traditional basketry and woodware from all over the country, as well as preserved foodstuffs. There is often an event or exhibition happening – if you're lucky you could catch a *wayang kulit* (shadow puppet) performance or *bangsawan* (traditional Malay theatre) production in full swing. Outside the building, buskers and medicine men give their own impromptu shows.

Besides Chinatown, there are several other districts in which it is pleasant to stroll and enjoy the sights. Northward from the Padang lies another area of interesting shops. The main road here is **Jalan Tuanku Abdul Rahman**, named after the country's first Prime Minister following independence. To the locals this road is often referred to as Batu Road. The street leads off the Padang; all along it lie shops, both old and new, as well as modern department stores, cheap hotels and many *kedai makan*, or eating stalls.

The **Coliseum Cinema**, built in the 1920s and one of KL's first, lies halfway down this road, and the **Coliseum Cafe and Hotel** next door is the most famous bar and restaurant in town, serving customers for more than 60 years. Off Batu Road where the Padang ends is Jalan Melayu, which was the site of one of the original *kampung* lying on the outskirts of the city. This area is principally interesting for its Indian shops.

Beyond Jalan Melayu is **Jalan Masjid India**, whose mosque sits on the same spot where one of the town's first mosques used to be. The road leads to what was formerly the red-light district and is now a thriving commercial area of shops, restaurants and hotels where Indian silks, flowery saris and glittering handmade jewellery are the order of the day. After 6pm every day, portable kitchens with tables and chairs take over the street, offering to passers-by food which is as spicy as you can stand it. ❑

RIGHT: night market in Kuala Lumpur. **BELOW:** shopping centre.

PENANG

It's a place with a colourful past, mysterious back alleys, palm-shrouded beaches and a stimulating cuisine. No wonder that it has lured visitors for centuries

Map on page 184

One of the most famous islands in Asia, **Penang ❶** is perhaps the best-known tourist destination in Malaysia. Since 1985, it has been connected to the mainland by the Penang Bridge, which has become a modern symbol of the island. It costs more than the ferry, but the 7-km (4½-mile) drive affords exhilarating views of the harbour, and you have the satisfaction of knowing that you have just driven over one of the longer bridges in the world.

Although once under the dominion of the Sultan of Kedah, 285 sq-km (115 sq-mile) Penang has always been on its own. Until the British came, it was largely deserted despite its strategic position. To encourage trade and commerce, the British made the island a free port; no taxes were levied on either imports or exports. This strategy worked, and in eight years the population increased to 8,000, comprising a diverse grouping of immigrants – Chinese, Indians and Bugis, among others.

Georgetown, named by the British after King George III of Great Britain, is also known by the Malays as Tanjong (or Headland) and is unmistakably a Chinese town. It has one of the most unusual waterfronts in Asia, what locals call the Clan Piers. It consists of villages built on stilts over the sea. As predominantly as the port is Chinese, the countryside beyond Georgetown is Malay, and the entrepreneurial fuss nearly disappears.

No visit should end without sampling the lip-smacking delights of the local cuisine: Indian curry to Malay *nasi* (rice), to Chinese *bah kut teh* (pork ribs in herbal soup). Much of the best food is found at unfashionable roadside stalls and cramped coffee shops in the old parts of Georgetown, especially along Gurney Drive and Jalan Burma.

Old Georgetown

Originally, **Fort Cornwallis** was a wooden structure. In the early 1800s, it was rebuilt with convict labour. Today, the old fort still stands, but its precincts have been converted into a public park and playground. Next to Fort Cornwallis lie the **Padang** (town green) and the **Esplanade** (Jalan Tun Syed Sheh Barakbah), which is the heart of old historical Georgetown. Handsome 19th-century colonial buildings stand at one end of the Padang, serving as government offices. At the other end, near the entrance to Fort Cornwallis, traffic circles the **Clock Tower**, presented to Penang by a rich Chinese *towkay* in commemoration of Queen Victoria's Diamond Jubilee.

The dignified and well designed **St George's Church**, built in 1818 on nearby Lebuh Farquhar, draws much attention as the oldest Anglican church in Southeast Asia. In the **Penang Museum** (Sat–Thurs 9am–5pm), on the other side of the street, visitors can

LEFT: sunset at Batu Ferringhi. **BELOW:** travelling salesman in Georgetown.

Rooftop patterns in Chinatown.

BELOW: municipal building evokes memories of colonial splendour.

peer into a Chinese bridal chamber created in the lavish style of the 19th century, or see a jewelled *keris*, the dagger Malays used for protection. The **Penang Art Gallery** upstairs displays batik paintings, oils, graphics and Chinese ink drawings. Further west along the waterfront, a traveller stumbles upon the stark white facade of the **Eastern & Oriental Hotel**, established in the late 19th century. It reopened in 2001 after renovation, and it once again looks set to stake its claim as one of Asia's grand hotels.

Jalan Penang (better known as Penang Road) is the main shopping bazaar, and it ends in the towering air-conditioned KOMTAR shopping complex at the top of a bus station, which also houses a tourist information centre and a Malaysia Airlines office. Take a ride up its probing circular tower for a bird's eye view of the city.

Take a walk through **Pasar Chowrasta** (Chowrasta Market), between Lebuh Campbell and Jalan Chowrasta. A wet market with the customary wet market pong, it has a section facing Penang Road that offers the Penang specialities of local biscuits and preserved nutmeg and mango prepared in a wide variety of styles. On Jalan Chowrasta is the row of *nasi kandar* (mixed curry rice) stalls whose food is reputed to be the best in the country.

Typical Malaysian institutions are the *pasar minggu* or *pasar malam*, the weekly market or night market. These are temporary markets that spring up in the street or an open space in the evenings or on the weekends. In Penang, they are called *pasar malam* and move from location to location every two weeks. The areas, wherever they might be, are well lit, and the bargains range from tiny trinkets to cheap Kelantan batik sarongs and plastic sandals and slippers. People-watching is especially enjoyable here.

Chinese heritage

Many of the Chinese immigrants arriving in Malaysia a hundred years ago fell under the "protection" and control of one of the clan associations, whose functions were not unlike those of medieval European guilds. The ancestral halls of these clan associations – such as the Khoo, Ong, Tan and Chung – are called *kongsi* and are scattered all over town. The most impressive is the clan hall built by the Khoo Kongsi. The **Khoo Kongsi** (daily 9am–5pm) stands at the junction of Jalan Masjid Kapitan Keling and Lebuh Acheh. Designed to capture the splendour of an imperial palace, it has a seven-tiered pavilion, "dragon" pillars and hand-painted walls engraved with the Khoo rose emblem. The original design was so ambitious that conservative Khoo clansmen cautioned against it, lest the emperor of China be offended. After eight years, the building was completed in 1902; but on the first night after it was finished, the roof mysteriously caught fire. Clan members interpreted this as a sign that even the deities considered the Khoo Kongsi too palatial for a clan house and rebuilt it on a more modest scale. A recent 15-month renovation process costing RM3 million and painstakingly put together by 16 Chinese artisans using traditional Chinese materials has restored the house to its former splendour.

Of all the Chinese temples, Penang's oldest is the **Kuan Yin Temple** in Lebuh Pitt, which is also the most humble and the most crowded. A Buddhist deity who refused to enter Nirvana as long as there was injustice on earth, Kuan Yin (Quanyin) typically personifies mercy, and is one of the most popular deities in the traditional Chinese pantheon of gods and goddesses. Set nearby, in direct contrast, is the Moorish **Kapitan Keling Mosque**, built in 1800 and the state's oldest mosque. The variety of Buddhist worship in Penang is so striking as to

Map on page 184

BELOW: Wat Chaya-mangkalaram.

Map
on page
184

TIP

The Penang Bird Park is a lush garden with over 200 species of tropical birds from around the world, housed in a huge walk-in aviary and geodesic domes.

RIGHT: Penang Bridge. **BELOW:** Kek Lok Si, the Temple of Paradise.

make sightseeing a new experience in every temple. One can enter the gigantic meditation hall at **Wat Chayamangkalaram** and find a workman polishing the left cheek of the 32-metre-long (100-ft) Reclining Buddha, the third-largest statue of its kind in the world.

High above the bustle of Georgetown on a hilltop at **Ayer Hita**, a few kilometres from downtown, looms the **Kek Lok Si** or Temple of Paradise. This temple is one of the largest Buddhist temples in Malaysia and one of the largest to be found in the region.

After nearly 200 years, the freshwater springs in the hills above Georgetown continue to lure visitors from the lowlands. Although labelled as **Waterfall Gardens**, situated about 3 km (2 miles) due northeast from Penang Hill, many locals refer to it as the **Botanical Gardens**, in the grounds of which grow some of Malaysia's most beautiful tropical plants.

Batu Maung, a fishing village on the southeast tip of the island about 3 km from the Bayan Lepas Airport, houses a shrine marking the sacred footprint of Zheng Ho, a eunuch of the ancient Chinese imperial court and admiral of an immense fleet of ships that explored not only Asia, but all the way to the east coast of Africa. On Pulau Langkawi, 100 km (60 miles) to the north, is a similar footprint said to belong to the admiral. The two are believed to be a pair and anyone who lights joss sticks and places them in the urns beside the footprint will have good luck and great fortune.

To the north

The road skirts around the southern end of the island and turns north. The scenery changes from flat rice land to rolling hills. Here, spice plantations of pepper, clove and nutmeg lured Arab, Spanish, Portuguese and other Western traders to this part of the world long ago. At **Titi Kerawang**, there are waterfalls and a serene view of the Indian Ocean.

Although the waters are not as clear as on the eastern coast of the Malay peninsula, the beaches of Penang are still quite seductive.

On the island's north shore, luxury hotels cluster around the beach at **Batu Ferringhi**. Activities include the typical resort sailing, horseback riding, hiking or just sprawling about smartly on stretches of white sand. Off the beach are the usual assortment of restaurants and galleries.

Also on the north coast is **Teluk Bahang**, a fine beach. Nearby is the **Pinang Cultural Centre**, which features arts and crafts, music and dance, and traditional architecture from all around Malaysia. Besides an exhibition gallery and theatre restaurant, the complex also sports a Malay *kampung* and Dayak longhouse imported from Sarawak. Further along the same road is the **Penang Butterfly Farm** (daily 9am–5pm), where some of the loveliest butterflies and most awesome insects of Malaysia are bred and displayed. A couple of minutes down the road is a 100-hectare (250-acre) **Forest Recreation Park** for trekking and picnicking. To get a taste of the "real" jungle, head for **Bukit Mertajam Recreational Park**, approximately 18 km (11 miles) from the mainland. ❏

SABAH AND SARAWAK

These sprawling states have hit the world's headlines because of their severe ecological problems. The problems remain, but so do fascinating remnants of ancient cultures

Map on page 212

S abah and Sarawak, two Malaysian states not on the main peninsula, cover the northwestern coast and northern tip of the world's third-largest island, commonly known as Borneo. Malaysia shares Borneo with Indonesia, whose part of the island is called Kalimantan. Together, Sabah and Sarawak bridge 1,000 km (600 miles) of sea to join the Malay peninsula as a federated nation. Although their population accounts for just 15 percent of the country's 21 million people, the land area is larger than the other 11 states combined.

Long a sanctuary of rain forest, unique fauna, and indigenous tribes of people, Borneo's ecosystems have suffered considerably in the past decade, first with extensive logging – much of it going to Japan as chopsticks and plywood – that denuded thousands of hectares, and in the late 1990s by extensive and highly destructive fires that burned out of control for months at a time. These fires, more often than not on the Indonesian side and lit by farmers seeking to clear land, clouded the air of Southeast Asia.

Sabah: Kota Kinabalu

The capital of Sabah, **Kota Kinabalu ❶**, is a sprawling, relaxed town on the west coast of the state. Within the past decade, the town has mushroomed with some of the most striking buildings in all Malaysia, as befits the capital of one of Malaysia's fastest-growing states, making the city a blend of ultramodern structures and old Chinese shophouses. Amongst the most impressive of these buildings, to the north of the city at the end of Likas Bay, is the gleaming tower of the Sabah Foundation, an institution created out of the timber royalties of the state. The monumental **Sabah Mosque** is also worth a visit to see its fine contemporary Islamic architecture. Nearby is the **Sabah Museum** (Mon–Thurs 10am–6pm; Sat–Sun 9am–6pm), built in the longhouse style of the Rungus and Murut tribes. The museum has a wealth of historical and tribal treasures, as well as a good section on Sabah's fascinating flora and fauna. One of the museum's most striking exhibits is a collection of 10 life-size traditional houses set in the museum gardens, each depicting the architecture of a different ethnic group. The complex also has a science centre with an exhibition on the oil and petroleum industry, and an art gallery.

South of town, off the road leading to the airport, is the famous beach at **Tanjung Aru**. The sea here is clear, the sand is clean and the coastal food stalls and restaurants offer delicious local seafood. Offshore is the **Tunku Abdul Rahman Park**, one of the most picturesque marine reserves in Southeast Asia. The park headquarters is on **Pulau Gaya**, the largest and most historically significant of the islands.

OPPOSITE: Mount Kinabalu. **BELOW:** atop Low's Peak.

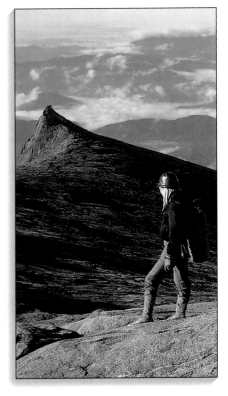

Sipadan's marine wealth makes it a coveted destination for divers.

Beyond Kota Kinabalu

Everyone in Malaysia knows about the mysterious **Gunung Kinabalu ❷**, Southeast Asia's highest peak at 4,101 metres (13,455 ft). To get to the top, one does not need to spend days cutting through tropical rain forest before reaching the granite slopes, unlike the first ascent of the mountain. Well-laid trails with steps and rails made of wood help today's climber ascend and descend the mountain in just two days. Accommodation is available both at the park headquarters and on the mountain slopes. Besides the mountain, **Kinabalu National Park** contains a treasure of other natural features, including a unique rain forest, a myriad of bird species, and Poring Hot Springs, which is found on the eastern side of the mountain.

Semporna is best known as the departure point for **Pulau Sipadan ❸**, Malaysia's only true oceanic island rising up 600 metres (2,000 ft) from the seabed. The marine life of Sipadan has been hailed by both Worldwide Fund for Nature and late Jacques Cousteau as among the best in the world. A local company, Borneo Divers, began building simple huts to accommodate scuba divers in 1990, and many other operators have since followed suit. Efforts are being made to protect the reefs and island, as over-exploitation of this tiny island could threaten its near-pristine condition.

In **Sandakan ❹**, in the heyday of the boom town of northeastern Sabah, people called the logs bobbing in the Sulu Sea "floating money". Logs floated down the Segama River from timber forests into the hands of Chinese entrepreneurs, who shipped them via freighter to Japan. So prosperous was Sandakan that at one time many investors thought the town would become another Hong Kong, but the speed of the region's deforestation has shattered that dream.

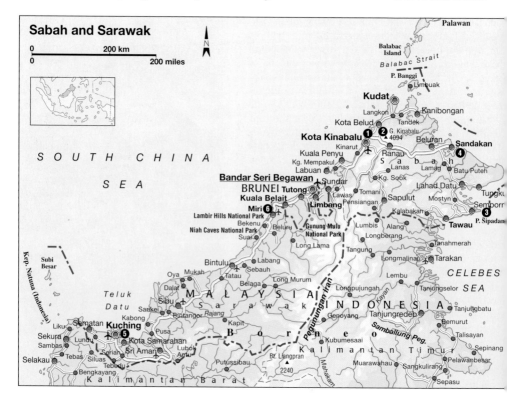

Sandakan's main source of tourist fame is the **Sepilok Orangutan Rehabilitation Centre** (daily 8am–4.30pm, feeding time 10am and 3pm), a 20-minute drive westward from town. The centre helps orang-utans who have lived in captivity or been orphaned to adjust gradually for a return to the wild.

Pulau Selingan is the largest of three islands within the confines of **Turtle Islands National Park**, off the coast of Sandakan. The other two islands within the national park are Pulau Bakingan and Pulau Gulisan. Green and hawksbill turtles come here to lay eggs nearly every night of the year, but the best time to watch is between July and September.

Another excursion that can be undertaken from Sandakan is a cruise up the Kinabatangan River. After crossing Sandakan Bay, the first stage of the journey is dominated by mangrove swamps and twisting waterways. The Kinabatangan and its tributaries are famed as the home of the long-nosed, pot-bellied proboscis monkey, and wild elephants can also be seen here.

Sarawak

The name of Sarawak still evokes romance rather than reality. White Rajahs and Borneo headhunters ring more nostalgic bells than 125,000 sq. km (48,000 sq. miles) of hills, jungle and swampland located just north of the equator. The days of the reign of the White Rajahs and head-hunting have now passed, it can be noted with certainty. Sarawak became a member of the Federation of Malaysia in 1963, and traces of colonialism soon began to disappear.

With colonialism's end, some of the old serenity went, too, accelerated by the advent of the oil industry, Kuala Lumpur's interest in developing the state, and in the logging disputes of recent decades.

Map on page 212

BELOW: Sarawak River, and traditional design.

Sarawak's national parks are home to some of the rarest orchid species in the world.

RIGHT: the Pinnacles of Gunung Mulu National Park.
BELOW: Kuching waterfront.

Sarawak's capital city, **Kuching ❺**, is suffused with memories, especially the many colonial buildings that have withstood the march of 20th-century progress. Charles Brooke's Astana, built in 1870 for the newly married rajah, still stands, although it has undergone several renovations since. Kuching's courthouse is a rather plain colonial building; Brooke obviously had functionalism in mind here. Built in 1874, the building later was joined by a clock tower in 1883. The Charles Brooke Memorial stands facing the courthouse, erected in 1924. The General Post Office, with its Corinthian columns, is more decorative and was built in 1931. An imaginative building is the Square Tower, built in 1879, the same year as the fort.

The most enthralling building is the marvellous **Sarawak Museum** (daily 9am–6pm), set in lush grounds between Jalan McDougall and Jalan Tun Haji Openg. Naturalist and co-founder of the theory of evolution along with Charles Darwin, Alfred Russell Wallace spent many years in Borneo and became a particular friend of Rajah Charles Brooke. With Wallace's encouragement, Brooke built the museum to house a permanent exhibition of native arts and crafts, as well as specimens from Wallace's extensive collection, many of which Wallace shot and preserved himself while exploring the jungle.

Where to relax

Outside of the urban pull, sun worshippers, beach lovers and golfers head for **Damai Beach**, near Santubong, just 30 minutes by road from downtown Kuching. The fishing village of **Santubong** is also worth a visit. For those interested in history, the village dates back to the Tang and Song dynasties of ancient China, between the 9th and 13th centuries when it was an important trading centre. Ancient rock carvings of Hindu and Buddhist influence have been discovered around the river delta here. Nearby is the state's popular tourist attraction, the **Sarawak Cultural Village** (daily 9am–5.30pm), which spreads across 6 hectares (15 acres) of jungle at the foot of Santubong Mountain.

In **Miri ❻**, northward and near the Brunei border, there are a couple of side-trips that attract many to Sarawak. The **Lambir Hills National Park**, just south of Miri, makes a pleasant excursion. The park's highlights are waterfalls with natural swimming pools and a climb up Bukit Lambir. Much more famous, and perhaps with more to offer, is **Niah Caves National Park**.

The limestone caves of Niah and their past inhabitants are the attraction. It was not until the 1950s that the Sarawak Museum learned of the caves as an archaeologist's gold mine. Haematite paintings, featuring stick figures with strange little boat-like objects along with other discoveries, revealed that people once living here worked with instruments made from bone and shell, made pottery, cut stone adzes, and carved wooden coffins and burial boats. To many, these discoveries were as significant as the unearthing of Java Man.

Twenty minutes by plane from Miri is **Gunung Mulu National Park**, an inland expanse of diverse terrain, including the spectacular Pinnacles. Accommodation ranges from simple lodges to a deluxe resort, not to mention longhouse stays. ❑

Map on page 212

BRUNEI

*A tiny Islamic sultanate on Borneo, Brunei is one of the
world's smallest countries and one of its wealthiest*

The Sultanate of Brunei, officially known as Negara Brunei
Darussalam (in Malay, "Abode of Peace"), is the only country to remain a sovereign entity in the Malay archipelago
throughout its contemporary history. Historically, Brunei endured
takeover attempts by more powerful sultanates, kept Spanish *con-
quistadores* and the Dutch East India Company at bay, resisted the
territorial ambitions of the White Rajahs of Sarawak, and quelled
an attempt in the 1960s to merge the tiny country into a much
larger Malaysia.

Today, Brunei is a bit of an anachronism – one of the few
nations in the world ruled by an absolute monarch, Sultan Haji
Hassanal Bolkiah Mu'izzaddin Waddaulah, the 29th ruler in a
long-surviving dynasty and perhaps the world's richest man. He
is also the country's prime minister and defence minister.

Oil money has transformed once sleepy Brunei into a thriving
modern nation. The population of about 336,000 enjoys a per
capita income of over US$17,000 a year, one of the highest in
the region. The gross domestic product exceeds US$5.5 billion
per year. The government has no foreign debt; treasury reserves
are said to be more than US$15 billion.

Bruneians have all benefited from their oil wealth. Nearly a
quarter of the government budget is spent on education and social
services, and Brunei has more than 95 percent literacy among
its young people. Many tropical diseases have been completely
eliminated. Life expectancy is high and infant mortality is low.

The population is about 62 percent Malay, 15 percent Chinese
and the remainder comprises various indigenous Dayak people
and Europeans. Islam is the official religion and the creed of two-
thirds of the people, but there are also sizeable communities of
Buddhists and Christians.

Geographically one of the world's smallest nations, Brunei has
just 5,770 sq. km (2,228 sq. miles) of land – about twice the size
of Luxembourg or the American state of Rhode Island. It is
bounded on the north by the South China Sea and on three sides
by the Malaysian state of Sarawak, which actually divides Brunei
into two parts. Over 70 percent of Brunei is still forested by
primary jungle that has never been logged.

Unique as it is, Brunei is a mixture of modern and ancient
influences, and at the same time it is a model of careful and well
managed development. ❏

BANDAR SERI BEGAWAN AND BEYOND

Islam and oil money are the two factors that demarcate this compact nation on Borneo, with few travellers making their way to Brunei

With only 60,000 people, Bandar Seri Begawan feels more like a small town than a capital city. It takes no more than 15 minutes to walk from one side of the central city to the other, even if people prefer their cars to walking. Oil money has transformed B.S.B. (as it is commonly known) into a modern if exceedingly compact city of skyscrapers and shopping malls and filling stations.

The **Sultan Omar Ali Saifuddien Mosque** dominates the downtown skyline. Built in 1958, its Arabic architecture features numerous arches, towers, columns, onion domes and minarets. The great golden dome rises to a height of 50 metres (170 ft), towering above the adjoining lagoon with a replica of a 16th-century royal barge. It is open daily except Thursdays.

Northwest of the mosque, obscured by modern apartment buildings, is the old **Istana Darussalam**. This green wooden structure, a classic example of local architecture, was the royal palace of Brunei until the 1960s.

At the junction of Jalan Stoney and Jalan Sultan is the **Royal Regalia Building**, which replaced the former Churchill Museum in 1992. On view inside are

BELOW: Istana Nurul Iman, the sultan's official residence.

the royal chariot, bejeweled crowns and ceremonial armoury. A gallery documents the constitutional history of the nation. The **Brunei Historical Centre** and the Dato Ibrahim Library, a research facility for Southeast Asian studies, are right next door.

Map
on page
223

Across the road is the **Lapau** (Royal Ceremonial Hall), which is used for important state occasions presided over by the sultan on his golden throne. Through the garden is the **Dewan Majlis** (Parliament House).

Nearby, at the intersection of Jalan Sungai Kianggeh and Jalan Elizabeth II, is a Daoist temple where Chinese Bruneian worship. Opposite is the *tamu* or open market, where one can watch boats off-loading coconuts, bananas, pineapples and other tropical produce, or else wander among the stalls, which are open from dawn to dusk. The night market is located in the carpark opposite.

Along a two-block stretch of Jalan Sultan that runs up from the waterfront are banks, embassies, airline offices, travel agents and luxury-good shops. Opposite Teck Guan Plaza, a kiosk sells tickets for high-speed ferries to Labuan, Lawas and Limbang in nearby East Malaysia. Money-changers and an open-air market are found in front of the municipal pier, the best jumping-off point for exploring the river. From the roof of the multi-storey car park on Jalan Cator there's a fine (and free) view over the city, the Brunei River and the vast water-village. On Jalan MacArthur near the waterfront is the Yayasan Sultan Haji Hassanal Bolkiah, the largest one-stop commercial and shopping centre in B.S.B.

Kampong Ayer, a riverine community built on stilts above the Brunei River, dates from the 15th century. It is home to 30,000 people – half the population of B.S.B. Yet don't think life in this village is not modern simply because it's built over water. There are mosques and schools, cafes and grocery

Although it's now one of the world's smallest nations, Brunei's rule during the 16th century extended over a vast area, including most of the northwest coast of Borneo and many southern Philippine islands.

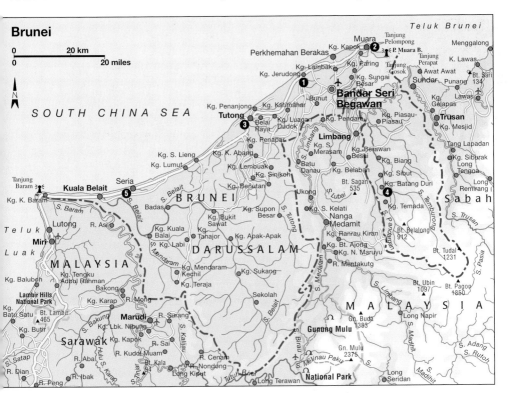

The Malay Muslim Monarchy

L ittle is known about the early history of Brunei, but recent archeological finds have determined that local inhabitants engaged in trade with China and other parts of mainland Asia as early as the 6th and 7th centuries AD.

During the 10th century, the area that is now Brunei was a Buddhist kingdom, part of the Srivijaya Empire of Sumatra. Later it became part of the Hindu Majapahit Empire of Java. By the 14th century, Brunei was a powerful seafaring state with a sultan based on Kota Batu on the Brunei River. Sharif Ali, a descendant of the Prophet Mohammed, came to Brunei at the start of the 15th century. Soon the sultan and most of his subjects converted to Islam, the foundation of a strong religious and cultural tradition that has endured to this day.

The remnants of Ferdinand Magellan's

fleet weighed anchor in Brunei in 1521 as the first Europeans to visit the sultanate. In the century that followed, other Spanish and Portuguese mariners explored the coast of Borneo. The Spanish made an attempt to conquer the sultanate, but instead had to settle upon dominance over the Philippines, including lands once ruled by Brunei.

Brunei's first permanent contact with Europe came at the end of the 16th century, when a trading relationship was established with the Dutch East India Company. Somehow, Brunei remained independent while Indonesia was absorbed into the Dutch colonial empire. The sultanate remained a power to be reckoned with until the arrival of the British in the 19th century.

Although James Brooke became Rajah of Sarawak as a result of helping the Sultan of Brunei, Brooke spent much of his energy chipping away at the power of the sultanate. Brooke's political manoeuvring and superior firepower forced the sultan into ceding large tracts of Brunei.

In order to preserve his nation from being completely swallowed up by Sarawak, the sultan asked for and received protection from Britain in 1888. The first British resident arrived in 1906 in order to advise the sultan on all matters except those pertaining to customs and religion.

The history of Brunei took a sudden and dramatic turn for the better in 1929 with the discovery of oil at Seria. Thirty years later, the nation achieved full internal self-rule, although Britain continued to administer its foreign affairs and defence. The first off-shore oil deposits were found in 1963.

Despite intense pressure, Brunei refused to become part of the Federation of Malaysia. Sultan Sir Omar Ali Saifuddin – the father of the present ruler – chose to keep Brunei under direct British protection. Sultan Omar abdicated in 1967 in favour of his 21-year-old eldest son, the Sandhurst-educated Prince Muda Hassanal Bolkiah, who became the 29th and current Sultan of Brunei.

In 1979, the sultan signed a treaty with Britain that set forth a five-year timetable for full independence. On 1 January 1984, the sultanate became the sovereign and independent nation of Brunei Darussalam. That same year it joined the UN. ❑

stores, police posts and fire stations, and even garages and gas stations that cater to boats. The water-villagers park their cars on land and get about in water-taxis.

Map on page 223

The portion of Kampong Ayer around the golden mosque and across Kedayan Creek is easily explored on foot along rickety wooden walkways and bridges. But to see the full extent of the water-village, take the river cruise.

The modern **Supreme Court** building sits next to the water as you cross the bridge, while on the right is a hill with an ancient Muslim cemetery and the modern RIPAS Hospital, reputedly the best in Borneo. In the same area is Brunei's largest mosque, the **Jame' Asr Hassanal Bolkiah**, known also as the Klarong Mosque. It has landscaped gardens, golden domes, and fountains. It was built to commemorate the sultan's 25th year of reign.

Continuing on, you come to the capital's wet market in Gadong, where housewives buy their seafood, meat, fruits and vegetables. A fast-growing district, Gadong has become a busy and popular office and shopping district with restaurants and department stores.

The impressive 1,788-room **Istana Nurul Iman**, home of the Sultan, is at Jalan Tutong. During the annual Hari Raya Aidilfitri festivities, the main doors are open to the public. Visitors are ushered in and feted with a buffet meal before meeting the royal family members. At other times, view the world's largest residential palace from the riverbank park, **Taman Persiaran Damuan**, with jogging paths, a playground, outdoor sculptures and foodstalls at night.

At the **Brunei Arts and Handicrafts Training Centre** in Jalan Residency, young artisans make silverware, brassware, baskets and brocade. Two specialties are toy cannons and *keris* knives. Nearby is the Ministry of Foreign Affairs.

The Sultan of Brunei is often said to be the world's richest man. But Bruneians generally have benefited from the oil boom: average incomes are the among the highest in Southeast Asia.

OPPOSITE: James Brooke. **BELOW:** water taxis.

Map on page 223

Brunei is the most Islamic country in Southeast Asia. In 1991, the sale of alcohol was banned and stricter dress codes have since been introduced.

RIGHT: Omar Ali Saifuddin Mosque. **BELOW:** Chinese temple.

Five km (3 miles) east of B.S.B is **Kota Batu**, where the superb **Brunei Museum** has exhibits of natural history, native customs and dress, and the oil industry in Brunei. Its Islamic gallery has a collection of illuminated Korans, pottery, weapons, carpets, brass and glass from the sultan's private collection.

Down the hill, the **Malay Technology Museum** galleries show the traditional crafts and technology of the land-dwelling Malays, water-village people, and the Dayak tribes of the interior. The adjacent Archaeology Park has the remains of Kota Batu, the old capital of Brunei, and the tomb of Sultan Bolkiah, the "Singing Admiral" who extended his realm into the southern Philippines during Brunei's golden age.

Another palace, Istana Nurul Izzah, is located in **Jerudong ❶**, about 25 km (15 miles) from B.S.B. This town has a polo field and club, royal stables, sports facilities and mini-palaces. Its chief lure is **Jerudong Park Playground**, a public amusement garden with free roller coaster and other fun rides. Nearby, the Jerudong Resort Hotel faces the South China Sea.

Fifteen minutes by car from B.S.B., via Jalan Berakas, is the site of the National Stadium and International Conventional Centre.

Beyond B.S.B.

Brunei has fine, unspoiled beaches along the northern coast. **Muara Beach ❷**, 27 km (17 miles) northeast of the capital, is near the main port where freighters and cruise liners dock. **Meragang** or Crocodile Beach is on the coastal road 7 km (4 miles) from Muara. **Serasa Beach**, about 10 minutes from Muara, has a watersports complex. **Pantai Seri Kenangan Beach**, 50 km (30 miles) west of the city near **Tutong ❸**, has the open ocean on one side and a lagoon on the other. **Tasek Merimbun**, Brunei's largest lake, is over an hour's drive from B.S.B., in Tutong district.

The Brunei government actively promotes ecotourism. Tour agencies organise trips to **Pulau Selirong**, a 2,570-hectare (6,350-acre) island some 45 minutes from Muara, with a 2-km wooden walkway and nature observation tower. The mangrove islands at the mouth of the Brunei River harbour the rare proboscis monkey, crocodiles and birds.

Across Brunei Bay is Temburong District's main town, **Bangar**, a jumping-off point for visiting Iban and Murut longhouses. The park at **Batang Duri ❹**, about 16 km (10 miles) away, offers walks and swimming. Within the **Batu Apoi Forest Reserve**, the Field Studies Centre near Kuala Belalong specialises in research on lowland tropical forest, while the 50,000-hectare (120,000-acre) **Ulu Temburong National Park** has a walkway through the forest canopy for examining tree-top life. It also offers Brunei's highest peak, Bukit Pagon, rising to 1,800 metres (5,900 ft).

The Seria oils fields, 90 km (50 miles) from B.S.B., is where the original Shell well that struck the first oil was drilled, in 1929. This oil strike ignited Brunei's economic growth for the next half century. Near **Seria ❺**, on the road leading out to Labi, is **Sungei Liang Forest Park**, a small jungle reserve offering nature trails, along with excellent facilities for picnics and recreation. ❑

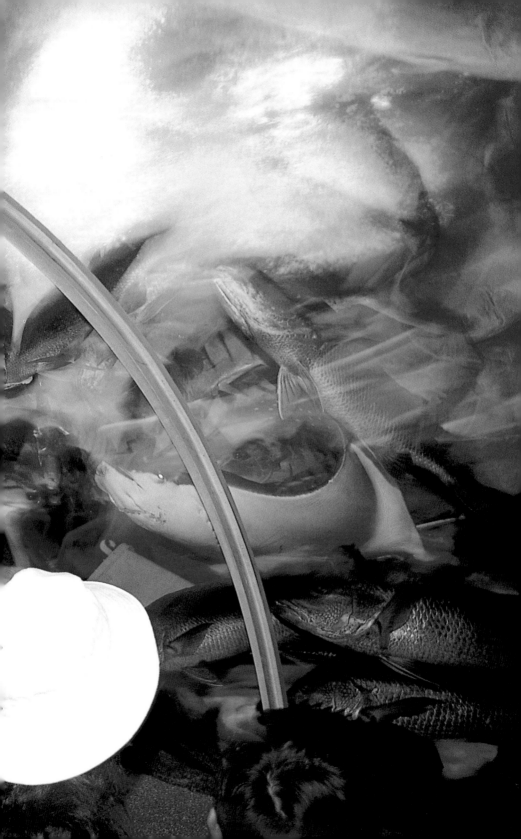

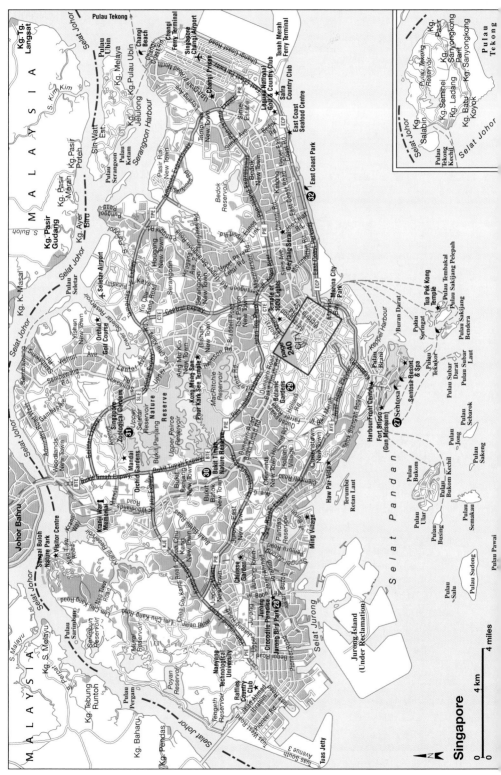

Singapore

SINGAPORE

The island's small size has allowed the government to manage

Singapore as one might operate a modern corporation

Minutes after landing at the stunningly efficient Changi Airport, the visitor is whisked down a wide highway lined with glorious tropical palms and bright bougainvillaea, and mile after mile of housing blocks, with probably the highest rate of home ownership in the world. Offshore, ships from all over the globe wait their turn in the world's busiest container port.

On a map of nearly any scale, the island of Singapore is just a dot at the tip of the Malay Peninsula. Despite well founded fears for its survival as an independent entity, the tiny 682 sq-km (263 sq-mile) island has blossomed into one of Asia's most successful economies. Its success has gone far beyond what Sir Stamford Raffles, its founder, envisioned when he bought the island from its Malay ruler in 1819 and set up as a trading post. From a sleepy Malay village, Singapore grew rapidly, drawing immigrants from China, India, Europe and neighbouring Malaya and Indonesia.

After independence from the British crown in 1965, the driving force behind Singapore's success was Lee Kuan Yew, who as Prime Minister (until 1990) led Singaporeans into a high-tech awakening and the second-highest standard of living in Asia, after Japan. Massive public housing projects and the establishment of educational facilities were initial priorities. Economic stability achieved through cooperation between unions and employers and an efficient infrastructure made Singapore attractive to multinationals. Indeed, some compare Singapore's style of governing to that of a corporation.

Singapore's population of 4.1 million is comprised of over 77 percent Chinese, 14 percent Malays, 7 percent Indians, and 1 percent other ethnic groups, including a sizeable number of expat employees of multinational corporations. In deference to the original settlers, Malay is the national language, but the *lingua franca* is English. Nearly every Singaporean is bilingual. English, Chinese, Malay and Tamil are official languages.

Asian and Western culture and values meet and mix in this cosmopolitan city. But Confucian precepts still temper ideals of personal freedom. Society and public discourse are kept on a tight rein, with fines for jaywalking, littering and other social misdemeanours. The result, however, is an uncommonly clean and efficient city, with probably the cleanest streets outside Switzerland. ❏

PRECEDING PAGES: walk-through aquarium at Sentosa; CBD skyline overlooking Singapore River.

Decisive Dates

The early years

2nd century AD: Sabara, a trading emporium, is identified in Ptolemy's *Geographic Huphegesis* as being at the southern tip of the "Golden Chersonese", possibly Singapore.

3rd century: Chinese said to have given the name Pa-luo-chung to the island.

1200s: Settlement called Tamasek reported on Singapore Island.

1300s: A settlement called Singapura is formed by Sultan Iskander Shah.

1330: Small settlement discovered by Chinese explorer and named Pancur. Singapore was probably founded around the middle of the 13th century by the Javanese Srivijayan empire.

14–18th centuries: Siam (modern-day Thailand), followed by Java's Majapahit empire, seizes the small island but shows little practical interest in it. At the beginning of the 16th century, the Portuguese capture Malacca, to the north, then an important centre in east–west trade. In the 17th century, the island of Singapore is settled by about 100 Orang Lauts, or sea nomads. At the end of the 18th century, the British and the British East India Company open a trading post in Penang and take Malacca from the Dutch, who dominate the region at the time.

British colonial rule

1819: Sir Thomas Stamford Raffles arrives in Singapore. His conviction is that the island, located at the crossroads of the South China Sea, will one day become important. The main items of trade are tea and silk from China, timber from Malaya, and spices from Indonesia.

1822: Raffles arrives from Bencoolen in October, declares principle of free trade in November.

1823: Raffles issues regulations outlawing gambling and slavery. Raffles leaves Singapore in June.

1824: The British agree to withdraw from Indonesia, in return for which the Dutch recognise British rights over Singapore. The Sultan cedes Singapore in perpetuity to the British.

1826: The trading stations at Penang, Malacca and Singapore are named the Straits Settlements, under the control of British India.

1839: First ship built in Singapore is launched.

1846: Chinese Funeral riots. First major secret society trouble in Singapore begins.

1851: Straits Settlements placed directly under the rule of the Governor-General of India.

1867: Straits Settlements become a Crown Colony, controlled by the Colonial Office in London.

late 1800s: The Suez Canal opens and the number of ships calling in at Singapore increases. Trade flourishes. John Ridley, director of the Botanical Gardens in Singapore, succeeds in growing a rubber tree. The Malaysian peninsula and Singapore develop into the world's main rubber producers.

World wars

1911: Population of Singapore grows to 250,000 and the census records 48 races on the island, speaking 54 languages.

1920s: The Great Depression's reverberations are felt in Singapore as the prices of commodities such as rubber collapse. But Singapore, even in its relative poverty, is secure – it is the greatest naval base of the British empire east of Suez.

1923: Singapore is linked to Malaysia by a causeway.

1941: Japan invades Malaysia, landing at Kota Bahru. Singapore is bombed on 8 December.

1942: British troops on Singapore surrender to Japan, whose troops surprise the British by coming down the Malay peninsula on bicycles. The Japanese rename Singapore as *Syonan*, "Light of the South". Under their occupation many civilians, particularly the Chinese, are killed or suffer unspeakable hardships.

1945: The Japanese three-and-a-half years' rule ends in August, with the landing of the Allied troops. The British make Singapore a Crown Colony.

Independence and federation

1948: The British allow a limited form of elections to the legislative council. A bill proscribing Pan-Malaya Federation of the Trade Unions is introduced in Malaysia. Emergency declared in June. Malayan Democratic Union dissolved.

1950: Lee Kuan Yew addresses Malayan Forum in London in January. Lee Kuan Yew and Goh Keng Swee return to Singapore in August.

1951: Legislative Council Election. Singapore formally proclaimed a city with a royal charter.

1955: Rendel Commission granted by the British leads to elections and David Marshall becomes chief minister. A legislative council consisting of 32 members, 25 of whom are elected, is established. The Labour Front have a majority, but the PAP (People's Action Party) forms a powerful opposition.

1956: PAP Central Executive Committee election in which Communists decline to run occurs in July. Chinese student riots; leftist PAP leaders are arrested.

1958: A constitutional agreement for partial independence for Singapore is finally signed in London.

1959: PAP wins general election with 43 of 51 seats, and 53 percent of the popular vote. Lee Kuan Yew becomes the country's first Prime Minister and Singapore is declared a state.

1962: Commission on colonialism rejects criticism of referendum.

1963: Malaysia agreement signed in London. The people of Malaya, Sarawak, North Borneo (now Sabah) and Singapore vote to form the Federation of Malaysia. Malaysia forms with Singapore as a component. PAP wins Singapore general election.

1964: PAP wins only one seat in Malaysian general election. Communal riots.

The Republic of Singapore

1965: PAP wins Hong Lim constituency's by-election. Singapore leaves the Federation of Malaysia and becomes an independent sovereign nation. of is made the 117th member of the United Nations and is admitted to the Commonwealth.

1966: Bukit Merah constituency by-election won by PAP against an independent. Chua Chu Kang, Crawford and Paya Lebar constituencies by-elections won by PAP uncontested.

1967: Singapore, Malaysia, Thailand, Indonesia, the Philippines and Brunei form a political and economic union known as ASEAN, the Association of Southeast Asian Nations.

LEFT: Sir Thomas Stamford Raffles.
RIGHT: former Prime Minister Lee Kuan Yew.

1968: PAP sweeps first Parliamentary general election, winning all 58 seats.

1970–89: The PAP continues to dominate parliament, but at the start of the 1980s, Lee Kuan Yew's party has to live with an opposition party.

1971: British Far East Command ceases.

1972: PAP wins all seats in general election.

1974: Combined Japanese Red Army and Popular Front for the Liberation of Palestine terrorists attack Shell Oil refinery at Pulau Bukom and take hostages.

1981: In a by-election, J.B. Jeyaratnam of the Workers' Party wins the first seat to be held by a member of an opposition party.

1984: PAP loses two of 79 seats in general election, its

first loss of a seat in a general election since 1964.

1990: Lee Kuan Yew steps aside as Prime Minister, and is replaced by Goh Chok Tong.

1995: Singapore ranks second in *World Competitive Report 1995;* remains high in subsequent years.

1996: As a result of a decision by the OECD, Singapore is no longer regarded as a "developing nation".

1999: The economy makes a dramatic recovery after the 1997 Asian crisis. S.R. Nathan is elected President.

2001: PAP wins 75 percent of the votes in the general elections. The economy takes a tumble in the face of the US and global economic slowdown.

2002: The economy continues to be plagued. An Al-Qaeda-linked terrorist plot to bomb the US embassy is uncovered. ❑

THE SINGAPOREANS

The island is a proverbial melting pot of cultures, and it is this diversity that gives the famously structured city-state its distinctive character

Today, the Chinese make up nearly 77 percent of the total population in Singapore. For centuries, Chinese junks roamed the neighbouring seas. A Buddhist pilgrim named Fa-Hsien passed through the Straits of Malacca from Ceylon in AD 414. A trader called Wang Ta-Yuan later visited in 1349 when Singapore was a swampy outpost named Temasek. He reported finding Chinese in residence in the area even then.

When Sir Stamford Raffles hoisted a Union Jack ashore and founded modern Singapore in 1819, Chinese planters, pirates, fishermen and traders were already installed. Five years after the colony was established, Singapore had 3,000 Chinese and more were arriving weekly.

The Straits Chinese began settling in the Malay Peninsula and Riau islands more than 400 years ago in order to take advantage of the rich trade along the Straits of Malacca. Straits Chinese culture is often called by a different name, Peranakan, and the people themselves are sometimes called Babas and Nonyas.

After centuries of melding, a hybrid Straits Chinese culture developed with its own distinct language, architecture, cuisine and clothing. Their *lingua franca* is Malay, but an idiosyncratic version of Malay. Peranakan food is unique in its lavish use of spices and shrimp paste for cooking and can be readily found all over the island.

Shortly after Singapore was founded, junks started bringing waves of immigrants from coastal areas of southern and eastern China. Some of the largest groups comprised Hokkien Chinese from southern Fujian province. These hardy Chinese were usually traders and businessmen, largely the roots of today's Hokkien population that account for two-fifths of the Chinese in Singapore. They are still mainly merchants and office workers. Other Chinese came in numbers, speaking distinct dialects,

cooking different foods and engaged in other work. The Chinese had fled from mainland China and the despotic Manchu dynasty. They took on the back-breaking jobs that no one else wanted to do.

Today's Singapore has a curious mixture of the new and old Chinese, broadly labelled

"English-educated" or "Chinese-educated". The latter tend more towards Chinese chauvinism and strong links to their heritage, responding more slowly to the new Singaporean identity. They sometimes look upon English-educated Chinese with shades of the contempt that their great ancestors held for barbarians not of the Middle Kingdom. The English-educated frequently perceive them, in return, as being conservative and unprogressive.

The Malays

Malays were here first, centuries before the Chinese, and today they make up 14 percent of Singapore's population. Malays, caught in the

LEFT: Singapore's children reflect Indian, Chinese, Malay and European heritage. **RIGHT:** Muslim women wear a head shawl when praying.

middle of a society driven by profit, are still Malays. And they are still at the heart of the island they sold to the British.

For all its Chinese influence, Singapore sings its national anthem in Malay. *Satay*, skewered pieces of grilled meat, is as much a symbol of Singapore as Hokkien *mee* (noodles).

Islam, followed closely by Malays, calls for hours of prayer and study of the Koran. The gentle drone of the *muezzin* echoes above traffic junctions from the lofty minarets of the

Sultan Mosque – centre of Islam in Singapore. The *surau*, or village mosque, lies at the heart of every Malay neighbourhood.

Today, many Malays have simply adopted the prevalent philosophy and melted into the economy. Still, at the risk of generalising, many Malays are less concerned with material wealth and the outward display of it, unlike many of Singapore's Chinese population. To the traditional Malay, a growing stack of financial assets is far less important than family life and religion. In Singapore, though, with historic nervousness, Malays must seek their own position and identity in the city-state – not so much as Malays but as Singaporeans.

INDIAN NAMESAKE

Ever since early settlers borrowed the Sanskrit words *Singha Pura* (Lion City) in the naming of the island, Singapore's society has continued to draw heavily from the Indian subcontinent.

The Indians

The aroma of incense and freshly pounded curry floats over several square kilometres of Little India. Sixty percent of Singapore's Indians are Tamils, from the eastern part of southern India, and approximately 20 percent Malayalis Hindus from the Kerala state on the other side of the subcontinent. The rest are Bengalis, Punjabis, and others – among whom one finds a colourful mixture of Hindus, Buddhists, Christians, Sikhs and the Parsis, a small yet close-knit community. A minority of just over 7 percent of Singapore's population, Indians nevertheless influence every aspect of life.

Much of the classical Indian culture has survived in Singapore, from old-style recipes to dance, art and literature. The casual traveller wanting a three-day taste of India might well find the taxi fare to Little India a better investment than a plane ticket to India.

Eurasians and others

The largest of the "minorities", the Eurasians, are a mixture from two continents. Some are half English, others part Dutch, many part Portuguese. Many of them are also partly Filipino, Chinese, Malay, Indian, Sri Lankan or Thai. Less than 1 percent of Singaporeans are Eurasians, and most trace their roots back to colonial times, when the Portuguese, Dutch and English married local women.

With its policy of attracting "foreign talent" to its shores, Singapore plays host to a significant number of foreigners, many of whom have acquired permanent residency status. Hailing from all corners of the globe, many work in white-collar professions, primarily the IT and finance industries. Also contributing their talents to the local workforce are Filipinos, Indonesians, Thai, Burmese, Sri Lankans and South Indians who work in construction, roadworks and environment maintainence as well as women who work as live-in domestic maids. They mainly take on the work that younger Singaporeans shun, and unfortunately, are marginalised in Singapore's affluent society. ❏

LEFT: Eurasians are a blend of cultures and races.
RIGHT: most Singaporeans are Chinese, reflected in the Chinese traditions such as *taiqi (tai chi)*.

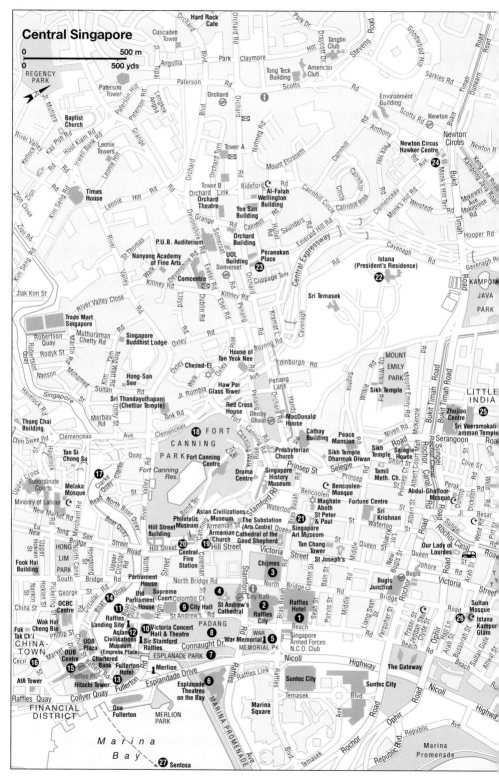

Central Singapore

0 ——————— 500 m
0 ——————— 500 yds

REGENCY PARK

Baptist Church

Times House

Trade Mart Singapore

Thong Chai Building

Tan Si Chong Su

Subordinate Courts

Ministry of Labour

Fook Hai Building

CHINA-TOWN

Wak Hai Cheng Bio

Fuk Tak Ch'i

AÏA Tower

FINANCIAL DISTRICT

Marina Bay

Hard Rock Cafe

Cuscaden Tower

Tong Teck Building

American Club

Environment Building

Newton Circus

Newton Circus Hawker Centre (24)

Orchard Theatre

Yen San Building

Al-Falah

Wellington Building

Orchard Building

UOL Building

Peranakan Place (23)

P.U.B. Auditorium

Nanyang Academy of Fine Arts

Comcentre

Istana (President's Residence) (22)

Sri Temasek

Singapore Buddhist Lodge

House of Tan Yeok Nee

Chesed-El

Hong-San See

Haw Par Glass Tower

Sri Thandayuthapani (Chettiar Temple)

Red Cross House

MacDonald House

Cathay Building

Peace Mansion

Sikh Temple

MOUNT EMILY PARK

Sikh Temple

Zhujiao Centre (25)

Sri Veeramakaliamman Temple

LITTLE INDIA

Melaka Mosque (17)

FORT CANNING PARK

Fort Canning Centre

Fort Canning Res.

Drama Centre

Singapore History Museum

Presbyterian Church

Sikh Temple Dharmak Diwan

Selegie House

Tamil Meth. Ch.

Bencoolen Mosque

Maghain Aboth

St Peter & Paul

Sri Krishnan

Fortune Centre

Abdul-Ghaffoor Mosque

Asian Civilizations Museum

Philatelic Museum

The Substation (Arts Centre)

Singapore Art Museum

Our Lady of Lourdes

Hill Street Building

Armenian Cathedral of the Good Shepherd

Armenian Church

Tan Chang Tower

St Joseph's

Bugis Junction

Central Fire Station (19)(20)

Hill Street

Chijmes (3)

Parliament House

Supreme Court

Old Parliament House

City Hall (9)

St Andrew's Cathedral

St Andrew's Rd

PADANG

Raffles City (2)

Raffles Hotel (1)

Sultan Mosque

Istana Kampong Glam (26)

HONG LIM PARK

OCBC Centre (11)

Raffles Landing Site

Asian Civilisations Museum (12)(10)

Victoria Concert Hall & Theatre

Sir Stamford Raffles

UOB Plaza

Chartered Bank

Fullerton Hotel

War Memorial (5)

Singapore Armed Forces N.C.O. Club

WAR MEMORIAL PK

Hitachi Tower

One Fullerton

Merlion

Esplanade Theatres on the Bay (6)

MERLION PARK

ESPLANADE PARK

Suntec City

The Gateway

Marina Square

Marina Promenade

Marina Bay

(27) Sentosa

SINGAPORE

Straddling the equator, this burgeoning city-state, despite being a tiny dot on the map, has made a reputation for itself as one of the most meticulously constructed societies in the world

Map on page 240

More than 170 years after Raffles first set foot in Singapore, the island is still governed from the colonial nucleus he established along the bank of the Singapore River. As well as being the hub of government, the old colonial district is also the location of Singapore's most famous landmark. Nearly everyone who comes to Singapore ends up at **Raffles Hotel ❶** at one point or another – usually to try the world famous Singapore Sling, a cocktail invented at Raffles in 1915 at the Long Bar. Opened in 1887 by the Sarkies brothers, Raffles has seen its fair share of kings and queens, presidents and prime ministers, movie actors and lions of literature, as well as millions of ordinary people who are attracted to this paragon of tropical elegance and style.

Towering beside the hotel is a silver monolith called **Raffles City ❷**, one of the island's largest retail, office and hotel complexes and a busy hub of the Mass Rapid Transit (MRT) network. Next door is **Swissôtel The Stamford**, the world's tallest hotel, with panoramic views offered from its penthouse restaurant at the top. Across the street from Raffles City is **Chijmes ❸**, a former Catholic convent and church dating back to 1860, but now restored into a pleasant hub of restaurants, bars and boutiques. South of Raffles City across Stamford Road is the graceful spire of **St Andrew's Cathedral ❹**. The church, built by Indian convict labour, owes its sparkling white surface to a plaster made of egg white, egg shell, lime, sugar, coconut husk and water. The cathedral, in the style of an early Gothic abbey, was consecrated in 1862. The stunning white exterior contrasts with the dark pews inside, and sunlight gently filters through the coloured stained-glass windows.

East of Raffles City across Beach Road is the **War Memorial Park ❺**, dedicated to civilians who suffered and died in Singapore at the hands of the Japanese during World War II. On the opposite side of the park are two huge developments on reclaimed land that was once part of the sea. One is a massive convention, hotel and shopping development called **Suntec City** and the other is **Marina Square**, a huge American-style mall with hundreds of shops.

BELOW:
The Esplanade – Theatres on the Bay.

new arts centre

South of Marina Square along Marina Bay is the prickly hedgehog-like outline of **The Esplanade – Theatres on the Bay ❻** (check www.esplanade.com for a schedule of programmes), a S$600 million performing arts centre with equally grandiose dreams of establishing itself as a cultural landmark akin to Australia's Sydney Opera House. Housing a concert hall, theatre, an open-air amphitheatre, practice studios, outdoor spaces for informal performances and sculpted gardens, its distinctive facade of sharp-edged metal sunshades has been likened to the thorny shell of the *durian* fruit. From this vantage point are expansive views of Singapore's CBD skyline with the statue of the water-spewing **Merlion** in the distance, the half-fish, half-lion creature that is associated with Singapore's mythical past.

Across Esplanade Drive is **Esplanade Park 7** with its tree-lined **Queen Elizabeth Walk**, formerly a seafront promenade where colonial-day Europeans spent their leisure time strolling or playing cricket. West of the park across Connaught Drive is an expanse of green called the **Padang 8** ("field" in Malay), a frequent venue of Singapore's annual National Day celebrations on 9 August. Flanking the Padang are two of Singapore's oldest leisure clubs, **Singapore Recreation Club** (1883) and the **Singapore Cricket Club** (1852) – the former newly rebuilt on its original site.

Facing the Padang is **City Hall 9**, completed in 1929 with a facade of Greek columns and a grand staircase. It was on these steps that Lord Louis Mountbatten accepted the surrender of Singapore by the Japanese General Itagaki on 12 September 1945. Lee Kuan Yew declared Singapore's independence from Britain on the same spot 14 years later, in 1959. Next door is **Supreme Court**, built in 1927 with its stout Corinthian columns and green dome. Across Parliament Place is the **Old Parliament House**, an 1820s structure currently being redeveloped into an arts venue while just beside it is the new **Parliament House**, completed in 1999. The colonial structure to the east is **Victoria Concert Hall and Theatre 10**, built in the 1880s to commemorate Queen Victoria's Diamond Jubilee. The building has long been the island's premier venue for opera, ballet and classical music. It features a distinctive clock tower with a Westminster chime that has never stopped pealing on the hour since its installation in 1906.

Singapore – the Lion City – was given its improbable name by a Sumatran prince, who thought he saw a lion when he landed on the island.

BELOW: Victoria Concert Hall and Theatre, a cultural haven in the city.

An 1887 bronze statue of Stamford Raffles graces the front of the theatre, a replica of which is found at the **Raffles' Landing Site ⓫** along the edge of the Singapore River. This is claimed to be the very spot where the founder of modern Singapore stepped ashore on 28 January 1819.

To its left is the stately **Asian Civilisations Museum, Empress Place ⓬** (open Mon 12–6pm, Tues–Sun 9am–6pm, Fri 9am–9pm), a neo-classical building that dates back to 1854 and formerly used as a courthouse and government offices. Having been beautifully restored, the museum displays a fine collection on the civilisations of East, Southeast, South and West Asia (a smaller second wing of the museum is found along Armenian Street). Nearby is the **Dalhousie Obelisk**, dedicated to Marquis Dalhousie – India's governor-general from 1848 to 1856 – who visited Singapore in 1850.

From here, cross the 1910 **Cavenagh Bridge** to get to Singapore's former General Post Office. This grand Palladian-style building has been restored to its current glory as the five-star **Fullerton Hotel ⓭**. Originally built in 1928 and named after Robert Fullerton, the first governor of the Straits Settlements, the building is a wonderful example of the Neo-Classical style that once dominated the district. Enter by the massive revolving door and see the central atrium, created by punching out several floors and the old ceiling.

For a study in architectural contrast, take the underpass beneath the Fullerton Hotel to the glass-and-steel **One Fullerton** structure, a new restaurant and nightlife hub by the waterfront. There are swanky restaurants and bars, most with floor-to-ceiling windows offering magnificent views of **Marina Bay**.

On the other side of the Singapore River is **Boat Quay ⓮**, an area of historic interest that has become something of a yuppie enclave. Dozens of Victorian-era shophouses have been restored and transformed into trendy bars and restaurants with outdoor seating.

The core of "Singapore Inc" runs along the water-front from south of Boat Quay to Keppel Road. The commercial area once centred on **Raffles Place ⓯**, which has been transformed into an open-air plaza with an MRT station below. Singapore's tallest sky-scrapers are centred here: OUB Centre (Overseas Union Bank), OUB Plaza (United Overseas Bank) and Republic Plaza, all of which reach a height of 280 metres (920 ft), the maximum allowed by civil aviation rules.

Chinatown

It may seem strange to have a **Chinatown ⓰** in a place that's over 75 percent Chinese, but the oddity can be traced back to Raffles, who subdivided his new town into various districts in the early 1820s. Narrow, noisy streets and shophouses huddle on the south bank of the Singapore River, stretching inland as far as Cantonment Road. The area is currently undergoing renewal and is surrounded by high-rises but Chinatown is still dominated by exotic sights and smells – dried fish, fried noodles, funeral offerings, incense sticks, wooden clogs and mountains of gaudy tourist tat. The heart of Chinatown is an area off South Bridge Road that embraces Pagoda, Temple and Trengganu streets. The basement of **Chinatown Complex** is worth exploring for its array of exotic ingredients on sale, from live fish, reptiles

BELOW:
Raffles Landing Site and surrounding skyscrapers.

Map on page 240

and poultry to fresh fruit, flowers and vegetables. Another good place to shop in the neighbourhood is **Chinatown Point**, at the corner of New Bridge Road and Cross Street, with its shops selling arts, crafts, souvenirs and antiques.

Chinatown has its fair share of Buddhist temples. But one of the most curious things about the neighbourhood is the fact that it harbours some of the island's best Hindu and Muslim shrines. Towering above the shophouses are the brightly painted figures adorning the *gopuram* (tower) at the entrance of the **Sri Mariamman Temple** on South Bridge Road, the oldest Hindu shrine in Singapore. Brightly clad devotees perform *pujas* amid gaudy statues and vivid ceiling frescoes. Built during the 1820s, this is the annual site of Thimiti – the fire walking festival – when the faithful work themselves into a trance and walk over burning embers to fulfil their vows to the goddess Droba-Devi.

A block away is the lovely **Jamae Mosque**, with its pagoda-like minarets rarely seen in mosque construction and reflecting strong Chinese influence. Telok Ayer Street once ran along the waterfront, but today the road is blocked from the sea by a wall of gleaming skyscrapers. It was here that seafarers and immigrants from China's Fujian Province set up a joss house in gratitude for their safe arrival after their long sea voyage from China in the early 1820s. The little joss house eventually became **Thian Hock Keng Temple** (Temple of Heavenly Happiness) dedicated to Ma-Chu-Po, Goddess of the Sea, who reputedly calms the ocean waters and rescues those in danger of drowning.

Further along the road is **Nagore Durgha Shrine**, also called Masjid Chulia, an architectural companion to the mosque on South Bridge Road. Built by Muslims from southern India in 1830, the mosque is another example of the ethnic and religious variety found in Chinatown.

Sri Mariamman Temple, on South Bridge Road.

BELOW: Chinatown calligrapher, a disappearing trade.

Upstream along the Singapore River, **Clarke Quay** ⓱ – bounded by River Valley Road, Tan Tye Place and North Boat Quay – features Singapore's first riverside festival village combining dining, shopping and nightlife by the water's edge. North of Clarke Quay is historic **Fort Canning Park** ⓲. Once known as Bukit Larangan (Forbidden Hill), in the early years of Singapore's history, this strategic location was the site of grand palaces protected by walls and swamps. In 1860, the British built a fort atop the hill, from where dawn, noon and dusk were announced each day by way of cannon fire.

At the base of the hill, at the junction of Coleman and Hill streets, is the **Armenian Church** ⓳, also called St Gregory the Illuminator. Built in 1835, this exquisite church is the oldest in Singapore. A cemetery in the church grounds is the final resting place of some eminent Singaporeans, among them Agnes Joaquim (1864–99), after whom Singapore's national flower, Vanda Miss Joaquim, is named. At No. 62 Hill Street is another architectural gem of a building, the old red and white **Central Fire Station** ⓴, headquarters of the Singapore Fire Brigade, which was completed in 1909. On the ground level is the **Civil Defence Heritage Gallery** (Tues–Sun 10am–5pm) where a gleaming red fire engine from 1905 occupies pride of place.

Down Hill Street and left into Stamford Road leads to the **Singapore History Museum**, which is unfortunately closed until 2006 for major renovations. Until then be content to gaze at the historic neo-classical building topped with a gleaming dome from the outside. At nearby Bras Basah Road, the former St Joseph's Institution is now the **Singapore Art Museum** ㉑ (open Mon 12–6pm, Tues–Sun 9am–6pm, Fri 9am–9pm). Beautifully renovated, with a nice cafe, the museum has rotating exhibits covering Singaporean, Asian and Western artists.

Map on page 240

Hell money is burned for the well-being of Chinese ancestors.

BELOW: the Armenian Church was built in 1835.

Orchard Road and environs

The de facto heart of modern Singapore is **Orchard Road**, which begins just north of the Raffles Hotel area. Plaza Singapura and Park Mall are the first of the big shopping centres that have given Orchard Road its international reputation. Near Plaza Singapura is the **Istana ㉒**, the official workplace and expansive residence of Singapore's president. The palace and its lavish garden are strictly off-limits to the public, except on National Day and certain public holidays, when the gates are thrown open to curious sightseers. The Istana was built in 1869 on the grounds of an old nutmeg plantation, and it served as the residence of the British governor until the island became self-governing in 1959.

Northwards on Orchard Road are the famous shopping centres that inspired one commentator to call Singapore the world's largest shopping centre with immigration controls. Near the Centrepoint mall is the charming **Peranakan Place ㉓**, a complex of six Peranakan-style terrace houses that have been transformed into a commercial hub. This area was once settled by the Peranakan people, or Straits-born Chinese, a unique culture that evolved through intermarriage between Chinese migrants and local Malay women in the 19th century. Take a walk behind Peranakan Place to **Emerald Hill**, where there are some lovely old restored homes that once belonged to wealthy Peranakan families.

Intersecting Orchard Road is Scotts Road, where there are more shopping malls and luxury hotels like the Grand Hyatt and Goodwood Park Hotel.

Little India

BELOW: Sri Srinivasa Perumal Temple.

A walk down Scotts Road leads to **Newton Circus Hawker Centre ㉔**, where one can sample the local fare for which Singapore is so famous for, and very cheaply too. Not far from here is **Serangoon Road**, where the visitor is plunged into a replica of the Asian subcontinent, with undulating music punctuated by car horns and bicycle bells, women drifting gracefully along in vivid *saris* and the pungent aromas of spices. **Little India ㉕** is filled with interesting religious sights – not just Hindu temples, but shrines representing the entire spectrum of Singapore's various faiths. Tucked away on Dunlop Street is the lovely old **Abdul Ghafor Mosque**, with its courtyard and small houses for Malay and Indian worshippers.

Hindus congregate at the **Sri Veeramakaliamman Temple**, dedicated to Kali, Shiva's consort, who epitomises the struggle against evil. She is shown ripping a hapless victim apart. Kali's sons – Ganesh, the elephant god, and Murugan, the child god – are depicted with her at the side of the temple. Further up Serangoon Road, the great *gopuram* (tower) of the **Sri Srinivasa Perumal Temple** is visible, showing the different incarnations of Vishnu. The annual Thaipusam procession sets off from here. Devotees, their tongues and cheeks pierced by great metal skewers supporting *kavadi* (cage-like constructions decorated with wire and peacock feathers) make their way to the **Sri Thandayuthapani Temple** (better known as Chettiar Temple) in Tank Road. This is done in gratitude or supplication to Lord Murugan.

Race Course Road may have lost its horses, but the

street is now renowned for its banana-leaf curry restaurants. Down the street are three very different Chinese temples. The small **Beo San Hood Chor** is dedicated to Kuan Yin, or the Goddess of Mercy. **Liong San See Temple**, also dedicated to Kuan Yin, is richly carved and ornately decorated. At the back is a spacious courtyard and numerous ancestral tablets. Over the road is the stunning **Temple of 1,000 Lights**, where a 15-metre-high (50-ft) Buddha sits in a halo of light, atop a base depicting scenes from the life of Prince Siddharta Gautama. There are also several Sikh temples in the Little India area. **Khalsa Jiwan Sudhar Sabha** on Kerbau Road is a small Sikh temple. For a most substantial example, visit **Khalsa Dharmak Sabha** on Niven Road behind the Selegie Complex.

At the very heart of the nearby Beach Road district is **Istana Kampung Glam**, the old royal palace built in the early 1840s by Sultan Ali Iskandar Shah. Arab traders – together with Bugis, Javanese, Sumatrans, Malays and people from the Riau islands – eventually settled in the area, transforming Kampung Glam into a commercial hub, especially the stretch along Arab Street, which still draws those looking for bargains. The palace is currently being restored and will open as a Malay Heritage Centre in the near future. Dominating the neighbourhood is the golden bulk of **Sultan Mosque ㉖**, the largest mosque in Singapore and where the *muezzin* calls the faithful to prayer five times a day, the women to their enclave located upstairs, the men to the mosque's main prayer hall.

Sentosa and the West Coast

Buried in the city and its shopping centres, it's easy to forget that Singapore is in the tropics, so take the opportunity to enjoy a little island hopping. The most accessible island is **Sentosa ㉗**, which has become a major resort and recreation

Map on page 232

TIP

During Ramadan – the fasting month for Muslims based on a lunar calendar – the area around the Sultan Mosque is festooned with bright lights and bustling activity at night, after the fast is broken at sundown.

BELOW: beachfront, Sentosa island.

Map on page 232

The Botanic Gardens are famous for its orchid collection.

RIGHT: much of old Singapore is undergoing renovation.
BELOW: bird life in the city.

area over the past few years, after its previous life as a military base. A cable car stretches from the **HarbourFront Centre**, on Telok Blangah Road, to Sentosa or one can reach the island via a very short ferry ride from the HarbourFront Centre. Don't be fooled by the island's name, which actually translates as "Island of Tranquillity". Sentosa is now a lively theme park that has become more of a giant amusement ride than a quiet island retreat. Still, on a quiet weekday, it may be possible to relax on its fine sandy beaches and soak up the sun. Several other islands surrounding Singapore can be easily reached, ranging from tiny specks like the Sisters Islands to larger places like St John's and Lazarus.

Flora and fauna retreats

Western Singapore embraces both industrial areas such as Jurong and Tuas with docks, factories and refineries, and a major recreation zone that includes some of Singapore's top green spaces and theme parks, such as the **Jurong Bird Park** ㉘ (8am–6pm daily). Scarlet ibis welcome visitors at the entrance of this 20-hectare (50 acre) park, which is home to 8,000 birds of 600 different species from all over the world.

The lovely **Botanic Gardens** ㉙ (daily 5am–midnight) off Holland Road have been in bloom for over a century, although its lineage can be traced back to the 1820s, when Sir Stamford Raffles planted an experimental spice garden near his bungalow. Its orchid gardens are not to be missed. For less manicured flora and fauna, jungle walks weave in all directions throughout the **Bukit Timah Nature Reserve** ㉚, about 12 km (8 miles) from the city centre. The thick tropical vegetation resembles the entire scenery of Singapore when Raffles first arrived. This 164-hectare (405-acre) park plays host to the island's highest point

and a rich collection of local wildlife, including long-tailed macaque monkeys, flying lemurs, tropical squirrels, civet cats and brilliant forest birds.

The **Singapore Zoological Gardens** ㉛ (daily 8.30am–6pm), regarded as one of the best zoos in the world, has the finest wildlife collection in Southeast Asia. The place bills itself as an "open zoo" – few of the animals are in cages or behind bars. Among the rare or endangered species are the Komodo dragon (the world's largest lizard), Malay tapir, clouded leopard, Sumatran tiger, Bawean hog deer and the largest group of orang-utans in captivity. For a different perspective, consider the unique **Night Safari** (daily 7.30pm–midnight), where nocturnal animals can be observed outside under special lighting.

East Coast

Millions of visitors have their first experience of Singapore while travelling into the city from **Changi Airport** along the east coast, with sandy beaches on one side of the coastal highway, and luxury condominium blocks on the other. The east coast is packed on weekends as Singaporeans escape for a day at the beach, but during the week the beaches and park areas are virtually deserted. **East Coast Park** ㉜ stretches for more than 10 km (6 miles) along the coast between Marina Bay and the airport, fringed with casuarinas, coconut palms and flowering trees. ❑

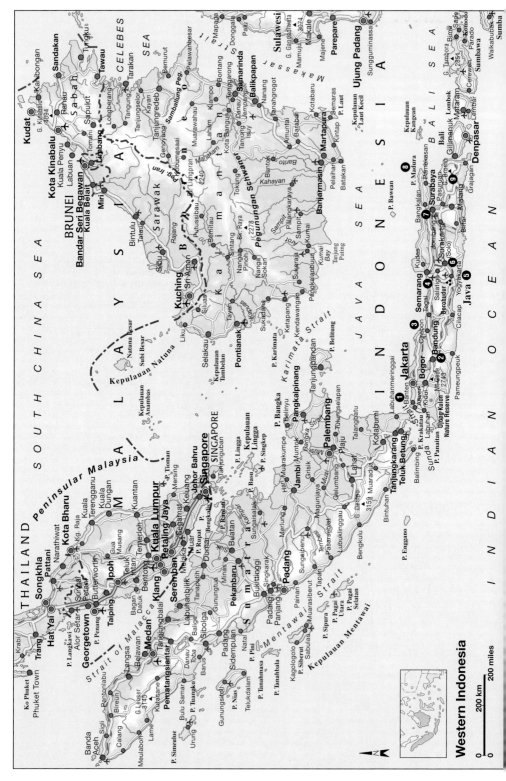

Western Indonesia

INDONESIA

An immense nation extending one-eighth of the world's circumference, Indonesia is Asia's most diverse country

Indonesia is one of the very few nations on earth to span such a broad spectrum of world history and human civilisation – from its ancient Hindu-Javanese temples to Bali's modern luxury resorts, and from the stone-age lifestyle in West Papua (Irian Jaya) to the immense metropolis that is Jakarta. The country's motto, *Bhinneka Tunggal Ika*, or Unity in Diversity, is no mere slogan. The population of nearly 220 million people is derived from 300 ethnic groups who speak over 250 distinct languages. The common element is the national language of Bahasa Indonesia, very similar to Malay.

Almost 90 percent of the people are Muslims, with a significant Christian population. There are also smaller numbers of Hindus and Buddhists. In most cases, at least in the rural areas, these beliefs are augmented by indigenous, centuries-old animistic traditions. The fourth most populous nation in the world, Indonesia straddles two geographically defined racial groups, the Asians to the west and the Melanesians in the east. The majority are Asians, particularly in the western part of the archipelago. Over the centuries, mostly through commerce and trade, Indians, Arabs and Europeans have mingled with the indigenous people. The largest non-indigenous ethnic group is the Chinese, who control nearly three-quarters of the nation's wealth while comprising only 3 percent of the population. This has not gone unnoticed, making them a favourite target of irate rioters.

Indonesia's people are unevenly distributed across the archipelago with more than half living in Java and Bali alone, which cover only 7 percent of the total land area. With more than 100 million people living in Java, the demands on its land and resources are considerable. As a result, the government has been relocating landless people from Java to the more remote provinces. But the programme's success is elusive and it has caused friction between the locals and the transplanted Javanese. It has also perhaps added to the push for greater autonomy in the outer islands, whose populations are unhappy that Jakarta continues to drain local resources in unfair exploitation. With East Timor having acquired its independence in 1999, others await their turn.

As the old Soeharto order is dismantled, the current leadership struggles to come to terms with the demands of a newly democratised system. However, it will take a while before the government can get its act together. Political infighting, a corrupt presidency, religious tensions, the clamour for autonomy and a weak economy all conspire against an immediate recovery. ❏

PRECEDING PAGES: planting rice, Lombok; Friendship Statue, Jakarta.

Decisive Dates

Prehistoric years

1.7 million years ago: Hominids live in Java, the largest island in the archipelago.

250,000 years ago: Evidence of Solo Man, the distinct evolutionary descendent of *Homo erectus*, have been found dating back 2,500 centuries.

40,000 years ago: Fossil records of modern humans (*Homo sapiens*) found in Indonesia.

5000 BC: Austronesian peoples begin moving into Indonesia from the Philippines.

3000 BC: Plain pottery pots and open bowls, together

with shell bracelets, discs, and beads found in southwestern Sulawesi and eastern Timor.

500 BC–AD 500: Dong Son bronze age. Characteristic of the period are the ceremonial bronze drums and axes, distinctively decorated with engraved geometric, animal and human motifs. This decorative style is highly influential in many fields of Indonesian art, and seems to have spread together with bronze casting techniques.

Indianised kingdoms

AD 400: Hindu kingdoms of Tarumanegara and Kutai emerge in West Java and East Kalimantan.

760: Construction of Sivaitic temples at Dieng.

850: Rakai Pikatan, a prince of the Sanjaya dynasty, marries a Sailendran princess and seizes control of central Java. The Sailendras flee to Srivijaya, blocking all Javanese shipping throughout the South China Sea for more than a century.

860–1000: The golden age of Srivijaya.

910: Political centre of Java moves to East Java; rise of Hindu kingdoms on Bali.

914–1080: First known Hindu kingdom.

1019: Airlangga, King Dharmawangsa's nephew, succeeds to the throne after the Srivijayan forces depart.

Singhasari and Majapahit

1222: Ken Arok founds Singhasari dynasty.

1275: Ken Arok sends first successful naval expeditions against Srivijaya to wrestle control of the important maritime trade.

1292: Civil war in Singhasari; Mongol invasion joins Wijaya against Jayakatwang.

1293: Wijaya founds kingdom of Majapahit and rules as Kertarajasa.

1297: Sultan Malek Saleh of Pasai first known Muslim ruler in the archipelago.

1330–50: Adityavarman rules Minangkabau.

1389: Majapahit's decline begins.

1403–06: Struggle for control erupts into civil war.

1429: Country reunited; Majapahit loses control of the western Java Sea and the straits to a new Islamic power located at Malacca.

15th century: Majapahit and Kediri are conquered by the new Islamic state of Demak, on Java's north coast, and it is said that the entire Hindu-Javanese aristocracy then fled into exile to nearby Bali. All trading ports of the western archipelago are brought within Malacca's orbit, including the important ports along the north coast of Java.

early 16th century: Islamisation of coastal kingdoms of Java begins.

1511: The Portuguese seize control of Malacca.

1522: Portuguese build fort in Ternate.

1552–70: Banten rises as independent state under Sultan Hasanuddin.

1570: Revolt against the Portuguese in Ternate.

Dutch colonial years

1596: First Dutch ships drop anchor in Banten.

1602: The Dutch form the United Dutch East Indies Company (VOC), one of the world's first joint-stock corporations.

1605: Dutch seize Ambon.

1621: Dutch take control of the Banda Islands.

1641: Dutch capture Malacca from the Portuguese.

1646–67: Despotic reign of Amangkurat I.

1666–69: Makassar wars.

1740–55: Great war in Java.

1799: Dutch financiers receive stunning news: the VOC is bankrupt.

1800: Dutch government assumes control of all former VOC possessions.

Raffles renaissance

1811–16: Brief period of English rule under Thomas Stamford Raffles.

1811: Raffles authors monumental *History of Java*. His invasion of Yogyakarta in 1812 leads to the cataclysmic Java War of 1825–30.

1830: In an attempt to remedy government debt, the Dutch introduce a land tax payable by labour or land use known as the "Cultivation System".

1821–38: Padri War between the Dutch and the Minangkabau of west Sumatra.

1840s: Englishman James Brooke establishes private empire in Sarawak, in northwestern Borneo.

National awakening

1908: Indonesians attending Dutch schools begin to form regional student organisations; new national consciousness takes shape.

1910: Indonesian Communist movement founded.

1910–30: Turbulent period of strikes, violence and organised rebellions.

1927: First major political party with Indonesian independence as its goal is founded by Soekarno.

1928: Second all-Indies student conference; importance of "one nation, one language, one people" is proclaimed.

1933: Crackdown ensues; Soekarno and all other student leaders are exiled to distant islands for 10 years.

World War II and independence

1942: Japanese invasion of Java.

1944: Japanese promise independence in attempt to maintain faltering Indonesian support; nationalist slogans are encouraged.

1945: Japan surrenders and its army retreats from Indonesia. Expecting to resume control of their former colony, the Dutch return. Nationalist leaders Soekarno and Muhammad Hatta declare Indonesia's independence as a republic. The Dutch resist.

1949: The Dutch acknowledge Indonesia's independence and sovereignty.

Late 1950s: A Communist insurgency prompts Soekarno to declare martial law. Soekarno resurrects the "revolutionary" constitution of 1945.

1960: Soekarno dissolves parliament; his anti-colonial sentiments become more militant.

1963: Confrontation with newly-independent Malaysia reveals Soekarno's brand of militant nationalism.

1965: Blood-letting ensues after failed Communist coup. The Chinese population is focus of anti-Communist attacks. Up to 500,000 people are killed.

1966: Soekarno persuaded to sign over powers to his protégé, Soeharto, who takes over presidency. Until 1998, he is re-elected 6 times.

1976: Indonesia annexes East Timor.

1990s: Indonesia joins Asia's "tiger" economies.

1996: Unrest ripples through Jakarta in response to the government's hard line against political oppo-

nents. Elsewhere, serious violence surfaces due to religious animosity between Christians and Moslems.

1997: Indonesia's economy is sucked into the regional crisis and the rupiah collapses.

1998: Soeharto refuses to reform economy; riots over rising prices and corruption. Troops kill six protestors in Jakarta. Soeharto is succeeded by B.J. Habibie.

1999: East Timor votes for independence. Abdurrahman Wahid wins Indonesia's first democratic elections in 40 years to become the country's fourth president.

2001: Wahid is impeached, and Megawati Sukarnoputri, daughter of Soekarno, is elected president.

2002: The Bali bombings are a wake-up call to the Megawati administration, prompting it to take action against the country's militant Muslim factions. ❑

LEFT: wife of Ken Arok depicted as a goddess.

RIGHT: Soekarno and Soeharto, early 1960s.

INDONESIA'S PEOPLE

An archipelago of 300 ethnic groups and 250 languages, Indonesia presents
the traveller with one of the world's most wide-ranging populations

For one travelling the length of Indonesia, the complexity and diversity of peoples, languages, customs and cultures found in the Indonesian archipelago are truly astounding, and thoroughly embracing. Living here are 250–300 distinct ethnic groups, each with its own cultural identity, who together speak a total of more than 250 mutually unintelligible languages, but all sharing the official Bahasa Indonesia as a common tongue.

Anyone travelling widely in Indonesia soon recognises the enormous physical differences of people from one end of the archipelago to the other – differences in pigmentation, hair type, stature and physiognomy. To explain this range of racial types, scholars once postulated a theory of wave migrations to the archipelago. According to this theory, various Indonesian groups arrived from the Asian mainland in a series of discrete but massive migratory waves, each separated by a period of several centuries. The wave theory, however, has lost considerable currency in recent years.

Migratory theories

The first wave of migrants, it was thought, were the primitive dark-skinned, wiry-haired negritos – people of pygmy stature who today inhabit remote forest enclaves on the Malay peninsula, in the Andaman Islands north of Sumatra, and on several of the Philippine islands. It has commonly been suggested that the negritos somehow migrated the length of the Eurasian continent, from Africa, eons ago.

The second wave, too, were thought to have arrived from Africa or perhaps India. These peoples were dubbed the Australoids, and are the Melanesian inhabitants of New Guinea, including Irian Jaya, and Australia. The third wave, proto-Malays, were thought to have migrated from China by way of Indochina.

The last wave, the deutero-Malays, were described as pure Mongoloids, hence related to

and much resembling the Chinese. These peoples today inhabit the plains and coastal region of all the major islands, and many developed large hierarchical kingdoms, attaining a level of pre-modern civilisation comparable to that found anywhere in the world.

The existence of *Homo erectus* (Java Man)

fossils in Indonesia – million-year-old remains of one of our earliest ancestors – suggests that the so-called negrito and Australoid people, with their sun-screening skin pigmentation, actually evolved partially or wholly in the tropical rain forests of Southeast Asia, just as the light-skinned Mongoloid types evolved in the cold temperate regions of east and central Asia. Of course, during the last Ice Ages, when land bridges linked the major islands of the Sunda shelf to the mainland, these peoples circulated freely and even crossed the oceans, populating Australia by about 50,000 years ago.

The wave theory of coordinated, coherent mass movements seems unlikely for a number

LEFT: Dayak woman with child and family wealth.
RIGHT: a Javanese soldier of yesteryear.

of reasons. In a fragmented region like the Indonesian archipelago, village and tribal groups have always been constantly on the move, at least in historic times, dissolving and absorbing each other as they go.

Many experts offer that perhaps it is more realistic, therefore, to imagine a situation in which small groups of Mongoloid hunters, gatherers and cultivators percolated into the region slowly, absorbing and replacing the original Australoid inhabitants over a period of many millennia.

SETTLED STABILITY

Great linguistic diversity has often been interpreted as indicating that an area has been settled and stable for a long period of time.

Cultural distinctions

One important distinction when considering Indonesia's people focuses on the two main agricultural patterns found in Indonesia: *ladang* and *sawah*. Ladang agriculture, also referred to by the Old English word swidden and by the descriptive expression slash-and-burn, is practised in forested terrains, generally outside of Java and Bali. The ladang farmer utilises fire as a tool, along with axe and bush knife, to clear a forest plot. By carefully timing the burn immediately to precede

Linguistic babel

Indonesians speak such a variety of different languages that the exact number would largely depend upon an arbitrary definition of what constitutes a distinct language, as opposed to a dialect. Most estimates place the total above 300, only a handful of which have been adequately studied. Languages such as Javanese, Balinese and Bahasa Indonesian (the national language, which derives from a literary dialect of Malay and is nearly identical to the language of Malaysia) are closely related, belonging to the Malayo-Polynesian branch of the Austronesian language family, but they are as different from one another as are French and Spanish.

the onset of rains, the farmer simultaneously fertilises and weeds the land. While these semi-nomadic swidden farmers now comprise less than a tenth of Indonesia's total population, they are scattered throughout more than two-thirds of the nation's land area. In the late 1990s, this practice on Sumatra, Java and Borneo ignited uncontrollable fires that sent clouds of haze over most of Southeast Asia for months.

Most Indonesians, by contrast, inhabit the narrow plains and coastal regions of the major islands, where the principal farming method is sawah, or wet-rice paddy cultivation. In fact, over half of Indonesia's population of 220 million lives on Java and Bali, which between them comprise only 7 percent of Indonesia's land. Here, the average rural population densities can soar as high as 2,000 people per sq. km (5,000 per sq. mile) – by far the world's highest population density, which has caused the government to relocate Javanese to less-populated provinces.

Sawah cultivation is a labour-intensive form of agriculture that can be successfully practised only under the special conditions of rich soil and adequate water, but one that seems capable of producing seemingly limitless quantities of food. The farmers who plant wet-rice paddies actually reshape their environment over a

As might be expected, the sawah societies of Java and Bali are strikingly different from the ladang communities of the outer islands. The Javanese, for example, put great emphasis on cooperation and social attitudes. Village deliberations are concluded not by majority or autocratic rule, but by a consensus of elders or esteemed individuals. *Rukun,* or harmony, is the primary goal, achieved through knowing one's place within society.

Time, balance and harmony

A favourite expression in Indonesia is *jam karet,* which translates, literally, as rubber time.

period of many generations, clearing the land, terracing, levelling and diking the plots, and constructing elaborate irrigation systems. As a result, this system has both required and rewarded a high degree of social cooperation. Particularly in Java and Bali, populous villages have long been linked with towns – economically and culturally – through a hierarchically defined framework that has coordinated labour to maintain the fragile irrigation works. The food surpluses produced by these villages have permitted an urban opulence.

LEFT: faces of Bali and Java. **ABOVE:** West Timorese, and working on a tea plantation, Java.

Rarely must a social event or a meeting start exactly at the appointed hour; time can be stretched to suit the occasion.

The notion of balance and harmony is also important in personal contacts. Great respect and deference are shown to superiors and elders, and there are distinct speech levels that are used according to the status of the person. These fine social divisions may hark back to the Hindu caste system: yet another example of Indonesia's Indian heritage.

Finally, to lose face, to be made ashamed *(malu)* is something to be avoided, and for this reason Indonesians often suggest that something can be done when they know it cannot. ❑

TEXTILES

From the colours and detail of batik to the textured dyeing of ikat, Indonesia's centuries-old tradition of textiles is unsurpassed in the world

Textile connoisseurs are quick to point out that Indonesia possesses the greatest diversity of traditional textiles in the world: the colourful bark cloths of Kalimantan, Irian Jaya, and Sulawesi; the plain weaves and exquisite *songket* silks of Sumatra; the beautiful *batik* of Java and Bali; and the renowned *ikat* of the eastern islands. For Indonesians, tex-

left its mark in textile use, and in the use of motifs derived from coins and porcelain.

Migrants as well as traders have played a role in the diffusion of textile techniques and motifs. For example, the northern coasts of Ceram and Irian Jaya were home to traditional weaving communities that may have originated in the Banggai islands, off the east coast of Sulawesi.

tiles reconfirm and maintain many old and hallowed sartorial associations, and also symbolise wealth, status and religious beliefs.

Each of Indonesia's hundreds of ethnic and linguistic groups appears to have had, at one time or another, its own distinctive textile tradition. Some of these may date back 2,000 years or more, and some are preserved today in remote upriver or mountainous areas. Many have also been influenced by foreign (especially Indian) textiles.

As early as the 14th century, Indian fabrics were imported on a large scale, and during the 16th and 17th centuries, Indian *patola* cloths were particularly influential. Colonial rule also

Symbolism

The production of textiles is interwoven with taboos that define gender roles to ensure the harmony of the community. The spinning, dyeing and weaving of yarn are symbolic of the process of creation, and of human birth in particular. Weaving is an exclusively female activity, and men are permitted to participate only in the dyeing of certain colours of the thread, analogous with their role in human conception. Dyeing requires the utmost privacy, with partitions often set up around the work area. Pregnant, menstruating or sick women are excluded from this work. In some areas, the mounting of the threads upon the loom is done on an auspicious day, otherwise the threads will break. In coastal villages, this means a full moon and a high tide. If a death occurs in the village, weaving stops at once. Otherwise, the spirit of the dead person will exact vengeance, bringing sickness upon the weaver and causing the threads to lose their strength.

Finished products are sanctified by metaphysical and psychological associations, and are regarded as powerful objects that can protect the weaver; they are also often necessary for life-cycle rituals.

FABRICATED CURRENCY

On many of Indonesia's islands, textiles were required in dowries, and small squares of cloth were used as currency.

of southern Sumatra and with a central motif that resembled a ship, or sometimes a bird. Human figures were generally depicted on the ships, often together with a variety of plants, animals and valuable objects. Up until the 19th century, a ship cloth was essential for the performance of all important life-cycle rituals in much of southern Sumatra, including birth, circumcision, marriage and death.

Bark and ikat

Textiles from all periods of Indonesia's history are still

LEFT: Timor cloth with characteristically bright colours, and *limar* cloth of *ikat* and *songket*.
ABOVE: tying off thread in ikat process before dyeing.

An entire language of textiles has developed. For example, the brown-and-white *ulos ragidup* (pattern of life) cloths of the Bataks of Sumatra were presented to a woman seven months' pregnant with her first child as a "soul cloth". Her in-laws drape this special cloth around her shoulders, and then the pattern is "read" by a knowledgeable elder.

Perhaps the best-known ritual textiles to be found in the Indonesian archipelago are the so-called ship cloths, once found in several areas

being produced. The bark cloths found among upland tribes in Kalimantan on Borneo, Sulawesi, and Irian Jaya display an extremely high degree of artistry, even though they date back to the prehistoric era.

The technique closely associated with the advent of cotton in Indonesia is warp *ikat*. This is a traditional method of design in which the warp threads of a cloth are tie-dyed prior to being woven. Spinning the threads and preparing the dyes, tying the warp threads and then repeatedly immersing and drying them to achieve the desired colour requires tremendous skill and patience, but in the hands of a master weaver the result can be intricate, with detailed motifs executed in very deep, rich colours.

A fine cloth produced with natural dyes once took from eight to 10 years to complete. Natural-dye recipes are extremely complex, some of them requiring sophisticated carriers and mordants. Traditionally, it appears that indigo, *mengkudu* root (a red dye) and *soga* (a brown dye from roots and barks) were the main dyes; Turkey red and cochineal were popularised by Islamic traders.

All warp ikat are distinguished by the grouping of motifs into horizontal or longitudinal bands, a logical and practical outcome of the warp-dyeing process.

People on the small arid islands of Roti and Sawu (between Sumba and Timor in the eastern part of the archipelago) also produce highly distinctive warp ikats recognisable by their narrow longitudinal bands, symmetrically patterned with rows of delicate flowers, and stars or diamonds in white and red against a background of indigo. Roses and tulips are commonly depicted, copied from traditional Dutch fabrics and porcelain.

Tenganan Pegeringsingan, in eastern Bali, is one of only three places in the world (the other two are in India and Japan) to traditionally produce the fabulously difficult double ikat – fabrics decorated by tie-dyeing both warp and weft before weaving. These *geringsing* cloths are dyed with indigo and mengkudu red, producing a reddish-purple design on a cream background. Loosely woven, some apparently imitate the Indian patola, also a double ikat. Others are clearly indigenous in design, such as the *geringsing wayang kebo,* with its symmetrical groupings of wayang figures around a central four-pointed star.

Magical cloths

Considered by the Balinese to be the most sacred of all textiles, geringsing cloths are used in many important ceremonies throughout the island, including tooth filings and cremations. Within the village of Tenganan, wearers of these cloths are said to be protected from evil influences and illness (geringsing means "without sickness").

It appears that a textile revolution took place in Indonesia after the 14th century, when Islamic (and later European) traders began to flood the archipelago with Indian textiles.

The use of cotton and silk had been the preserve of the Indonesian aristocracy, but a democratisation of textiles occurred as a result of the spice trade. Traders discovered that they could obtain valuable Indonesian spices in exchange for Indian cottons and silks. Indonesians, meanwhile, found that they could have fine imported textiles in exchange for easily gathered cloves, nutmeg, peppers and aromatic woods.

Weaving the future

Perhaps the most important innovation of this period was the cotton plain weave, now found throughout Indonesia and worn by the majority as the all-purpose *sarong* or body wrap.

Another textile inspired by the flowering of trade with the Islamic world is the songket – weavings produced with gold or silver thread imported from India. The Minangkabau of western Sumatra are also known for their silver-threaded songket, produced against a background of wine-red silk. And in Bali, that idyllic island that is so rich in creativity, a whole range of songket are produced, from simple sarongs to exuberant festive costumes in silks of purple, green, yellow and blue. ❑

Left: a Lembata woman spinning cotton.
Right: *geringsing* cloth, a double *ikat* weave found in only three places in the world, including Bali, where it is considered to be a sacred cloth.

Jakarta

N

0   1000 m
0   1000 yds

Pluit Reservoir

J a k a r t a   B a y

Jl. Pluit Timur Raya
Jl. Muara Baru
Cikampek T

Sunda Kelapa Harbour ❺

Ancol "Dreamland" Amusement Park
Dunia Fantasy
Jl. Pantal Indah ❼
TAMAN IMPIAN JAYA ANCOL
Sea World
P. Tritis Raya
Kr. Bolong 5
Pesar Seni (Art Market)
Jl. Lodan Raya

Jl. Pluit Selatan Raya
Bahari Museum ❻
Pasar Ikan (Fish Market)
Lookout Tower
Jl. Lodan Raya
Jl. Toll Pelabuhan
Jl. R. E. Martadinata

Jl. Pluit Raya
Jl. Pakin
Tongkol

Harbour Tollroad
Gedong Panjang
Ut. Sel.

Taman Fatahillah ❶
Wayang Museum ❷
Red House
Jakarta Museum
Jl. Sengkeh
Balai Seni Rupa (Fine Arts Museum) ❸
Kota Station
Kp. Bandan Station
Jl. R. E. Martadinata
Jl. Budi Mulia
BIRD SANCTUARY

KOTA
Jl. Bandengan
Jl. Bandengan
Jl. Jembatan Batu
Jl. Mangga Dua
PADEMANGAN
URBAN FOREST PARK
Jl. Landas Pacu Utara
Jl. Griya Utama

International Trade Centre
Jl. Perniagaan
Jl. Perniagaan
Jl. Pintu Besar Sel.
Pancoran
Portuguese Church
Jl. Pangeran Jayakarta
Gunung Sahari
Jl. Hidup Baru

Angke Station
Jl. Duri Selatan
Jl. Tambora 4
Jl. Tambora
Jl. Perniagaan
Glodok Plaza ❹
Jayakarta Station
Mangga Besar 13
Banjir Kanal
Selatan
Jl. Rajawali

GLODOK
Jl. Hayam Wuruk
Jl. Mangga Besar 1
Jl. Mangga Besar
Jl. Industri
Jl. Landes Pacu Barat/Timur

TAMBORA
Jl. Moh Mansyur
Petak Sembilan Chinese Temple
Jl. Tanah Sereal
Mangga Besar Market
Jl. Mangga
Besar
Mangga Besar Station
Jl. Mangga Besar 4
Jl. Mangga Besar 4
Kr. Anyar Utara
Jl. Kartini
Jl. Landasan Sel.

Jl. Kalianjar g
Jl. Duri Selatan
National Archives
Jl. Tanah Sereal
TAMAN SARI
Jl. Galah Mada
Kr. Anyar Market
Jl. Angkasa

Jl. Dr. Muwardi
Jl. K.H. Zainul Arifin
Jl. Wiryopranoto
Peceningan
SAWAH BESAR
Jl. Kartini
Jl. Garuda

GROGOL
Jl. Kyai Tapa
Jl. AM.
Jl. Batu Jajar
Jl. KH. Samanhudi
Pasar Senen
KEMAYORAN
Kalibaru Market
Jl. Bugur Besar
Jl. Tanah Tinggi Barat
Jl. Tanah Tinggi Timur

Jl. Tomang Utara 1
Jl. Blak
Sangaji
Jl. KH. Hasyim Asyhari
Jl. Ir. Juanda
Jl. Veteran
Cathedral
Jl. Pos
Central Post Office
Freedom Memorial
Senen Station

TOMANG
Jl. Tomang Raya
Jl. Kamboja
Jl. Kyai Caringin
Jl. Balikpapan
Istana Negara (Presidential Palace)
Jl. Medan Merdeka Utara
❾ Istiqlal Mesjid
Senen Raya
Jl. Kramat Bunder

Jl. Madala
Ancient Inscription Museum
Jl. Ciding Timur
Jl. Tn. Abang 2
Jl. Ciding Barat
Muis
Abdul
Jl. Medan Merdeka Barat
Monas National Monument ❽
Gambir Station
Immanuel Church
Jl. Prapatan
SENEN
Jl. Kwitang
Jl. Pilo Gundul

TANAH ABANG
Tanah Abang Station
Jl. Jatibaru
Banjir Kanal Barat
National Museum ❿
Jl. Kebon Siwih
GAMBIR
Jl. Medan Merdeka Timur
Jl. Medan Merdeka Selatan
Ciliwung
JOHOR BARU

Textile Museum
Jl. Kebon Jati
Jl. Kebon Siwih
Jl. K.H. Wahid Hasyim
Jl. M. H. Thamrin
Jl. K.H. Wahid Hasyim
Taman Ismail Marzuki (Ismail Marzuki Arts Centre) ⓫
Jl. Cikini 6
Jl. Cikini
Jl. Raden Saleh
Jl. Paseban

Jl. Brigjen. Katamso Dharmokusomo
Said Na'um Mosque
Plaza Indonesia
Jl. Kebon Kacang
Welcome Statue ⓬
Jl. Sultan Syahrir
University of Indonesia
Jl. Diponegoro
Jl. Salemba Raya

Merak, Cilegon
Jl. Lentjen S. Parman
Jl. Slipi 3
Jl. Slipi 5
Jl. K. H.
Jl. Hos. Cokroaminoto
Jl. Iman
MENTENG
Jl. Bonjol
Jl. Diponegoro
Adam Malik Museum
Jl. Mataram

Jl. Palmerah Utara
SENAYAN
Taman Mini, ⓭
Bogor
Jl. Karet Pasar Baru Barat
Jl. Mangsyur
Jl. Karet Pasar Baru Tumur
Jl. Jend. Sudirman
Blok M
Jl. Latuharhari
Jl. Sultan Agung
Jl. Surabaya

JAKARTA

Map
on page
266

Don't look for rustic charm in the huge sprawling metropolis of the capital city. Jakarta dwellers themselves are proud of the cultural and intellectual life in this ever-changing, chaotic capital

Capital of the world's fourth most populous nation and home to more than 15 million Indonesians, Jakarta is a metropolis that verges on the chaotic. The city has grown tremendously in recent years with the addition of skyscrapers, motorways and middle-class suburbs. The busy Thamrin–Sudirman boulevard corridor through the heart of the city is a wall of glimmering glass and steel, with some of the most interesting high-rise architecture in Asia. The busy Glodok and Blok M districts throb with neon signs and modern shopping centres. Tanjung Priok is the nation's busiest port, and nearby Ancol and Pluit are being developed into waterfront resort communities.

In fact, much of Jakarta is hardly recognisable from a decade ago. Yet there are other parts of the city that seem frozen in time. Small residential districts with market gardens and makeshift *kampung* dwellings impart something of a village atmosphere to many back alleys.

Jakarta is located at the mouth of the Ciliwung River, on the site of a pepper-trading port that flourished here in the 16th century. In 1618, the architect of the Dutch empire in the Indies, Jan Pieterszoon Coen, ordered construction of a new town: Batavia. Under the Dutch East India Company (VOC), Batavia at first prospered, but then it began to decline as official corruption, decreasing market prices and frequent epidemics of malaria, cholera and typhoid took their toll. In the 19th century, the old city was demolished to provide building materials for a new one a couple of kilometres to the south, around what is Medan Merdeka (Freedom Square) today.

During the brief Japanese occupation of World War II, Batavia was renamed Jakarta (Djakarta), quickly transforming into a city of more than 1 million people. Since then, it has become the unrivalled political, cultural and economic centre of the post-war nation.

BELOW: early map of Batavia Harbour, late 1780s.

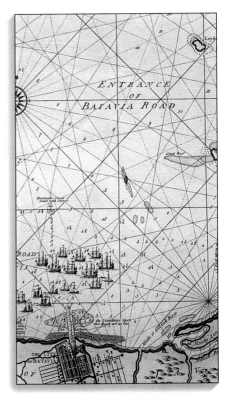

Political problems

In 1998, the worst riots in decades broke out in Jakarta and elsewhere in Indonesia, ignited by the collapse of the economy and centred on the removal of President Soeharto and his family from political and economic power. Hard-hit in the riots were businesses and buildings owned by Chinese Indonesians, a small minority of whom control most of the economy. Glodok, Jakarta's Chinatown, was devastated in some areas. Many gleaming high-rises went wanting for office tenants after the collapse of the rupiah, as foreign corporations, which had seen Jakarta as an up-and-coming financial and business centre, packed and left. Many have yet to return, and Indonesia continues to suffer from an economic malaise that will take years to recover from.

Old Batavia

Known as **Kota**, the area of the old town of Batavia came to life in the 1620s as a tiny, walled town modelled after Amsterdam. Most of the original settlement – Old Batavia – was demolished at the beginning of the 19th century. Only the town square area survived. It was restored and renamed **Taman Fatahillah ❶**. On the north side of the square is Si Jagur, an old cannon regarded by many as a fertility symbol. Surrounding colonial edifices have been converted into the History Museum, the Fine Arts Museum and the Wayang Museum. The **Museum Wayang ❷** (Puppet Museum; Tues–Fri and Sun 9am–4pm, Sat 9am–3pm) on the western side of the square, displays puppets and masks from all over Indonesia. There is also a collection of *topeng* masks, and tombstones of several early Dutch governors are on display.

The **Museum Seni Rupa ❸** (Fine Arts Museum; Tues–Fri and Sun 9am–4pm, Sat 9am–3pm) on the east side of Taman Fatahillah is housed in the former Court of Justice building, completed in 1879. The museum has mediocre collections of paintings and sculptures by modern Indonesian artists, and an exhibition of rare porcelains.

Behind the Wayang Museum are two Dutch houses dating from the 18th century. The first, across the canal and to the left, is a solid red-brick townhouse (Jalan Kali Besar Barat No. 11) that was built around 1730 by the soon-to-be governor-general. The design, and particularly the fine Chinese-style woodwork, is typical of old Batavian residences. Three doors to the left stands the only other house from the same period, now the offices of a bank. Several blocks to the north along the fetid and polluted canal, an old red wooden drawbridge straddles the canal, recalling the days when Batavia was laced with waterways.

BELOW: on the site of Jayakarta, the new town of Batavia sported features of Amsterdam.

Jakarta's Chinatown, **Glodok** ❹, is adjacent to the old European quarter. Unlike Chinatowns elsewhere, you'll see no signs in Chinese here, except in the two Buddhist temples deep within the convoluted back alleys. The public use of Chinese characters was banned in the 1960s during the failed but bloody Communist insurgency. Riots in 1998 destroyed large numbers of buildings here.

To the north lies the old spice trading harbour, **Sunda Kelapa Harbour** ❺, with a mile-long wharf in use since 1817. Early morning is the best time to walk along the 2-km (1¼-mile) wharf among the ships' prows and gangways and witness one of the world's last remaining commercial sailing fleets. Filled with the romance of a bygone era, watch the unloading of cargo from the majestic wooden *pinisi* schooners built by the seafaring Bugis people of South Sulawesi.

The area around Sunda Kelapa is rich in history, and the best way to survey the area is on foot. Near the river stands a 19th-century **Dutch lookout tower** (Uitkik), constructed by the Dutch upon the site of the original customs house (Pabean) of Jayakarta. This is where traders once rendered their gifts and tribute to the local ruler in return for the privilege of trading here.

Behind the tower stands a long, two-storey structure dating from VOC times, now the **Museum Bahari** ❻ (Tues–Thur 9am–2.30pm; Fri and Sun 9am–3pm; Sat 9am–noon). This former warehouse was erected by the Dutch in 1652 and was used for many years to store coffee, tea and Indian cloth. Inside are displays of traditional sailing craft from all corners of the Indonesian archipelago, as well as some old maps and photographs of Batavia. Down a narrow lane and around a corner behind the museum lies **Pasar Ikan**, the fish market, beyond which are numerous stalls selling nautical gear.

Further east along the waterfront is a giant seaside recreation area called

Map on page 266

BELOW: vessels at Sunda Kelapa.

*A page from an
ancient edition of
the Koran, Islam's
holy book.*

Ancol Dreamland ⑦, once swampland and now featuring beach-front hotels, a golf course, bowling alley, arts and crafts market, drive-in theatre, and swimming pools. There are also several theme parks in the area, including **Sea World** (Sun–Fri and public holidays 9am–8pm; Sat 9am–9pm) and **Dunia Fantasi**, Indonesia's only real amusement park complete with roller coaster and Ferris wheel. Hundreds of Indonesians converge here on the weekends and holidays.

Ferries to some of the 600 offshore islands, known collectively as **Kepulauan Seribu** (Thousand Islands) leave from Ancol Marina. The islands are a popular escape for residents of Jakarta. Several of the closer islands, notably Onrust, were used by the Dutch East Indies Company as locations for warehouses and drydocks. The ruins of these colonial installations from the 17th and 18th centuries can still be seen.

Around Medan Merdeka

A circumnavigation of central Jakarta begins at the top of the **Monas** (National Monument; Tues–Fri and Sun 9am–4pm; Sat 9am–3pm), a 137-metre-tall (450-ft) marble obelisk set in the centre of **Medan Merdeka ⑧** (Freedom Square). The monument is surmounted by an observation deck and a 14-metre (45-ft) bronze flame sheathed in 33 kilograms (73 lbs) of gold. It was commissioned by Soekarno and completed in 1961 – a combination Olympic flame and Washington Monument with the phallic overtones of an ancient Hindu-Javanese *lingga*. A high-speed elevator rises to the observation deck, where on a clear day you can enjoy a fabulous 360-degree view of Jakarta.

East of Medan Merdeka is the imposing white marble **Mesjid Istiqlal ⑨**, with its massive dome and rakish minarets, on Jalan Veteran. The largest mosque in

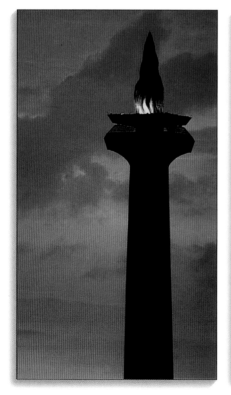

Southeast Asia, it was built on the former site of the Dutch Benteng (Fort) Noordwijk. During the Islamic fasting period of Ramadan, the mosques are filled to capacity. Tours of the mosque are available.

On the west side of Medan Merdeka lies one of Indonesia's great cultural treasures, the excellent **National Museum** ❿ (Tues–Thurs and Sun 8.30am–2.30pm, Fri to 11.30am, Sat to 1.30pm). Opened in 1868 by the Batavian Society for Arts and Sciences – the first scholarly organisation in colonial Asia and founded in 1778 – the museum houses enormously valuable collections of antiquities, books and ethnographic artifacts acquired by the Dutch during the 19th and early 20th centuries. The objects exhibited are fascinating: Hindu-Javanese stone statuary, prehistoric bronze wares and Chinese porcelains are among the exhibits that will need hours to be viewed properly. The star collection, however, is housed in the Treasure Room – a stupendous hoard of royal Indonesian heirlooms. Southeast of the square, a short ride down Jalan Cikini, are two other noteworthy attractions. **Taman Ismail Marzuki** (TIM) ⓫ is a multifaceted cultural centre that presents a continuing bill of drama, dance and music from around the Indonesian archipelago.

Nearby, Jalan Surabaya is the city's so-called "antique street", with dozens of stalls selling everything from wayang puppets to vintage ship fittings. Be aware that most of it is brand new.

South Jakarta

Hail a cab and cruise west across the upper-class residential area of Menteng to the **Welcome Statue** ⓬, a busy roundabout with a statue of two waving youths and a fountain. Jalan Thamrin, lined with shopping malls and office buildings,

Map on page 266

BELOW: the bronze Welcome Statue is one of several grand monuments which dot the city.

Map on page 266

runs north and south here, turning into Jalan Sudirman a few more blocks south. The roundabout fountain is an urban anchor of Jakarta, built by Soekarno in the early 1960s. Surrounding the roundabout are the Hotel Indonesia, the nation's first international-class hotel, and the ritzy Grand Hyatt. The hotel is perched atop Jakarta's finest mall, Plaza Indonesia, offering numerous food outlets and a Western-style market stocked with imported goods.

Adjacent to the Hilton Hotel is the **Jakarta Convention Centre**. Everything from art exhibits and cultural events to rock concerts is held here. Close by is the **Taman Rai**, an amusement park with arcade games, nightclubs and fashionable eateries very popular with Jakarta's young crowd. Further south on Jalan Sudirman, behind the Senyan sports field, home to the national soccer games, is the **Senayan Plaza**, one of the newest shopping malls.

Blok M, in the southwest of the city, is where Jakarta's middle class does much of its shopping. The area bustles with street stalls, hundreds of shops and half a dozen modern shopping malls, including two giant shopping centres: Blok M Plaza and Blok M Mall. This is also the home of the Pasaraya department store, which features two entire floors of clothing and handicrafts from all over Indonesia. After the shopping is done, try one of the trendy restaurants or pubs in the Blok M area. To get a different view of Jakarta, drive through the nearby residential neighbourhoods like Pondok Indah or Cipete to see how wealthy Indonesians and many expatriates live. The **Pondak Indah Mall** is one of Jakarta's busiest malls, and there's a water slide park in the same complex if you get bored with shopping.

Still heading south about 15 km (9 miles) from the centre of the city is the **Ragunan Zoo** (daily 9am–6pm). With a pleasant, relaxed atmosphere set in a tropical garden park, there are over 3,000 animals indigenous to Indonesia. This may be your only chance to see the infamous Komodo dragon, along with orangutan and Sumatran tigers.

Just off the super highway leading south to Bogor is a theme park called **Taman Mini-Indonesia** ⓭ (Indonesia in Miniature Park; daily 9am–5pm), which compresses the entire archipelago into a single attraction. While this is surely an impossible feat, the park does at least permit you to see something of the thousands of Indonesian islands you will not visit. In any case, it is worth a visit, for the fine bird park if nothing else. Encompassing nearly 100 hectares (250 acres), Taman Mini has 27 main pavilions, one for each of Indonesia's provinces. These are clustered around a lake containing a three-dimensional relief map of the Indonesian archipelago. The pavilions have been constructed using authentic materials and workmanship to exhibit a traditional style of architecture from each province. Inside are displays of handicrafts, traditional costumes, musical instruments and artifacts indigenous to the regions.

The park contains at least 30 other attractions, including the orchid garden, IMAX cinema, cable-car ride (useful for orientating one's self), transport museum, swimming pool, and the splendid **Museum Indonesia** (daily 9am–5pm) – a three-storey Balinese palace filled with Indonesia's cultural arts. ❑

OPPOSITE: Jakarta at night. **BELOW:** West Sumatran wedding clothes, Taman Mini.

JAVA

Map
on page
254

The island of Java is Indonesia's most populated, and is perhaps its culturally richest island. The country's large urban centres are on Java, along with important cultural and natural retreats

lthough most visitors to Indonesia are inclined to make a beeline for Bali, the island of Java has as much to offer to the intrepid traveller, whether the rich and complex ancient cultures of eastern Java to the cool mountain retreats south of Jakarta. (In fact, many of the crafts sold on Bali as "antiques" come from Java.) While Java is Indonesia's most populated island – the government has long encouraged people on Java to resettle on other islands – there are large areas that are as pristine as anywhere. Getting around is the easiest anywhere in Indonesia, with trains, long-distance buses, air links and modern if somewhat chaotic highways. All that's needed is a bit of time and a desire to stray from the beaten track.

In the uplands of West Java, beyond the sprawl of Jakarta, the inhabitants are mainly Sundanese, a people with their own language and identity. The Javanese themselves constitute about two-thirds of the total population and inhabit the fertile plains of central and east Java, plus much of the island's northern coast. Madura and the adjoining coast of east Java are home of the Madurese people. There are also small pockets of Tenggerese and Badui peoples living in isolated highland sanctuaries in eastern and western Java, respectively. Lastly, the trading ports of the north coast also harbour immigrant Chinese, Arabs and Europeans, as well as other people from the Indonesian archipelago.

LEFT: colonial Dutch architecture, Banten.
BELOW: misty montane forest.

Beyond Jakarta: West Java

West Java may be roughly divided into two distinct regions: the Parahyangan (Abode of the Gods) or volcanic highlands centred around the provincial capital of Bandung, and the northern coastal plain. The coast is much more mixed, having absorbed a multitude of immigrants and influences via its trading ports for many centuries. In certain coastal areas (notably around Jakarta and Banten), Javanese and Bahasa Indonesian are more commonly spoken.

A quick getaway from Jakarta is the jaunt to Java's sandy and secluded west coast beaches. Stop along the way at the village of **Banten ❶**, which was one of the most vibrant towns in Asia during the 16th century. Banten was razed by the Dutch in 1808, and today is but a tiny fishing village straddling a tidal creek. But there are the ruins of two massive palaces and a Dutch fortress, plus an interesting old mosque, with its adjacent museum, and a Chinese temple. Twenty km (12 miles) further south is **Carita Beach**, a popular weekend retreat for Jakartans that offers beach-side bungalows with swimming, sailing, diving and dining. This palm-fringed coast is famous for its views of the volcanic islands of **Krakatau**.

Only two hours from Jakarta by high-speed train (the *Argo Gede*), four or more by road, the highland city of **Bandung ❷** offers a cool alternative to the capital's oppressive heat. There is plenty for travellers, with an abundance of Dutch-colonial, art-deco architecture, including the magnificent **Gedung Sate**. You can also browse factory outlet shops along Jalan Ciampelas or check out the famed "Java Man" at the Geological Museum on Jalan Diponegoro. The town has a hilly contour, which adds to its character.

The northern coastal ports of Java were once the busiest and richest towns on the island. In **Cirebon ❸**, the Kraton Kesepuhan (Palace of the Elder Brother), built in 1678, sits on the site of the 15th-century Pakungwati palace of Cirebon's earlier Hindu rulers. Just next to the palace stands the Masjid Agung (Grand Mosque), constructed around 1500.

Another 90 km (55 miles) and two hours to the east, the substantial city of **Semarang ❹** overflows out across a narrow coastal plain and up onto steeply rising foothills. Known during Islamic times for its skilled shipwrights, Semarang today is the commerical hub and provincial capital of Central Java. Relics of the past bear witness to the presence of a large population of Dutch traders and officials, and a generous sprinkling of affluent Chinese merchants. The old Dutch Church on Jalan Suprapto downtown, with its copper-clad dome and Greek cross floor plan, was consecrated in 1753 and stands at the centre of the town's 18th-century European commercial district. Semarang's most interesting district, however, is Pacinan, its Chinatown – a grid of narrow lanes tucked away in the centre of the city, and reached by walking due south from the old church along Jalan Suari to Jalan Pekojan. Here, some old townhouses retain the distinctive Nanyang style of elaborately-carved doors and shutters.

Javanese mountains.

BELOW: colourful Cirebon boats.

Yogyakarta and Borobudur

The green crescent of fertile rice lands that blankets Gunung Merapi's southern flanks – with historic Yogyakarta as its focal point – is today inhabited by over 10 million Javanese, with at least 3 million urban residents. Rural population densities here soar above 1,000 people per sq. km (2,500 per sq. mile), and in some areas, a square kilometre feeds an astounding 2,000 people with labour-intensive farming.

Although it was founded only in 1755, the sprawling city of **Yogyakarta** ❺ is situated at the very core of an ancient region known as Mataram, site of the first great central-Javanese empires. From the 8th until the early 10th centuries, this fertile and sloping plain between the Progo and the Opak rivers was ruled by a succession of Indianised kings – the builders of Borobudur, Prambanan and dozens of other elaborate stone monuments. In about AD 900, however, these rulers suddenly and inexplicably shifted their capital to eastern Java, and for more than six centuries thereafter, Mataram was deserted.

The first stop for all visitors to Yogyakarta is the **Keraton** (Sultan's Palace; Sat–Thur 8am–1pm; Fri 8–11am), a 200-year-old palace complex that stands at the very heart of the city. According to traditional cosmological beliefs, the Javanese ruler is literally the "navel" or central "spike" of the universe, anchoring the temporal world and communicating with the mystical realm of powerful deities. In this scheme of things, the Keraton is both the capital of the kingdom and the hub of the cosmos. It houses not only the sultan and his family, but also the powerful dynastic regalia *(pusaka)*, private meditation and ceremonial chambers, a magnificent throne hall, several audience and performance pavilions, a mosque, an immense royal garden, stables, barracks, an armaments foundry and

Map on page 254

BELOW: Dutch colonial buildings, downtown Yogya.

two parade grounds planted with sacred banyan trees. All of this is in a carefully conceived complex of walled compounds, narrow lanes and massive gateways, and bounded by a fortified outer wall measuring 2 km (1½ miles) on every side. Construction of Yogyakarta's Keraton began in 1755 and continued for almost 40 years. Today, only the innermost compound is considered part of the Keraton proper, while the maze of lanes and lesser compounds, the mosque and the two vast squares have been integrated into the city. Long sections of the outermost wall *(benteng)* still stand, however, and many if not most of the residences inside are still owned and occupied by members of the royal family.

There is much else to see within the Keraton, including the museum, ancient gamelan sets, two great gateways and several spacious courtyards. Behind and just west of the Keraton stand the ruins of the opulent and architecturally ingenious royal pleasure garden called **Taman Sari** (Sat–Thur 8am–1pm; Fri 8–11am). Dutch representatives to the sultan's court marvelled at its construction: a large artificial lake, underground and underwater passageways, meditational retreats, a series of sunken bathing pools, and an imposing two-storey mansion of European design.

Face of nobility in Yogyakarta.

Main Street, Yogyakarta

Yogyakarta's main thoroughfare, **Jalan Malioboro**, begins directly in front of the royal audience pavilion, at the front of the palace, and ends at a phallic *lingga* some 2 km (1½ miles) to the north, a shrine dedicated to the local guardian spirit, Kyai Jaga. It was laid out by Hamengkubuwono I as a ceremonial boulevard for colourful state processions, and also as a symbolic meridian along which to orient his domain. Today, Jalan Malioboro is a busy avenue lined with shop fronts and teeming with vehicles and pedicabs; it's primarily a shopping district, but also an area of historical and cultural interest. Begin at the town square *(alun-alun)* and stroll up this latter-day processional, stopping first at the Sono Budaya Museum, on the northwestern side of the square. It was opened in 1935 by the Java Institute, a cultural foundation of wealthy Javanese and Dutch art patrons, and today houses important collections of prehistoric artefacts, Hindu-Buddhist bronzes, *wayang* puppets, dance costumes and traditional Javanese weapons.

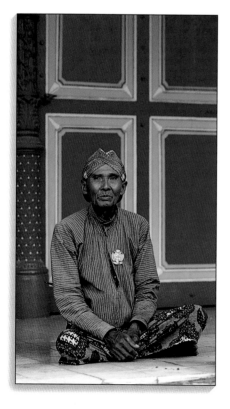

BELOW: Keraton guard.

Proceed northward from the square through the main gates and out across Yogya's main intersection. Immediately ahead on the right stands the old Dutch garrison, **Benteng Budaya** (Fort Vredeburgh), now a cultural centre, complete with exhibition and performance halls. Opposite it on the left stands the former Dutch Resident's mansion. Used during the revolution as the presidential palace, it is now the governor's residence. Farther along on the right, past the fort, is the huge covered central market, Pasar Beringan, a dimly lit women's world of small stalls.

A leisurely one-hour drive across the river beds and rice fields leads to the steps of fabled **Borobudur**, 40 km (25 miles) northwest of Yogyakarta. This huge stupa, the world's largest Buddhist monument, was built sometime during the relatively short reign of the Sailendra dynasty in central Java, between AD 778 and 856 – 300 years before Angkor Wat and 200 years before Notre Dame. Yet, within little more than a century of its completion, Borobudur and all of central Java were abandoned. At about this time, neighbouring Gunung Merapi erupted violently, covering Borobudur in volcanic ash and concealing it for centuries.

It's unlikely that we shall ever know the full import of Borobudur as a religious monument. It is estimated that 30,000 stonecutters and sculptors, 15,000 carriers and thousands more masons worked anywhere from 20 to 75 years to build the monument. At a time when the entire population of central Java numbered less than 1 million, this represents a commitment of perhaps 10 percent of the available work force to a single effort. Seen from the air, Borobudur forms a mandala, or geometric aid for meditation. Seen from a distance on the ground, Borobudur is a stupa or reliquary, a model of the cosmos in three vertical parts: a square base supporting a hemispheric body and a crowning spire. As one approaches along the traditional pilgrimage route from the east and then ascends the terraced monument, circumambulating each terrace clockwise in succession, every relief and carving contributes to the whole.

East of Yogyakarta is a volcanic plain littered with ancient ruins. Because these *candi* are considered by the Javanese to be royal mausoleums, this region is known by them as the Valley of the Kings. In the centre of the plain, 17 km (11 miles) from Yogya, lies the town of **Prambanan** (daily 6am–sunset). The temple complex of Prambanan was completed sometime around AD 856 to commemorate an important military victory. It was deserted within a few years of its completion, however, and eventually collapsed. Restoration work begun on the central temple in 1918 was finally completed in 1953. The Indonesian Government is continuing a long-term restoration project on the other temples.

Map on page 254

Ancient temple at Prambanan.

BELOW: Borobudur.

Map
on page
254

Morning rounds.

Surakarta (Solo)

The quiet, old court city of **Surakarta ❻** (more commonly known as **Solo**) lies just an hour east of Yogyakarta by car. The main attraction, a functioning 18th-century palace called the **Keraton Kasunanan** (Sat–Thur 8.30am–1pm), was constructed between 1743 and 1746 on the banks of the mighty Benagawan Solo River.

The **Keraton Museum** was established in 1963 and contains ancient Hindu-Javanese bronzes, traditional weapons, and coaches dating back to the 1740s. Also be sure to visit **Sasana Mulya,** a music and dance pavilion of the Indonesian Arts College (STSI), just to the west of the main or north palace gate. Here you may see *gamelan* rehearsals, dance performances and *wayang kulit* shows. Another branch of the royal family has constructed their own keraton around a kilometre northwest of the main palace. Completed in 1866, **Keraton Mangkunegaran** (Sat–Thur 9am–2pm; Fri 9am–12.30pm) houses the private collections of Mankunegara IV: dance ornaments, *topeng* masks, jewellery (including two silver chastity belts), ancient Javanese and Chinese coins, bronze figures, and a superb set of ceremonial *keris* blades.

Surabaya and eastern Java

Until the turn of the 20th century, the East Java provincial capital of **Surabaya ❼** was the largest and most important seaport in the archipelago. It still ranks second (after Jakarta's Tanjung Priok), with more than 400 years of colourful history behind it.

In the centre of town is the **Hotel Majapahit**, built nearly a century ago in the tradition of the Strand in Rangoon and the Raffles in Singapore. Now managed by Mandarin Oriental, it has been completely renovated and is worth visiting for its combination of colonial elegance and Art Deco trimmings. Just to the south is the **Hong Tik Hian Temple**, where Chinese hand-puppet *(potehi)* performances are put on daily for the benefit of the assembled deities. And just across Jalan Kembang Jepun, on Jalan Selompretan, stands Surabaya's oldest Chinese shrine, the 18th-century **Hok An Kiong Temple**, built entirely of wood by native Chinese craftsmen.

Just north of Surabaya, off the coast in the Java Sea, is **Madura ❽**, famous for its straightforward people, and for the annual *kerapan sapi* or bull races in early autumn. According to the Madurese, bull-racing began long ago when plow teams raced one another across rice fields. Today's bulls are never used for plowing, but are specially bred and are a considerable source of regional pride. Races take place in August and September, with a grand finale in **Pamekasan**, the island's capital.

One of the best bases for explorations of any sort in East Java is the delightful mountain resort of **Tretes**, just 55 km (35 miles) south of Surabaya, where you can walk or ride on horseback to one of three valley waterfalls in the vicinity. This area is also studded with ancient monuments.

The steep slopes of the active volcanos of eastern Java have been the home of the Tenggerese people for several hundred years. The region has become a major vegetable-growing area, and the spectacular gardens and high-altitude pine trees are a great sight. **Gunung Bromo ❾** itself is a squat volcanic cone inside the much larger Bromo Caldera. The views from the rim of this caldera, developed for tourism, and from the narrow lip of Gunung Bromo itself are an other-worldly experience, especially if Bromo is belching steam. The traditional visit to Gunung Bromo has been a midnight ascent (by car) to position oneself on the volcanic lip at dawn. The light of the rising sun slowly illuminates the caldera, full of fog. On clear mornings, the cone of **Gunung Semeru**, Java's highest volcano, looms south. ❑

TIP

Most visitors, eager to escape Surabaya's heat, head for the inviting hills to the south of the city, including the delightful town of Malang. Check out the exquisite antiques and art, and unique rooms, at the Hotel Tugu Malang.

OPPOSITE: banteng bull in a nature reserve.

BALI

Map on page 285

Everyone knows Bali, even if they don't know that it's part of Indonesia. Intense commercialisation has changed the southern part of the island, but elsewhere the magical ambience remains

The island of Bali is, first and foremost, a masterpiece of nature formed by an east-to-west range of volcanoes and dominated by two towering peaks, Gunung Batur and Gunung Agung. The Balinese have done much to turn the natural blessings to their advantage. All but the steepest land has been painstakingly terraced over the centuries with rice paddies that hug the volcanic slopes like steps. Each watery patch is efficiently irrigated through an elaborate system of aqueducts, dams and sluices regulated since ancient times by village agricultural cooperatives called *subak.*

The land repays these efforts with abundant harvests, which in turn give the people extra time and energy to devote to their renowned cultural pursuits, especially the arts.

Abundant harvests are attributed to the benign efforts of the goddess of rice and fertility, Dewi Sri. Her symbol is the *cili,* two triangles connected in the form of a shapely woman. Divine spirits dwell in the lofty mountains; dark and inimitable forces lurk in the seas. The human's rightful place is the middle ground between these two extremes, and each home, village and kingdom in Bali has traditionally been aligned along this mountain–sea axis.

LEFT: temple's kala-head gateway.
BELOW: the beach at Sanur.

Isolation and confrontation

Bali was settled and civilised relatively early, as evidenced by stone megaliths like Gunung Kawi. Around a thousand years ago, Bali became a vassal of the great Hindu empires of eastern Java. Yet Balinese culture developed a sophisticated persona all its own. Bali was united in 1550 under an independent ruler, and for two generations, Bali experienced a cultural golden age in which an elaborate ceremonial life, and also the arts, flourished.

Due to their traditional fear of the sea and suspicion of foreigners, the Balinese lived in virtual isolation from the rest of the world until the early 20th century. Throughout this period, its traditions of dance, music, painting, sculpture, poetry, drama and architecture were refined and elaborated, ostensibly for the benefit of Bali's numerous gods.

Throughout the 19th century, the Dutch, under the guise of seeking treaties of friendship and commerce, attempted to establish sovereignty over the island. Their incursions culminated in horrific mass suicides *(puputan)* in the early 1900s, in which Balinese kings and courtiers threw themselves on *keris* knives, or ran headlong into Dutch gunfire, rather than face the humiliation of surrender. But Bali has always been adept in absorbing influences from the outside, while retaining, if not strengthening, its local cultural touchstones.

Southern Bali

As the focus for Bali's tourism, commerce and government, the south is by far the island's busiest region. But don't be deceived by the area's development. The south's temple festivals are legendary for the intensity of their trance dances and the earthiness of their rituals. Denpasar's palace ceremonies rank among the most regal on the island, and Kuta establishments host highly professional dance performances nightly. During Nyepi (Balinese New Year), thousands of villagers, arrayed in their ceremonial finery, flood the southern shores of Kuta bearing offerings of food for the *melis* purification rites.

South of the **Ngurah Rai International Airport** ❶, the island's only airport, a bulbous peninsula fans out to form the **Bukit Badung**, once the hunting grounds of Denpasar's rajas. Geologically and climatically, this area is Mediterranean, a dry and mostly barren plateau lying well above sea level. The western and southern shoreline is rimmed with sharp, jutting cliffs, the site of the region's most illustrious temple, **Pura Luhur Uluwatu** ❷. Giant sea turtles swim in the ocean 300 metres (1,000 ft) below the temple's cliff-top perch.

The mangroves lining **Benoa Harbour**, on the northwest coast of Bukit Peninsula, give way to superb beaches along the northeastern shore of the peninsula – a place called **Nusa Dua** ❸, which has been developed into an extensive planned-resort project over the last decade.

Whereas Nusa Dua caters to more up-market visitors, **Kuta** ❹ has become a kind of cluttered, traffic-packed tinseltown with a cosmopolitan feel, especially during peak season (July–August and December–January). Kuta's natural attractions are a broad beach, pounding surf and sunsets. Deserted stretches of sandy beach and the serenity of the Balinese countryside are, thankfully, never more

Chosen by the Balinese saint Pedenda Sakti Wawu Ruah as the "stage" for his moksa *reunion with the godhead, Pura Luhur Uluwatu is unrivaled for sheer grandeur of location.*

BELOW: net fishing, and the cliffs at the temple of Uluwatu.

Map on page 285

than a few minutes away. Past the Bali Oberoi Hotel is the important estuary temple of **Peti Tenget**. Farther along the main road lies **Kerobokan**, a village of rural charm and as instant a trip into the "real" Bali as one can hope to find in short order. Further north along the eastern coast is **Sanur ❺**, a relatively quiet cluster of resort facilities, but with an excellent beach and choice of water activities.

Denpasar

Denpasar ❻ has swollen some tenfold over the years into a metropolis of more than 200,000 people, especially after it replaced the northern port of Singaraja as the island's capital in 1945. Denpasar's main square was the scene of the horrific mass suicide in 1906, when almost the entire royal house of Denpasar rushed headlong into blazing Dutch guns. Successive governments have erected monuments commemorating the event. East of the square stands the town's state temple, **Pura Jagatnata**, a figurine of Tintya, the almighty godhead, glinting from its sea high on the temple's central shrine. The **Museum Bali** (Tues–Sun 8am–5pm) next door houses a fine collection of archaeological artefacts and examples of Balinese craftsmanship. Denpasar means "the market". The centre of town is the **Pasar Badung**, a four-storey building housing Bali's largest traditional market.

Central Bali

One of the most important temples between Denpasar and Ubud, dating from the 12th century, is Pura Sada, in **Kapal**. It has 64 stone seats resembling megalithic ancestral shrines. These are believed to commemorate loyal warriors who fell

TIP

For some insight and appreciation of Balinese performing arts, visitors can observe dance and music classes in progress at STSI, in Denpasar.

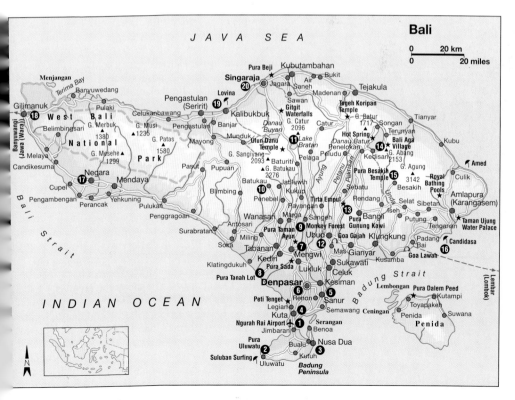

in battle. Past Kapal, a turn-off toward the mountains leads to **Mengwi** ❼, a few kilometres north of Kapal. In 1634, the Raja of Mengwi built a magnificent garden temple, Pura Taman Ayun. The temple's spacious compound is surrounded by a moat and is adjacent to a lotus lake. In the surrounding pavilions, priests recite their vedic incantations.

Southwest of Mengwi on the southern coast, west of Denpasar, is **Pura Tanah Lot** ❽, perched on a large rock just offshore and founded by the proselytising Hindu saint, Naratha, during his wanderings.

Northeast at **Sangeh** ❾ is Bali's famed monkey forest. According to Balinese versions of the *Ramayana* epic, this is where part of Hanuman's monkey army landed when the monkey king lifted the sacred mountain, Mahameru, and broke it apart in order to crush Rawana. A moss-covered temple lies hidden deep within the jungle.

Popular with travellers is Pura Luhur, near **Batukau** ❿, on the slopes of Gunung Batukau, 2,278 metres (7,474 ft) in altitude. One of Bali's most venerated temples, every other temple in Bali in western Bali has a shrine dedicated to Pura Luhur, located within solitary grounds far above the farmlands. There are no ornate carvings or gilded shrines to be found in this mountain sanctuary. At **Danau Bratan** ⓫, a lake on the road crest to the north shore and a water source for surrounding farmlands, is Pura Ulun Danau Bratan, which honours Dewi Danau, goddess of the lake.

With more gold leaf per square metre than imperial China, more artists than Montmartre, and the most glamourous traditional culture in the modern world, the magical middle kingdom is Bali's most exotic and artistic region. Ever since the great Hindu-Balinese renaissance of the 17th century, the realm within a 15-km (9-mile) radius of Ubud, north of Denpasar, has been the main centre of Balinese art. The village of **Sukawati**, halfway between Denpasar and Ubud, was once an important kingdom and centre for Chinese traders during the Dalem dynasty period. A phalanx of shops and a market now conceal the grand Puri Sukawati palace. Further north is **Mas**, a village of master carvers. In former times, woodcarvers worked only on religious or royal projects, but now they mostly produce decorative works for export.

Crossing the Petanu River immediately to the east of Peliatan on the road to Bedulu, the mysterious although exceedingly commercial **Goa Gajah** (Elephant Cave) is just visible on the lower side of the road, opposite a row of souvenir stands. The cave's gaping mouth is fantastically carved with leaves, rocks, animals, waves and demons, and when it was discovered in 1923, these carvings were apparently mistaken for an elephant, hence the cave's name.

For many years, **Ubud** ⓬ has been a mecca for foreign and local artists who enjoy the creative atmosphere in this area of Bali. Artists have thrived in Ubud since the 1930s, when a local aristocrat named Cokorda Sukawati formed the Pita Maha art society together with German painter Walter Spies and Dutch artist Rudolf Bonnet. Many of the finest works of the early Pita Maha years, which show clearly the transition from traditional to modern Balinese painting

Pura Luhur is a pura taman, or a temple with a garden pond and maintained by a king. Rituals here include veneration of lakes and a blessing for irrigation water.

BELOW: a banana balancing act.

styles, are exhibited in the Puri Lukisan Museum. Also visit the Neka Museum, west of downtown, for a superb collection of Balinese art.

Map on page 285

Pura Penataran Sasih (Lunar Governance), in **Pejeng**, contains Indonesia's most important bronze-age antiquity: the 2,000-year-old Moon of Pejeng drum. Shaped like an hourglass, beautifully etched, and over 3 metres (10 ft) long, it is the largest drum in the world to be cast as a single piece. According to Balinese legend, it fell from the sky, but the discovery of an ancient, similarly shaped stone mould in Bali proves that sophisticated bronze-casting techniques were known here from an early time.

Pura Gunung Kawi ⓫ is a complex of stone-hewn *candi* and monk's cells reached by descending a long, steep stairway through a stone arch into a watery canyon. The Balinese refer to their religion as Agama Tirta – the religion of the waters. It's not surprising then that a pilgrimage to the Pura Tirta Empul spring at **Tampaksiring**, 2 km (1½ miles) upstream from Gunung Kawi, is an essential part of every major Balinese ceremony and ritual. Further north, in the old crater of Gunung Batur, is **Danau Batur** ⓮. Here, Pura Ulun Danu Batur is one of two major *subak* (irrigation society) temples on Bali.

The waters of Tampaksiring are believed to have magical curative and restorative powers.

Eastern Bali

The direction "east" is greatly revered by the Balinese, as it is the realm of the Hindu god Shiva in his manifestation as Surya, the sun god. Balinese myth tells how the gods set down towering **Gunung Agung** in the east and placed their thrones upon it. Coming from Ubud or the south, the major roads pass through **Gianyar**, centre of Bali's famous weaving industry. Many workshops and factories still produce a variety of beautiful hand-woven and hand-dyed textiles,

BELOW: the most revered of all Balinese temples, Pura Besakih.

Map
on page
285

although the use of machine-spun cotton thread, quick chemical dyes and tinsel foil cannot match the quality of the older cloths, with their hand-spun threads, elaborate vegetable dyes, and gold and silver ornamentation.

The mountain road north from **Klungkung** climbs along some of Bali's most spectacular rice terraces, passing through several villages on the way to the island's holiest spot, the temple of **Pura Besakih** ⓯ (daily 8am–6pm). With the massive peak of Gunung Agung as a backdrop, the broad and stepped granite terraces and slender, pointed black pagodas of this 60-temple complex are a fitting residence for the gods. Regarded as a holy place since pre-historic times, the first record of Besakih's existence is an inscription dating from AD 1007. From at least the 15th century – when Pura Besakih was designated as the sanctuary of the deified ancestors of the Gelgel god-kings and their very extended family – this has been the "mother" temple for the entire island.

Several kilometres after **Kusamba**, at the foot of a rocky escarpment, gapes the entrance to **Goa Lawah** (daily 7am–6pm), one of the nine great temples of Bali. About 15 km (9 miles) past Goa Lawah, a side road to the right leads to the picturesque harbour town of **Padang Bai**. This is where the Lombok ferry departs, and where cruise ships anchor.

Candidasa ⓰ is a perfect base for exploring **Tenganan**, home of a pre-Hindu Bali Aga tribe. Located several kilometres inland in an area of lush bamboo forests and mystical banyan trees, Tenganan was for some reason never assimilated to the island's Hindu-Balinese culture, and thus it has retained its own traditions of architecture, kinship, government, religion, dance and music, supplying the rest of the island with several valuable items, notably the double-ikat *geringsing* fabrics, some of which are considered to be sacred.

Twenty-five km (16 miles) farther east, the road crosses a wide lava bed and enters **Amlapura**, a medium-size town formerly known as Karangasem and once the capital of Bali's cultured king. Puri Kanginan, the palace where the last raja was born, is an eclectic creation reflecting the strong European influence of his education, and of his architect – a Chinese by the name of Tung.

Northern and western Bali

The drive along the southwestern coast is splendid, and uncongested after the traffic chaos of southern Bali. There are excellent and splendid black-sand beaches along the way. The district capital of **Negara** ⓱, near the western end of Bali and on the southwestern coast, is famed mostly for its bull races. A secular entertainment introduced from eastern Java and Madura less than a century ago, bull-racing takes place regularly between July and October.

At the western extreme of Bali is **Gilimanuk** ⓲, a rather nondescript town that is the main ferry terminal for frequent ferries to eastern Java. Just before Gilimanuk is **Culik**, headquarters for the **West Bali National Park**. Trekking in the park requires hiring the services of a guide in Culik. The island of **Menjangan**, within the park, offers Bali's best scuba diving.

The nearly extinct Bali starling is protected within West Bali National Park.

The north coast is peppered with quiet villages and fields of agriculture, including numerous spices. The culture of the north is different in several ways: the language is faster and less refined, the music is more allegro, and the temple ornamentation more fanciful. The towns comprising **Lovina Beach** ⓳ offer countless bungalows for wayward travellers, mostly foreigners seeking an alternative to the overdeveloped southern part of the island.

Further on, the port city of **Singaraja** ⓴, the capital of Bali under the Dutch, has sizeable communities of Chinese and Muslims. From **Penulisan**, the winding road seems to drop straight out of the sky, flattening out several kilometres before the village of **Kubutambahan**, on the coast. ❑

OPPOSITE: scene from *Ramayana*.

Ramayana

One of the two main Indian epics informing Indonesian theatre and dance, including that of Bali, is the *Ramayana*. (The other is the *Mahabharata*.) It is a moral tale, full of instructions and examples on how to lead the good life. It praises the rectitude, wisdom and perseverance of the noble *satriya* or warrior class, and stresses faithfulness, integrity and filial devotion.

The *Ramayana* acknowledges that the trek along the path of virtue demands humility, self-sacrifice, deprivation and compassion. It is a cautionary tale, less a battle between good and evil (in which evil must always lose) than a recognition of the perpetual ebb and flow of the spirits of darkness and light.

In its homeland, India, the *Ramayana* has been known for 3,000 years. With the spread of Indian religions and culture through Southeast Asia, the *Ramayana* became part of the mythology of Burma, Thailand, Laos, Cambodia, the Malay Peninsula, and of Java and Bali. The epic is long and complex.

The characters: In the *Ramayana*, the chief characters are Rama, his wife Sita, his brother Laksmana, the monkey general Hanuman, the demon-king Rawana, and Rawana's brother, Wibisana. Rama is semi-divine (an incarnation of Vishnu), and a consummate archer. He is of noble birth, for he moves in a refined manner. Even in battle, he is graceful and delicate, using his mind as much as his muscles. Rawana, Rama's implacable foe, thrusts and struts upon the stage, every step filled with menace. His head turns sharply with each movement. His face is impassioned, furious red in keeping with his aggressive, hostile nature.

The story: Rama, Laksmana, and their half-brother Barata are the sons of the king of Ayodya. An accomplished bowman, Rama wins the hand of the beautiful Sita in an archery contest, but through the intervention of Barata's mother, Rama is prevented from succeeding his father as king. Rama, Sita and Laksmana go into exile. In the forest they meet the sister of Rawana, king of the demons; she falls in love with Rama, is spurned, and then she turns to Laksmana, who promptly cuts off her nose and ears.

Rawana, determined to avenge this indignity, sends off a servant in the form of a golden deer. Rama stalks the animal and kills it. Its dying cries sound like Rama calling for help, and Laksmana goes in search of his brother. Rawana appears, abducts Sita, and flies off with her.

Searching for Sita, the brothers meet Hanuman, a general in the kingdom of apes. Rama assists the king of the apes, who then places his army at Rama's disposal. Rama and Laksmana set off with Hanuman and the ape army to Langka, Rawana's homeland. Hanuman undertakes a daring reconnaissance of Langka and finds Sita in Rawana's palace. He gives her a token from Rama, and Sita gives Hanuman one of her rings. Hanuman is caught and sentenced to be burned at the stake, but escapes back to Rama.

The ape army builds a giant causeway across the sea to Langka and attacks it. One of Rama's magic arrows eventually fells Rawana, and the victors return home with Sita. Rama receives a boisterous welcome and the throne of the kingdom. ❑

THE PERFORMING ARTS OF BALI

The performing arts of Bali reflect an integration of environment, religion and community, in which every individual is a part of the experience

Wayang kulit (shadow-puppet theatre) is perhaps the most popular of all Balinese performing arts. The two-dimensional puppets are carved from leather and jointed from the elbows and the knees. Most of the puppets are based on characters from epic Indian tales such as the *Ramayana* or the *Mahbharata*. Suspended at the centre of a white screen is the *damar*, a coconut-oil lamp that illuminates and casts a shadow on the screen, though today electric light bulbs are also common. The audience usually sits on the other side of the screen and is entertained by the shadows; the *dalang* – the storyteller and puppeteer – remains behind the screen with his assistants (right and left) and musicians. On the *dalang*'s left is his puppet chest *(grobag)*, while a quartet of musicians, playing the accompaniment on the ten-keyed *gangsa* instruments, sit behind him. A performance can last for up to nine hours.

DANCE-DRAMA

The exuberance of Balinese dance gives it an air of spontaneity, yet beneath lies a learned set of motions presented in a highly stylised form. Each gesture has a name that describes its action; for example a sidestep may be named after the way a raven jumps. No play is complete without music, no dance without a story or meaning.

△ **DANCE SCHOOL**
Dance pupils learn one dance only. After teaching the basic moves, the teacher adjusts the pupil's body into position.

△ **PUPPET MASTER**
The *dalang,* or puppet master, is a consecrated priest. He moves the puppets while narrating the story.

▷ **GAMELAN GONGS**
Gamelan gongs are made from bronze and are still crafted in Bali. Most villages have clubs *(sekaa)* that own and cooperatively maintain the village gamelan.

◁ **LEGONG DANCE**
The classical Balinese *legong* dance is performed by young girls wearing elaborate costumes and headdresses.

◁ KECAK (MONKEY) DANCE

The *kecak* dance originates from a trance dance in which a central person communicates with a god or ancestor. The dance gets its name from the rhythmic chanting of *kecak* by the chorus to encourage the state of trance.

▽ TOPENG PLAYS

Topeng, or *tapel*, means something pressed against the face – a mask. Today's mask plays, commemorating historical exploits of local kings and heroes, was influenced by the *gambuh* dance.

GAMELAN – THE MUSIC OF BALI

The term *gamelan* derives from *gamel*, an old Javanese word for hammer, as most instruments in the orchestra are percussive. The *gamelan* orchestra performs at *wayang* plays, important occasions and temple ceremonies, with the composition of the orchestra changing accordingly. Each octave is split into scales of either five or seven notes, and the instruments are usually designed for one or the other. A principal of *gamelan* music is that the instruments with a higher range of notes are struck more frequently than those with lower ranges. At given intervals, gongs of various sizes mark off the structure of the music, while the other instruments add the complicated ornamentation. Lots of musicians play *gangsa* metalphones, which consist of bronze bars hung over bamboo resonators. The lead *gangsa* player cues the orchestra. The two drums or *kendang* players control the tempo. The small hand cymbals *(cengceng)* accent the music, while the small and single gong or *(kempli)* helps to keep the orchestra together.

◁ COMMUNITY ART

A crowd gathers around the gamelan orchestra at a popular village *wayang kulit* performance.

▷ WAYANG

A *wayang kulit* puppet representing Kresna, a king and spiritual guide of Ajuna, a warrior and hero in the *Pandawa* cycle of plays.

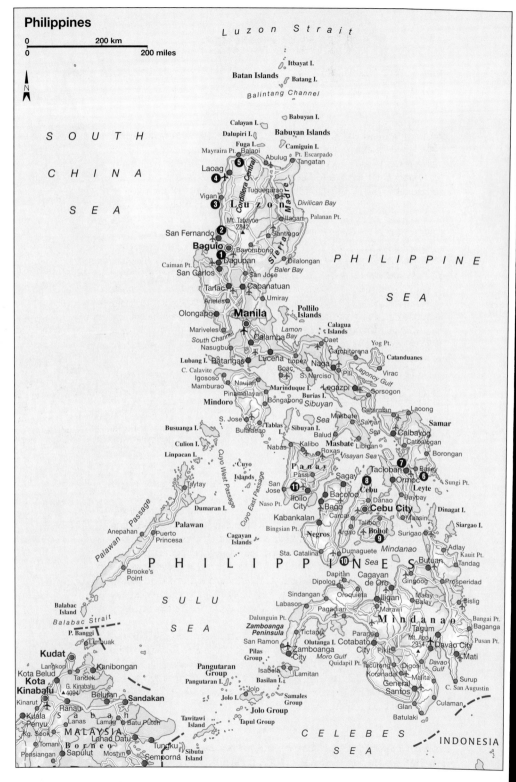

Philippines

0 _____ 200 km
0 _____ 200 miles

N

Luzon Strait

Itbayat I.
Batan Islands   Batang I.
Balintang Channel

Babuyan I.
Calayan I.   **Babuyan Islands**
Dalupiri I.
Fuga I.   Camiguin I.
Mayraira Pt.   Balaoi
Abulug   Pt. Escarpado
⑤   Tangatan
Laoag
④
Tuguegarao

③ Vigan   **Luzon**   *Divilican Bay*
Ilagan   Palanan Pt.
Mt. Tabayoc   *Sierra Madre*
② San Fernando   2842
Santiago
Baguio   Bayombong
① Dagupan   Dilalongan
Caiman Pt.   San Jose   *Baler Bay*
San Carlos
Tarlac   Cabanatuan
Angeles   Umiray

S O U T H

C H I N A

S E A

Cordillera Central

P H I L I P P I N E

S E A

Olongapo   **Manila**   Pollilo Islands
Mariveles   Calauag Islands
Calamba   *Lamon Bay*
Nasugbu   Daet   Garchitorena
Lubang I. **Batangas**   Lucena   Catanduanes
C. Calavite   Boac   Naga
Igososo   S. Narciso   Pili   Virac
Mamburao   Naujan   Legazpi
Mindoro Pinamalayan   Marinduque I.   Sorsogon
S. Jose   Bongabong   Burias I.   Catarman
Masbate   *Sibuyan*   Laoong
Sea   **Samar**
Busuanga I.   Tablas   Sibuyan I.   Calbayog
Catbalogan
Culion I.   **Masbate**   Libigan
Nabas   Roxas   Borongan
Linpacan I.   Kalibo
Visayan Sea   Basey
Cuyo   **⑦**
Islands   Tacloban   **⑥**
Taytay   Passi   **Panay**   Sagay   Ormoc   Sungi Pt.
San   **⑪**   **⑧**   **Leyte**
Dumaran I.   Jose   Iloilo   Bacolod   Cebu   Baybay
Palawan   City   Bago   Danao
Anepahan   Naso Pt.   Kabankalan   Carcar   **Cebu City**   Dinagat I.
Puerto   Talibon   Maasin
Princesa   Bingsian Pt.   **Negros**   Argao   Siargao I.
Cagayan   Sta. Catalina   **Bohol**   Surigao
Islands   **⑨**
Dumaguete   *Mindanao*   Adlay
Brooke's   **⑩**   Dapitan   *Sea*   Butuan   Kauit Pt.
Point   Dipolog   Cagayan   Gingoog   Tandag
S U L U   Sindangan   de Oro   Prosperidad
Oroquieta   Iligan   Malay
S E A   Labason   Marawi   Balay   Bislig
Pagadian
Balabac   Dalunguin Pt.   **Mindanao**   Bangai Pt.
Island   **Zamboanga**   Tictapul   Baganga
Balabac Strait   **Peninsula**   Parang   Mt. Apo   Tagum   Pusan Pt.
P. Banggi   San Ramon   Cotabato   2954   Davao City
Pilas   Olutanga I.   City   Pikit   Digos   **Mati**
Kudat   Group   **Zamboanga**   Quidapil Pt. Tacurong   *Davao*
Langkon   Isabela   City   Koronadal   *Gulf*
Kota Belud   **Pangutaran**   Lamitan   Malita   Surup
Kota   Tandek   **Group**   Basilan I.   **General**   C. San Augustin
Kinabalu   G. Kinabalu   Pangutaran I.   Jolo   **Santos**
Kinarut   4094   Jolo I.   **Samales**   Glan   Culaman
Kuala   Beluran   **Group**
Penyu   Sandakan   **Jolo Group**   Batulaki
Tomani   Ranau   Tawitawi   Tapul Group   **C E L E B E S**
Lanas   Lamag Batu Puteh   Island
MALAYSIA   Sibutu   **S E A**   **INDONESIA**
Kg. Sook   **Borneo**   Island
Pensiangan   Sapulut   Tungku
Mostyn   Semporna

PHILIPPINES

Spanish and American influence over four centuries has made this intriguing archipelago Asia's unexpected surprise

They lie like lovely gems atop Asia's continental shelf, these 7,107 islands, straddling where two tectonic plates collide to create islands with fluid names like Luzon, Mindoro, Palawan and Sulu. Only a couple thousand of these islands can be considered inhabited by the 80 million Filipinos, or as they call themselves, Pinoy, who represent 111 different linguistic, cultural and racial groups. Their national languages are Pilipino, based on Tagalog, a dialect of the Tagalog people of southern Luzon, and English.

Geographically, the Philippines is a sprawl of half-drowned mountains, part of a great cordillera extending from Japan south to Indonesia. The nation's archipelago stretches 1,840 km (1,140 miles) north to south, spanning 1,100 km (690 miles) at its widest.

This archipelago was born from powerful forces – great tectonic pressures pushing islands upwards and mighty volcanoes depositing their ash to enrich plains nurtured by monsoon rains. The first humans to see this land walked here during the ice ages, when seas were hundreds of metres lower. Later, after the ocean once again flooded the land bridges, waves of colonisers came from Borneo in seagoing *barangay* to settle the coastal areas, pushing the earlier arrivals into the mountains. Nearly everything that the Malay people brought has lasted, including language, custom and culture. To this foundation the endowments of the Spanish and Americans have been added. Three centuries in a convent followed by 50 years in Hollywood, goes the old saying.

Manila, the in-your-face capital, is the usual starting point for most journeys in the Philippines. The traveller leaving Europe or North America for the first time finds the city immensely intimidating in its chaos and frantic energy. Worry not, for aside from the predictable scam artists and the like, it is a city with merit for the traveller. It is an old city, with a history that lingers in its architecture: Malacañang Palace, the inner city of Intramuros, the statues and boulevards.

Manila is on the southern end of Luzon, the largest island, and on the northern end of the archipelago. Northward out of Manila leads into the lofty highlands of Baguio and beyond, or along the western coast of Ilocos. This is the land of immense cascading rice terraces, stretching away beyond the horizon.

South of Luzon are the Visayas, a gathering of variously shaped islands that can keep travellers engaged for years. Central to the Visayas is the island, and city, of Cebu. This is not only the gateway to resorts and coral reefs, it is an entrepreneurial city, noted within and outside the Philippines as the nation's place to do efficient business – but also famous for its guitars. ❑

PRECEDING PAGES: Mt Mayon, southern Luzon, has erupted nearly 50 times since 1616; wedding at San Augustin Church, Intramuros, Manila.

Decisive Dates

Early days

Pre-history: Migrants cross land bridge from Asian mainland and settle archipelago.

AD 900: Chinese establish coastal trading posts over the next 300 years.

1400: Muslim clergy start to bring Islam to the Philippines from Malaya.

1494: The Treaty of Tordesillas is signed between Portugal and Spain, dividing much of the world between the two colonial powers. Everything to the east of a line 370 leagues west of the Cape Verde Islands

belongs to Portugal, while everything to the west belongs to Spain.

Early colonial intrusions

1521: Magellan lands on Cebu, claims region for Spain. Lapu Lapu (Rajah Cilapulapu), in defending the island from the Spaniards, slays Magellan, thus driving expedition from Islands.

1543: Ruy de Villabos sails from Mexico to Mindanao and names archipelago after Crown Prince Felipe II.

1565: Miguel Lopez de Legazpi sails from Mexico and gains a foothold in Cebu.

1571: Legazpi builds walled Spanish city of Intramuros. Intramuros is menaced from the outset by enemies: Japanese *wako*, Dutch fleets, Chinese

pirates and disgruntled Filipinos. The core of modern Manila begins to form outside of Intramuros.

1762: Late in the year, as a minor episode in the Seven Years' War with Spain, Intramuros is seized by England's General William Draper.

1764: End of the British occupation.

Rise of nationalism

1872: Uprising in Cavite. Spain executes Filipino priests Jose Burgos, Mariano Gomez and Jacinto Zamora, who continue to be martyrs today.

1892: Jose Rizal returns from Europe. Andres Bonifacio founds the Katipunan.

1896: Spanish colonists imprison and kill hundreds of Filipinos in Manila. Bonifacio and the Katipunan launch the Philippine revolution. Emilio Aguinaldo and rebel forces capture Cavite, south of Manila. Colonial authorities execute Rizal.

1898: The United States goes to war with Spain, and wins. Treaty between the US and Spain grants the US authority over the Philippines, along with Puerto Rico and Guam.

1899: War breaks out between the US and the Philippines. Aguinaldo is inaugurated as president of the first Philippine republic in 1899.

1901: Aguinaldo captured after guerrilla war of resistance and swears allegiance to the US. Scattered resistance continues throughout the decade.

1916: The US Congress authorises the gradual independence of the Philippines.

1935: Quezon elected president. The Philippines is made an American commonwealth with the promise of independence in 1945; but World War II intervenes. General Douglas MacArthur takes charge of the Philippines' defence against Japan.

World War II

1941: On 22 December, Japanese land on Luzon.

1942: Japan takes Manila. Quezon proposes and Roosevelt rejects Philippine neutrality. MacArthur retreats to Australia. *Hukbalahap (Huk)* established with PKP member Luis Taruc in command. Quezon and Osmena flee to the United States, where they establish a government in exile.

1943: Japanese install puppet republic with Jose Laurel as president. The Japanese rule over the country is exceedingly brutal.

1944: Quezon dies. MacArthur and Osmena land in Leyte, beginning the Allied effort to retake the Philippine archipelago from the Japanese.

1945: The Allies recapture Manila, declared an "open city" by the Allies and thus subject to unlimited bombardment. Much of the city is destroyed.

Problems and opportunities

1946: Roxas defeats Osmena for presidency. On 4 July, the Philippines proclaims independence.

1951: US-Philippine mutual defence treaty signed.

1965: Ferdinand Marcos defeats Macapagal in his bid for re-election to the presidency.

1969: Ferdinand Marcos becomes the first Philippines president to be re-elected.

1970: Peso devaluation fuels price increases, food shortages, unemployment and unrest. Radical students and others stage a series of anti-Marcos, anti-US demonstrations. American senators accuse the Philippines of misusing funds supplied for Philippine forces in Vietnam. Marcos threatens to impose martial law.

1972–81: Martial law imposed by Marcos, who rules with an iron fist during this period, erecting monuments to himself and accumulating a vast fortune. His wife, Imelda, dominates Manila government.

1981: Martial law lifted but Marcos keeps power to rule by decree. Marcos re-elected in contest boycotted by opposition.

1983: Leading opposition leader Benito Aquino returns to Manila from exile in the US, is assassinated on arrival at the Manila airport. Circumstances point to government involvement.

1984: Legislative elections held. "Parliament of the street" holds frequent anti-Marcos demonstrations. Spiralling economic crises.

1985: General Fabian C. Ver and 25 others charged with slaying Aquino, but are acquitted. Marcos announces snap election. Over a million people petition Cory Aquino, widow of the assassinated Aquino, to run against Marcos. Aquino agrees.

1986: Violence escalates before the elections, at least 30 killed on election day. Election rigging enrages Filipinos, and millions join in uprising against Marcos regime. On 26 February, the Marcoses flee. Aquino, elected to the presidency, orders release of political prisoners. First two anti-Aquino coup attempts foiled (Aquino would survive 7 coup attempts in all). New constitution drafted. Labour leader Rolando Olalia murdered. Ceasefire with the New People's Army (NPA).

1987: Ceasefire breaks down, and the military kills 13 peasant demonstrators near presidential palace. Public ratifies constitution after third military mutiny put down. Concern grows about renewed human rights abuses. Pro-Aquino forces win majorities in House and Senate elections. Another bloody coup attempt fails. Activist Lean Alejandro murdered.

1988: Provincial elections. The US agrees to pay $481 million a year for use of American military bases in the Philippines. Marcoses indicted by a US grand jury for fraud and embezzlement.

1989: Ferdinand Marcos dies in Hawaii. Coup attempt splits military; government calls on the US for air support of Aquino government.

1990: Cabinet revamped. Negotiations start on status of American military bases.

1991: Bilateral posturing regarding the US bases ends abruptly with the dramatic eruption of Mount Pinatubo. Americans simply pack up and leave.

1992: Fidel Ramos, Aquino's defence minister and a strong ally who backed her during coup attempts, wins presidential election. His pragmatic leadership and problem-solving defy traditional perceptions of inept Filipino government. Foreign investors return.

1998: Joseph Estrada, popular film actor with a reputation for women and wine, is elected president.

2000: Estrada is impeached for bribery, betrayal of public trust and violation of the constitution.

2001: Estrada is ousted from office against his will and Gloria Macapagal Arroyo his vice-president takes over.

2002: US military joins the Philippines in large-scale exercises in southern Philippines to rescue kidnapped foreign hostages. Arroyo announces that she will not run for the next presidential elections in 2004. ❏

LEFT: Spanish expedition leaders Villabos, Legazpi and Magellan are fancifully juxtaposed in an old engraving. **RIGHT:** former president Fidel Ramos tends to important matters.

FNO WAYS

From Christian fervour to ancestral worship, and from clans to mountain tribes,
the richness of Filipino culture creates one of Asia's most vibrant societies

Filipinos have a justifiable reputation as one of the most hospitable people in the world, especially in rural areas where traditional attitudes still survive. Clans are the rule of survival, and are both the main strength and source of corruption in Filipino society. They operate as custodians of common experiences (many old families religiously keep family trees), and as the memory of geographical and racial origins. Clans also act as disciplinary mechanisms, employment agencies and informal social security systems.

Perhaps the crowning glory of local sociology is the Filipino expression that one anthropologist has traced to a linguistic root in *Bahala na*, or "leave it to God". This is a typical Filipino reaction to crises and insoluble problems. Development experts have often decried Bahala na as passive and fatalist, the sole factor in the delayed maturity of the Filipino nation. Others, however, praise its philosophical origins.

Filipina and friar

The image of today's Filipina emerged from a checkered history. It is no longer well remembered, but the majority of the Philippines' early tribes relied on the woman to perform their most sacred rites. *Catalonan* to the Tagalog, *baliana* to the Bicolano, *managanito* to the Pangasinense, *babaylan* to the Bisaya – the priestess healed with herbs, exorcised those who were devil-possessed and, receiving the spirits in trance, guided her tribe or clan through crucial junctures of communal life.

There is no cause for wonder, then, that women furiously fought the Europeans' arrival. Feeling the cornerstone of tribal life threatened, priestesses of Cagayan, Pangasinan and the Visayas let out one long wail of incantation against the conqueror. As Catholic missionaries cursed them for being agents of the devil, the priestesses moved their tribes to poison the cowled strangers, burn their Christian altars,

and all else failing, flee to thick forest and higher if not safer ground.

The Filipina who stayed behind to be Christianised proved to be the colonist's delight. She traded and parlayed with the white man, often helping him pacify war-like neighbouring tribes. Here began the special relationship

between friar and Filipina. Once daughter and consort to proud and free men, she became an adopted waif to be cast in the Castellan mould. The friar who was father figure to whole villages fancied her a naive child, tenderheartedly teaching her his alphabet. He gave her only enough to keep her serving and worshipful, withholding higher education from her eager grasp until as late as the 19th century.

It was a relatively easy thing to declare political independence. It has been a totally different matter coping with the loose ends of colonial thinking. Under two kinds of white rule, the relationship between the sexes in the Philippines has lived through severe imbalances, giv-

LEFT: Filipinas in traditional dress of the Philippines.
RIGHT: young Filipina.

ing it both comedy and tragedy. The Spaniard moulded the Filipina to an Old World charm. The American touched her ambitions to the quick, kindling a fire that still smoulders today. Yet society continues to remind the Filipina of her former status as a friar ward. She cannot draw up or sign contracts without her husband's consent, and her adultery is more stiffly punished than his.

Religion

Kinship was the glue of early Filipino society, and in no time at all, the souls of departed

The difference can be seen today in the oldest churches of the country, particularly in the Tagalog provinces, and in Cagayan, Ilocos, Cebu and Panay islands.

Propaganda was part and parcel of the missionary kit. Friars made sure that every important event in the lives of their flock was attributed to divine intervention. Thus Mary and her son (along with the various patron saints of particular places) became the agents for fire prevention, earthquake-proofing (especially of churches), the

ancestors, the spirits of nature, and not a few mythical monsters were replaced by (and in many cases, incorporated within) an extended Christian family that consisted of both the human and the divine.

Depending on the temperamental and cultural quirks of the settlement, emphasis varied between either Mother, the Virgin Mary, or the Child Jesus. In the shrines and churches of Luzon, where women's equality with men had long ago extended into roles of power as priestesses, Mary became the standard-bearer of Catholicism. In the Visayas of Queen Juana, where children to this day are indulged in extended childhood, the Santo Niño was king.

countering of spells to outside invasions by the Dutch, British, Muslim, Portuguese and Chinese, as well as deities of rain, fertility and the entire range of human needs and concerns.

In the same tradition, there is hardly a Catholic home without its own enshrined Virgin and Child, usually near the master bedroom. Just a generation ago, it was a standard practice to affix a *Maria* or a *Jesus Maria* to a Filipino child's given name.

Ethnic and minority groups

Of the Philippine population, now just under 80 million, some 10 percent are classified as cultural or ethnic minorities. Most of these people live outside the cultural mainstream of lowland Filipino Christians. They comprise the most diverse and exotic population of the nation, with the vast majority of these minorities, some 60 percent, made up of various Muslim groups living on the southern islands of Mindanao and the Sulu Archipelago.

The remaining peoples, who are mostly animists, inhabit the mountain provinces of northern and central Luzon, and the highland plains, rain forests and the isolated seashores of Mindanao and Palawan. These people often live as they have for generations, but are also accessible to outsiders.

There are five major ethnic groups spread across the Cordillera highlands of northern Luzon: Benguet, Bontoc, Ifugao, Kalinga and Apayao. Other indigenous groups of northern Luzon include the Kalinga and Tingguian.

These are the unconquered people of the north who have evolved robust indigenous cultures and traditions in highland seclusion, far removed from lowland colonial history. These mountain tribes live sedentary lives based upon a highly developed agricultural economy. They worship tribal ancestors or spirits of nature, and

LEFT: a ritual cult practice on Mt. Banahaw, south of Manila. **ABOVE:** Ifugao elder, northern Luzon.

turn a suspicious face upon the "intruders" from the lowlands.

Cordillera is home to various tribes, including the gold- and copper-mining Benguet and the mountain people of Bontoc. Probably the best-known people of the mountains, the Bontoc combine American missionary teaching with their ancestral religion.

The Ifugao of the eastern and central Cordillera are the master architects of the most famous rice terraces in the world. The Ifugao rice terraces, first constructed between 2,000 and 3,000 years ago, cover over 260 sq. km (100 sq. miles) of steep mountain slopes in Ifugao Province.

Muslims

Considered as a whole, the Muslims of the south constitute the largest cultural minority of the Philippines. The Muslims, also known as Moros and equally known as fiercely independent and combative, are classified into five major groups: Tausug, Maranao, Maguindanao, Samal and Badjao.

Another unique cultural group, living on Basilan Island south of Zamboanga amidst the Sulu Islands, are the Yakan. They are of partial Polynesian origin, with mixed Muslim and animistic beliefs. They are the most superb textile weavers of the southern archipelago.

The non-Muslim ethnic tribes of the Mindanao highlands are the least studied of the Philippine cultural minorities, and among the most highly costumed and colourful. There are over 10 tribes living in relative isolation in the Mindanao interior, including the Tiruray, the Bagobo and the Subannon.

The debatable Tasaday

The cave-dwelling Tasaday of southern Mindanao have been the focus of furious anthropological debate since their so-called discovery in 1971. They were portrayed as a stone-age tribe of some two dozen people living in harmony with nature, with no prior contact to the outside world. However, many anthropologists consider the Tasaday a hoax of the Marcos regime. They argue that the tribe's habitat cannot support their hunter-gatherer existence; the Tasaday language is closely related to the nearby Manobo tribe; and that no trash heaps, showing long-term occupation, have been found anywhere near their caves. ❑

FIESTAS AND FESTIVALS

Splashes of colour, raucous laughter, and an air of insouciance can be found at
any Filipino celebration – and celebrations are a Filipino speciality

The present textures of the Filipino fiesta comes from the wisdom of old Spanish friars, who were disturbed by early symptoms of forced – and seemingly incomplete – conversion of Filipinos to Catholicism. When natural calamities and tribal enemies threatened the life of Christian settlements, the friars took

10 Bornean lords escaping religious tyranny in the south fled northward with their followers. Upon their arrival in Panay, they sought rights to this island and struck an accord with the local king. Later, the peace pact was reinforced by a lavish harvest feast prepared by the Bornean immigrants for their Ati neighbours. Ever eager

the opportunity to lead everyone to the church in quest of a "miracle". The guardian spirits of traditional harvest feasts were slowly replaced by Christian saints, and as summer heat rose in the blood, friars would scurry through their memories of Spain for songs, dances and colours to woo a musical people in the worship of the Virgin Mary.

January

Kalibo's Ati-Atihan festival, held during the third week of January, is the Philippines' most famous fiesta. *Ati-Atihan* means "making like Atis", and refers to the black Negrito aborigines, the original inhabitants of Panay. In 1212,

to please, the Borneans enlivened up the welcome with gongs and cymbals, smeared soot on their faces and started dancing in the streets in merry imitation of their Ati guests. The Christ-child figure of Santo Niño was introduced in later years, when the Borneans successfully fought off marauding Muslim attackers.

February

The giant ring road encircling Metro Manila, Epifanio de los Santos Avenue, or EDSA, was the focus for the February 1986 revolution that toppled former dictator Ferdinand Marcos without violence or bloodshed. Despite their fears, hundreds of thousands of Filipinos converged on this road of resistance to form a protective human wall. Since then, Filipinos have celebrated the EDSA People's Power anniversary with moving church masses, stage shows, dancing, displays, singing and fireworks.

March

During Holy Week, there are colourful Easter celebrations throughout the Philippines. The heart-shaped island of Marinduque especially turns into a stage for a unique spectacle: the Moriones festival and the re-

In the late 1960s, a Manila-based oil company, in a flash of public relations genius, launched a search for a so-called Jeepney King.

Amid the typical hoopla of a local Filipino fiesta, jeepney drivers from all over the archipelago compete in contests designed to test their judgement and reflexes on the road and steadiness at the wheel, not to mention a showy parade of wondrous and unique jeepneys.

MAY FLOWERS

Sampaguita, ilang-ilang and hibiscus surround the month-long May tribute to the Queen of Heaven, or the Virgin Mary.

May

The first of May is an important day throughout the Philip-

LEFT: fire-breathing during Ati-Atihan, and fiesta clown. ABOVE: mask used in Marindugue's Moriones festival during Holy Week.

enactment of the ancient Biblical legend of Longinus and his miracle. On Good Friday, Christ's resurrection is then dramatically re-enacted.

April

Filipino, jeepneys have for years served as the country's most important mode of transport. They were originally a solution to the problem of what to do with army jeeps abandoned by American soldiers at the end of World War II.

pines, as it marks the beginning of a merry month of flowers, dainty maidens in pretty gowns and the Queen of the Philippine festivals, the Santacruzan, or Queen of Heaven. The Santacruzan is a Spanish legacy that commemorates the search for the True Cross of Christ.

June

At the centrepiece of any Filipino fiesta table, the *lechon*, or whole roast pig, is king. So revered is the aroma of this succulent dish that the people of Balayan and Batangas provinces have highlighted the feast of their patron saint, St John, with a tribute to the golden-red and crispy lechon.

July

A colourful procession highlights the festival of Santa Ana Kahimonan Abayan, held on 27 July in the northern Mindanao city of Butuan. In earlier times, human-eating crocodiles infested the Agusan River, biting, so to speak, into the townpeople's life.

Faced with a common enemy, the townspeople implored their patron saint Santa Ana to give them bountiful harvests and safe passage over the river. Santa Ana heard their prayers and destroyed the creatures.

Today, the river-people honour their patron saint by staging a waterborne high mass. Hun-

dreds of boats strung with multicoloured bunting and festooned with decorations are linked side by side to form a long platform spanning the river.

August

Four-metre-high (14-ft) papier-mâché *gigantes* strut through the Quezon town of Lucban representing Juan Cruz, a farmer, his wife and their two children. During the month of August, a full-blown fiesta is dedicated to these symbolic, fun-loving gigantes.

Heightening the fun is the *toro*, an enormous papier-mâché bull brightly painted red and rigged with firecrackers. Throughout the

parade, the enormous bull scampers around the town plaza, scattering spectators as fireworks inside are ignited.

September

The religious observance surrounding one September festival involves the ritual transfer, known as the *translucion*, of the statue of Our Lady of Peñafrancia to the Metropolitan Cathedral. Devotees travel by any means to catch a glimpse of her at the festival in Naga. A nine-day *novena* is then held before the statue is returned to her shrine down the Bicol River.

October

The Masskara festival was first conceived in 1980 to add colour and gaiety to the Negros city of Bacolod's celebration of its Charter Day anniversary, on 19 October. *Masskara* is coined from two words: *mass*, meaning crowd or many, and the Spanish word *cara*, or face; thus the double meaning for "mask" and "many faces". The symbol of the festival – a smiling mask – was adopted by the organisers to dramatise the Negrense's happy spirit, despite periodic economic downturns in the sugar industry.

November

Built in the 16th century, Manila's Intramuros district is a stellar example of a medieval fortress town. In November is a festival of regal revelry, when the walled city relives its colonial golden age. The underlying theme of the varied activities, including a choral competition, is the traditions observed during the Spanish colonial period.

December

This month is host to the Christmas lantern festival. Three days before Christmas, at sunset, lanterns glow like phantasmagorical stars along the streets, illuminating the night. Townspeople dance through the streets to the beat of a lively brass band, the air cool and filled with the sound of Christmas carols. The lanterns, or *parols* as they are known, are specimens of pyrotechnic splendour, representing the synergistic endeavour of every town barrio. On the 22nd, the lanterns go on parade accompanied by music, feasting and dancing. ❑

LEFT: Christmas lantern of San Fernando.
RIGHT: painted "warriors" for the Pintados fiesta, Leyte.

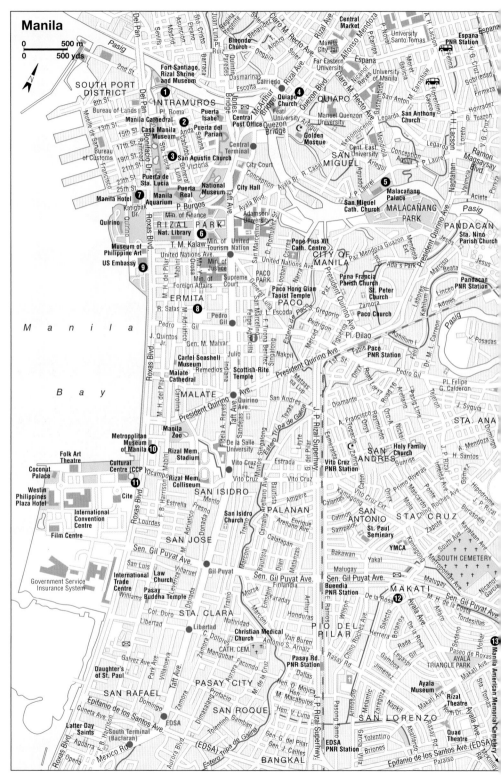

Manila

0 ____ 500 m
0 ____ 500 yds

MANILA

*Over the years, the legacies of different eras in Manila
have melded with contemporary demands, holding this capital city
of the Philippines in a heady flux of never-ending motion*

Map
on page
308

Of course, Manila is not the Philippines, although countless visitors leave Manila with what they think is an image of the Philippines: happily Westernised Asians on the move and in the know, flashing their best hospitality smiles. It is a shallow impression, and false, too. To go beyond the facade for a deeper understanding of Philippine people and history, start in Old Manila, the centre of the archipelago.

What is commonly called Metro Manila is bisected by the **Pasig River**, so that most city areas are known as either north or south of the Pasig. The Spanish conquistador Miguel Lopez de Legazpi arrived in the area in 1571. After a battle, he took over the ruins of the ruler's fortress at the mouth of the Pasig. According to legend, the ruler, Sulayman, razed his palace at his impending defeat to Legazpi. Legazpi founded Spanish Manila that same year, beginning construction of a medieval fortified town that was to become Spain's most durable monument in Asia, Intramuros.

Intramuros

The city fortress, which stands today and was an expanded version of the original Fort Santiago, was defended by moats and walls 10 metres (30 ft) thick with well positioned batteries. It was called **Intramuros** or "Within the Walls". **Fort Santiago ❶** (daily 8am–6pm) is situated close to where the Pasig empties itself into Manila Bay. On this site four centuries ago stood the bamboo fortress of Rajah Sulayman, the young warrior who ruled the palisaded city state of about 2,000 inhabitants before losing it to Legazpi. Four gates connected Intramuros to the outlying boroughs, where lived the *indios* (as the Spaniards called the natives), *mestizos*, Chinese, Indians and other foreigners, including a number of Spanish commoners. Trade and commerce flourished to such an extent in these suburbs that they soon outstripped the city proper in area and population.

Though Intramuros is a far cry from the bustling Spanish city it once was, it has come a long way from the ravages of wartime. Once a jumble of broken buildings, portions of the old city have been restored, including the *Ayuntamiento* (Municipal Hall), once the grandest structure here. Part of the continuing restoration plan is to replicate eight houses to illustrate different styles of local architecture. A few are already open to the public, including the splendid **Casa Manila** (Tues–Sun 9am–6pm), a restored Spanish merchant's house from the late 1800s.

From Fort Santiago, cross over to the **Manila Cathedral ❷**, an imposing Romanesque structure. A

BELOW: Casa
Manila, Intramuros.

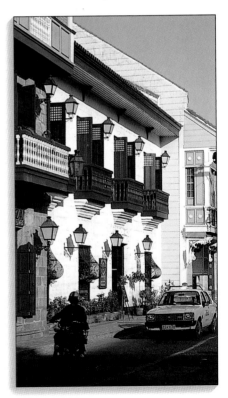

plaque on its facade tells of a phoenix-like cycle that holds true for most old churches in the country: a relentless history beginning in 1571 of construction and reconstruction after the repeated ravages of fire, typhoon, earthquakes and war.

Fronting the cathedral is **Plaza Roma**, where bullfighters imported from Spain performed in the 18th century. Colonial soldiers once drilled in the plaza, originally called Plaza de Armas. Later the Spanish rechristened it Plaza Mayor when it became the government centre in Intramuros. It was also briefly known as Plaza McKinley during the American occupation at the end of World War II.

At this point, facing Manila Cathedral, imagine the former Intramuros laid out as a rough pentagon or triangle. The perimeter measured nearly 4.5 km (3 miles). Following Legazpi's blueprint for the capital, succeeding Spanish governors constructed 18 churches and chapels, convents, schools, a hospital, publishing house, university (as early as 1611), palaces for the governor-general and the archbishop, soldiers' barracks, and houses for the assorted elite.

From Plaza Roma, walk down General Luna Street, past the western side of the cathedral, for four blocks to the intersection of General Luna Street and Calle Real. Here, incongruous Chinese *fu* dogs carved of granite guard the entrance to the courtyard of the only structure in Intramuros that was completely spared the ravages of World War II: **San Agustin Church** ❸ (daily 9am–noon, 1–5pm).

The church facade is notable for its combination of styles – Doric lower columns and Corinthian upper columns – and the evident absence of its original left tower, victim to the violent earthquakes of 1863 and 1889. The remarkable main door is carved out of a Philippine hardwood called *molave*, and it is divided into four panels depicting Augustinian symbols and the figures of St Augustine and his mother, Santa Monica.

The Spanish called Manila the Noble and Ever Loyal City – El Insigne y Siempre Leal Ciudad.

BELOW:
overview of old Manila, with Rizal Park on the left.

Map on page 308

From San Agustin Church, there are several options. Turn right at Calle Real and prowl the remains of Intramuros until reaching Muralla Street. Here, follow the walls or pass through one of the restored gates leading back to the Pasig River, or to a plaza, **Liwasang Bonifacio**. On this busy square is a statue of the revolutionary leader Andres Bonifacio, with the **Central Post Office** just to the north.

Between these two landmarks is a system of overpasses and underpasses handling, at all hours, the great bulk of Manila's traffic. The left lane leads to Jones Bridge, the centre lane to MacArthur Bridge, and the right one to Quezon Bridge. These three bridges are the major passageways across the river, leading to the half of Manila north of the Pasig.

Quiapo

The area north of the Pasig includes the district of Quiapo. Recto Avenue is marked by a stretch of small shops selling new and second-hand schoolbooks for the university belt, an area that begins right after Recto Avenue's juncture with Quezon Boulevard. Quiapo is saturated with colleges, offering degrees in just about everything.Turning left at Quezon Boulevard leads to **Central Market**, really more of a textile emporium, and eventually to España, which leads to the vast residential and governmental area of Quezon City.

Turning right at Quezon Boulevard from Recto Avenue will end up at **Quiapo Church ❹**. The area beside the church is the terminal for most public road transport plying north–south routes of the metropolis. A frenzied quarter, it has long been considered the heart (some say the armpit) of downtown Manila. Close to where Recto Avenue becomes Mendiola Street is the **San Sabastion Church**, reputedly the only prefabricated steel church in the world.

TIP

Just next to the post office, beneath MacArthur Bridge, board the Metro Ferry and chug along the Pasig River to Guadeloupe, near Makati, glimpsing river life, old buildings and Malacañang Palace.

BELOW: Manila kids.

Mendiola Street threads past private colleges to **Malacañang Palace** ❺ (Thurs–Fri 9am–3pm), formerly the office and residence of Philippine presidents. It is now open to the public as a museum, housing memorabilia of all past Philippine presidents. Originally a country estate owned by a Spanish nobleman, Malacañang became the summer residence of Spanish governor-generals in the middle 1800s. Since Independence Day in 1946, ten Filipino chief executives have set up shop in the Presidential Palace, including Ferdinand Marcos. His successor after the People's Revolution, Corazon Aquino, broke with tradition by choosing to operate from the adjacent Guest House. Joseph Estrada, in contrast, fully entrenched himself in Malacañang.

Mother and child.

Rizal Park

Formerly known as Luneta (Little Moon, for its crescent shape), **Rizal Park** ❻ is a large rectangular field broken up into three sections, with an elevated strolling ground bounded by Roxas Boulevard and ending at the sea wall facing Manila Bay. On the harbour end is the legendary **Manila Hotel** ❼, once the most exclusive address in the Pacific.

At the central portion of Rizal Park is **Rizal Monument**, a memorial to the national hero and the object of much wreath-laying by visiting dignitaries. Under 24-hour guard, the regular drill manoeuvres of the sentries are an attraction in themselves. Behind the monument is a series of plaques on which are inscribed Rizal's poem *Mi Ultimo Adios (My Last Farewell)* in the original Spanish and in various translations. A marble slab marks the spot where Rizal met his martyr's death by firing squad, while an obelisk stands on the site of the earlier executions of three Filipino priests.

BELOW: jeepney colours, and Malacañang Palace.

This central section of the park, where the Rizal Monument is located, is bordered by Roxas Boulevard to the west, T.M. Kalaw Street to the south, M. Orosa Street to the east, and Padre Burgos Street to the north. Close to the Burgos side are the Japanese and Chinese gardens, and an orchidarium, all of which charge token fees for entrance. On this side, too, is the city planetarium, where an interesting audiovisual show is conducted twice a day for a nominal charge.

The eastern side of the park is bounded by Taft Avenue, one of the major arteries cutting through Manila south of the river. Burgos Street, on the park's northern side, leads past the Old Congress Building, which once housed the Philippine Senate and still houses the **National Museum** (Tues–Sun 9am–5pm). Northward is Manila City Hall, and beyond, Liwasang Bonifacio, from where the three bridges noted earlier lead to north of the Pasig River.

Ermita

From Taft, turn right at any of the perpendicular streets beginning with United Nations Avenue; this will lead to **Ermita ❽**, an unusual district in many respects. Its tourist-belt reputation is built on the strength of its proximity to Rizal Park, the seawall along Manila Bay, and a number of government buildings, such as the Department of Justice on Padre Faura Street. Consequently, many hotels and lodging houses exist in the area, in turn attracting a conglomeration of eateries, nightspots, boutiques, antique shops, handicraft and curio stalls, and travel agency offices.

Legend has it that around 1590, a Mexican secular and hermit made the small seaside village his retreat. Four years later, an Augustinian priest founded the hermitage dedicated to Nuestra Señora de Guia, and the label *Ermita* ("her-

Map on page 308

BELOW: Manila Bay sunset from Roxas Boulevard.

Map
on page
308

Jeepneys are a novel form of Philippine transport.

RIGHT: Manila's Coconut Palace.
BELOW: Makati by night.

mitage") has stuck ever since. By the 19th century, the district had become an aristocratic suburb, together with the adjacent district of **Malate** further south.

Ermita offers diverse nightspots featuring Filipino folk singers, rock bands, and jazz groups. Here, still, another facet of the Ermita spirit may be glimpsed – the bohemian lifestyle of its younger and well educated residents made up of artists, writers, musicians and dancers.

Roxas Boulevard

Parallelling Manila Bay and Ermita is Roxas Boulevard and its seawall fronting the bay. The seawall begins, not without some hint of appropriateness, where the sprawling grounds of the **US Embassy ❾** – hard to miss with the long lines of visa seekers outside – end. Along President Quirino Avenue on the landward side is a government complex that includes the Ospital ng Maynila (Manila Hospital), the **Metropolitan Museum of Manila ❿** (Mon–Sat 10am–6pm) and the Central Bank of the Philippines. Behind the hospital are the **Manila Zoological and Botanical Gardens** (daily 7am–6pm).

Past the Navy Headquarters and on the seaward side of Roxas Boulevard is the immense **Cultural Centre of the Philippines ⓫**, the centrepiece of a spit of reclaimed land called CCP complex. The main building houses two theatres and two art galleries, and a museum and library. In the northwest corner is a former Marcos guesthouse, the **Coconut Palace** (Tues–Sun 9–11.30am, 1–4.30pm), built entirely of indigenous materials like narra and molave hardwoods in addition to coconut wood and husks. The palace is available for private functions, often hosting lavish parties for Manila's rich and famous. Although guided tours are available, it's best to call in advance to avoid a private event.

Makati

From NAIA Avenue, take a short bus or taxi ride to **Makati ⓬** via Epifanio de los Santos Avenue (EDSA), Makati's main east–west boulevard and focus of the 1986 People's Power demonstrations. Makati's main north–south street, Ayala Avenue, has been dubbed the Philippine Wall Street, as it is the financial hub of the Philippines. On Makati Avenue is the **Ayala Museum Galleries** (Tues–Sat 8am–6pm). It has an outstanding archive and a permanent exhibit of dioramas portraying significant episodes in Philippine history, and detailed replicas of ships that have plied Philippine waters.

From Ayala Avenue's end at the EDSA, cross the highway to upscale if not ritzy **Forbes Park**, a swanky housing area built by the Ayala family, one of the country's top business empires. Forbes Park's McKinley Road leads to the Manila Polo Club and to **Fort Bonifacio**, a military camp once housing the headquarters of the Philippine Army.

Nearby is the **Manila American Memorial Cemetery ⓭** (daily 6.30am–5pm), where the remains of 17,000 Allied dead rest below seemingly endless rows of white crosses. The Libingan ng Mga Bayani (Graveyard of Heroes) is close by with its eternal flame burning by the Tomb of the Unknown Soldier. ❑

NORTH TO ILOCOS

The northwestern part of Luzon island, far beyond the congestion of Manila, embraces misty highlands and rocky coastline, and also tribal people who retain their traditions

Map on page 296

T here is a rugged symmetry to Ilocos that sets it, and its people, apart from others in the Philippines. Perched on a narrow ledge along the rugged northwest, the coast rises from the South China Sea to rocky bluffs and rolling sand dunes. Behind it, a slim, arable strip of land is tucked under the towering Cordillera Mountains. In this narrow confine lie the Ilocano provinces of La Union, Ilocos Sur (South), and Ilocos Norte (North).

Sometime after the first century, waves of migration swelled out of Borneo to crest along the Philippine coast. Late-comers to the archipelago, the immigrants were pushed ever northward along the coast by those who had come earlier. By the time they reached the northwestern coast, there was no where else to go but ashore. The migrants flooded into the hundreds of coves along the jagged coast and shifted up onto the narrow plains. With superior numbers and metal weapons, the immigrants pushed the region's indigenous tribes, who had lived here for centuries, high into the bordering mountains. The people became known for the coves *(looc)* around which they built their communities *(ylocos)*.

The conquistador Juan de Salcedo landed in Vigan, Ilocos Sur, in the late 16th century. Soon, the Spanish introduced corn, cocoa, tobacco and, of course, Christianity. Chapels were built alongside the garrisons, schools were organised, and soon the missions were pulling converts into the town square. Compulsory native labour and hired Chinese masons and artisans soon resulted in Spain's most lasting landmarks in the Ilocos – the churches, like the grand old cathedral of Vigan. Fascinating architectural specimens, nicknamed "earthquake baroque" by Filipino historians, they were built as much to dramatise the power of the Old World god as to withstand natural disasters. Indeed, the 17th and 18th centuries saw a flowering of baroque that filtered into the Philippines.

LEFT: churchyard basketball.
BELOW: Spanish baroque church, Bantay.

Baguio and environs

Leaving the flat plains of Pangasinan, the National Highway begins to climb over the rolling hills of southern Ilocos. The first province along the way is La Union. It was carved out of Pangasinan, Ilocos Sur and the Cordilleras by royal decree in 1854. Entering La Union, the sea begins to glint behind the palms, where creamy sand beaches await.

At **Agoo-Damortis National Seashore Park** in Lingayen Gulf, near **Agoo** the sands are nearly black because of the iron deposits. The Shrine of Our Lady of Charity, in the baroque-style Agoo basilica, attracts visitors on a Good Friday, when patron saints are paraded through the streets. The Museo de Iloko, in the old Presidencia of Agoo, houses artefacts of Ilocos culture.

Inland from Agoo is the famous highland town of **Baguio** , more or less the gateway to Luzon's highlands if coming north from the Manila area. By road it's four hours from Manila; by plane, just an hour. Nestled atop a 1,500-metre-high (5,000-ft) plateau, Baguio's cool climate and pine-clad hills have long lured visitors. Baguio was severely damaged by an earthquake in 1990, but little evidence of the quake is visible today.

Baguio is not noted for any tourist hot-spots, but rather for a sense of leisure that the environs nurture in both Filipinos and foreigners. Baguio seduces with cool air, clean parks, lovely gardens, quaint churches, and a variety of restaurants and hotels. The main avenue for the easy life is Session Road, with its gamut of bookstores, bakeries, Indian bazaars, coffee houses, Chinese restaurants, pizza parlours, and antique stores.

Back along the coast and a few kilometres inland sits **Naguilian**, the *basi*-making capital of the Ilocos. Basi, the local Ilocano wine, is a fermented sugarcane concoction, coloured with *duhat* bark.

San Fernando ❷ produces bursts of sound and an array of colours on market day: loud gourd hats from up north, burnished earthenware from San Juan, and bright blankets from Bangar line the stalls and shops. Overlooking it all is a dragon-encrusted Chinese temple, Macho. Six km (4 miles) north of San Fernando, along Monalisa Beach, runs some of the best surf in Ilocos.

Bacnotan to Bangar

In **Bacnotan**, local silk production can be seen at the state university. In the mountains to the east, around **Bagulin**, trails along the Bagulin-Naguilian River offer some trekking opportunities. The century-old church of St Catherine, in

Catholic relic in wood.

BELOW: the women of Ilocos are known to smoke what must be the world's largest cigars.

Luna, houses an image of Our Lady of Namacpacan, the patroness of Ilocano travellers. **Bangar**, on the northern border of La Union Province, is a blanket-weaving centre, where the best woven blankets and handcrafted bolos in the region are made.

Map on page 296

Ilocos Sur

Ilocos Sur Province twists along the coast as the narrowest province in Ilocos. In some places, the Cordilleras range extends right down to water's edge. Because the land is ill-suited for agriculture, most people in Ilocos Sur have turned to trade and handicrafts, and each town in the region seems to have its own specialty. In San Esteban, there is a quarry from which mortars and grindstones are made. San Vicente, Vigan and San Ildefonso specialise in woodcarving, importing their raw material from the mountain provinces. Skilled silversmiths work in Bantay. Other towns make saddles, mats, brooms and hats. Sisal and hemp-fibre weaving are household industries everywhere.

The first town in Ilocos Sur along the National Highway is **Tagudin**, where a sundial built by the Spanish in 1848 sits in front of the Municipal Hall. The next town, **San Esteban**, has a round, stone watch tower built by the Spanish to keep lookout for Moro pirates, and Apatot Beach.

The small burg of **Santa Maria** has a centuries-old church nestled atop a hill, which served as a fortress during the 1986 revolution and now stands as a national landmark. Near Santa Maria is Pinsal Falls, a favourite setting for many films, and where the legendary footprints of the Ilocano giant, Angalo, can be seen. **Santa** has a small picturesque church with a pure-white facade and slight greenish tint standing by the sea.

BELOW: Vigan's quiet ambiance, and piling into a jeepney.

Map
on page
296

TIP

In Currimao it is worth stopping for the old abandoned tobacco warehouses at the port – vestiges of the great tobacco monopoly once dominating the region.

Vigan

A living, breathing repository of Spanish architecture and Filipino culture, **Vigan ❸** was the third Spanish city to be built in the Philippines, in 1572, following the first in Cebu and the second, Intramuros, in what is now Manila. The **Cathedral of St Paul**, built in 1641, is the centre of Vigan. Stretching out in front of St Paul's is Plaza Salcedo, an elliptical plaza with the Salcedo Monument and a towering bell tower. Across the plaza to the west is the **Ayala Museum** (Mon–Fri 8.30–11.30am, 1.30–4.30pm), also called the Burgos House.

Probably the best attractions in Vigan are the old ancestral houses in the former Mestizo District, known as **Vigan Heritage Village**, south of St Paul's along Mena Crisologo Street. Each building in the district has been lovingly preserved, and many now house antique shops, bakeries, and craft shops. Other Vigan attractions include the Crisologo Memorial Museum on Liberation Boulevard. Stop at RG Potter, at the southwest end of Liberation Avenue, where the famous Ilocano jars, or *burnay*, are made for storing vinegar and basil. Walk back into the kiln area to see one of the best examples of a Chinese dragon kiln anywhere in the world.

Outside of Vigan, the church in **Bantay** features Philippine earthquake baroque with Gothic influences. Its belfry, a few metres away from the church, was used as a lookout for Moro pirates. Further north, in **Magsingal**, the Museum of Ilocano Culture and Artifacts has a collection of early trade porcelains, neolithic tools, weaponry, baskets, and old Ilocano beadwear.

Ilocos Norte

Unlike its poorer cousin to the south, Ilocos Norte stands rich in timber, minerals, fisheries, and agriculture. Garlic is the principle cash crop, and it gives the province its flavour and aroma. It also did not economically hurt that the Philippines' longest-serving president, Ferdinand Marcos, was an Ilocano Norte.

The first town in Ilocos Norte is **Badoc**. Exhibited at Luna House here are reproductions of a renowned 19th-century Filipino painter, Juan Luna. The Badoc Church is also worth a visit.

Past Badoc, at the kilometre-460 junction, turn left for **Currimao**. From Currimao, take the side road to **Paoay**. The church here is a real stunner and perhaps the most famous in Ilocos. It is a successful hybrid creation wedding the strong features of "earthquake baroque" (such as massive lateral buttresses) with an exotic Asian quality, reminiscent of Javanese temples. Built of coral blocks at the turn of the 18th century, its bell tower served as a observation post during the Philippine revolution and was used by guerrillas during the Japanese occupation. Paoay Church has been declared a UNESCO World Heritage Site. Not far from the town is Lake Paoay where loom weaving is a major activity, producing textiles with ethnic Ilocano designs.

South of **San Nicolas**, back down the National Highway in **Batac**, is the mausoleum of Ferdinand Marcos and the house in which he grew up. Across the bridge from San Nicolas is the capital of Ilocos Norte, **Laoag ❹**, the Sunshine City. St William's Cathedral, dating back to the 16th century, is another notable example of earthquake baroque.

Further north, **Pagudpud** on Bangui Bay has some of the best coral reefs in the archipelago. The reef is virtually untouched and swarms with countless tropical fish. The beaches here are some of the finest in the Philippines.

Balaoi ❺ is the last town in Ilocos Norte before passing into Cagayan Province. The town sits on the eastern side of the northernmost point of Luzon and overlooks Paseleng Bay. Along the shore of Paseleng Bay is what some consider one of the best hideaway resorts in the islands, Saud Beach Resort. ❑

Nipa-hut smile.

OPPOSITE: Catholic church in Luzon's mountains.

THE VISAYAS

Map on page 296

Six major islands and other fringe groups of isles parade together in a series of idyllic images – the calm waters, shimmering coves, rocky coasts and palm-fringed beaches that are the Visayas

Hanging like a necklace of uneven beads strung together by various geographic threads, the islands of the Visayas lend themselves to the sort of languid exploration that is perhaps more identifiable with the South Pacific. People from Luzon, when asked about these southern islands, generally point out the slower pace, the seductive lilt to the Visayan speech, and perhaps, chauvinistically, the sensuousness of the women.

In 1521, Ferdinand Magellan anchored off the tiny island of Homonhon in Leyte Gulf. He had sailed up through the Canigao Channel to the island of Cebu, where he Christianised the local rajah and 500 of his followers. A minor rajah of Mactan – a flat, muddy island where Cebu's international airport now stands – stood in rebellion to the rajah of Cebu and his new foreign guests. Now known to all Filipinos as Lapu Lapu, Rajah Cilapulapu (the *ci* simply means, "the") defended his island with some 2,000 warriors against 48 armour-clad Spaniards shortly after their arrival. During the battle that raged for just over an hour, Magellan was slain.

LEFT: Cebu is known for quality guitars.
BELOW: Visayan beach.

Samar

This large island lies opposite the southern tip of Luzon and can easily be reached from Manila via the National Highway. The first landfall of Samar is the town of **Allen** with its nearby hot springs. The main roads wind along the northern coast to **Catarman**, capital of Northern Samar Province. Several interesting waterfalls are found in the interior of this part of the island, but reaching them requires considerable hiking through roadless terrain.

In the southwest corner of the island is the San Juanico Bridge, the longest in the Philippines and linking Samar to the adjacent island of Leyte. Near the approach to the bridge is **Basey ❻**, known for Sohotan Caves, Sohotan Natural Bridge, and **Sohotan National Park**. Basey is also the home of mat weavers whose designs have become popular items in the markets of Tacloban, on Leyte across the bridge.

Leyte

Trading centre of the eastern Visayas is **Tacloban ❼**, the capital of Leyte Province. The Capitol Building features the scene of Gen. Douglas MacArthur's historic landing on Leyte in 1945. In the centre of town is an attractive Spanish-style museum and shrine, the Santo Niño Shrine, housing Imelda Marcos' collection of statues of the infant Jesus. (Leyte is her home province.) The island has several fine beaches on its western coast, notably Agta Beach in Almeria and

Banderrahan Beach in Naval. The town of **Caibiran**, on the eastern coast, has the spring-fed San Bernardo pool and the falls of Tumalistis, once claimed as having the sweetest water in the world.

From Tacloban, the National Highway follows the eastern coastline southward past Palo and **Tolosa**, the home-town of Imelda Marcos, where a visit to her former grand residence should not be missed. Past Abuyog, the road veers west and crosses Leyte's Central Cordillera Mountains to the town of Baybay.

The road then follows the western coastline to southern Leyte's provincial capital of **Maasin**.

Cebu

On the island of Cebu, the oldest city in the Philippines, **Cebu ❽**, is the commercial and education centre of the Visayas, and the hub of air and sea travel throughout southern Philippines. Cebu is a busy capital, second in commercial activity only to Manila, but considerably more entrepreneurial than Manila.

On Juan Luna Street is **Santo Niño Basilica and Musuem** (open on request), built in 1565 to house the country's oldest religious relic, the Image of the Holy Child Jesus, presented by Magellan to Queen Juana of Cebu on her conversion to Christianity.

As the oldest Spanish settlement in the country, Cebu has plenty of spots that depict its rich colonial heritage. The foremost is **Fort San Pedro** (daily 9am–5pm), a Spanish fort built in the early 1700s to repel the attacks of Muslim raiders. Close to the fort runs Colon Street, the oldest street in the country, situated within the Parian district, which was Cebu's original Chinatown. A piece of a wooden crucifix that was left by Magellan in 1521 commemorates the

BELOW: Daoist
temple, Cebu.

archipelago's first encounter with the West. Magellan's cross is Cebu's most important historical landmark. The **Magellan's Marker**, erected in 1886, marks the spot where he was slain on Mactan's shore, while the **Lapu Lapu Monument** stands at the plaza fronting the Lapulapu City Hall.

Cebu is well-known for its pristine, sun-drenched white beaches and year-round tropical climate. The coastal waters off Cebu offer fantastic scuba-diving sites. Among them are **Mactan Island**, the Olango Islands and Moalboal, all of which have complete facilities and international-standard accommodations. On the southwest coast, **Moalboal** is a haven for scuba diving enthusiasts as well as budget travellers.

For many travellers, Cebu means handcrafted guitars and ukeleles made of soft jackfruit wood. The guitar-making industry is centred in Maribago and Abuno on Mactan.

Bohol

A 20-minute flight southeast of Cebu's airport is **Bohol ❾**, which is one of the largest coconut-growing areas in the country. Miguel Lopez de Legazpi, the Spanish conqueror and coloniser of the Philippines, anchored briefly near the island in 1563 and is said to have sealed a blood pact with a chieftain, Sikatuna.

For its relatively small size, Bohol has much to offer in history and natural attractions. A good road system traverses the island. The coastline is marked by picturesque coves and clean, white-sand beaches, most of them a short ride from **Tagbilaran**, the provincial capital and Bohol's main port of entry. Seven km (4 miles) from Tagbilaran is Baclayon Church, built by Jesuits in 1727. Also known as the Church of La Purisima Concepcion (Immaculate Conception), it

Map on page 296

Surfing instructor.

BELOW: Chocolate Hills, Bohol.

Map on page 296

A recent theory of dubious merit purports that Filipino faith healers are descendants of the kahuna, *the ancient healers of old Tahiti and Hawaii. The shamans are said to have had the ability to dematerialise tissues and bones and to rematerialise them in perfect order.*

RIGHT: Boracay.
BELOW: Ati-Atihan, Panay.

has an interesting museum housing a rich collection of religious relics, ecclesiastical vestments, and old librettos of church music in Latin on animal skins.

But what remains Bohol's most famous attraction, with which in fact the island has become synonymous, is a unique panorama in the vicinity of **Carmen**, a town 55 km (34 miles) northeast of Tagbilaran in Bohol's central regions. Here, several hundred haycock hills – formed by limestone, shale, and sandstone – rise some 30 metres (100 ft) above the flat terrain. These are the **Chocolate Hills**, so-called for the confectionery-like spectacle they present at the height of summer, when their sparse grass cover turns dry and brown.

Negros

The capital of Negros Oriental (Eastern Negros) Province, **Dumaguete ⑩** is a small university town built around the Protestant-run Silliman University. Offshore is **Siquijor Island**, accessible by an hour's fast ferry from Dumaguete. This small island has long been considered the centre of sorcery in the southern Philippines. There are some 50 *mananambal*, or folk healer-sorcerers, on the tiny island. They are classified as "white" or "black" sorcerers, depending upon the nature of their abilities and intents.

Dominating the northwest shore is **Bacolod,** the capital of Negros Occidental (Western Negros) Province. Its points of interest do not go beyond several fine antique collections, ceramic shops, and weaving centres producing principally *hablon* fabric – a textile originally developed in Bacolod and much in vogue in the 1960s.

A few minutes' drive north is **Silay**, small and sleepy, but with several interesting old houses recalling the Castilian past. A bit further north is Victorias Milling Company, reputedly the largest sugar-cane mill and refinery in the world. Within the Vicmico compound is St Joseph, the workers' chapel noted for its psychedelic mosaic made from pop bottles depicting an angry Jesus and saints as Filipinos in native dress. It is still sometimes referred to as the Chapel of the Angry Christ.

Panay

From Bacolod, it's a two-hour ferry ride to **Iloilo ⑪** on Panay Island. By the river's mouth is **Fort San Pedro**, originally built in 1616 with earthworks and wooden palisades, and transformed into a stone fort in 1738. In 1937 the fort became the quarters for the Philippine Army. The fort has since been turned into a promenade area, popular in the early evening. The Museo ng Iloilo (Iloilo Museum) on Bonifacio Drive showcases prehistoric artifacts from the many burial sites excavated on Panay, including gold-leaf masks for the dead, seashell jewellery, and other ornaments worn by pre-Spanish islanders.

The district of **Molo**, 3 km (2 miles) from the city centre, has a Gothic-Renaissance church completed in the 1800s and the Asilo de Molo, an orphanage where little girls hand-embroider church vestments. Panaderia de Molo (Molo Bakery), the oldest bakery in the South is a favourite. Biscuits and breads are packed in tins for convenient take-home gifts. ❑

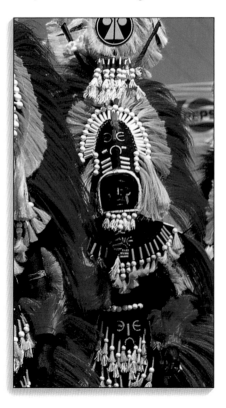

Boracay

In an archipelago of over 7,000 islands, there's bound to be one island that really stands out. Boracay, in the Visayas off Panay Island, is shaped like a slender butterfly drawn in sugar-fine white sand.

It was first "discovered" back in the 1960s, when beachcombers went looking for its rare *puka* shells. By the 1970s, Boracay was on the must list of every intrepid adventurer in Asia. They came in small numbers at first, staying in the *nipa* huts along White Beach for a couple of dollars a night.

But like every other magical spot – with a pristine environment and an increasing cachet amongst backpack travellers – the word spread. By the 1980s, the adventurers had become the hordes, and boutique resorts sprang up all along White Beach. It was still a journey to reach, as it remains today, but that was part of the draw.

Today, Boracay has moved way up-market. Since the mid 1980s, it has attracted the well-heeled of Europe, America and Asia, who rush to Boracay to get an off-the-beaten-track feeling. But not without just cause. The sight greeting arrivals is nothing but spectacular: a gentle sea, the whitest of white beaches, and tall palms swaying in the breeze.

And yet, not all seems well in paradise. The resorts, restaurants and bars that had sprung up to serve the tourists were found to have been dumping their sewage into the sea. In 1997, the Philippine Department of Health declared the waters around Boracay to be severely polluted. The waters are now regularly monitored. If bacteria levels are within an acceptable range blue flags are raised along the beach.

Still, new arrivals continue to stake out a stretch of white sand beneath Boracay's special sun. Meanwhile, the locals in *maong* pants and T-shirts quietly serve the outsiders' needs.

Visitors can hire sailboats and windsurfing boards, and an instructor, if needed, at any of the score of rental shops that have sprung up along White Beach. Pathetic little horses wait above the beach for those who have always dreamed of riding along the sands. Further back, the tennis courts await,

and of course, snorkel or scuba boats bob everywhere. For those who still feel the need for exploration, bicycles are available to explore the tiny island, 8 km long by 3 km wide (5 miles by 2 miles). Thirty minutes of pedalling leads through the corn and cassava fields to fishing villages that have been there for, well, nearly forever. Yap-ak village on the northern end is where everyone heads for puka shells.

Accommodations can be found everywhere nowadays. There're still some basic nipa huts, but it's mostly resorts that splatter the beach now. It has gotten so crowded that resorts are even springing up along the less spectacular eastern coast. Boracay dining, which was once simple but good island fare, now ranges from haute Filipino to haute French, with Indonesian, Thai, Italian, Swiss, and even English food available.

Getting there is not quite the adventure it once was. Fly from Manila to Caticlan and take the 15-minute boat ride to Boracay, or fly to Kalibo, take a jeepney (2–3 hrs) to Caticlan, and then make the crossing. ❑

✵ INSIGHT GUIDES
TRAVEL TIPS

CONTENTS

Getting Acquainted

The Place

Situation In the South China Sea, bordered by Malaysia on the south, Burma to the west, Laos across the Mekong River to the northeast and Cambodia to the east.
Area 514,000 sq km (198,000 sq mi), nearly the size of France or twice as large as England, with 2,600 km (1,600 mi) of coastline.
Population 62 million, of whom 75 percent are Thais and 10–15 percent Chinese.
Capital Bangkok.
Time Zone 7 hours ahead of Greenwich Mean Time (GMT), so New York is 12 hours, Los Angeles 15 hours and London 7 hours behind, Australia 3 hours ahead.
Currency The *baht*.
Weights and Measures Metric.
Electricity 220 volts, with flat-pronged or round-pronged plugs.
International Dialling Code 66.

Climate

There are three seasons: hot, rainy and cool. But for most tourists, Thailand has only one temperature: hot. To make things worse, it drops only a few degrees during the night and is accompanied 24 hours by humidity above 70 percent. Only air-conditioning makes Bangkok and other towns tolerable during the hot season. The countryside is cooler, but the northern regions can be hotter in March/April than Bangkok.
Hot season (March to mid-June), 28°–38°C (82°–100°F).
Rainy season (June to October), 24°–32°C (75°–90°F).
Cool season (November to February), 18°–32°C (65°–90°F), but with less humidity.

Economy

Nearly 70 percent of Thailand's 62 million people are farmers who till alluvial land so rich that Thailand is a world leader in the export of tapioca, rice, rubber, canned pineapple, and is a top-ranked exporter of sugar, maize and tin. Increasingly, Thailand is turning to manufacturing, especially in clothing, machinery, and electronics.

Government

Thailand is a constitutional monarchy headed by His Majesty King Bhumibol. Although he no longer rules as did the absolute monarchs of previous centuries, he can influence important decisions merely by a word or two. He is still regarded as one of the three pillars of the society – monarchy, religion and the nation. This concept is represented in the five-banded national flag of Thailand: the outer red bands symbolising the nation; the inner white bands the purity of the Buddhist religion; and the thick blue band at the centre representing the monarchy.

The king's dedication over many years to improving farmers' lands and yields, and her Majesty Queen Sirikit and others' promotion of the interests of poorer Thais have gained the royal family genuine respect. Photographs of the king and queen hang in nearly every home, shop and office.

A constitution passed in 1997 aimed to place power in the hands of the people, but certain groups, especially the military, have sometimes abused their power. Modelled loosely on the British system, the Thai government consists of three branches: legislative, executive and judiciary, each acting independently of the others in a system of checks and balances.

The legislative branch is composed of a senate and a house of representatives. The senate consists of 200 leading members of society, including business people, educators and a pre-ponderance of high-ranking military officers. Members have traditionally been selected by the prime minister and approved by the king. Under the 1997 constitution they were elected in 2000. The house of representatives comprises 500 members elected by popular vote.

The executive branch is represented by a prime minister, who must be an elected member of parliament. He is selected by a single party or coalition of parties and rules through a cabinet of ministers. They implement their programmes through the very powerful civil service.

Public Holidays

1 January New Year's Day
February full moon* Magha Puja
6 April Chakri Day
13–15 April Songkran (Thai New Year)
1 May Labor Day
5 May Coronation Day
May* Ploughing Ceremony
May full moon* Visakha Puja
July full moon* Asalaha Puja
July* Khao Phansa
12 August Queen's Birthday
23 October Chulalongkorn Day
5 December King's Birthday
10 December Constitution Day
31 December New Year's Eve

Chinese New Year in January/February is not an official public holiday, but many businesses are closed for several days.
* Variable

Business Hours

Government offices 8.30am–4.30pm Monday to Friday.
Offices 8am or 8.30am–5.30pm Monday to Friday. Some open 8.30am–noon on Saturday
Banks 9.30am–3.30pm Monday to Friday, but many operate money-changing kiosks open until 8pm daily.
Shops 8.30–9am to 6pm–8pm.
Restaurants generally close at 10pm.
Coffee shops Most close at midnight; some stay open 24 hours.

Planning the Trip

Visas & Passports

Travellers should check visa regulations at a Thai embassy or consulate before starting their journey. All foreign nationals entering Thailand must have valid passports. At the airport, nationals from most countries will be granted a free transit visa valid up to 30 days, provided that they have a fully paid ticket out of Thailand.

Tourist visas allowing for a 60-day stay, or a 30-day transit visa may also be issued. Visas can be extended before they expire by applying at the **Immigration Bureau** on Soi Suan Plu, Sathorn Tai Road, tel: (02) 286 4231, 287 3101, ext. 2271 (8.30am–4pm, Monday–Friday). Visitors wishing to leave Thailand and return before their visas have expired can apply for a re-entry permit prior to their departure at immigration offices in

Tourist Information

Tourism Authority of Thailand's (www.tat.or.th) overseas offices are at the following locations:
● **Australia**
2F 75 Pitt Street, Sydney 2000.
Tel: (02) 9247 7549.
Fax: (02) 9251 2465.
● **United Kingdom**
3rd Floor, Brook House
98–99 Jermyn Street
London SWIY GEE.
Tel: 207-925 2511.
Fax: 207-925 2512.
● **United States**
304 Park Avenue South
8th Floor, NY 10010.
Tel: (212) 219 4655.
Fax: (212) 219 4697.

Bangkok, Chiang Mai, Pattaya, Phuket and Hat Yai. An exit visa is not required.

Customs

The Thai government prohibits the import of drugs, dangerous chemicals, pornography, firearms and ammunition. Attempting to smuggle heroin or other hard drugs may be punishable by death.

Foreign guests are allowed to import, without tax, one camera with five rolls of film, 200 cigarettes, and one litre of wine or alcoholic spirits.

Health

Visitors are no longer required to show evidence of vaccination for smallpox or cholera. The cholera vaccine is of limited effectiveness and is no longer recommended for travellers. Before you leave, check that your tetanus boosters are up to date.

Malaria is still very dangerous in some regions of Thailand. Mosquitoes in several areas are resistant to many brands of anti-malarial drugs, so seek advice on medication from a tropical institute before your departure. Should you contract malaria, there is a network of malaria centres and hospitals throughout Thailand. The most dangerous form appears disguised as a heavy cold, so if you have flu symptoms see a doctor at once.

Aids is not confined to "high risk" sections of the population in Thailand. You're at risk from casual sex if you don't use condoms.

Establishments catering to foreigners are generally careful with food and drink preparation and sanitation. But Bangkok water pipes are somewhat less than new, so drink bottled water or soft drinks.

Money Matters

The *baht* is divided into 100 *satang*. Banknote denominations include 1,000 (grey), 500 (purple), 100 (red), 50 (blue), 20 (green) and 10 (brown) baht.

Credit Card Warning

Credit card fraud is a major problem in Thailand, so do not leave your cards in hotel safe deposit boxes.

There are 10-baht coins (brass centre with a silver rim), two different 5-baht coins (silver pieces with copper rims), three varieties of 1-baht coin (silver; usually only the small size will fit in a public telephone), and two small coins of 50 and 25 satang (both are brass-coloured).

Thailand has a sophisticated banking system with representation by the major banks of most foreign countries. Money is best imported in cash or traveller's cheques and converted into baht. There is no minimum requirement on the amount of money that must be converted. Foreign tourists may freely bring in foreign banknotes or other types of foreign exchange. For travellers leaving Thailand, the maximum amount permitted to be taken out in Thai currency without prior authorisation is 50,000 baht.

Both cash and traveller's cheques can be changed in hundreds of bank branches; rates are more favourable for traveller's cheques than for cash. Hotels generally give poor exchange rates.

Most banks now have 24-hour ATM machines outside where cash (in baht only) can be withdrawn with credit or debit cards. Note, however, that many banks only accept ATM cards linked directly to Thai bank accounts; for those with ATM cards on the Plus or Cirrus networks who wish to withdraw funds directly from their home bank accounts, HongKong and Bangkok banks are good bets.

Occasionally, an ATM card may not work at one machine – simply try another branch. Periodically, cards are accepted at machines with no related sign out front.

Credit cards are widely accepted throughout Bangkok. In provincial destinations, it is better to check that plastic is accepted, and not to count on using cards.

What to Bring/Wear

Bangkok, Chiang Mai, Pattaya and Phuket are modern destinations with most of the modern amenities found in Europe or North America.

Lip balm and moisturisers are needed in the north during the cool season. Sunglasses, sunblock and hats are essential. Clothes should be light and loose. Open shoes (sandals during the height of the rainy season, when some Bangkok streets get flooded) and sleeveless dresses for women or short-sleeved shirts for men are appropriate. A sweatshirt or fleece is needed for nights in the north. Suits are worn for business and in many large hotels but, in general, Thailand lacks the formal dress code of Hong Kong or Tokyo. Casual but neat and clean clothes are suitable for most occasions.

One exception is the clothing code for Buddhist temples and Muslim mosques. Shorts are taboo for both women and men wanting to enter some of the important temples. Those wearing sleeveless dresses may also be barred from certain temples. Improperly dressed and unkempt visitors will be turned away from large temples like the Wat Phra Kaeo (Temple of the Emerald Buddha) and from the Grand Palace.

Getting There

BY AIR

Bangkok is a gateway between east and west and a transport hub for Southeast Asia served by most of the major airlines. In addition to Bangkok, Thailand has five other international airports: Chiang Mai, Phuket, Hat Yai, Chiang Rai and Ubon Ratchathani. **Thai Airways** flies to more than 50 cities on four continents.

BY SEA

The days when travellers sailed up the Chao Phraya River to view the golden spires of Bangkok are long gone. Luxury liners now call at Pattaya and Phuket but have ceased serving Bangkok. Check with a travel agent or shipping company for details.

A regular cruise ship, *Andaman Princess*, operates between Bangkok and Singapore. Details from Siam Cruise Co., Bangkok. Tel: (02) 255 8950. Fax: (02) 255 8961.

BY RAIL

Trains operated by the **State Railways of Thailand** (www.srt.or.th) are clean, cheap and reliable, albeit slow. There are only two entry points into Thailand, both from Malaysia on the southern Thai border. The trip north to Bangkok serves as a scenic introduction to southern Thailand.

The *Malay Mail* travels from Kuala Lumpur to Butterworth, the port opposite Malaysia's Penang Island, five times daily. A daily train leaves Butterworth at 1.40pm and arrives in Bangkok at 9.30 the next morning. There are second-class cars with seats which are made into upper and lower sleeping berths at night. There are also air-conditioned first-class sleepers and dining cars.

Trains leave Bangkok's Hua Lampong Station daily at 3.15pm for the return journey to Malaysia.

BY ROAD

Malaysia provides the main road access into Thailand, with crossings near Betong and Sungai Kolok. It is possible to cross to and from Laos from Nong Khai by using the Friendship Bridge across the Mekong River. Visitors need visas. Most Thai roads are modern, paved and usually well maintained.

Arrive in Style

The Eastern & Oriental Express is Asia's most exclusive travel experience. Travelling between Singapore, Kuala Lumpur and Bangkok, the 22-carriage train with its distinctive green-and-cream livery passes through spectacular scenery. It's expensive but classy. www.orient-express.com

Practical Tips

Media

PRESS

There are two national English-language dailies, *Bangkok Post* and *The Nation*. The *Asian Wall Street Journal* and *International Herald Tribune* are printed in Bangkok. Newsstands in major hotel gift shops carry air-freighted, and therefore expensive, editions of British, French, American, German and Italian newspapers. Newsagents on Soi 3 (Soi Nana Nua), Sukhumvit Road, Bangkok also offer Arabic newspapers.

In addition, check out *Bangkok Metro*, a well put-together monthly magazine which features interesting writing; book, film and restaurant reviews; shopping information; and a calendar of Bangkok events, including sport, health and kids' activities. Several pages are also devoted to Phuket and Samui.

In Pattaya, the weekly *Pattaya Mail* contains local news and features, as well as information on events, special offers and new facilities and services in the area.

RADIO

AM radio is devoted entirely to Thai-language programmes. FM frequencies include Radio Thailand (92.5 FM) with a variety of English-language programmes, and Chulalongkorn University (101.5) which plays jazz 5pm–6pm and classical music 8pm–10pm. Other popular stations can be found at 89 FM (Thai rock); 95.5 FM (English-speaking DJs playing hits from the 70s, 80s and 90s); 105 FM (easy listening with hourly international, local and traffic news); 107 FM (50s–90s hits with hourly CNN broadcasts).

In addition, Voice of America, BBC World Service, Radio Canada, Radio Australia and Radio New Zealand all offer shortwave radio broadcasts in English and Thai. Check newspapers for current frequencies and programme schedules.

TELEVISION

Bangkok has five Thai language television channels, and there is a wide variety of satellite and cable television services.

Postal Services

Thailand has a comprehensive and reliable postal service. Major towns offer regular air mail services, as well as express courier services.

In Bangkok, the General Post Office (GPO), on Charoen Krung (New) Road between Suriwongse and Si Phraya roads, tel: (02) 233 1050/9, 235 2834, is open 8am–8pm during the week, and 8am–1pm on weekends and holidays. (Note that it is easier to conduct business in person, rather than by phone.) A building to the right of the main GPO provides telecommunications services (telephone, telegram, fax and telex) around the clock.

Tourist Information

The **Tourism Authority of Thailand (TAT)** offers brochures, maps and videos of the country's many attractions. Bangkok's head office at 1600 New Phetburi Road, Makkason, Rachathewi, (tel: (02) 250 5500) provides essential information; also try the office at 4 Ratchadamnern Nok Avenue (tel: (02) 282 9775/6).

The TAT's website is www.tat.or.th; its e-mail address for enquiries is center@tat.or.th. It also has a 24-hour hotline: dial 1155.

Branch post offices are located throughout the country, many staying open until 6pm. Post office kiosks along some of the city's busier streets sell stamps, aerograms and ship small parcels. Hotel reception desks will also send letters and postcards for no extra charge.

Telecommunications

Thailand has a sophisticated communications system, not that it always works; the lines have a way of getting jammed, like the traffic, especially after a heavy rain. Most hotels have telephone, telegram, e-mail, and fax facilities.

Area Codes

Since 2002, area codes (including the prefix zero) must always be dialled when making local calls and when calling from one province to another. If calling from overseas, drop the prefix zero.

TELEPHONE

Most international telephone calls can be dialled direct from Bangkok. International telephone calls can be placed at the **General Post Office** (GPO) 24 hours a day. Most provincial capitals have telephone offices at the GPO; hours are generally 7am–11pm.

Note that any telephone number beginning with 01 indicates a cellular telephone. Telephone calls to Malaysia do not require a country code; simply prefix the number, including the area code, with 09.

Operator Assistance

For directory assistance in English in Bangkok and in the provinces, dial 1133.

For operator assistance with a domestic call (including those to Malaysia and Laos), dial 101; for assistance with an international call (including collect/reverse charges calls), dial 100. Operators at these numbers speak English.

Emergencies

- **Police** 191
- **Tourist Police** 1155
(The Tourist Police are assigned specially to assist travellers, and are likely to speak English.)
- **Bangkok**
26/56 South Salom
Tel: (02) 678 6800-9
Tourist Assistance Centre, 1600 New Phetburi Road, Tel: (02) 250 5500. Booths can also be found in many tourist areas including Lumpini Park (near the intersection of Rama IV and Silom Roads) and Patpong (at the Silom Road intersection).
- **Chiang Mai**
Below the TAT office, 105/1 Chiang Mai–Lamphun Road. Tel: (053) 248 604/5, 248 607.
- **Pattaya**
382/1 Chaihat Road.
Tel: (038) 427 667.
- **Phuket**
TAT office, 73-75 Phuket Road.
Tel: (076) 217 138, 211 036.

International Telephone Calls

The international prefix from Thailand is 001. Home Direct is a service whereby one can reach an international operator in a number of countries worldwide. Home Direct is accessible from most private telephones, the GPO in Bangkok, many post office telephone offices in the provinces, and at the airports in Bangkok, Chiang Mai and Phuket. It is not, unfortunately, widely available from hotel telephones.

To access Home Direct, dial 001 999, and then the following: Australia, 61 1000; Canada, 15 1000; New Zealand, 64 1066; United Kingdom, 44 1066; USA, 1111 (AT&T); 12001 (MCI); 13877 (Sprint).

TELEGRAM, E-MAIL AND FAX SERVICES

Main post offices in nearly every city offer telegram, telex and fax services to all parts of the world. Many small shops throughout the country also offer a variety of telephone and fax services, although prices may be steep, particularly for faxes.

Internet cafés can now be found on almost every street in Bangkok, and even the least developed provinces have places to check e-mail and surf the web. Some of the larger facilities serve hot and cold food.

Medical Services

HOSPITALS

First-class hotels in Bangkok, Chiang Mai and Phuket have doctors on call for medical emergencies. The hospitals in these three destinations are the equivalent of those in any major western city. Most small towns have clinics which treat minor ailments and accidents.

Bangkok
BNH Hospital, 9/1 Convent Road. Tel: (02) 632 0550, www.bangkoknursinghome.com.
Samitivej Hospital, 133 Soi 49, Sukhumvit Road. Tel: (02) 392 0010/9, 655 1024/5, www.samitivej.co.th.
Thai Nakharin Hospital, 345 Bang Na Trat Road. Tel: (02) 361 2712/61.

Chiang Mai
Chiang Mai Maharaj Hospital, 110 Inthavarorod, Sriphum, Muang. Tel: (053) 221 122, 221 075, fax: (053) 221 141, www.med.cmu.ac.th.
Chiang Mai Ram Hospital, 8 Boonmuangrit Road, Tamboon Sripoom, Muang. Tel: (053) 224 861, fax: (053) 224 871, www.chiangmairam.com.

Phuket
Bangkok-Phuket Hospital, 2/1 Hongyok Utit Road, Phuket town. Tel: (076) 254 421/9. Emergencies: ext. 1060.
Patong-Kathu Hospital, Sawatdirak Road, Patong Beach. Tel: (076) 340 444.

Phuket International Hospital, Chalermprakiat Road, Phuket. Tel: (076) 249 400. Emergencies: (076) 210 936.

Embassies in Bangkok

Australia
37 Sathorn Tai Road.
Tel: (02) 287 2680.
Canada
Boonmitr Bldg., 11th Floor, 138 Silom Road.
Tel: (02) 237 4126.
United Kingdom
1031 Witthayu Road.
Tel: (02) 253 0191/9.
United States
120/122 Witthayu Road.
Tel: (02) 205 4000.

MEDICAL CLINICS

For minor problems, there are numerous clinics in all major towns and cities. In Bangkok, the **British Dispensary**, at 109 Sukhumvit Road (between Soi 3 and 5), tel: (02) 252 9179, has British doctors on its staff.

In Chiang Mai, go to **Loi Kroh Clinic** on Loi Kroh Road, tel: (053) 271 571. Most international hotels also have an on-premises clinic or doctor on call.

Tipping

Tipping is not a custom in Thailand, although it is becoming more prevalent. A service charge of 10 percent is generally included in restaurant bills and is divided among the staff. A bit extra for the waitress would not go unappreciated.

Do not tip non-metered taxi or *tuk-tuk* drivers unless the traffic has been particularly bad; 10 baht would suffice for a journey costing over 60 baht. Hotel bellmen and room porters are becoming used to being tipped in urban centres but will not hover with hand extended.

Getting Around

On Arrival

BANGKOK AIRPORT

The once nightmarish journey from Bangkok's Don Muang International Airport into the city centre has vastly improved with the completion of an elevated highway and several linking expressways. Still, be prepared for gridlocked traffic at the city centre during peak hours.

Limousine Service
Thai Airways runs a limousine service from the airport to the city. The limousines are nothing more than air-conditioned taxis with the Thai Airways logo on them. Fares start from 650 baht (plus toll fees of 30–70 baht), depending on your destination. Air-conditioned metered taxis *(see below)* are just as comfortable and cost much less. Most people use the limousine service to get to Pattaya; the fare costs about 2,500 baht.

Airport Bus
A special express bus service operates from the airport to four areas of Bangkok: **route A1** goes to the Silom Road area; **route A2** goes to Banglumpoo; **route A3** runs along Sukhumvit Road; and **route A4** ends at Hua Lampong railway station. Detailed maps of the routes are available at the bus counter. Buses run daily every 15 minutes from 6am to midnight and tickets cost 100 baht.

Taxis
Getting a metered taxi into Bangkok from the airport used to be hectic, but the system established in the last couple of years has changed all

Bangkok Taxi Talk

Thai taxi drivers are not renowned for their fluency in English, so it's often wise to have your destination written in Thai to hand to the driver.

Note that in Bangkok, Wireless Road, base of many embassies, a large hotel and several banks, is more commonly known by its Thai name, Thanon Witthayu. Similarly, Sathorn Road, a main thoroughfare divided into north and south which runs between Lumpini Park and the river, is often referred to as Sathorn Nua (north) and Sathorn Tai (south).

that. Taxi stands are located just outside the arrivals hall at the kerb. Simply get in line and tell the woman at the counter where you want to go. Your destination is recorded along with the license plate number of a waiting taxi that you'll be directed to. The air-conditioned taxi will take you to your destination using the meter. Once you arrive, add 50 baht to what is on the meter (plus any toll or expressway fees – 30 to 70 baht) and that is your fare.

Sometimes when the queue is long, cabbies waiting for fares will wave at you, trying to get you to leave the queue and negotiate with them directly. Simply ignore them. The system has been put in place to protect passengers from fraud.

Public Buses

For budget travellers (without much luggage), air-conditioned buses – Nos. 4, 13 and 29 – stop in front of the airport. The trip into town costs about 18 baht. The last buses leave at around 8pm.

CHIANG MAI AIRPORT

Chiang Mai's airport is a 10-minute drive from the city centre. There is no bus service, visitors should choose between one of the following services:

Taxis: If you have not made arrangements with your hotel to pick you up, airport taxis are available for the 15–20 minute ride to the city for 100–120 baht.

Minibus: Thai Airways operates a minibus between the airport and its town office on Phra Poklao Road.

PHUKET AIRPORT

Taxis: If you have not made arrangements with your hotel to pick you up, Thai Airways offers air-conditioned taxis to the major beaches. The price is computed per vehicle, and each vehicle holds up to four persons.

Minibus: The Thai Airways minibus runs hourly between the airport and its Phuket town office on Ranong Road. You must then find your own way from the office to the hotel. Some hotels operate minibuses to ferry guests with reservations direct to their hotels.

Domestic Travel

BY AIR

The domestic arm of **Thai Airways** (www.thaiairways.com) operates a network of daily flights to 21 of Thailand's major towns aboard a fleet of 737s and Airbuses. Thai Airways offers a "Discover Thailand" visitor's pass, allowing four domestic flights, for about US$250. Certain conditions apply, notably that this pass must be purchased outside Thailand. Contact a TAT office for further details *(see page 333)*.

In addition, **Bangkok Airways** (www.bangkokairways.com) flies from Bangkok to Ko Samui several times daily; to Sukhothai and Chiang Mai twice daily; and to Ranong once daily.

Note that if you are planning a trip to the tropical island of Ko Samui from Bangkok, you will save much travelling time if you go by air, a journey of less than two hours; the same trip by road and boat may take as long as 14 hours.

BY RAIL

The **State Railways of Thailand** (www.srt.or.th) operates three principal routes from Hua Lampong Station. The northern route passes through Ayutthaya, Phitsanulok, Lampang and terminates at Chiang Mai. The northeastern route passes through Ayutthaya, Saraburi, Nakhon Ratchasima, Khon Kaen, Udon Thani and terminates at Nong Khai. The southern route crosses the Rama VI bridge and calls at Nakhon Pathom, Phetchaburi, Hua Hin and Chumphon. It branches at Hat Yai, one branch running southwest through Betong and on down the western coast of Malaysia to Singapore. The southeastern branch goes via Pattani and Yala to the Thai border opposite the Malaysian town of Kota Bharu.

In addition, there is a line from Makkasan to Aranya Prathet on the Cambodian border.

Another line leaves Bangkok Noi station, in Thonburi, on the western bank of the Chao Phraya River, for Kanchanaburi and other destinations in western Thailand. There is also a short route leaving Bangkok Noi that travels west along the rim of the Gulf of Thailand to Samut Sakhon and then on to Samut Songkram.

Express and rapid services on the main lines offer first-class, air-conditioned or second-class, fan-cooled cars with sleeping cabins or berths and dining cars. There are also special air-conditioned express day coaches that travel to key towns along the main lines.

20-day rail passes are available.

Booking Train Tickets

The easiest way to book your train trip is through hotel or a local travel agency. There will likely be a small service charge, but it will save the headaches of trying to get through by phone.

Also, make certain that you know from which station your train leaves, particularly if travelling west to Kanchanaburi.

Reservations can be made at the station or with any travel agent within 30 days prior to departure.

In Bangkok, details from: **Hua Lampong Station**: Rama IV Road. Tel: (02) 233 7010, 233 7020 (information), (02) 223 3762, 224 7788, 225 6964 (reservations), fax: (02) 225 6068. **Bangkok Noi (Thonburi) Station**, Arun Amarin Road (near Siriraj Hospital). Tel: (02) 225 0300.

BY ROAD

Bus services are reliable, frequent and very affordable to most destinations in Thailand. Rest stops are regular, and in some cases refreshments are available.

Fan-cooled buses, painted orange, are the slowest since they make stops in every village along the way. For short distances, they can be an entertaining means of travel, particularly in the cool season when the fan and the open windows make the trip reasonably comfortable.

Blue air-conditioned buses are generally a faster, more comfortable way to travel. VIP buses are available on some of the longer routes; these usually have larger seats, more leg room and toilets.

Bus Stations

For bus and coach journeys to destinations outside of Bangkok, the major terminals are:
Eastern, Sukhumvit Road, opposite Soi 63 (Soi Ekamai). Tel: (02) 391 2504, 391 9829, 392 2520/1. Departures for Pattaya, Rayong, Chanthaburi.
Northern and Northeastern, Moh Chit Mai. Tel: (02) 936 0667. Departures for Ayutthaya, Lopburi, Nakhon Ratchasima, Chiang Mai.
Southern, Boromrat Chonnani Road (western bank of Chao Phraya). Tel: (02) 435 1199/1200, 391 9829, 435 0511, 434 5557/8. Departures for Nakhon Pathom, Kanchanaburi, Phuket, Surat Thani.

To reach a small town from a large one, or to get around on some of the islands, *song tao* (meaning two benches), pick-up trucks with

Guard Your Bags!

Pocket-picking and bag-slashing are not uncommon on Bangkok buses. Keep your wallet in a front pocket and your bag in front of you at all times.

benches along either side of the bed, function as taxis.

Public Transport

BANGKOK

Taxis, Tuk-Tuks & Motorcycles
There are two types of taxi available in Bangkok: metered and non-metered. Both are air-conditioned and reliable, but the drivers' command of English is usually minimal. This might present a problem, not only in conveying your destination, but with non-metered taxis, in bargaining the price.

Do not step into a non-metered taxi without having first agreed on a price, which can fluctuate depending on the hour of the day and the amount of traffic, rain, and the number of one-way streets he must negotiate. The basic fare for all journeys is 35 baht. Taxi drivers do not charge you an extra fee for baggage stowage or extra passengers, and there is no tipping. Check at hotels for typical fares.

The metered taxis are a much better choice if you do not know the precise distance to your intended destination. Taxi drivers are experts at outwitting their less knowledgeable passengers, so if you are just a casual tourist, stick to the metered taxis. The minimum

Bangkok's Waterways

Chao Phraya River express boats (white with red trim) run regular routes at 15- to 20-minute intervals up and down the Chao Phraya River, going all the way to Nonthaburi, 10 km (6 miles) north of the city. The service runs from 6am to 6pm.The fares are collected on board.

basic fare is 35 baht, and it rises in two-baht increments depending on the length of time and distance involved in the trip. Make sure the driver of the metered taxi turns his meter on after you get in.

Occasionally a driver will try to negotiate a flat fare from you instead of turning on his meter; this practice is particularly common in the area of the World Trade Centre and the Erawan Shrine. Sometimes the fare quoted amounts to thievery; you will nearly always get a better rate from a metered taxi. Note that any trips made along the expressway ("highway" to some drivers) will involve an additional toll of 40 baht, which you will be expected to pay. Also, most taxi drivers do not maintain a ready supply of small change; it's best not to offer anything larger than a 100-baht note in payment of fare.

If the English fluency of taxi drivers is limited, that of *tuk-tuk* (also called *samlor*, meaning three wheels) drivers is even less. *Tuk-tuks* are the brightly coloured three-wheeled taxis whose nickname comes from the noise their two-cycle engines make. They are fun for short trips, but choose a taxi for longer journeys, particularly during the heat of the day. A *tuk-tuk* driver on an open stretch of road can seldom resist racing, and the resultant journey can be a hair-raising experience. For very short trips, the fare is 20 baht.

As the traffic situation worsens in Bangkok, motorcycle taxis have proliferated; their drivers wear single-colour vests. Passengers are required to wear helmets on the major roads, but the drivers do not

Ferries, often red, cross the river at dozens of points and are very cheap. They begin operating at 6am and stop at midnight.

It is also possible to catch a long-tail taxi to many points along the Chao Phraya or the canals; it helps to be fairly familiar with the waterways before doing so.

always supply them. In the case of an accident, not a rare occurrence, the driver will likely not hold any insurance. In spite of the risks, this means of travel is worth trying when the streets are jammed.

Buses and Minibuses
Bangkok buses come in four varieties: executive, air-conditioned, ordinary, and the green minibuses. They operate every two or three minutes along more than 100 routes and are an excellent way to see the outer areas of the city. Bus maps give the routes for all buses.

Buses are especially useful during rush hours when travelling up one-way streets because they can speed along specially marked bus lanes going against on-coming traffic. Conductors prowl through the aisles collecting fares and issuing tickets. Destinations are only noted in Thai so a bus map is needed. Most routes cease operating around midnight, though some run all through the night.

Red executive micro-buses hold 20 seated passengers in air-conditioned comfort; they charge a flat fare regardless of destination, but serve fewer routes. Ordinary buses come in two varieties: red and white (more expensive) and blue and white. Aside from the price, there is no difference in service routes. Both can be very crowded. (It is a sight to see one leaning heavily to one side while students cling to the open doors.) Their drivers usually drive in very colourful fashion and deck out their buses with stereo sets and even TVs.

Skytrain
The Bangkok Transit System (BTS), or **Syktrain**, opened in December 1999 (tel: (02) 617 7300, fax: (02) 617 7133, www.bts.co.th). Trains arrive every three-to-five minutes, and no journey exceeds 30 minutes. It consists of two lines: the **Sukhumvit Line** runs from On Nut along Sukhumvit Road to Siam Square, Phaya Thai Road, Victory Monument and Mo Chit. The **Silom Line** extends from Saphan Taksin through Silom's business district, Siam Square and

ends at the National Stadium. The two lines cross at Siam Square.

A 21-km (13-mile) underground subway system with 18 stations is due to open in late 2004.

CHIANG MAI

Buses: Chiang Mai has red minibuses known locally as *song tao*. They will carry passengers almost anywhere within the town.

Tuk-tuk: They charge according to distance, starting at 20 baht. You must bargain for the price before you get in.

Samlor. These pedal trishaws charge 5 baht for short distances. Bargain before you board.

PHUKET

Buses: Picturesque wooden buses ply regular routes from the market to the beaches. They depart every 30 minutes between 8am and 6pm between Phuket town market and all beaches except Rawai and Nai Harn. Buses to Rawai and Nai Harn leave from the traffic circle on Bangkok Road. They prowl the beach roads in search of passengers. Flag one down; 15–20 baht per person.

Tuk-tuk: The small cramped *tuk-tuks* function as taxis, and they'll go anywhere. Barter your fare before

Motorcycle Rental

Motorcycles can be rented in Chiang Mai, Pattaya and Phuket (just about everywhere, in fact) for economical rates. Remember that when you rent a motorcycle, you must surrender your passport for the duration.

Motorcycles range in size from 90cc models to giant 750cc behemoths. The majority are 125cc trailbikes. Rental outlets can be found along beach roads and main roads in each town.

It is not uncommon for rental bikes to be stolen; lock them up when not in use, and only park them in areas with supervision.

getting on. For example, Patong to Karon, 120 baht, Patong to airport, 300 baht. Within town, 10–20 baht.

Motorcycle taxis: 10–20 baht per ride. A convenient if dangerous way to get around.

Private Transport

LIMOUSINES

Most major hotels operate air-conditioned limousine services. Although the prices are at least twice those of ordinary taxis, they offer English-speaking drivers and door-to-door service.

RENTAL CARS

Thailand has a good road system with over 50,000 km (31,000 miles) of paved highways. Road signs are in both Thai and English, and you should have no difficulty following a map. An international driver's license is required.

Driving on a narrow but busy road can be a terrifying experience; right of way is generally determined by size. It is not unusual for a bus to overtake a truck despite the fact that the oncoming lane is filled with vehicles. It is little wonder that, when collisions occur, several dozen lives are often lost. In addition, many of the long-distance drivers consume pep pills and have the throttle to the floor because they are getting paid for beating schedules. You are strongly advised to avoid driving at night.

Avis, Hertz Budget and numerous local agencies offer late-model cars with and without drivers, and with insurance coverage for Bangkok and upcountry trips. A deposit is usually required except with credit cards.

In the provinces, agencies can be found in major towns like Chiang Mai, Pattaya and Phuket. These also rent four-wheel-drive jeeps and minibuses. When renting a jeep, read the fine print carefully and be aware that you are liable for all damages to the vehicle. Ask for first class insurance, which covers both you and the other vehicle involved in a collision.

Where to Stay

Choosing a Hotel

Thailand's hotels and guesthouses are equal to the very best anywhere in the world. The facilities in the first-class hotels may include as many as six or more different restaurants serving Western and Asian cuisines, coffee shops, swimming pools, fitness centres, business centres, shopping arcades, and cable and satellite television.

Expect the level of service to be second to none. It is not surprising, therefore, that top hotels like the Oriental and the Shangri-La in Bangkok, the Amanpuri in Phuket, and the Regent Resort in Chiang Mai are consistently voted among the best in the world. Even budget and inexpensive hotels will invariably have a swimming pool and more than one food outlet.

In first class hotels add 10 percent service charge and 7 percent value-added tax to the prices. It is acceptable to bargain, especially during the low season (May–October).

BANGKOK

Bangkok Marriot Resort and Spa
257 Charoen Nakhon Road
Tel: (02) 476 0022
Fax: (02) 476 1120
www.marriott.com
A resort hotel with the conveniences of nearby downtown. Located on the western side of the Chao Phraya River. The warren of streets nearby offers a glimpse of old Bangkok life. $$$$
Dusit Thani
946 Rama IV Road
Tel: (02) 236 9999
Fax: (02) 236 6400

www.dusit.com
Bangkok's first high-rise hotel. Adjacent to major banks and businesses on Silom Road. Views of Bangkok from the rooftop restaurant are excellent. Close to the Patpong nightlife scene. $$$$
Four Seasons Bangkok
155 Ratchadamri Road
Tel: (02) 251 6127
Fax: (02) 253 9195
www.fourseasons.com
High luxury in the heart of the city. With music and tea in the lobby lounge, there are echoes of the old Orient. The best hotel pool in Bangkok. Faces the Royal Bangkok Sports Club. $$$$
Grand Hyatt Erawan
494 Ratchadamri Road
Tel: (02) 254 1234
Fax: (02) 254 6308
www.bangkok.hyatt.com
On a major intersection and close to the famous Erawan Shrine, one of the best known religious symbols in Bangkok. Just adjacent are major shopping malls. The hotel has a good mix of restaurants and high standards of service. $$$$

Price Guide

A general guide for a standard double room, excluding taxes.
$$$$ = above US$150
$$$ = US$100–150
$$ = US$50–100
$ = under US$50

Shangri-La
89 Soi Wat Suan Plu,
Charoen Krung Road
Tel: (02) 236 7777
Fax: (02) 236 8579
www.shangri-la.com
Every room has a river view. The evening buffet on the riverside terrace is famous. Other services include a helicopter transfer service to Don Muang International Airport. The biggest hotel on the river. $$$$
The Oriental
48 Oriental Ave
Tel: ((02) 659 9000
Fax: (02) 659 0000
www.mandarinoriental.com
A visit is a must, even if it is only to

have a drink on the river terrace or afternoon tea in the Author's Lounge. The Oriental is part of the history of East meeting West. Repeatedly voted one of the world's best hotels. $$$$
The Sukhothai Bangkok
13/3 Sathorn Tai Road
Tel: (02) 287 0222
Fax: (02) 287 4980
www.sukhothai.com
A quiet and luxurious oasis with its interior design inspired by Thailand's myriad arts and crafts. Near the city's centre on a busy thoroughfare but set well back amid tropical gardens. $$$$
Amari Airport
333 Chert Wudthakas Road
Tel: (02) 566 1020/1
Fax: (02) 566 1941
www.amari.com/airport
Closest hotel to the airport and popular with travellers arriving late and departing early. Connected to airport by footbridge and shuttle bus. $$$
Ambassador
171 Sukhumvit Road
Tel: ((02) 254 0444
Fax: (02) 253 4123
www.amtel.co.th/bangkok
A sprawling complex with more than 1,000 rooms and an array of Asian and European restaurants. The attached food mall is a great place to sample a variety of Thai dishes. $$$
Emporium Suites
622 Sukhumvit Road (Soi 24)
Tel: (02) 664 9999
Fax: (02) 664 9990
www.emporiumsuites.com
Convenically located above the upmarket Emporium shopping mall and close to the Phrom Pong BTS station, this stylish service apartment complex offers a range of accommodations – from studio and one-bedroom suites to 3-bedroom apartments. Ideal for long-term stays. $$$
Holiday Inn Crowne Plaza
981 Silom Road
Tel: (02) 238 4300
Fax: (02) 238 5289
www. crowneplazabangkok.com
Located between the business centre and the Chao Phraya River. A choice location with small shops nearby. $$$

Novotel Bangkok
Siam Square Soi 6
Tel: (02) 255 6888
Fax: (02) 255 1824
www.novotelbkk.com
Located in the middle of Siam
Square, a busy shopping area with
a huge variety of shops, cinemas
and eating places. **$$$**

Royal Orchid Sheraton
Si Chao Phraya Road
Tel: (02) 266 0123
Fax: (02) 236 8320
www.royalorchidsheraton.com
A large hotel located on the river.
Once one of the big three riverside
hotels (together with the Oriental and
the Shangri-La), now a good medium-
priced hotel with good facilities. **$$$**

The Landmark
138 Sukhumvit Road
Tel: (02) 254 0404
Fax: (02) 253 4259
www.landmarkbangkok.com
Centrally located with a Skytrain
station opposite the hotel. Well-
equipped for business travellers
and shoppers. **$$$**

Asia Bangkok
296 Phayathai Road
Tel: (02) 215 0808
Fax: (02) 215 2642
www.asiahotel.co.th
Great location for shopping with
Siam Square, Siam Discovery
Centre and the World Trade Centre
all close. Good facilities include a
sauna and health club plus a
Brazilian restaurant. **$$**

Tai Pan Hotel
25 Sukhumvit Road Soi 23
Tel: (02) 260 9888
Fax: (02) 259 7908
www.taipanhotel.com
A tasteful hotel in the busy Sukhmvit
area. The Pan Kitchen serves
excellent lunch and evening buffets.
Other facilities include a fitness
centre and swimming pool. **$$**

A-One Inn
25/13-15 Soi Kasem San 1
Tel: (02) 216 4770
Fax: (02) 216 4771
www.aoneinn.com
A great little guest house located on
a quiet lane close to Siam Square
and not far from the World Trade
Centre. Spacious rooms and
friendly service. **$**

Atlanta
78 Sukhumvit Road Soi 2
Tel: (02) 252 1650
Fax: (02) 656 8123
www.theatlantahotel.bizland.com
Well located for shopping and night
entertainment. One of Bangkok's
oldest and most respected
establishments. Good value for
money. Well regarded by return
visitors. **$**

CHIANG MAI

Four Seasons Chiang Mai
Mae Rim-Samoeng Road
Tel: (053) 298 181
Fax: (053) 298 190
www.fourseasons.com
True to the Four Seasons name, this
is the most luxurious accommodation
in northern Thailand. The 'Modern
Lanna' pavilion-style rooms are set
amid rice fields that are still worked.
A true world-class resort. You need to
plan early if you want to stay here
during the high season. **$$$$**

Amari Rincome
1 Nimmanhemin Road
Tel: (053) 221 130
Fax: (053) 221 915
www.amari.com/rincome
One of the oldest and best known
hotels in Chiang Mai. A low-rise
hotel that offers a quiet ambience,
good restaurants and a superb
swimming pool. **$$**

River View Lodge
25 Charoen Prathet Road
Tel: (053) 271 109/10
Fax: (053) 279 019
www.riverviewlodgch.com
A modest hotel with a lovely view
overlooking the Ping River. Breakfast
on the terrace is a great way to start
the day. It's close to Chiang Mai's
famous Night Bazaar. **$$**

PHUKET

Dusit Laguna
390 Srisoonthorn Road, Bang Thao
Beach
Tel: (076) 324 320/32
Fax: (076) 324 174
www.dusit.com
Part of the Dusit chain of deluxe

hotels in Thailand, this five-star
resort reflects its Thai heritage,
apparent in its decor, staff
costumes and the acclaimed Ruen
Thai restaurant. Note: broad,
sweeping Bang Thao Bay is
exposed and it is unsafe to swim in
the monsoon season. **$$$$**

Kata Thani Hotel & Beach Resort
3/24 Patak Road
Tel: (076) 330 124/6
Fax: (076) 330 127
www.katathani.com
A four-star property with 433 rooms.
Located on quiet Kata Noi where
guests get pretty much the run of the
stunning beach. Four swimming pools
and full facilities. Five restaurants,
serving seafood, German, Brazilian,
Italian and Asian fare. **$$$$**

Club Andaman Beach Resort
2 Hadpatong Road, Patong Beach
Tel: (076) 340 530
Fax: (076) 340 527
www.clubandaman.com
Large hotel in expansive manicured
gardens close to but not on the
beach. Cottage accommodation in
addition to hotel wing. Tennis
courts, gym, pool. Well-appointed
rooms with in-house video, fridge
and safe deposit box. **$$$**

Marina Cottage
47 Karon Road, Karon Beach
Tel: (076) 330 625
Fax: (076) 330 516
www.marinaphuket.com
Thai-style cottages exquisitely
landscaped into a hilly coconut
plantation. There are also two
excellent restaurants at the
cottages: Sala Thai (offering mostly
central Thai cuisine) and On the
Rock (mostly seafood). **$$$**

**Mom Tri's Boathouse and Villa
Royale**
2/2 Patak Road, Kata Beach
Tel: (076) 330 015/7
Fax: (076) 330 561
www.theboathousephuket.com
Situated on the quiet end of Kata,
this small and elegant beachfront
'boutique' hotel prides itself on
attentive and personalised service.
The main building is built in the
Ayutthaya-style with steep sloping
roofs. Beautifully appointed
bedrooms and one of the best
restaurants on the island. **$$$–$$$$**

Concerts

The Fine Arts Department offers concerts of Thai music and dance/drama at the **National Theatre**. At 2pm on Saturdays, Thai classical dance is presented at the auditorium of the **Public Relations Building** on Ratchadamnern Klang Avenue opposite the Royal Hotel. At 5pm on Fridays, Bangkok Bank offers traditional Thai music performances on the top floor of its **Pan Fah** branch (Ratchadamnern Avenue at the intersection with Phra Sumen Road).

Concerts of European music and dance are now regular events. The Bangkok Symphony Orchestra gives frequent concerts, as do groups from western countries. See *Bangkok Post*'s Sunday magazine.

Art Galleries

The **National Gallery**, to the north of the National Museum in Bangkok, across the approach to the Phra Pinklao Bridge at 4 Chao Fa Road, tel: (02) 281 2224, displays works by Thai artists and offers frequent film shows. Exhibitions of paintings, sculpture, ceramics, photographs and weaving are numerous.

Silpakorn University, opposite the Grand Palace on Na Phralan Road, is the country's premier fine arts college. It frequently stages exhibitions of students' work. Other promoters of Thai art and photography are the British Council, the Goethe Institute and Alliance Française, all of which sponsor various exhibitions.

Art galleries seem more interested in selling mass market and "tourist" works than in promoting experimental art; but one, **Visual Dhamma**, takes an active role in ensuring that talented artists exhibit their works. As its name implies, it is interested primarily in a new school of Thai art which attempts to re-interpret Buddhist themes. It is located at 44/28 Soi 21 (Soi Asoke), Sukhumvit Road. Tel: (02) 258 5879.

Thailand's Nightlife

For years, Thailand has enjoyed a lusty reputation as a centre for sex of every persuasion and interest. But times and clienteles have changed. The American GIs of the 1960s and the German and Japanese sex tourists of the 1970s and 80s have been replaced by upmarket tourists, usually couples. While there has been no diminution in massage parlours and bars, there has been an increase in activities for the new breed of travellers.

Nightlife
Jazz clubs, videotheques, discos and open-air restaurants are the most popular form of nocturnal entertainment in towns. The queen of nighttime activities in Bangkok is shopping, with night markets along Sukhumvit and Silom roads. Even in that wrinkled old harlot of a street, Patpong, vendors' tables choke the street, drawing more patrons than the bars, with their counterfeit watches, shirts and tapes. The change has rubbed off on the bars as well. Many of Patpong's bars have metamorphosed into discos.

The scene is essentially the same in Chiang Mai, where the night bazaar on Chang Klan Road attracts more tourists than the bars along Loi Kroh Road.

In Phuket, "barbeers" (a bar which serves beer) line the streets of Patong beach's Soi Bangla and similar areas of Karon and Kata.

Massages
"Traditional Thai Massage" and "Ancient Thai Massage" are therapeutic according to age-old traditions. The best place for this is at Wat Po. "Special" massages are sexual. Punters pick a woman from behind a one-way mirror and spend the next hour getting a bath and whatever else they arrange.

Shopping

Whatever part of your budget you have allocated for shopping, double it or regret it. Keep a tight grip on your wallet or you will find yourself being seduced by the low prices and walking off with more than you can possibly carry home. The widest range of handicraft items is found in Bangkok and Chiang Mai, but if you never have a chance to leave Bangkok, do not despair; nearly everything you might want to buy can be found in the capital.

What to Buy

REAL/FAKE ANTIQUES

Wood, bronze, terracotta and stone statues from all Thailand and Burma can be found in Bangkok and Chiang Mai. There are religious figures and characters from classical literature, carved wooden angels, mythical animals, temple bargeboards and eave brackets. Most fake antiques passed off as real are crafted in Chiang Mai and surrounding villages.

Although the Thai government bans export of Buddha images, there are numerous deities and disciples that can be sent abroad, such as bronze deer, angels and characters from the *Ramakien* cast in bronze. It is also possible to export Burmese Buddha images.

BASKETS

Thailand's abundant bamboo, wicker and grasses are transformed into lamps, storage boxes, tables, colourful mats, handbags, letter holders, tissue boxes and slippers. Wicker and bamboo are turned into storage lockers with brass fittings and furniture to fill the house.

Shoppers' Map

Nancy Chandler's *Map of Bangkok*, available in bookstores and hotels, is an invaluable reference for shoppers. It is not the best map for finding specific addresses, but for pointing you in the direction of the top shopping areas, restaurants and sights, it is unparalleled. Also, the brightly coloured, hand-lettered map makes a wonderful souvenir.

Yan lipao, a thin, sturdy grass, is woven into delicate patterns to create purses and bags for formal occasions. Although expensive, the bags retain their beauty for years.

CERAMICS

Best known among the distinctive Thai ceramics is the jade green celadon, which is distinguished by its finely glazed surface. Statues, lamps, ashtrays and other items are also produced in dark green, brown and cobalt blue hues.

Modelled on its Chinese cousin, blue-and-white porcelain includes pots, lamp bases, household items and figurines. Quality varies according to the skill of the artist, and of the firing and glazing.

Bencharong (meaning five colours) describes a style of porcelain derived from 16th-century Chinese art. Normally reserved for bowls, containers and fine chinaware, its classic pattern features a small religious figure surrounded by intricate floral designs, usually green, blue, yellow, rose and black.

DECORATIVE ARTS

Lacquerware comes in two styles: the gleaming gold-and-black variety normally seen on temple shutters, and the matte red type with black and/or green details, which originated in northern Thailand and Burma. The range includes ornate containers and trays, wooden

figurines, woven bamboo baskets and Burmese-inspired Buddhist manuscripts. Pieces may also be bejeweled with tiny glass mosaics and gilded ornaments.

Black lacquer is also the base into which shaped bits of mother-of-pearl are pressed. Scenes from religious or classical literature are rendered on presentation trays, containers and plaques.

GEMS AND JEWELLERY

Thailand is one of the world's exporters of cut rubies and sapphires. Customers should patronise only those shops that display the trade's official emblem: a gold ring mounted with a ruby.

Thailand is now regarded as the world's leading cutter of gemstones, the "Bangkok cut" rapidly becoming one of the most popular. Artisans set the stones in gold and silver to create jewellery and bejeweled containers. Light green Burmese jade (jadeite) is carved into jewellery and art objects. Phuket produces international standard natural, cultured Mob (teardrop) and artificial pearls. Costume jewellery is a major Thai business.

HILL-TRIBE CRAFTS

Northern hill tribes produce brightly coloured needlepoint in a variety of geometric and floral patterns. These are sold as produced, or else incorporated into shirts, coats, bags, pillowcases and other items.

Hill-tribe silver work is valued less for its silver content (which is low) than for the intricate work and imagination that goes into it. Other hill-tribe items one might consider include knives, baskets, pipes and gourd flutes that look and sound like bagpipes.

METAL ART OBJECTS

Although Thai craftsmen have produced some of Asia's most

beautiful Buddha images, modern bronze sculpture tends to be of less exalted subjects and execution.

Silver and gold are pounded into jewellery, boxes and other decorative pieces, many set with gems. Tin, mined near Phuket, is the prime ingredient in pewterware, of which Thailand is a major producer. Items range from clocks and steins to egg cups and figurines.

Thai Silk and Fabrics

● **Silk** is perhaps Thailand's internationally best-known craft. First brought to world attention by American entrepreneur Jim Thompson, Thai silk has enjoyed enduring popularity and is on the shopping list of many visitors. Sold in a wide variety of colours, it is characterised by the tiny nubs which, like embossings, rise from its surface – and, of course, by its smooth silkiness.

But unlike sheer Indian silks and shiny Chinese-patterned silks, Thai silk is a thick cloth that lends itself to clothes, curtains and upholstery, but is also used to cover purses, tissue boxes and picture frames.

Mudmee is a silk from the northeast of Thailand and whose colours are sombre and muted. A form of tie-dyed cloth, it is sold both in lengths and as finished clothing or accessories.

● **Cotton** is popular for shirts and dresses, since it breathes in Thailand's hot, humid air.

● **Batik** Southern Thailand is a batik centre and offers ready-made clothes and batik paintings.

● **Wall hangings** Burmese in origin and style, *kalaga* wall hangings are popular. The figures are stuffed with *kapok* to make them stand out from the surface in relief.

Getting Acquainted

Situation In the Indian Ocean, bordering Thailand and Laos to the east, Bangladesh to the west and India and China to the north.
Area 671,000 sq km (260,000 sq mi).
Capital Yangon.
Population 48 million, about 5 million of whom live in Yangon.
Highest Point Hkakabo Razi (5,889 m/19,320 ft) is the highest mountain in Southeast Asia.
Time Zone 6.5 hours ahead of Greenwich Meridian Time (GMT), so New York is 11.5 hours, Los Angeles 14.5 hours and London 6.5 hours behind, Australia 2.5 hours ahead. Bangkok is half an hour behind.
Currency *Kyat* (pronounced *chat*).
Weights and Measures Imperial.
Electricity 230 volts, using three-pin plugs, but the power supply is intermittent and unreliable.
International Dialling Code 95.

National Flag

The Burmese national flag is red in colour with a dark blue canton in the top left corner. Within the blue field are a white pinion and ears of paddy rice, surrounded by 14 white stars. The pinion represents industry, the rice symbolises agriculture, and the stars correspond to the 14 administrative states and divisions of Burma. The three colours of the flag represent decisiveness (red), purity and virtue (white) and peace and integrity (blue). The state flag was adopted in 1974.

Climate

Like all countries in South and Southeast Asia's monsoonal region, Burma's year is divided into three seasons. The rains begin in May, and are most intense between June and August. The central inland is drier than other parts of the country, but is subject to much rain during this time.

In October, the rains let up. The ensuing winter "cool season" (November through to February) is the most pleasant time to visit Burma. The average mean temperature along the Ayeyarwady plain, from Yangon to Mandalay, is 21–28°C (70–82°F), although in the mountains on the north and east, the temperature can drop below freezing and snow can fall.

During the months of March and April, Burma has its "dry season". Temperatures in the central plain, particularly around Bagan (Pagan), can climb to 45°C (113°F).

Annual rainfall along the rain-shadow coasts of Rakhine (Arakan) and Tanintharyi (Tenasserim) ranges from 300 to 500 cm (120 to 200 in). The Ayeyarwady Delta gets about 150 to 200 cm (60 to 78 in), while the central Burma region, between Mandalay and Bagan and the surrounding areas, averages 50–100 cm (20–40 in) of rain each year. In the far north, the melting snows of the Himalayan foothills keep rivers fed with water.

The People

Burma has seven minority-dominated states: Rakhaing (Arakan), Chin, Kachin, Kayin (Karen), Kayah, Mon and Shan. There are seven divisions populated mainly by Bamars (Burmans): Ayeyarwady (Irrawaddy), Magway (Magwe), Mandalay, Bago (Pegu), Yangon (Rangoon), Sagaing and Tanintharyi. Eighty percent of the population live in the country and 20 percent in towns. Population density is 46.9 per sq km. (123 per sq mi). Annual growth rate is around 1.8 percent. Life

Public Holidays

All offices are closed on the following days:
● **4 January** Independence Day commemorates the date in 1948 that Burma left the British Commonwealth and became a sovereign independent nation.
● **12 February** Union Day marks the date in 1947 that Aung San concluded an agreement with Burma's ethnic minorities at Panglong in the Shan State.

The Union of Myanmar (Burma) flag, which has been carried by runners to each of Burma's state capitals, is returned to Yangon amid the roar of hundreds of thousands of people from all over the nation.
● **2 March** Peasants' Day honours the farming population.
● **27 March** Resistance (Tatmadaw) Day commemorates the World War II struggle against Japan. It is celebrated with parades and fireworks. Ironically, Burma spent most of the war on the Japanese side fighting Allied forces, but switched allegiance in early 1945.
● **1 May Workers'/May Day** The working people's holiday.

● **19 July** Martyrs' Day is a memorial to Burma's founding father, Aung San, and his cabinet who were assassinated in 1947. Ceremonies take place at the Martyrs' Mausoleum, Yangon.
Non-Buddhist religious holidays: Minority groups celebrate holidays not on the Burmese calendar: the Hindu festival *Dewali* in October, the Islamic observance of *Bakri Idd* with changing dates, the Christian holidays of Christmas and Easter, and the Kayin (Karen) New Year Festival on or about 1 January.

Business Hours

- **Government offices/post offices** 9.30am–4.30pm Monday to Friday, 9.30am–12.30pm Saturday.
- **Myanmar Airways** 9.30am–4.30pm Monday to Friday.
- **Banks** 10am–2pm weekdays.
- **Central Telegraph Office** 8am–9pm weekdays, 8am–8pm Sunday and holidays.
- **Myanmar Travels & Tours** information counter 8am–8pm seven days a week.
- **Restaurants** Most close by 10pm, although some tea and coffee shops will stay open later.

expectancy is 57 years for men and 61 for women; the infant mortality rate is 79 per 1,000 (1996).

Economy

Burma's gross national product is around US$34.8 billion, a per capita GNP of US$765. It is growing by about 5 percent per annum. The national labour force numbers 15 million, of whom 67 percent are employed in agriculture and 13 percent in industry.

Government

In 1990 the first free elections were held in 30 years, and Nobel laureate Aung San Suu Kyi's NLD (National League for Democracy) won by a large majority. The military-led "State Peace and Development Council" (SLORC) responded by raiding NLD headquarters and arresting key members. Since then, SLORC has been fighting a war of attrition with the NLD. Several attempts have since been made to adopt a new constitution for the Union of Myanmar (in Burmese, Myanmar Naing-Ngan). In 1997 SLORC transformed itself into the State Peace and Development Council (SPDC).

Planning the Trip

What To Wear/Bring

Unless you are conducting business in Yangon, you won't be expected to wear a tie. Long trousers for men and dresses or long skirts for women, lightweight and appropriate for the weather, are the generally accepted mode of dress for Westerners. Quick-drying clothes are a good idea for visits during the rainy season or *Thingyan* ("water festival"). Shorts or mini-skirts are frowned upon by the Burmese. A sweater or jacket should be carried if you plan a visit to the hill stations or Shan Plateau, especially in the cool season. Open shoes, such as sandals, are acceptable, but remember to remove footwear when entering religious institutions.

Sunblock, sunhat and sunglasses are essential.

Visas & Passports

Visitors to Burma must present a valid passport and a tourist or business visa obtained at one of Burma's overseas embassies or consulates *(right)*. An entry visa for tourists (EVT) is valid for 28 days. These visas can now easily be extended for another four weeks at the Yangon immigration office. It is also possible to obtain a multiple journey entry visa for those operating a business in Burma.

Children above seven years of age, even when included on their parents' passport, must have their own visas.

Independent travel is allowed around Burma, but you may find it easier to travel as part of an organised group, particularly in border areas.

Health

Malaria is a danger in Burma. The risk is highest at altitudes below 1,000 m (3,000 ft) between May and December. Mosquitoes in several areas are resistant to many brands of anti-malaria drugs, so seek advice on medication from a tropical institute before you leave. Many upcountry hotels have mosquito nets, but they're worthless if they have holes in them. It can be a worthwhile investment to carry your own mosquito net and pack mosquito coils to burn while you sleep.

Amoebic dysentery is a danger to those who do not take precautions: under no circumstances should you drink water unless you know it has been boiled; all fruit should be carefully peeled before being eaten, and no raw vegetables or salads should be eaten.

Health standards in much of Burma are still relatively low, so it is essential to buy private medical insurance before your departure.

Money Matters

When entering Burma every visitor has to exchange US$200 into FECS (Foreign Exchange Currency, commonly called tourist money). Children up to 12 years and members of package tours are exempt. These 200 FECS cannot be reconverted when leaving the

Embassies Abroad

Visas can be obtained from the following embassies abroad:
- **Australia**
22 Arkana Street
Yarralumla
ACT 2600
Tel: (06) 6273 3811.
- **United Kingdom**
19a Charles Street
London W1X 8ER
Tel: (020) 7629 6966/499 8841.
- **United States**
2300 S Street NW
Washington DC 20008
Tel: (202) 332 9044/5/6.

Tourist Information

There is a limited amount of literature on Burma and no official overseas tourist offices. Burma embassies abroad have brochures and leaflets, and specialist tour operators can supply helpful details, but the best source of information (albeit lacking in brochures) is **Myanmar Travels & Tours** (MTT), which is part of the government tourist board. Though it provides little in the way of brochures, it sells tours and can arrange various types of transport around Burma. Head office: 77–91 Sule Pagoda Road, Yangon. Tel: (01) 283 997/282 013. e-mail: mtt.mht@mptmail.net.mm www.myanmars.net/mtt

Within Burma, there is also: **Myanmar Tourism Promotion Board** (MTPB), 5 Signal Pagoda Road, Yangon. Tel: (01) 243 639, Fax: (01) 245 001 www.myanmar-tourism.com

In addition, you may wish to check the following websites: www.myanmar.com www.shwenet.com www.myanmars.net

country. Visitors can exchange as many dollars into FECS as needed during their stay and can reconvert the surplus.

Among the required documents is a currency form. There is no limit to the amount of foreign currency you can bring into Burma, as long as it is declared upon entry. However, the import and export of Burmese *kyats* is forbidden, and the export of foreign currency is limited to the amount declared upon entry. The currency form must be presented whenever money is converted into FECS, and again when you leave the country.

FECS or US dollars must be used to pay for hotel rooms, air tickets and guide services. You can legally exchange FECS for kyats, at the official rate of exchange which is about six to one US dollar or FEC. However, you would be quite crazy

to exchange your money at that rate. The black market rate for both dollars and FECS has oscillated between 315 and 1,100 in the past years. Caution: When dealing in the black market, you open yourself up to being cheated by unscrupulous money changers. Kyats can be used to pay for meals, souvenirs, tips, bus and car transportation and occasionally (in the outlying districts) for accommodation.

US dollars and UK pounds sterling and a variety of other currencies can officially be exchanged into FECS at the Foreign Trade Bank (in Yangon, it's on Barr Street; in Mandalay, on B Road at 82nd Street). This is also where you can draw advances on your credit cards, but, only payable in FECS.

Credit Cards

Visa, American Express and MasterCard are only accepted at Myanmar Travels & Tours, all the major hotels, at airline offices and at the Yangon Duty Free Shop.

Getting There

BY AIR

Most of Burma's visitors arrive at Yangon's **Mingaladon Airport**. Situated 19 km (12 miles) northwest of the capital, it is where most scheduled international flights arrive. Others have begun to arrive in Mandalay from Chiang Mai, Thailand. There are plans to make the new **Mandalay International Airport** eventually a regional hub of Indochina. The largest number of international flights connect Yangon and Bangkok. **Thai Airways** and Burma's international carrier, **Myanmar Airways International**, each have two roundtrip flights daily. MAI also operates daily flights to Singapore, three flights a week to Hong Kong, two a week to Kuala Lumpur and one per week to Dhaka. **Silk Air** flies daily from Singapore, **Malaysian Airlines** (MAS) has two roundtrip flights from Kuala Lumpur, **Biman** of Bangladesh flies once a week from Chittagong via Yangon to Bangkok and back. **Air Mandalay**, a

private domestic airline, operates a biweekly service between Yangon and Chiang Mai. **Air China** (CAAC) has a weekly flight between Yangon and Kunming (Yunnan). Newcomers are **Druk Airlines** (Bhutan) and ANA (All Nippon Airways of Japan), connecting their respective countries. Travellers from the US, Australia and Europe probably will find it easiest to reach Burma via Bangkok or Singapore. Some 80 airlines connect these cities with other world capitals.

BY LAND

Burma's frontiers have long been closed to overland international travel, primarily due to the continuing rebellions by various ethnic groups in the border areas. It is, however, possible to visit Tachilek and Kyaingtong (Kengtung) in Shan State from Mae Sai in northern Thailand. For a day trip the visa is available at the border post. Similarly, the island of Kawthaung (the former Victoria Point) in the Myeik (Mergui) archipelago can be reached from Ranong in southern Thailand. On the Burma-Yunnan frontier border posts have been opened at Lwe-ge from where organised group tours can go to Bhamo, Muse, Namkham and Kunlon. Organised groups are also permitted to continue up to Lashio. The Thai and Burmese governments have constructed a bridge across the Moei River between Mae Sot and Myawaddy but so far travel is still not permitted between the two countries except for the visit to a casino within sight of the bridge. If the present development plan is carried through, it should eventually be possible to travel by car from Singapore through Burma to India or China and on to Europe.

Practical Tips

Media

Newspapers
The daily English language newspaper is called *The New Light of Myanmar* and is available at newsstands and in all hotels. Western publications can be read at the British and American Libraries in Yangon. The English-language *Myanmar Times* is available online at www.myanmar.com.

The International Press Club is at 245–247, Anawratha Street, Yangon. Tel: (01) 222 023.

Television and Radio
Both are government controlled and censored. For English radio programmes, the BBC World Service broadcasts Burma's news from 8.15 to 9pm on Wednesdays. TV Myanmar has news in English at 9.15pm every night.

Telecommunications

Although there are automatic exchanges in Burma's largest towns, the majority of places operate on manual exchanges so you need to go through the operator to place a call.

Moves are being made to update the phone system, however. Burma now has direct satellite links to seven countries: Japan, Hong Kong, Singapore, Thailand, India, UK and Australia. Siemens of Germany has installed additional satellite communication lines that should bring telecommunication connections up to Western standard. Most of the new hotels now offer an IDD telephone and fax service to foreign countries.

It is always cheaper if you telephone or send your fax through the nearest post office, but you may have to wait for a few hours until you get a connection.

The area code for Yangon is 01; Mandalay is 02; for Bagan it is 35; and for Taunggyi 81. Local calls are free of charge.

Call 101 for an overseas or inland booking between 7am to 7pm. The operator will call you when the line is open.

For further information, call the information line, tel: 103, or the trunk supervisor, tel: (01) 272 001.

The **Central Telegraph Office**, tel: (01) 281 133, located one block east of the Sule Pagoda on Mahabandoola Street, is open from 8am to 9pm Monday to Saturday, and from 8am to 8pm on Sundays and public holidays.

If you encounter problems with any of the communications systems, contact the **Myanmar Posts and Telecommunications**, 43 Bo Aung Gyaw Street. Tel: (01) 285 499.

Postal Services

The **Yangon General Post Office**, tel: (01) 285 499, is located on Strand Road at the corner of Bo Aung Gyaw Street. All post offices in Burma are open 9.30am to 4.30pm Monday to Friday, and 9.30am to 12.30pm Saturday. They are closed Sunday and public holidays.

The only exception is the Mingaladon (Yangon) Airport mail sorting office, which is open round-the-clock every day for receipt and dispatch of foreign mail and ordinary letters and postcards.

Registered letters can be taken

Embassies in Yangon

● **Australia**
88 Strand Road.
Tel: (01) 251 809/10.
● **United Kingdom**
80 Strand Road.
Tel: (01) 281 702.
● **United States**
581 Merchant Street.
Tel: (01) 282 055.

Emergency Numbers

The following Yangon numbers can be called in emergencies:
● **Police** 199
● **Fire Brigade** 191/192
● **Ambulance** (01) 208 204, 281 722
● **Immigration** (01) 286 434
● **Customs** (01) 284 533

at the airport postal counter only during normal government working hours.

Medical Treatment

By Western standards, healthcare provision is still primitive in Burma. The **Kandawgyi Clinic** on Natmauk Road, Yangon (tel: (01) 530 083) is the best on offer, or there are reasonable private military hospitals in Yangon, Mandalay and Pathein. For more serious problems, however, you are probably best flying out to Bangkok or Singapore.

For minor problems, pharmacies operate an out-of-hours rota, which should be posted in their windows.

Security & Crime

Although terrorist attacks are always a possibility in Burma, the country is basically safe and hospitable to tourists. Look after your belongings, though, as Western goods can be attractive to impoverished Burmese. Avoid driving at night, too, as highwaymen are not uncommon.

Getting Around

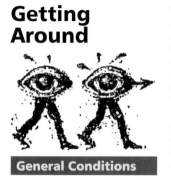

General Conditions

In Burma, it is not the distance that you should concern yourself with but rather the road conditions in the particular area in question. Average speeds achievable on road or rail are well below those in neighbouring countries. Many roads are pot-holed while others are mere dirt tracks.

From The Airport

There are two ways to get from **Mingaladon Airport** to downtown Yangon, a distance of 19 km (12 miles). You have the option of getting a "limousine" (actually just a better-looking taxi) for US$5 to anywhere in the city, payable in advance at the counter. Otherwise taxi drivers will besiege you in a bid to drive you into the city. If you book a room through the hotel desk at the airport, transport into town is usually arranged free of charge. On departure, the fare from Yangon to the airport usually can be paid in local currency.

Domestic Travel

BY AIR

Three different domestic airlines ply a network of air routes to 37 localities within Burma. Privately owned **Air Mandalay** (AM) serves several domestic destinations and Chiang Mai in Thailand with French ATR72-210 planes and offers Western standard service, check-in procedures and flight safety. The newer **Yangon Airways** (YA) has similar standards. Government-owned **Myanma Airways** (UB) has a fleet consisting of ageing Fokker F-28 jets and Fokker F-27 turboprop planes; it has a reputation for unreliable service and a questionable safety record and cannot be recommended. Air Mandalay and Yangon Airways tickets can be purchased in Bangkok, or through many travel agents in Yangon or Mandalay. Myanma Airways tickets may only be purchased at offices of Myanma Airways or Myanmar Travels & Tours (see page 346).

BY RIVER/SEA

Burma's rivers provide more than 8,000 km (5,000 miles) of navigable routes, and as a result, shipping is the most important means of transport for people and goods throughout much of the country.

Popular River Routes

The most interesting and most travelled river route for tourists is the stretch of the Ayeyarwady between Mandalay and Bagan.

A local slowboat leaves Mandalay at 5am, arriving in Bagan (Pagan) in the evening. You can travel deck class or "first class" but be forewarned that facilities are very basic. Two modern and faster express boats, Shwe Kein Nayi 1 & 2, sail the same route daily except Sunday and Wednesday, leaving at 6am from both Mandalay and Bagan for the 9-hour journey. For all bookings, contact the **Inland Waterways Transport** office (for foreigners) near the Kaingdan Jetty

Official Priority

The Burmese government runs an unofficial but nevertheless rigid priority list which can disrupt flight bookings right up to the last minute. Burmese VIPs, of course, have priority. Behind them, in order, come tour parties, individual foreign visitors, foreign expatriate residents, and – last and least – native residents of Burma.

Buying Air Tickets

Domestic flight schedules of Yangon Airways can be checked at www.yangonairways.com while Air Mandalay's is found at www.airmandalay.com. Travel agents sometimes sell domestic air tickets below their recommended published fares. But note that travel agents accept cash payment only, while airlines can accept credit cards.

in Yangon, tel: (01) 284 055; and in Mandalay near the Gawein Jetty on 35th Street, tel: (02) 86035.

If you have the money to burn, book yourself on the Road to Mandalay (operated by Orient-Express Trains & Cruises), which sails the Ayeyarwady between Mandalay and Bagan in great splendour. Five-and six-night itineraries spending three and four nights respectively aboard the luxury ship are offered. Contact **Orient-Express Trains & Cruises** in Yangon, tel: (01) 296 680, www.orient-express.com.

A smaller cruise boat, the Irrawaddy Princess, runs on a regular basis between Bagan and Mandalay. Contact **Barani Cruise & Trading** in Yangon, tel: (01) 225 377, e-mail: barani-cruise@mptmail.net.mm

A third option for the Mandalay-Bagan stretch is on board the Pandaw III, a newly-built river steamer that recalls the experience of river travel during colonial times. Operated by the London-based Irrawaddy Flotilla Company (IFC), the Pandaw III has 39 comfortable cabins with attached bathrooms. There are overnight as well as 2-night cruises from Mandalay to Bagan and vice versa. Contact the **Irrawaddy Flotilla Company** at its Yangon office, tel: (01) 298 085 or check its website: www.pandaw.com

A short popular ferry trip for tourists is the one up the Ayeyarwady from Mandalay to Mingun. Boats leave from Mandalay's B Road Jetty several times daily for the one-hour voyage.

BY TRAIN

Myanmar Railways has a network of more than 4,500 km (2,800 miles) of track. Yangon's Central Railway Station is the nation's hub. By day and night, express trains, mail trains and local trains depart on journeys of varying lengths. Most popular are the daily services between Yangon and Mandalay.

Ordinary (second class) and Upper Class (first class) seating is available on all trains. Upper Class seats cost almost three times that of Ordinary Class. Sleepers are not readily available for overnight trips. Foreigners can purchase their tickets through **Myanmar Travels & Tours** *(see page 344)* or at the **railway station**, tel: (01) 274 027, advisably 24 hours in advance.

Yangon to Mandalay

For the main train route most often used by tourists, the 716-km (445-mile) **Yangon-Mandalay Line** uses reasonably comfortable Korean and Chinese coaches. This is the country's most acceptable railway and is recommended for the scenes of Burmese village life it offers from its windows. Passengers however must be willing to put up with a little discomfort, and often long delays (the train often arrives in Mandalay four or more hours later tahn scheduled).

BY BUS & COACH

Government Bus Transport
Public bus travel aboard government-owned **Road Transport Company** vehicles tend to be long and tedious. Many roads are poor, vehicles are overcrowded, and in the event a bus breaks down, it can be hours before mechanical assistance becomes available.

Yangon city is served by an extensive network of local buses which connect Yangon with the new satellite towns that were created after 1989.

Private Bus Service
Several companies run comfortable air-conditioned buses from Yangon to Mandalay, Bagan, Taunggyi/Inle Lake for the approximate equivalent of US$7. These companies operate from one station, the **Highway Bus Centre** at the intersection of Pyay and Station roads, southwest of Mingaladon Airport. Some also maintain ticket offices opposite the Central Railway Station.

Travel from Yangon to other major tourist destinations is overnight and you can choose between several companies. Some travellers prefer bus to train, it's less than a quarter of the price (as you can pay in kyats) and the arrival times are more reliable than that of trains. Regular stops for food and refreshments are also made.

Among the companies providing reliable service and vehicles are:
Leo Express – tel: (01) 249 512
Sun Moon Express – tel: (01) 642 903

City Transport
Bicycle trishaws *(sai-kaa)* or motorised three-wheelers *(thoun bein)* are the most popular means of getting around the streets of the larger cities – less so in Yangon where taxis have taken over. Easily available and cheap, they take their passengers anywhere they want to go in the city for US$1 or less per trip. For longer trips in the vicinity of Yangon, Mandalay and other large population centres, jeep collectives or "pick-ups" *(kaa)* – similar to the Thai *songthaew* – do yeomen's work carrying large numbers of riders. They don't follow a set schedule; instead, they take off whenever the last seat is taken.

TAXIS

Cab drivers wait in front of all the big tourist hotels in Yangon; their vehicles nowadays are second-hand Japanese cars or retired Singapore taxis.

Taxis are not metered although they charge by the trip. Ask at your hotel or guesthouse for the proper fare, which shouldn't exceed US$1 within the city. Rates for a full day's charter run is about US$20 within Yangon; a little more if the driver speaks good English, and about US$25 for a day trip into the countryside (Bago or Thanlyin). Taxis are by far the best way to explore the countryside surrounding Yangon, especially if one is able or willing to share the fare with other passengers.

Tour Operators in Yangon

Abercrombie & Kent
64, B-2 Shwe Gon Plaza
Tel: (01) 542 949/542 902
Fax: (01) 542 992
e-mail: tun@mptmail.net.mm
www.abercrombieandkent.com
Ainda Travel Associates Limited
10 Highland Avenue, Mayangon
Tel: (01) 660 266
Fax: (01) 544 014
e-mail: ainda@mptmail.net.mm
Asian Trails Tour Ltd.
73 Pyay Road
Tel: (01) 211 212/727 422
Fax: (01) 211 670
e-mail: res@asiantrails.com.mm
www.asiantrails.com
Diethelm Travel
I Inya Road
Tel: (01) 527 110/527 117
Fax: (01) 527 135
e-mail: leisure@diethelm.com.mm
www.diethelm-travel.com
Exotissimo
#0303 Sakura Tower
339 Bo Gyoke Aung San Street
Tel: (01) 255 266
Fax: (01) 255 428
e-mail: myanmar@exotissimo.com
www.exotissimo.com
Golden Express Ltd
97B, Wardan Street
Tel: (01) 226 779
Fax: (01) 227 636
e-mail: getours@mptmail.net.mm
Woodland Travels
422/426 Strand Road
Tel: (01) 202 071
Fax: (01) 202 076
e-mail:
woodlandtravels@mptmail.net.mm
www.woodlandgroups.com

Where to Stay

Choosing a Hotel

Burma is fast becoming a tourist destination. After only 32,000 tourists in 1989 and 100,000 in 1994, an estimated 230,000 visitors arrived in 2000. Following the privatisation of hotels in 1992, Yangon and to some extent Mandalay have experienced a great hotel building boom. As a result many of the larger hotels have very low occupancy rates. For the savvy traveller, this may present an opportunity to ask for better-than-advertised rates.

Most hotels operate a two-tier pricing system whereby tourists pay in US dollars or FECs and locals in kyats, the latter being up to only one tenth of the dollar rate. In the case of some of the remaining government-owned hotels, rates can be high compared to those of similar standards offered in the rest of Southeast Asia. With increased competition from the private sector, government-operated hotels are getting the message.

YANGON

The Strand
92 Strand Road
Tel: (01) 243 377
Fax: (01) 289 880
www.ghmhotels.com
In a class of its own in price, but also in its tasteful décor and appointments. Originally built in 1903 by the Sarkies brothers and completely renovated in 1993, it reflects the epoch of the 1920s and 30s. It has 52 guest rooms including 32 suites, and a business centre. The Strand Grill, an elegant evening restaurant, and the Strand

Café serve Burmese, Southeast Asian and Continental fare. The Strand Bar offers a full range of drinks in a club-like atmosphere. The Strand's restaurants and bar provide rewarding experiences. **$$$$**

Hotel Nikko Royal Lake Yangon
40 Natmauk Road
Tel: (01) 544 500
Fax: (01) 544 400
www.nikkoyangon.com
Overlooking Kandawgyi Lake, this 303-room hotel is geared towards the business traveller with facilities that include internet access, business centre and secretarial services. Excellent Japanese restaurant. Swimming pool and fitness centre. **$$$**

Price Guide

A general guide for a standard double room, excluding taxes.
$$$$ = above US$200
$$$ = US$80–200
$$ = US$20–80
$ = under US$20

Inya Lake Hotel
Kaba Aye Pagoda Road
Tel: (01) 662 857
Fax: (01) 665 537
www.inyalakehotel.com
Built by the Russians in 1961 and completely renovated and modernised in 1995, the Inya Lake offers a complete range of facilities including a swimming pool, tennis courts, putting green, barber shop, beauty salon and conference facilities. **$$$**

Kandawgyi Palace Hotel
Kanyeiktha Road
Tel: (01) 249 255
Fax: (01) 280 412
e-mail: kphotel@mptmail.net.mm
At the lake shore. Located on the site of the former Museum of Natural History and the Orient Boat Club, the Kandawgyi Palace Hotel was renovated in 1996. Facilities include a fitness centre, swimming pool and business centre. **$$$**

Pansea Yangon
35 Taw Win Road
Tel: (01) 229 860
Fax: (01) 228 260

www.pansea.com
A beautiful 45-room hotel set in spacious grounds. Its superb restaurant is known for its French and Asian cuisines. **$$$**

Sedona Hotel
1 Kaba Aye Pagoda Road (near Inya Lake)
Tel: (01) 666 900
Fax: (01) 666 911
www.sedonamyanmar.com
The Sedona has a business centre, fitness centre with sauna, swimming pool and a lively pub/disco, one of the few in town. **$$$**

Sofitel Plaza Yangon
33 Alan Pya Paya Lan
Tel: (01) 250 388
Fax: (01) 252 478
www.accorhotels.com
Located north of the centre of Yangon and containing 350 rooms, this is one of the newer hotels in the town. The décor features rattan and wood. Along with a business centre, disco/pub, swimming pool and fitness centre there are Chinese and Japanese restaurants. **$$$**

Traders Hotel
Bogyoke Aung San Street and Sule Pagoda Road
Tel: (01) 242 828
Fax: (01) 242 800
www.shangri-la.com
Elegant décor with Oriental touches, four excellent restaurants and bar establishments; business centre with e-mail facility; gym, sauna, pool. Contains 407 rooms. **$$$**

Comfort Inn
4 Shwe Lin Street
Tel: (01) 533 377
Fax: (01) 524 256
Located in spacious grounds which include a putting green. Comfortable rooms; breakfast included; provides transfers to the airport. **$$**

Summit Parkview
350 Ahlone Road
Tel: (01) 227 966
Fax: (01) 227 993
e-mail: summit@mptmail.net.mm
One of the first modern hotels in Yangon, this hotel contains 252 rooms. Its facilities include a swimming pool, health club, coffee

shop and a shopping arcade including an art gallery. Popular with business travellers and Japanese visitors. Some rooms face Shwedagon Pagoda which is magnificent at night. **$$**

Thamada Hotel
37 Kaba Aye Pagoda Road
Tel: (01) 243 639-43
Fax: (01) 245 001
www.inyalakehotel.com
Managed by the same company than runs the deluxe Inya Lake Hotel, this comfortable moderate class hotel is located next to the Yangon railway station. Popular with both business and leisure travelers. **$$**

MANDALAY

Mandalay Swan Hotel
Corner of 26th Road and 68th streets facing Mandalay Palace
Tel: (02) 31625
Fax: (02) 35677
e-mail: mdyswan@mptmail.net.mm
The restored former Mandalay Hotel, with comfortable 120 rooms ranging from economy to suites. Coffee shop, restaurant, pool and tennis courts. MTT travel office on premises. **$$$**

Novotel Mandalay
9 Kwin (416B), 10th Street
Tel: (02) 35638
Fax: (02) 35639
www.accorhotels.com
206 rooms; high-rise hotel at base of Mandalay Hill. Café, restaurant, disco, large pool, tennis courts. Room rates include breakfast. **$$$**

Sedona Hotel Mandalay
Corner of 26th and 66th streets
Tel: (02) 36488
Fax: (02) 36499
www.sedonamyanmar.com
247 rooms. Great location opposite southeast corner of Mandalay Palace with view of Mandalay Hill. Easily the best hotel in town; pool, fitness centre, business centre with e-mail facility. All room rates include breakfast. **$$$**

Emerald Land Inn
14th Street between 87th and 88th streets
Tel: (02) 39471/72

Fax: (02) 35645
Comfortable hotel in a garden setting located in a residential area northwest of the Mandalay Palace. Restaurant, bar and swimming pool **$$**

AD–1 Hotel
Corner of 87th and 28th streets, near the Eindawya Pagoda
Tel: (02) 34505
One of the best budget hotels. Clean rooms with fans and showers or with air-conditioning. Breakfast included in the room rate **$**

Silver Cloud Hotel
Corner of 73rd and 29th streets
Tel: (02) 27059
40 rooms. Good atmosphere and good value economy rooms with fans and attached bath. Larger rooms have air-conditioning, fridge and TV. Breakfast is included. **$**

BAGAN

Bagan Hotel
Tel: (062) 70146
Fax: (062) 70313
www.oldbaganhotel.com
108 rooms, on the river near Gawdawpalin Pagoda; new hotel with air-conditioned rooms, satellite TV and IDD telephones. Pretty gardens, good value and well located. **$$$**

Thazin Garden Hotel
22 Thazin Road, Anawrahta Ward
Tel: (062) 70020
Fax: (01) 512 715 (Yangon)
e-mail:
thazingarden@mptmail.net.mm
Charming hotel in a quiet location. Low-rise wood-panelled rooms furnished with Burmese artefacts are located amid well tended gardens. Restaurant serving Burmese and Western fare. Staff are very helpful and go out of their way to make you feel welcome. **$$**

Thante Hotel
Tel: (062) 70144
Fax: (062) 70143
Old Bagan, near Archaeological Museum overlooking the river; 42 rooms and attractive bungalow units. Dining room and bar. Breakfast included in the room rate. Good value for money. **$–$$**

Where to Eat

What to Eat

Due to the economic improvements in Burma's main towns over the last decade it is no longer difficult to find good Burmese food. Good Chinese, Indian and European food is also available at restaurants throughout the country. Reservations are seldom needed and restaurants, except those located in the larger hotels, tend to close early in the evening. Burmese take their main meal at lunchtime and usually have an early dinner, around 6pm. Below is a categorised list of a few food items and their respective English translations easily available on any Burmese restaurant menu.

Soups
Chin Ye Hin. Spicy fish soup.
Bu Thee Hin Khar. Clear soup with vermicelli and gourd.
Kin Mone Ywet Hin Khar. Clear soup with herbal leaves.

Appetizers
Pa Zun nga paung kyaw. Deep-fried prawns with onions.
Ginn Thoke. Pickled ginger salad with fried condiments.
Nga Paung Kyaw. Deep fried beansprouts with fish.
Ah Kyaw Sone. Selection of deep fried appetisers.

Salads
Pe Thee Thoke. Long bean salad.
Pa Zun Thoke. Prawn salad.
Myin Khwar Ywet Thoke. Herbal leaves salad.
Ngar Phe Thoke. Pounded fish salad.
Kyet Thar Thoke. Burmese chicken salad.

Vegetables

Ah Sone Kyaw. Mixed-fried vegetables.
The Sone Hin. Vegetables in curry sauce.
Kha Yan Thee Hnat. Eggplant curry with shrimps.

Curries

Kyet Tha Hin. Chicken curry.
Wet Tha Hin Lay. Pork curry.
Ah Mae Tha Hnat. Beef curry.
Ngar See Pyan. Fish curry with tomatoes.
Pa Zun Ne Ahloo Hin. Prawn curry and potatoes.

Seafood

Ngar Doke Kha. Red snapper with garlic and parsley.
Pa Zun Oh Kat. Shrimp with chilli.
Nga Su See. Yangon fish fillet.
Mawlamyine Nga Thalauk Paung. Fish steamed in lemongrass, ginger and garlic.

Meat Dishes

Wet Tha A Sat Kyaw. Pork with chillies and onions.
Kyet Tha Cho Chet. Chicken with basil.

Desserts

Rakhine Nget Pyaw Paung. Steamed banana with coconut milk.
Mote Kyar Sae. Sticky rice, lotus seeds and syrup.
Thaku Pyin. Sago with coconut milk.

Restaurant Listing

YANGON

50th Street Bar & Grill
9/13 50th Street, Botataung
Tel: (01) 298 096
Colonial atmosphere; popular with the expat community and locals. Serves good pizza and pasta. Bar stays open until late. **$$–$$$**

Aung Thuka
17A 1st Street (between Shwegondine Street and Dhammazedi Road)
A clean, reasonably priced Bamar restaurant. Easy to order as all you have to do is point at the array of cooked food in clay pots to indicate your choice. **$**

Danubyu Daw Sawyi
175/177 29th Street
Tel: (01) 275 397
Modern looking restaurant, serving traditional Bamar dishes. Good place to go for breakfast as it serves noodles and other local snacks. **$**

Green Elephant
519A Thirimingalar Road, off Pyay Road
Tel: (01) 531 231
Recommended. Serves very good Bamar food in air-conditioned atmosphere. The pennywort salad is excellent. Popular with both visitors and locals. **$–$$**

Restaurant Price Guide

A general guide for dinner for two person excluding beverage:

$$$ = above US$20
$$ = US$10–20
$ = under US$10

Hla Myanma Htamin Zain
27 5th Street
Simple restaurant offering a wide variety of Bamar and Shan dishes displayed in pots, plus some Chinese and Indian food. **$**

Le Planteur
16 Sawmaha Street
Tel: (01) 549 389
Serves very good French-Swiss food with smoked ham and salami. The house punch is excellent. **$$$**

Nan Yu Restaurant
81 Pansodan Street
Tel: (01) 252 702
Old well-established air-conditioned restaurant offering Cantonese specialities. **$–$$**

New Delhi Restaurant
Anawrahta Street between 29th and Shwebontha streets
Tel: (01) 275 447
Wide range of North and South Indian dishes available. Excellent *masala dosa.* Longer opening hours than most Indian restaurants. **$**

Strand Grill and Strand Café
Strand Hotel
Tel: (01) 243 377
The Grill is one of the most elegant restaurants in Yangon. Both the Grill and the Café have similar menus

that offer excellent Burmese dishes, among others. The Grill is open only for dinner while the Café serves lunch and dinner at slightly lower prices too. **$$–$$$**

MANDALAY

Everqueen Restaurant
Old Bagan
Fine garden setting, but can be a bit breezy at night. Tucked along a sandy road before the old city gate. Offers good variety of Burmese food, especially fish dishes. **$**

Lashio Lay Restaurant
23rd Street between 83rd and 84th streets
Very tasty and spicy Shan food and a few vegetarian dishes. It's easy to order as dishes are on display. **$**

Pyi Gyi Mon Royal Barge
Tel: (02) 26779
Replica of the floating Karaweik restaurant in Yangon and located in the southeastern corner of the moat at Mandalay Palace. Mostly Burmese and Chinese dishes and dinner is accompanied by a puppet show.

Sakantha Restaurant
24 72nd Street, between 27th and 28th streets
Tel: (02) 21066
The good Bamar food justifies the higher than average prices. Setting is pleasant as its dining room looks out onto a garden. **$–$$**

Sarabha Restaurant
Old Bagan
Offers a choice of Bamar, Shan, Thai and Chinese dishes either indoors or outdoors. Great location near the Tharaba Gate.

Culture

Pagodas & Temples

There are two main types of Buddhist monuments in Burma: pagodas and temples.

A pagoda consists of a stupa and its surrounding enclosure. The stupa (also known as a *zedi*, *cetiya* or *dagoba*) is a monument of commemoration containing a relic chamber beneath (or sometimes over) the bell-shaped central structure. Burmese stupas are generally built on several terraces; these are passages upon which the devotees should walk in a clockwise direction.

The term "temple" is applied to Buddhist structures in Burma only because a more specific terminology does not exist in English. In Theravada Buddhism a temple is not a place of worship of a higher being; the Buddha is not a god, and Theravada Buddhism in its pure form does not recognise any form of divine worship. The temple is instead seen as a place of meditation. The Burmese word is *ku*, derived from the Pali *guba*, which roughly translated means "cave". This word also reflects the cultural heritage of the edifice – these buildings were formerly constructed as artificial caves used

Spirit Worship

Before Burma adopted Buddhism, people worshiped *nat* or spirits (usually in hills, trees and natural features). Though the young generally don't subscribe to this superstitious world, drivers of all ages tie red and white strips of cloth to their car mirrors to protect them from *nats*.

Images of Buddha

Just as temples and pagodas are created in different styles, so are Buddha images. The various body postures and hand and leg positions have symbolic meanings, each of considerable importance to students of Buddhism. These positions, called the *mudra*, are thousands of years old.

by monks where there were no overhanging slopes.

The main feature of a *ku* is that it is dark and cool inside. This feature characterises the Mon-style ("hollow cube") Bagan temples, into which only a little light is able to enter through the perforated stone windows. The Bamar-style ("central pillar") temples are totally different: they were built with huge entrances and two tiers of windows to make the interiors bright and airy.

One can trace the development of the "central pillar" type from the stupas. During festivals, it was the custom to stretch huge awnings from the stupa to the surrounding wall of the enclosure to offer protection from rain and sun. As a result, a covered walkway surrounds the central sanctuary. When this was copied in solid materials, it gave the impression that the upper part of a stupa had been built on the temple roof. The same principle applies to the multi-storeyed Bamar-style temples.

The "hollow cube" type of temples are not actually hollow inside; they may seem to be so, but the majority have a central supporting pillar. From the outside, their pointed, bell-shaped domes resemble Gothic buildings. But the temples of Bagan could not be more different. Instead of spanning the greatest possible space, the Buddhist temple interiors consist of a multitude of walls enclosing narrow passageways and chambers, thereby satisfying the *ku*'s original purpose as a sanctuary for inner peace and meditation. The exteriors of these

temples – white, and invariably decorated with a gold finial – represent Mount Meru and the devout Buddhist's striving for a spiritual goal via the ever-valid *dharma*, or law of life.

Museums

Burma's myriad pagodas and temples are her finest museums. The following have also assembled various items of historical and anthropological interest:

National Museum
Payay Road and Pyidaungsu Yeiktha Road, Yangon. It contains the Mandalay Regalia from Burma's last royal court and various artefacts of ancient history. Open 10am–3pm Sunday to Thursday, and 1–3pm Saturday. Closed Friday and holidays.

National Museum and Library
24th Road and West Moat Road, Mandalay. Contains a variety of memorabilia from many eras of Burmese history, and a fine collection of Buddhist literature.

Bagan Museum
Near Thiripyitsaya Hotel, Bagan. A good introduction to the images and architectural styles of this ancient city.

Taunggyi Museum
Main Road, Taunggyi. Displays traditional costumes and cultural artefacts of the 30-plus ethnic groups living in the Shan Plateau region.

Theatres

The best place to view a Burmese *pwe* (or traditional ceremonial dance to propitiate the spirits) is at city streets or pagoda grounds at festival times. For those whose visit doesn't coincide with a festival, however, there are two public theatres in Yangon and one in Mandalay that have irregular performances of various types:

Garrison Theatre, U Wisara Road.
Open-Air Theatre, Lanmadaw Road.
Myanmar Marionette, Mandalay Marionette, Garden Villa Theatre, 66th Street (between 26th and 27th Streets), Mandalay.

Festivals

When the moon waxes full, there is a Burmese celebration, the mood of which varies from season to season: frivolity during the water dousings of the New Year in March/April, solemnity for Buddhist Lent in July, and joyousness during the October Festival of Light.

Thingyan – Changing Over is the year's biggest party *(see below)*.

Day of Buddha *Kason* (April/May) is a month of anticipation, as the annual monsoon could break at any time. On the full moon, the birth, enlightenment and death of the Buddha is celebrated. People join in a procession of musicians and dancers to the local pagoda.

Scriptures Exam During the full moon day of *Nayon* (May/June), after the rains have begun, Burmese students are tested on their knowledge of the *Tipitaka*, the Buddhist scriptures. *Sayadaw* lecture before large crowds, schools operated by monasteries are opened to the public.

Beginning of Lent The monsoon begin season marks the beginning of the Buddhist Lent. On *Dhammasetkya*, the full moon day of *Waso* (June/July), the people celebrate the Buddha's conception, his renunciation of worldly goods, and his first sermon after enlightenment. Those who wish to devote their lives to the Sangha are ordained. During the next three months, members of the Sangha go into retreat for study and meditation.

"Draw-a-Lot" Festival The full moon of *Wagaung* (July/August) is purely a religious time for merit-making. The name of each member of the local Sangha is written on a piece of paper, which is then rolled up and deposited in a large basket. A representative from each household draws a slip of paper from the basket, and the next day provides an elaborate feast for the *pongyi* named on the piece of paper. One layman will have drawn a paper containing the name of the Gautama Buddha. He is the most fortunate of all, because he will have the opportunity to host the Buddha.

Boat Racing Festival By the time of *Tawthalin* (August/ September), Burma's rivers are full and flowing and boat races are held in rivers and lakes. At Inle Lake, the Phaung Daw U Festival is held this month or next, with leg-rowing competitions and the voyage of a recreated royal *karaweik* barge.

Festival of Light Buddhist Lent comes to an end with the arrival of the full moon of *Thadingyut* (September/October), indicating the approach of clear blue skies. On this full moon night, the Burmese celebrate the descent of the Buddha and his followers to earth from *Tavatimsa* (heaven) where, according to legend, he travelled to preach the doctrine to his mother.

The Weaving Festival During *Tazaungmone* (October/ November), unmarried girls sit under the full moon in the pagoda grounds, engaged in weaving competitions to make new robes for monks.

Month of temple festivals *Pyatho* (December/January) is when gifts are presented to monks and offerings made for temple upkeep. These are also occasions for merrymaking, lasting three or more days. A bazaar, boat and pony races, magic acts and sideshows, and evening *pwe* performances are commonplace. Burmese culinary delicacies are also offered.

Harvest festival When *Tabodwe* (January/ February) arrives, it is time to harvest the paddy and celebrate the harvest festival. After the first harvest is offered to the monastery, elaborate meals are prepared, and Burmese women show off their cooking prowess. The celebration is named *Htamane* after a food offering of rice, sesame, peanuts, ginger and coconut.

Thingyan: Burma's New Year

The year's biggest party is the *Thingyan* Festival in the month of *Tagu* (March/April), when the Burmese celebrate New Year. For 3–4 days (the length of the celebration is determined annually by *ponnas*, or Brahman astrologers), government, farm labour and business come to a virtual standstill.

Thingyan is best known as the Water Throwing Festival. The old year must be washed away and the new anointed with water. No one, Burmese or visitor, is safe from deluges that seem to appear from nowhere out of the hot blue sky.

Celebrations begin when Thagyamin, king of the *nat*, descends to earth to bring blessings for the new year. He also carries two books with him: one bound in gold to record the names of children who have been well-behaved in the past year, and one bound in dog skin with the names of naughty children.

Thagyamin comes riding a winged golden horse and bearing a water jar, symbolic of peace and prosperity in Burma in the coming year. Every house greets him with flowers and palm leaves at their front doors. Guns fire in salute and

music resounds from all corners of the land. Gaily decorated floats parade up and down the streets of the cities and larger towns.

Yet there are times of tranquillity in the midst of this exuberance. All revellers find a quiet moment each day to make offerings at pagodas and at the homes of their elders. Buddha images are given a thorough washing on this holiday by devout elderly women.

In medieval times, *Thingyan* was observed with a public hair-washing by the Burmese king, a ritual purification.

Shopping

Markets & Bazaars

Burma's markets and bazaars are the most interesting, and at the same time the most reasonable, places to shop for native arts and crafts. In Yangon the **Bogyoke Aung San Market** is open 9.30am–4.30pm Monday to Saturday. It is the place where most tourists do their last shopping before leaving the country. Some of the shops in the market offering reasonable prices include:

Lacquerware, Daw Chit Khin Lacquerware, Shop 43, East (C) Block.
Jade, Colourful Jade Store, Shop 42, West "D" Arcade.
Mother of Pearl, Myanmar Variety Store, Shop 75, Centre Arcade.
Silverware, William Tan, Shop 33, Main Line. This shop offers beautiful hammered silverware.
Other markets, including

Where to Buy Gifts

● **Markets** Burma's numerous bazaars and markets, the most popular of which is Yangon's Bogyoke Aung San *(see above)*, are full of gift ideas.
● **Tourist Department Stores** A pricey selection of all types of Burmese handicrafts is always for sale at the tourist stores at 143–144 Sule Pagoda Road in Yangon. Open 10am–4pm Monday to Friday and 10am–1pm Saturday, the stores will accept only foreign exchange.
● **Hotels** There are gift shops at Inya Lake and Strand hotels. Both are open 9.30am–5pm Monday to Saturday.

Mandalay's **Zegyo Market**, generally stay open from early in the morning until dark. The best shopping for lacquerware is in New Bagan, the residential area about 8 km (5 miles) from the archaeological zone.

There are also night markets that set up after dark. The best are in Yangon's Chinese and Indian quarters, and in Mandalay on 84th Street between 26th and 28th Roads.

Bazaars and markets thrive in Yangon. There are open-air markets across Bogyoke Aung San Street from the Bogyoke Market; at the corner of St John's Road and Pyay Road; and east of the Botataung Pagoda. The **Thein Gyi Zay** Indian market is just off Anawrahta Street, and there's a Chinese market at the corner of Maha Bandoola Street and Lanmadaw Road.

The entrances to the **Shwedagon Pagoda** are also bazaars – of some length, in fact, covering both sides of the stairways. The bazaar at the east entrance is most interesting; among items frequently sold are puppets, drums, masks, toys, brassware and metal goods, including swords. The bazaar at the pagoda's south entrance is notable for wood and ivory carvings.

Wood carvings are also sold in quantity and quality at the **New Carving Shop**, 20 University Avenue. For other types of artwork, try the **Beik Thano Art Gallery**, 113/3 Kaba Aye Pagoda Road, tel: (01) 542 560; **Ivy Art Gallery**, 159 45th Street, tel: 297654; **J's Irrawaddy Dream**, 59 Taw Win Road; **Myanmar Gallery of Contemporary Art**, 5 Kaba Aye Pagoda Road, tel: (01) 548 058; **Orient Art Gallery**, 121E Thanlwin Road, tel: (01) 530 821.

Other Shops in Yangon

Art
Golden Valley Art Centre, 54 D, Golden Valley. Tel: (01) 533 830.
Traditional Arts and Sculpture Sales Shop, 188–192, East Wing Bogyoke Aung San Market.

Bargaining

Few prices are seen to be believed in Burma – bargaining is a way of life. Except for at top-of-the-range hotels, restaurants and department stores, you should be able to get a few kyats off the "fixed" price of most things. Even room prices are negotiable. Offer half the asking price, work up, and expect to settle for a bit more than 50 percent. Bartering is also an accepted means of payment in markets: stall holders are all too happy to accept jeans, watches and T-shirts.

If you are looking for a special producer or distributor, look at the Myanmar Business Directory. Chamber of Commerce, 74-86, Bo Sun Pat Street. Tel: (01) 877 103/70749.

Antiques
Charlie Antique, 17 Kaba Aye Pagoda Road.

Furniture
Hla Gabar, Burmese furniture, 166 Maha Bandoola Road. Tel: (01) 291 311.
Green Elephant, 12 Inya Road. Tel: (01) 530 263.

Jewellery
Myanmar Silve & Ruby Co. Ltd., 35, Myazabe Street and International Airport Departure Hall. Tel: (01) 664 900.
Myanmar VES Joint Venture Co. Ltd., 66 Kaba Aye Pagoda Road. Tel: (01) 661 902.
Golden Owl, Jewellery and Gem Laboratory, 724 Merchant Street. Tel: (01) 281 863.

Books
Innwa Book Store, 232 Sule Pagoda Road.
Myanmar Book Centre, 477 Pyay Road.

Longyi
Pan Sa Gar Longyi, 386 Mahabandoola Panchan Upper Street. Tel: (01) 874 870.

these countries is relatively low, it is essential to arrange vaccinations and private medical insurance (preferably covering evacuation in an emergency) before departure.

Money Matters

Laos The official currency, the *kip,* comes in 5,000, 2,000, 1,000, 500, 100 notes. There are no coins, and notes smaller than 100 have been rendered obsolete.

Officially and legally, purchases must be made in local currency; however, US dollars and Thai baht are widely accepted and can readily be exchanged at official exchange booths or banks. It is not recommended to convert much currency to Lao kip. Even restaurant and noodle vendors are usually happy to accept dollars and baht.

Credit cards are accepted at a limited number of establishments, mainly those that cater for upmarket travellers. You may encounter difficulty in using MasterCard; American Express and Visa are both popular, however.

Visa cash-withdrawal service is available at the Banque pour le Commerce Extérieur du Lao (BCEL), the agent for Visa in Vientiane.

Traveller's cheques are accepted at banks but can be expensive to cash because of the commission. They should be in US dollars only.

What to Wear/Bring

Clothes should be light and loose, preferably cotton. Open shoes and sleeveless dresses for women or short-sleeved shirts for men are appropriate, but visitors should abide by local ideas of modesty (see *Etiquette* opposite) when visiting pagodas, temples and official places. A sweater or sweatshirt is needed for nights.

Lip balm and moisturisers are needed just about anytime, as are sunblocks, sunglasses and hats. Women should not count on obtaining tampons and sanitary towels.

Just about every major Thai bank has a branch in Vientiane, and most have English-speaking staff familiar with the needs of foreign travellers, whether currency exchange or wire transfers of money. There are no ATM machines.

Cambodia Although the local currency is the *riel,* for most purposes, the US dollar seems to be the money of the realm.

Getting There

BY AIR

Arriving in Vientiane is relatively easy. International flights arrive from Bangkok, Chiang Mai, Hanoi, Ho Chi Minh City, Kunming, Kuala Lumpur, Phnom Penh, Yangon and Singapore.

Access to Angkor/Siem Reap is via Phnom Penh or direct from Bangkok or Sukhothai.

BY LAND

Increasingly, it is becoming easier to enter Laos by land, although the situation can change. Also, be warned that although the following places are official points of entry, foreign travellers may not be permitted to make the crossing. Check with your home country's Lao embassy before attempting a border crossing.
From Thailand:
Nongkhai to Vientiane
Mukdahan to Savannakhet
Chiangkhong to Houeyxay
Chong Mek/Champasak
Nakhon Phanom/Tha Kaek
From Vietnam:
Dong Ha/Lao Bao
Cau Treo to Kaew Neua
From China:
Mengla to Botem

Land crossings to Cambodia are now safe and reasonably easy from Thailand via Aranyaprathat and from Vietnam via Moc Bai.

Practical Tips

Postal Services

Laos The **General Post Office** (GPO) is on the corner of Thanon Khou Vieng and Lan Xang Avenue. It offers postal services and public telephones for local, national and international calls. Most areas of the Post Office are open during normal business hours. There is no mail delivery service in Laos; mail is collected from the boxes at the GPO.

The mail service is inexpensive and usually reliable. For urgent or important mail (to or from Laos), however, use either EMS (express mail service) or a commercial courier.

Incoming parcels and packets must be inspected by a Customs official. All mail should use the official title of the country: Lao PDR, in preference to Laos.

Cambodia The postal service, like many other services, has improved over the last few years. Mail is forwarded via Bangkok and arrives much more quickly than before.

Tips and Bargaining

Tipping is not customary in Southeast Asia. But as the income of the average person in Laos and Cambodia is so low, small tips are welcome. Be prepared for bargaining, however, as few prices are fixed except for in department stores, hotels and guest houses. A good general rule is to start with half the price indicated, and aim to pay a bit more than this.

Embassies

- **Vientiane**
Australia: Nehru Street,
Vat Phonsay area.
Tel: (21) 413 610, 413 815.
United States: Bartholomie Road,
Ban Thatdam.
Tel: (21) 213 966, 212 581/2.
Fax: (21) 212 548.

- **Phnom Penh**
Australia/Canada: 11 254 Street.
Tel: (23) 213 470.
Fax: (23) 426 003.
UK: 27-29 Street 75.
Tel: (23) 428 295.
Fax: (23) 427 125.
United States: 27 Street 240.
Tel: (23) 216 436.
Fax: (23) 216 437.

Telecommunications

Laos
Telephone: International Direct
Dialing (IDD) is available in
Vientiane, and the operators speak
English. The central telephone
office is located on Setthathilath
Road, Vientiane, near Nam Phu
Fountain. It is open 8am–10pm
daily. Fax services are also
available.

A limited number of public
telephones using prepaid phone
cards are available in the major
cities of Laos: Vientiane, Luang
Prabang, Khammouane, Pakse,
Savannakhet. Cards for the phones
are available in three values: 3,000
kip for 100 units, 9,000 kip for 300
units, and 15,000 kip for 500 units.

The code for Luang Prabang is
71, and for Phnom Penh 23.
E-mail and Internet: Until recently
there was no e-mail service at all in
Laos, but Internet access is now
easily available to foreigners in
Vientiane and Luang Prabang (and
some smaller cities too). There is a
local server in Vientiane run by the
American Globenet company. Its
lines are notoriously busy, but it
offers reliable access from its
office on the second floor of the
Lao Hotel Plaza and in computer
shops and cafés in the town.

Cambodia
Both local and international calls
are expensive. Phone boxes that
accept phonecards are now found
across the country. There are
currently two Internet providers:
Camnet and BigPond. Internet
access is easy and increasingly
common.

Medical Treatment

Standards of healthcare in Laos
and Cambodia are generally pretty
dire by Western standards. But the
following reasonable facilities are
available in emergencies:
Laos In Vientiane, an international
medical clinic is operated by the
Mahosot Hospital, located near the
Mekong River on Fa Ngum road.
It is open daily 24 hours.
Tel: (21) 214 018.

The Australian embassy operates
a modern medical clinic primarily for
embassy staff. However,
consultation and treatment of non-
staff is available with payment.
Australian Embassy Clinic, Phonsay
Road. Tel: (21) 413 603, 511 462.
Open Mon, Tues, Thurs, Fri
8.30am–noon and 2–5pm, and Wed
8.30am–noon.

Cambodia Good hospitals are few
and far between in Cambodia, and
for anything major it would be best
to go to Bangkok.
Calmette Hospital, Monivong
Boulevard, Phnom Penh. Tel: (23)
723 173.
European Medical Clinic, Hong
Kong Centre, Sisowath Boulevard,
Phnom Penh. Tel: (23) 916 413,
Fax: (23) 364 656.

Media

Laos The *Bangkok Post* and *The
Nation* are both good Thai
newspapers in English and are
available in many shops and most
hotels. International English-
language newspapers, such as the
International Herald-Tribune, *Asian
Wall Street Journal*, or the *Financial
Times* are often available in major
hotels, but delivery to Vientiane is
not always reliable. *Passason* and

Etiquette

Family structure is very strong in
Laos. Most people are extremely
polite and well mannered.
Remember that local standards
and expectations of efficiency
and procedure can be very
different from Western
perceptions. Be patient, and
remember that you are a guest,
not a client and hopefully not a
revisionist colonialist.

The traditional form of
greeting among Lao people is the
nop: one's palms are placed
together in a position of praying,
at chest level, but not touching
the body. The higher the hands,
the greater the respect. This is
accompanied by a slight bow to
show respect. The *nop* is a
greeting, thanks, expression of
regret and goodbye.

As elsewhere in Southeast
Asia, the head is thought to be
the most sacred part of the body,
the soles of the feet the lowliest.

Dress: Visitors should dress
modestly, especially near and in
pagodas, temples and public
places. Shorts should not be
worn when visiting pagodas
and monasteries, and all
footwear must be taken off
when entering them.

As elsewhere in Asia, it serves
no purpose to show anger when
conversing with the locals,
whether on the street or in a
shop. Public displays of anger or
discontent are considered a
weakness and will garner no
respect. Similarly, most
traditional Asian customs also
apply in Laos, including:

- don't touch people,
including children, on the head
- don't point your foot at a
person
- women should wear clothing
that covers more rather than less
of the body, especially when
eating.
- Buddha images are sacred
objects and to be treated with
the utmost respect.

Vientiane Mai are two Lao-language daily newspapers.

The local English-language newspaper is the *Vientiane Times*, published weekly. There is also *Le Mekong*, a monthly newspaper in French, covering the Mekong River countries.

Cambodia The weekly *Phnom Penh Post* reports national news, while the *Cambodia Daily*, *Bangkok Post* and *International Herald Tribune* cover international events.

In both countries there is little in English on TV or radio. In Vientiane and Phnom Penh satellite TV is now available, offering channels like CNN, MTV and BBC world service.

Tourist Information

Dielthelm Travel
www.diethelmtravel.com
Reputable agent with many years of experience in the region. Has offices in the following locations:
● **Vientiane**
Namphu Circle
Tel: (21) 213 833.
Fax: (21) 216 294.
● **Luang Prabang**
Phothisarat Road
Tel: (71) 212 277.
Fax: (71) 212 032.
● **Phnom Penh**
No. 65, Street 240
Tel: (23) 219 151.
Fax: (23) 219 150.
e-mail: dtc@dtc.com.kh
● **Siem Reap/Angkor**
House Nr. 4, Road Nr. 6,
Phum Taphul
Tel: (23) 57524.
Fax: (23) 57694.

Useful Websites
The following websites provide useful travel information on travel in Laos and Cambodia:
www.visit-mekong.com
www.cambodia-hotels.com
www.cambodian-online.com
www.khmernet.com
www.visit-laos.com
www.laos-travel.net
www.laos-hotels.com

Getting Around

The safest way of getting around Cambodia is by air, but flights are scarce and can be booked only the day before travelling. Road and river transport is slowly improving. Laos is more hospitable to tourists, with the following modes of transport.

By Air

Laos All flights in Laos are handled by the state-run **Lao Aviation**. It runs the popular Vientiane–Luang Prabang route. There is also a daily flight from Vientiane to Pakse in the south. Flights to Savannakhet leave every day except Friday. These three destinations, Luang Prabang, Pakse and Savannakhet, have the only scheduled flights you can really rely on. There are also less frequent flights to and from other places such as Luang Nam Tha, Muang Sing, Phonsavan, Sam Neua and Muang Xai.

Lao Aviation
2 Pangkham Street, Vientiane
Tel: (21) 212 051.
Fax: (21) 212 056.
www.lao-aviation.com

Cambodia Three local airlines, **Royal Phnom Penh**, **President** and **Siem Reap Airways**, run regular flights between Phnom Penh and Siem Reap (for Angkor), Battambang, Koh Kong, Stung Treng and Ratanakiri. There are at least four flights per day to Siem Reap.

President Airlines
50, Norodom, Phnom Penh
Tel: (23) 427 402
Fax: (23) 212 992
e-mail: presidentair@bigpond.com.kh
Royal Phnom Penh Airways
209, Street 19, Phnom Penh
Tel: (23) 217 419

Fax: (23) 217 420
www.royalpnhair.com
Siem Reap Airways
61A, No. 61, Street 214, Phnom Penh
Tel: (23) 720 022
Fax: (23) 720 522
www.siemreapairways.com

River Transport

It is possible to take transport up and down the **Mekong River** year-round. Check with a travel agent in Vientiane for up-to-date information.

There are speedboats on the upper reaches of the Mekong that travel from Luang Prabang to northern Thailand, and even to the Chinese border. Rates are reasonable, usually under US$50. Bookings can be made in northern Thailand and Luang Prabang. Slow boats travel the rest of the Mekong from Luang Prabang southward to the Cambodian border.

In Cambodia, comfortable modern boats now ply the routes between Phnom Penh and Siem Reap/Stung Treng.

By Road

Laos Although it is improving, the road system is lousy, with only a quarter of the roads tarred. Unless blessed with an awful lot of time and stamina, most visitors will find travelling by air preferable. Still, travel overland offers the greater adventure. Public buses are not air-conditioned, and seats can be hard. Many locals travel in converted pickup trucks. Travel agents can provide cars and minibuses for anywhere. Rates are high, averaging close to US$100 per day with driver.

Cambodia There are three air-conditioned bus services now offering comfortable trips between Phnom Penh and the seaside resort of Kompong Som (Sihanoukville) – by far the best road in the country. There are buses to Siem Reap, but as the road is still in poor condition it is a long and tedious journey. It is still not possible to hire your own vehicle, but hotels and travel agents can arrange cars with drivers.

Where to Stay

Laos

Accommodation in both Laos and Cambodia has improved over the last few years but it is still limited. Good quality hotels are restricted to the capitals and a few major centres. Mid-level accommodation can be found in most areas and is usually quite comfortable. At the lower end, guesthouses are now becoming more and more common and some of them are really quite good. Hotels which charge more than US$20 per night will have rooms that are air-conditioned and equipped with satellite television and a refrigerator. Hot water is usually available even in the cheaper guesthouses.

Price Guide

A general guide for a standard double room, excluding taxes.

$$$$ = above US$100
$$$ = US$50–100
$$ = US$20–50
$ = under US$20

VIENTIANE

Lao Plaza Hotel
63 Samsenthai Road
Tel: (21) 222 741
Fax: (21) 222 740
www.laoplazahotel.com
One of Vientiane's newest luxury hotels, located right smack in the centre of the city. Has all the services expected of an international standard hotel, including a pool, fitness centre, nightclub, and e-mail access. **$$$$**

Settha Palace Hotel
6 Pang Kham Street
Tel: (21) 217 581
Fax: (21) 217 583
www.setthapalace.com
Once known as the grandest hotel in Indochina, and built at the turn of the century, this place underwent renovation in 1998. It has now been returned to its former glory. Offers spacious guest rooms and suites with private terraces in a graceful colonial-era building. **$$$$**

Royal Dokmaideng Hotel
Lane Xang Avenue
Tel: (21) 214 455
Fax: (21) 214 454
www.dokmaidenghotel.laopdr.com
Near the Morning Market on Vientiane's main avenue, the Royal offers a Chinese restaurant and night club (with occasional traditional Lao music and dance performances), and a swimming pool and fitness centre. **$$$**

Anou Hotel
3 Heng Boun Road
Tel: (21) 213 360
Fax: (21) 213 632
www.anouhotel.laopdr.com
Includes satellite television in all rooms and downstairs there's the Anou Cabaret. Also serves a good lunchtime buffet. **$$**

Day Inn Hotel
59/3 Pangkham Street
Tel: (21) 223 847, 223 848
Fax: (21) 222 984
Popular with UNDP staff on temporary stints in Vientiane, this recently refurbished colonial structure downtown has a refreshingly light and airy interior, large rooms and an excellent location. **$$**

Lani Guest House
281 Setthathirat Road
Tel: (21) 214 919
Fax: (21) 215 639
www.lanigh.laotel.com
A charming converted residence set back from a main road in the heart of Vientiane's central district, the Lani offers 12 spacious rooms, each with phone and hot shower. **$$**

Le Parasol Blanc Hotel
263 Sibounheuang Road
Tel: (21) 215 090, 216 091
Fax: (21) 222 290, 215 444
e-mail: vicogrp@laotel.com
Among the best in this category, the hotel has bungalow-style rooms with beautiful hardwood floors, satellite TV, swimming pool and a shaded garden. A bar and restaurant (with occasional live piano music) serves good French, Lao and Thai food in one of the more charming surroundings in town. **$$**

Auberge du Temple
184/1 Sikhotabang Road
Tel and Fax: (21) 214 844
Small French-owned villa just out of town, this hotel offers large rooms, with verandas overlooking Wat Khunta temple across the street. **$**

LUANG PRABANG

The Grand Luang Prabang
Baan Xiengkeo, Khet Sangkalok
Tel: (71) 253 851
Fax: (71) 253 027
www.grandluangprabang.com
This beautiful hotel is situated in the grounds of the old Xiengkeo Palace. The palace was once the home of Prince Phetsarath, Lao national hero. All rooms combine the best of the art deco style of the 1920s with modern amenities. **$$$**

The Pansea Phu Vao
Tel: (71) 212 530
Fax: (71) 212 534
www.pansea.com
On a hilltop overlooking Luang Prabang, this hotel was recently refurbished by Pansea, a French hotel company. Neither in town nor too far away, the hotel has an attractive ambience and a swimming pool with a view. **$$$**

The Villa Santi Resort
Tel: (71) 252 157
Fax: (71) 252 158
www.villasantihotel.com
Managed by the same group as the well-known Villa Santi Hotel in Luang Prabang town, this resort 4km (2 miles) south of the town offers 55 charming rooms in a rural setting with mountain views. Set on 10 hectares of rolling hills, the resort also has a swimming pool. **$$$**

Ban Lao
Ban Mano
Tel: (71) 252 078
www.banlao.laopdr.com
Comfortable family-run hotel and restaurant with 28 rooms, some with air-conditioning. **$$**

Cambodia

PHNOM PENH

Raffles Hotel Le Royal
92 Rukhak Vithei Daun Penh (off
Monivong Boulevard)
Tel: (23) 981 888
Fax: (23) 981 168
www.raffles.com
Established in 1929 this is a luxury
hotel with a history. It has seen a
succession of foreign guests
including all the top journalists of
the Vietnam War and also UN aid
workers after the defeat of the
Khmer Rouge. All rooms are
decorated with traditional
Cambodian folk art. **$$$$**
Hotel Cambodiana
313 Sisowath Quay
Tel: (23) 426 288
Fax: (23) 426 290
www.hotelcambodiana.com
A splendid hotel, overlooking the
confluence of the Sap, Bassac and
Mekong rivers. Contains all the
amenities of a top modern hotel.
$$$
Inter-Continental
Regency Square, 296 Mao Tse Tung
Boulevard (Issarak Street)
Tel: (23) 720 888
Fax: (23) 720 885
www.interconti.com
A five-star hotel with all the
amenities of this world-wide chain.
Good business facilities and one of
the best Cantonese restaurants in
Phnom Penh. **$$$**
Royal Phnom Penh
Samdech Sothearos Street
Tel: (23) 360 026
Fax: (23) 360 036
www.royalphnompenhhotel.com
South of the city centre, with very
good restaurants, a large pool,
fitness centre and tennis courts.
$$$
Sunway
1, Street 92, Sangkat Wat Phnom
Tel: (23) 430 333
Fax: (23) 430 339
www.allsonhotels.com
Situated at the heart of old colonial
Phnom Penh. Facilities include
Jacuzzi, swimming pool and sauna.
$$$

Goldiana Hotel
10-12, 280 Street
Tel: (23) 727 085
www.goldiana.com
An excellent mid-range hotel with a
good fitness centre and swimming
pool. Very popular with diplomats,
UN personnel and consultants. **$$**

SIEM REAP

Raffles Grand Hotel D'Angkor
1 Vithei Charles de Gaulle
Tel: (63) 963 888
Fax: (63) 963 168
www.raffles.com
This fabulous hotel sits in the
centre of Siem Reap opposite King
Sihanouk's villa. It was recently
completely refurbished by the
Raffles Group and can rightly claim
to be one of Southeast Asia's
grandest hotels. **$$$$**

Price Guide

A general guide for a standard
double room, excluding taxes.
$$$$ = above US$150
$$$ = US$80–150
$$ = US$20–80
$ = under US$20

Sofitel Royal Angkor
Angkor Wat Road
Tel: (63) 964 600
Fax: (63) 964 610
www.accorhotels-asia.com
A charming low-rise but a bit out of
town. Beautiful garden and pools
plus a variety of restaurants and a
bar. Ideal for relaxing after the
artistic overload at the temples. **$$$**
Angkor Hotel
Street 6, Phum Sala Kanseng
Tel: (63) 964 301
Fax: (63) 964 302
www.angkor-hotel-cambodia.com
A resort-style hotel with swimming
pool and well located for the Angkor
complex. Excellent restaurant **$$$**
Ta Prohm Hotel
Near Old Market
Tel: (63) 380 117
Fax: (63) 380 116
Very well situated next to the river,
in the old French quarter. **$$**

Where to Eat

Laos

WHAT TO EAT

Lao cuisine, like that of
neighbouring Southeast Asian
countries, revolves around rice. This
isn't the long grain rice that
Vietnamese, Central Thai and most
Westerners are used to eating,
however, but *khao niaw*, or
glutinous 'sticky rice', deftly rolled
into a neat, small ball and eaten
with the hand. In Vientiane, the Lao
capital, as indeed in all other large
towns, long grain rice or *khao jao* is
readily available – but *khao niaw*
remains the basic staple of the Lao
people, and is the single most
distinctive feature of Lao cuisine.
Another essential is fish sauce or
naam paa, which is the universal
Lao condiment.

This sticky rice is generally
accompanied by a selection of dips,
parboiled vegetables, salad, soup
and various curried meat dishes or
fish dishes. The sticky rice is
usually served in a woven bamboo
container called a *tip khao*. Whilst
sticky rice is eaten by hand, long
grain rice is always eaten with a
spoon and fork.

Popular Lao dishes include *tam
som*, a spicy salad made of sliced
green papaya mixed with chilli
peppers, garlic, tomatoes, ground
peanuts, field crab, lime juice and
fish sauce. This is often eaten with
sticky rice and *ping kai* or grilled
chicken. Another standby is *laap*, a
spicy dish of minced meat, poultry
or fish mixed with lime juice, garlic,
chilli pepper, onion and mint. Meats
used in *laap* are generally cooked,
but can also be raw. If you are
concerned about this, ask for *laap
suk*, or cooked *laap*.

RESTAURANT LISTING

Vientiane
Bunmala
Khu Vieng Road
Tel: (21) 313 249
Famous among Lao and expats alike for its excellent grilled chicken, duck and fish, papaya salad, sticky rice and fresh beer. **$**
Kua Lao
111 Samsenthai Road
Tel: (21) 215 777
An upscale Lao restaurant – which you might say is an oxymoron – offering good Lao and Thai food in a beautiful French colonial mansion. Nightly traditional Lao music and dance performances. **$$**
L'Opera
Namphu Circle
Tel: (21) 215 099
One of the best restaurants in town, L'Opera offers excellent Italian food in a romantic setting. The charismatic Italian owner ensures that the service is impeccable and that his favourite opera music is always playing. The restaurant's takeout *gelati* bar is a highlight. **$$$**
Namphu
Namphu Circle
Tel: (21) 216 248
One of the oldest high-end establishments in town, the Namphu has a good bar and serves excellent French and German food, and some impressive desserts. Also has a few Lao specialities. **$$$**
Santisouk Restaurant
Nokeo Khumman Road
Tel: (21) 215 303
Has been around since the revolution days, and is known for its sizzling steak platters, good breakfasts, and retro atmosphere. Also serves Lao food. Probably the best value French restaurant in town. **$**

Luang Prabang
Luang Prabang Bakery
Sisavang Vong Road
Tel: (71) 212 617
Café serving good salads, quiches, sandwiches and pastries. **$$**
Pak Huoy Mixay
47/5 Ban Vatnong,
Savang Vatthana Road
Tel: (71) 212 260

Probably the best place in town for Lao specialities, this place serves excellent fresh fish from the Mekong; they also have a barbecue out on the terrace. **$$**
Restaurant l'Elephant
Ban Vat Nong
Tel: (71) 252 482
An elegant French brasserie situated in the most picturesque part of the old city. A daytime tea salon and a variety of daily specials including vegetarian meals make this many visitors' favourite restaurant in Luang Prabang. **$$**

Restaurant Price Guide

A general guide for dinner for two people excluding beverages:
$$$ = above US$20
$$ = US$10–20
$ = under US$10

Cambodia

WHAT TO EAT

Cambodian food draws heavily on the traditions of both its Thai neighbours and Chinese residents. Often referred to as Thai food but without the spiciness. The main national staple is of course rice, but French colonial influence has dictated that the Cambodians eat more bread than any other Southeast Asian country. Because of the country's vast waterways, freshwater fish and prawns are especially popular. Beef, pork, chicken and duck are widely available. Visitors up country will generally find only Cambodian cuisine or eateries serving only fairly ubiquitous baguette and paté. In towns of any size Chinese food will also be available. In the west of the country Thai food is widespread. Similarly in the east Vietnamese influence is common.

RESTAURANT LISTING

Phnom Penh
Eid Restaurant
327 Sisowath Quay
Tel: (23) 367 614

Serves some very good Khmer dishes as well as special Thai dishes prepared by a Thai cook. **$**
Foreign Correspondents Club of Cambodia
363 Sisowath Quay (Riverfront)
Tel: (23) 210 142, Fax: (23) 427 758
Great setting overlooking the confluence of the rivers. In the early evenings watch the fishermen on the Sap River. Draught beer available and always an interesting international menu. **$$**
La Croisette
241 Sisowath Quay (Riverfront)
Tel: (012) 876 032
Another great riverside location with the emphasis on charcoal grilling. One of the house specialities is "Beef Skewers A La Corsaire", they also serve good breakfasts. **$$**
Ponlok
232 Sisowath Quay
Tel: (23) 426 051
Overlooks the Sap River. There are two air-conditioned floors and a terrace. An extensive menu with many Khmer specialities. **$$**
Veiyo Tonle
237 Sisowath Quay
Tel: (012) 847 419
A selection of Khmer dishes plus an array of pizza and pasta dishes. Also some other international favourites on the menu. Overlooks the Sap River. **$$**

Siem Reap
Bayon
Wat Bo Street, just off Route 6
Tel: (012) 855 219
Standard Khmer food with the emphasis on curries. Serves fine French wine. Also good Western breakfasts. **$**
Chivit Thai
Wat Bo Street
Excellent Thai food served in a traditional atmosphere in an old wooden house. **$**
Continental Café
Psar Chas (Old French Quarter, next to the river)
Tel: (63) 964 036, Fax: (63) 380 065
A varied European menu with great salads and a small selection of wines. It's also one of the few places you can get Bayon beer. **$$**

Getting Acquainted

Situation A thin 1,600-km strip extending from China down to the Gulf of Thailand.
Area 329,556 sq km (127,242 sq miles).
Terrain Variable, from low mountains to mangrove swamps of the Mekong Delta. 75 per cent of the country is mountainous, 3,200km coastline.
Population 78 million, two-thirds of whom are under 25.
Capital Hanoi.
Language Vietnamese.
Religion Buddhism with Confucian/Taoist influences, Christianity.
Ethnic origins Over 85 percent of the population are Vietnamese (known as Viet or Kinh), one million Chinese (Hoa), around 100,000 Chams (in the central and south provinces, whose descendants now live in Cambodia); 6–8 million Montagnards (hill tribes in the north and centre).
Time zone 7 hours ahead of GMT, so New York is 12 hours, Los Angeles 15 and London 7 hours behind, Australia 3 hours ahead. Note: the sun sets around 5.30pm in winter and 8pm in summer.
Currency Dong (pronounced *dome*).
Weights and Measures Metric.
Electricity Mainly 220 volts, with rounded two-pin plugs. 110 volts in some areas. Expect frequent power cuts and surges.
International Dialling Code 84.

Economy

Vietnam is essentially an agricultural country, with rice cultivation accounting for 45 percent of the GNP and employing around 70 percent of the population. Other major crops include tea, coffee, maize, bananas, manioc, cotton, tobacco, coconut and rubber.

Industry represents 32 percent of the country's GNP and occupies 11 percent of the active population. Electricity, steel, cement, cotton fabrics, fish sauce, sea fish, wood, paper and the growing oil exploration and production industry represent Vietnam's major areas of industrial production.

Ho Chi Minh City now has a small oil refinery and has become Vietnam's economic capital, accounting for 30 percent of the national industrial production.

The country's standard of living ranks among the lowest in the world. Despite a protracted effort to revive the nation's rural economy, disastrous economic polices, coupled with the drain of more than 50 percent of the country's budget on supporting its occupation forces in Cambodia and Laos until 1989, have had devastating effects on the economy of Vietnam.

In an effort to revive the ailing economy the country has recently opened its doors to encourage foreign investment and tourism, while further reform policies have been geared to re-establishing a market economy and encouraging production in the private sector, agriculture and light industry.

Business Hours

Offices and public services generally open from around 7.30am and close for lunch at around noon or 12.30pm, opening again around 1pm until 4.30pm Monday to Saturday.
Banks 8am to 3pm Monday to Friday and closed on Saturday afternoons and Sundays.
Shops are open from 8.30am until late in the evening seven days a week.
Food markets generally close around 5pm.

Government

Vietnam has been a socialist republic ruled by the Vietnamese Communist Party since the fall of Saigon in 1975, and the country's subsequent imposed reunification in 1976. Vietnam's domestic policy is shaped primarily by the party and its Secretary General. The Prime Minister presides over drafting of laws and day-to-day governing. The President oversees state policy, the military and police.

The government is nominated by the National Assembly, proposed by the party and theoretically elected by the people.

Climate

Vietnam has a monsoon climate. The south's dry season runs from December to May, with rains May to November. Temperatures rarely fall below 20°C (68°F). The centre is similar but cooler. Along the coast, the "dry" season is March to August, but can be fairly wet. North Vietnam's dry season is October to December. The summer months tend to be hot and sticky, with temperatures up to 40°C (104°F). Hanoi's average is 30°C (86°F).

Public Holidays

The most important holiday is *Tet*, or New Year (late January/early February).
Other public holidays include:
1 January New Year's Day
3 February Founding of the Communist Party of Vietnam
8 March Women's Day
26 March Youth Day
30 April Liberation of Saigon
1 May International Labour Day
7 May Victory over France
19 May Ho Chi Minh's birthday
1 June Children's Day
27 July Memorial Day for war martyrs
19 August August Revolution of 1945
2 September National Day
20 November Teacher's Day
22 December Army Day

Planning the Trip

Visas & Passports

It used to be incredibly difficult for independent travellers to gain entry to Vietnam, but today it is fairly straightforward. It is possible to get a tourist visa for US$65 in four working days from a number of travel agents in Bangkok and Hong Kong. Bangkok is definitely the best place in Asia to pick one up and many travel agents offer attractive round-trip flight and visa packages.

Other types of visa available include: business, press, family visit, and official visit. To enter Vietnam on business, you must contact your Vietnamese sponsor who will then submit an application and letter to the embassy you are applying to. This process can often take weeks, so make sure you get a head start. Certain Vietnamese companies have the connections to have visas issued on arrival in Hanoi and Ho Chi Minh City for US$50. If you do enter Vietnam without a visa in hand, and there is a problem with immigration, remain calm. Usually the worst thing that will happen is you'll be put in the airport hotel for a night while your host hopefully secures your visa.

Without the right connections, it can be very difficult to get any type of visa issued for more than one month. Most must be used within one month of their issue. While it was once fairly easy to receive an extension to your visa in Vietnam, recently the government has changed its rules and tightened restrictions. Now, no extensions will be given for tourist visas. Foreigners who enter on tourist visas and conduct business or government activities will be deported when caught. They may also be fined.

Overseas Vietnamese may be granted extensions for as long as six months, but family reasons must be proven. Visa extensions may also be granted for foreigners working in joint-venture offices, foreign representative offices and who have proper visas.

You will be given a copy of your landing card on arrival. This, along with your visa, must be kept with you at all times and handed back on your departure.

Customs

When you arrive you have to fill in a form declaring your valuables, including cameras and video cameras. You keep a photocopy of this form to show to Customs on your departure, so it's worth declaring as much as you can just in case you lose your luggage or Customs question anything as you leave. Visitors are allowed to import 200 cigarettes and 1.5 litres of alcohol duty free.

Export of anything of "cultural or historical significance" is forbidden. So if you buy antiques you must apply for an export license, and if you want to take any fakes home it's worth getting them cleared as fakes by the ministry so there is no hassle at Customs.

Health

The only vaccination required is for yellow fever, for travellers coming from Africa. Immunisation against hepatitis (A & B), Japanese encephalitis and tetanus are strongly urged. It is a good idea to consult a doctor a month to six weeks before departing to leave enough time to get the injections.

Malaria is widespread in Vietnam, especially in the Central Highlands and the Mekong Delta. The best protection is prevention. Always sleep under a mosquito net when visiting rural areas, use a strong repellent and wear long sleeves and trousers from dusk to dawn. Mosquitoes in several areas are resistant to many brands of anti-malaria drugs, so seek advice on medication from a tropical institute before you leave.

Do not drink tap water unless it has been boiled and avoid ice in drinks, especially in the country. Imported bottled water is available in most cities, but beware of bottles that are refilled with tap water.

Caution should be taken when eating, because food is often not prepared in sanitary conditions. Doctors advise abstaining from shellfish, especially shrimps. Fruit and vegetables should be peeled before eating; cooking them is a better idea. Avoid mayonnaise and raw eggs, raw vegetables like the herbs and lettuce served with *pho*, the noodle soup, and spring rolls. Eat in restaurants that are crowded. Because most places do not have refrigeration, eat at places where you know food will not be spoilt – if it is crowded, it is a good sign.

Should you have an accident or an emergency health problem in Vietnam, you may want to consider evacuation to Singapore or Bangkok for treatment. Vietnam has no shortage of well trained doctors, but hospital services and supplies are in very short supply. It is essential to take out private medical insurance before you leave.

Money Matters

The dong (pronounced *dome*) currently circulates in bank notes of 100,000, 50,000, 20,000, 10,000, 5,000, 2,000, 1,000, 500, 200 and 100 denominations. Care should be taken when exchanging money or receiving change. The 20,000 dong notes and 5,000 notes (both widely used) are the same size and colour (blue) and easily confused.

Vietnam's black market for US dollars isn't what it used to be. The difference between the street rate and the bank rate is very small – if any. Changing money on the street is foolish. Because the dong notes are so similar, you can easily be given the wrong denomination. As the old saying goes, you get what you pay for. Better to stick to a

Dong or Dollars?

Although the government issued a decree that all transactions be conducted in Vietnamese dong, in reality the country still uses a dual-currency system. That is, most purchases can be made in US dollars as well as Vietnamese dong. However, often shops, restaurants and taxi drivers insist on a lower exchange rate when using dollars – such as 14,000 dong to US$1 instead of the current rate of exchange (about 15,000 dong to US$1). To avoid haggling, its better to carry some Vietnamese dong with you.

One other potential problem is the quality of the notes. Although Vietnamese dong notes are often ripped, faded and crumpled, Vietnamese are reluctant to accept US dollars that are not crisp and new. Before taking US dollars from a bank, you should inspect them to make sure they have no stray marks or tears, or appear old.

Note: the Vietnamese currency is not convertible so you cannot legally bring in or take out dong as a foreigner.

bank or currency exchange booth, of which there are many in all the major cities.

After banking hours, it is possible to change dollars at almost any jewellery or gold shop; sometimes the rate is slightly higher than the bank rate. These shops are called *hieu van* or *hieu kim hoan* and are easily identifiable because their signs usually have bright gold-coloured letters.

Be prepared to be offered two exchange rates: one for denominations of 50 and 100 USD, a lower rate for smaller denominations. It is better to change larger bills.

Some banks will also exchange Vietnamese dong for other currencies: French francs, German marks, Japanese yen, Australian dollars, for example. But gold shops will not. Better to bring US dollars. Traveller's checks in US dollars are accepted in most banks and in major hotels, but not in shops and smaller hotels and restaurants.

Major credit cards are accepted. Sometimes a high commission – 4 percent is standard – is charged when using them, however. Cash advances can be collected from major credit cards (again with the 4 percent commission) from major banks, including Vietcombank.

When you arrive in Vietnam, the Customs form requires you to note currency brought into the country if it is worth more than 2,000 US dollars. However, visitors no longer have to account for money exchanged or spent during trips.

What to Wear/Bring

The main thing to consider is the weather, as it can be freezing cold in the mountainous north and at the same time hot and humid on the Central Coast. If you are travelling in the north or the Central Highlands during the winter months definitely bring jeans and a warm coat or sweater. It seems that it is always raining somewhere in Vietnam, so bring lightweight rain gear. Sunblock, sunglasses and hat are also essential.

In the hot months, dress cool but conservative. Many Vietnamese cannot understand why foreigners insist on wearing shorts and sleeveless tops when they have the money to dress well. For them, appearance is very important, so if you are dealing with an official of any rank make sure you are dressed appropriately.

Imported pharmaceutical drugs are widely available in Hanoi and Ho Chi Minh City, but it is best to bring a small supply of medicine to cope with diarrhoea, dysentery, eye infections, insect bites, fungal infections, and the common cold.

There is an extensive black market for smuggled consumer goods in Hanoi and Ho Chi Minh City, so don't worry about running out of something. However, there are two things that are difficult to find in Vietnam: sunscreen and tampons.

It is still quite difficult to get access to news in Vietnam, so you may want to consider bringing a small short-wave radio to keep up with the world. Film, both print and slide, is available in the cities, but look at the expiry dates and make sure it hasn't been sitting in the sun.

Getting There

BY AIR

The easiest way to get to Vietnam is by air. International flights are available to Hanoi and Ho Chi Minh City, and a direct service to Danang is available from Bangkok on Thai Airways.

Hanoi

Noi Bai Airport is served by direct flights from Bangkok (Thai, Vietnam Airlines, Air France), Berlin (Vietnam Airlines), Dubai (Vietnam Airlines), Guangzhou (China Southern Airlines), Hong Kong (Cathay Pacific, Vietnam Airlines), Moscow (Aeroflot, Vietnam Airlines), Paris (Air France), Seoul (Vietnam Airlines), Singapore (Singapore Airlines), Taipei (China Airlines, Vietnam Airlines) and Vientiane (Lao Aviation, Vietnam Airlines).

There are bus and taxi services from the airport into central Hanoi. Vietnam Airlines operates a shuttle bus between its central Hanoi office and the airport for US$4. An official Vietnam Airlines taxi costs US$20.

Tickets for a taxi and the shuttle can be purchased near the baggage claim area. Freelance taxi drivers will swarm around visitors (see below for how to deal with them). There are also metered taxis, although they are difficult to find.

Ho Chi Minh City

The **Tan Son Nhat Airport** is served by flights from Amsterdam (KLM Airlines), Bangkok (Thai, Vietnam Airlines), Berlin (Vietnam Airlines), Dubai (Vietnam Airlines), Frankfurt

Taxi Driver Menace

Freelance taxi drivers are a menace at Hanoi's Noi Bai Airport, accosting visitors the moment they arrive. They will try to charge as much as they can; a car in good condition with air conditioning should cost around US$15. For an older car without air conditioning, US$10. Drivers will grab your arm and try to pick up your bags; negotiate the fare before letting anyone lead you away. If a driver refuses to come down in price, walk away – there are more than enough drivers. They may also try to charge you for a road toll, which you should not pay. If a driver insists, demand that you pay for the toll and keep the receipt. Also try to steer the driver onto the new highway; it will save you about 20 minutes. (Say: *Di duong bac thang long – noi bai* or simply *cau thang long*.)

(Lufthansa), Hong Kong (Cathay Pacific, Vietnam Airlines), Jakarta (Garuda Indonesia), Kuala Lumpur (Malaysia Air), Manila (Philippine Airlines), Osaka (Vietnam Airlines), Paris (Air France), Phnom Penh (Vietnam Airlines, Cambodia Air), Seoul (Vietnam Air), Singapore (Vietnam Airlines, Singapore Airlines), Sydney (Qantas), Taipei (Eva Air, Vietnam Airlines, China Airlines).

Tan Son Nhat is just 15 minutes from the centre of the city. Here the taxi scene is not as chaotic as at Hanoi. There is a somewhat orderly system for metered taxis, with an attendant directing taxis to passengers. A metered fare is reasonable and should cost less than US$10 to the city centre; there are no extra charges for baggage or extra passengers. You can also hire a freelance taxi driver, but the fare will not be much less.

BY SEA

Cruise ships sometimes make stops in Ho Chi Minh City and Danang as part of South China Sea cruises, but there is no regular service. Anyone considering arriving by sea on a freighter or private vessel should contact the Hanoi immigration office directly to receive authorisation. It is possible to take a ferry between Cambodia and Chau Doc in the Mekong Delta, but travellers have reported difficulties with immigration officers on arrival.

BY ROAD

It is also possible to enter Vietnam from China (and vice versa) at the Lang Son border crossing. Border tensions between the two countries routinely flare, so find out what the situation is when making plans.

It's now easy to cross from Laos to Vinh by the Lao Bao border crossing. It is also possible, but less common, to enter Laos via Cau Treo. You can also enter Vietnam from Cambodia.

When applying for a visa, you must specify where you intend to enter and exit Vietnam. If you do not do the immigration police may turn you away. Exit points can be changed by the immigration offices in Hanoi and Ho Chi Minh City.

Practical Tips

Media

Outside Hanoi and Ho Chi Minh City, getting your hands on accurate news in Vietnam can be difficult.

Foreign newspapers, including the *International Herald Tribune*, *Bangkok Post*, *The Nation* (from Bangkok), and *The Asian Wall Street Journal* can be purchased in Hanoi and Ho Chi Minh City. Usually you can buy the same day's paper in Ho Chi Minh City and Hanoi, but not elsewhere.

News magazines such as *Newsweek*, *Time*, *The Economist* and the *Far Eastern Economic Review* are also sold. French newspapers and magazines are readily available, and there are some English-language Vietnamese publications as well. The daily *Vietnam News*, published in Hanoi, contains official news from the Vietnam News Agency (a government-run service), stories from Reuters, reprints of articles from Vietnamese newspapers, some foreign news and sports scores. News about Vietnam itself tends to be sanitised.

Tipping & Bargaining

Tipping is not expected, although small gratuities are always welcome. But bargaining is usual (except in department stores and large hotels and restaurants). The impoverished Vietnamese see tourists as fair game for making a dong or two. The rule of thumb is stay friendly and if you reach stalemate remember you're probably haggling over a few cents.

Postal Services

Post offices are open every day from 7am to 8pm. Every city, town and village has one of some sort, and the domestic service is remarkably reliable and fast (unlike overseas mail). Within the country, mail reaches its destination within three days, sometimes faster. There is also an express mail service for overnight delivery.

Stamps come in small denominations, which means you need so many to mail a postcard that little room is left for writing a message. However, many post offices now have meter machines so stamps are no longer necessary.

City post offices
Can Tho Hoa Binh Street.
Da Lat 14-16 Tran Phu Street.
Da Nang 45 Tran Phu.
Hai Phong 5 Nguyen Tri Phuong.
Hanoi 75 Dinh Tien Hoang.
Tel: (04) 825 2730.
Ho Chi Minh City 2 Cong Xa Paris.
Tel: (08) 823 2541.
Hue 8 Hoang Hoa Tham.
Nha Trang 4 Le Loi.
Tel: (073) 828 000
Vung Tau 4 Ha Long Street.
Tel: (064) 852 689

Telecommunications

International telephone connections are quite clear from Vietnam. However, the costs of calling overseas are among the highest in the world. Direct calls can be placed from hotels, the post office and homes. Reverse charges are not allowed. Expect to pay from US$4–5 a minute to call the US, Europe or Australia. Hotels will add a surcharge that can make calls about US$7 a minute.

Domestic calling is still haphazard. The circuits between Hanoi and Ho Chi Minh City tend to be quite busy, so getting through can take a long time.

Telex services are available 24 hours a day in post offices larger cities. Fax machines are available in post offices and hotels, but the cost is high. Both Hanoi and

Emergency Numbers

- ● **Ambulance** 15
- ● **Fire** 14
- ● **Police** 13

Ho Chi Minh City have mobile telephone and paging services. Internet and e-mail services are provided by cybercafés, some post offices and most large hotels.

To call within the country, dial 01 followed by the area code followed by the number. Phone numbers are either five or six digits.

International access codes: MCI: 1201 1022; Sprint: 1201 1111 (AT&T: not available).

Medical Treatment

Hospitals
While Vietnam has well trained medical-care professionals, it lacks adequate equipment, medicine and facilities, especially by Western standards. The Ministry of Health has designated five hospitals to treat foreigners. Although in an emergency any hospital is allowed to help tourists, people are most often directed to the officially designated facilities:

Hanoi
Bach Mai Hospital, 35 Gia Phong Street. Tel: (04) 852 2089.

Ho Chi Minh City
Cho Ray Hospital, 201B Nguyen Chi Thanh Street, Dist. 5. Tel: (08) 855 4137.

Embassies and Consulates

HANOI
Australia
8 Dao Tan Street. Tel: (04) 831 7755, Fax: (04) 831 7711, www.ausinvn.com
New Zealand
63 Ly Thai To. Tel: (04) 824 1481, Fax: (04) 824 1480.
United Kingdom
31 Hai Ba Trung. Tel: (04) 936 0500, Fax: (04) 936 0561. www.uk-vietnam.org

Thong Nhat Hospital, 1 Ly Thuong Kiet, Tan Binh Dist.
Tel: (08) 864 0339.
Danang: C Hospital
Hai Phong: Viet Tiep Hospital

Doctors
Foreign doctors run two out-patient clinics, which is probably the best alternative to hospitals for medical care. They have a supply of pharmaceuticals. (Medicine of almost every kind can be bought on the street or at pharmacies – nha thuoc – but there is a problem that fake drugs are often sold.) The one recommended below is affiliated to emergency evacuation companies:
The Swedish Clinic, across from the Swedish Embassy at the entrance of the Van Phuc living quarters on Kim Ma Road.
Tel: (04) 825 2464; after-hours emergency. Tel: (04) 821 3555.

Traditional Medicine
Acupuncture and therapeutic massage are available at:
National Institute and Hospital of Traditional Medicine, 29 Nguyen Binh Khiem, Hanoi. Tel: (04) 822 6775.

Tourist Information

Vietnam's tourist industry is being developed along the organised tour line. **Vietnam Tourism**, which is the official representative of the National Office of Tourism, has a network of offices throughout the country, providing information and services such as tours, transport hire and hotel reservations.

United States
7 Lang Ha. Tel: (04) 772 1500, Fax: (04) 772 1510, http:// usembassy.state.gov/vietnam

HO CHI MINH CITY
Australia
5-B Ton Duc Thang, Dist. 1. Tel: (08) 829 6035, Fax: (08) 829 6031.
United Kingdom
25 Le Duan, Dist. 1. Tel: (08) 823 2604, Fax: (08) 822 1971.

Vietnam Tourism
80 Quan Su, Hanoi
Tel: (04) 942 1061
e-mail: vnat@vietnam-tourism.com
www.vietnamtourism.com

Useful Websites

There isn't much information on Vietnam on the Internet but visitors should check out the following websites (which offer links to numerous associated websites on Vietnam and the region).
www.vietnam-travel.com
www.visit-mekong.com

Crime & Security

In general, Vietnam is a very safe country to travel in and violent crimes against foreigners are rare. However, there are dangers. In Ho Chi Minh City, tourists are increasingly becoming the victims of pickpockets, snatch-and-grab thieves, and hotel burglars. Always leave valuables in a hotel safe, and when you must carry cash, put it in a money belt inside your clothes. When walking or travelling in a cyclo, keep one hand firmly on handbags and cameras.

Vietnamese police can be less than friendly. Corruption among them is commonplace due to low wages. Don't get conned into paying a trumped-up fine: if you have genuinely broken the law, they must hand you a fine ticket; if the charge is false, patience, a few calm words and cigarettes usually do the trick. Never take photographs of military sites.

Women should take care when travelling alone, especially at night. Paying a reliable driver extra to wait for you is better than having to find a lift home in a deserted area.

Getting Around

By road

In Hanoi and Ho Chi Minh City it is possible to hire good Japanese cars and minivans to go on day trips or week-long excursions. In Ho Chi Minh City you can even hire a convertible Mustang or Citroen to drive the scenic coastal road north to Hue. Hiring a driver and vehicle in Vietnam is good value if your travelling party is large enough to spread the cost. Self-drive is not yet possible.

By train

Train travel in Vietnam is very slow. The fastest Hanoi–Ho Chi Minh City express train covers 1,730 km (1,073 miles) in 36 hours, so if you need to get somewhere fast forget about the train. However, if you want to soak in the Vietnamese countryside leisurely the train has a lot to offer, including mountain passes, ocean views, tunnels, French-era bridges, and an opportunity to get to know the Vietnamese up close and personal. However, there have been burglaries on board so make sure you secure your bags properly.

There are two express trains every day and berths are reserved fast, so try to make reservations two days in advance. There are also local train services on the Hanoi–Ho Chi Minh City line that serve coastal cities. Lines also run from Hanoi West to Pho Lu, East to Hai Phong and North to Lang Son. In **Ho Chi Minh City**, the train station is at 1 Nguyen Thong Street, tel: (08) 823 0105. In **Hanoi**, go to 120 Le Duan Street, tel: (04) 825 2770.

By air

Flying is by far the best way to travel if you intend only to visit a few cities in Vietnam. A Vietnam Airlines flight from Hanoi to Ho Chi Minh City costs about US$200, whereas the train for the same distance, if you figure in meals for two days, is roughly the same price. Scheduled **Vietnam Airlines** flights (www.vietnamairlines.com) from Ho Chi Minh City serve Buon Me Thuot, Da Lat, Danang, Hai Phong, Hanoi, Hue, Nha Trang, Phu Quoc, Pleiku, Qui Nhon and Rach Gia. From Hanoi there are scheduled flights to Danang, Ho Chi Minh City, Hue, Vinh and Nha Trang.

The major problem with flying is finding space. Popular flights fill up a few days before departure, so it is imperative to book flights early. It is very common for Vietnam Airlines to bump Vietnamese passengers off domestic flights when foreigners are on the waiting list, as foreign ticket prices are twice the Vietnamese price.

You can use credit cards to buy airline tickets in Hanoi and Ho Chi Minh City, but in other cities you may be asked to pay cash.

Vietnam Airlines' **Hanoi** office is located at 1 Quang Trung Street, tel: (04) 832 0320, and the **Ho Chi Minh City** office at 116 Nguyen Hue, District 1, tel: (08) 832 0320.

By bike

In the cities the best way to get around is by bicycle or *cyclo* (trishaw). Bicycles can be rented for as little as US$5 per day from tourist cafés in Hanoi and Ho Chi Minh City. If you have a mechanical problem or a tire puncture, don't worry as there are stands set up on practically every street corner where most repairs will cost a few thousand dong.

No trip to Vietnam is complete without a ride in a cyclo. Vietnam has thousands of waiting cyclo drivers who can be hired by the kilometre or the hour. Expect to pay at least 3,000 dong for a short ride or 10,000 dong for an hour. It is essential to bargain with cyclo drivers. As a rule, halve their first offer and work up. Most cyclo drivers in the South are former ARVN soldiers and speak a little English. Cyclo drivers are indispensable as guides, sources of historical information, and as the procurers of hard to find items.

By motorcycle taxi

A faster way to get around town in Hanoi and Ho Chi Minh City is a motorcycle taxi, called a *xe om* (pron. *say ome*) or Honda *om*, which literally means "hugging taxi" as passengers grab on to the driver's waist. Fares are actually cheaper than on cycles, and of course the ride is quicker. Some of the drivers navigate the roads badly, however, so be careful. If a driver seems unsafe, tell him to stop, get off and pay him, then find another driver. Some women travellers have reported problems with *xe om* drivers getting too friendly; be careful late at night, especially.

By taxi

Taxis in Hanoi and Ho Chi Minh City are generally comfortable, with meters and air-conditioning and are generally reasonably priced.

In **Ho Chi Minh City**, **Vinataxis**, tel: (08) 811 0888 and **Airport Taxis**, tel: (08) 844 6666, provide an efficient metered service. **Hanoi Taxi**, tel: (04) 853 5252 and **Taxi PT**, tel: (04) 853 3171, in the capital city, **Hanoi**, do the same. Taxis are seldom found outside these two cities, but thanks to the enterprising nature of the Vietnamese, old jalopy-style cars are available for hire as taxis in many areas.

By bus

Large express buses travel between all the major towns and cities. These can be slow and often break down, but they are cheap and one of those typically Asian experiences some travellers like to try.

Where to Stay

Choosing a Hotel

You will find the best and widest range of accommodation in the country in Ho Chi Minh City. Here, hotels like the Caravelle have set new standards in the luxury-class category of hotels. To keep up with the times and to cater to increasing numbers of businessmen in the city, many of the older hotels have been refurbished to international standards.

Hanoi has also witnessed a hotel boom in the last few years, but most accommodation tends to be somewhat overpriced. Elsewhere, standards can vary. If you're on a tight budget, try the so-called 'minihotels', small, often family-run hotels with fairly modern facilities. These abound in Hanoi and Ho Chi Minh City and are beginning to make an appearance in popular resort towns. Rates are subject to 10–15 percent government tax.

HANOI

Sofitel Metropole Hanoi
15 Ngo Quyen Street
Tel: (04) 826 6919
Fax: (04) 826 6920
www.accorhotels-asia.com
The Metropole is the center of international business in Hanoi, and its guests are primarily American, French and Asian business people. It is the ultimate hotel in Vietnam, especially after major renovations by a French company in 1992. You would be well advised to book at least one month in advance. **$$$$**
Hanoi Horison Hotel
40 Cat Linh Street
Tel: (04) 733 0808
Fax: (04) 733 0888

www.hanoihorisonhotel.com
Comfortable five-star hotel with attractive rooms. All the usual amenities plus a great health club and large swimming pool. Well located for the Temple of Literature. **$$$**
Melia Hanoi
44B Ly Thuong Kiet Street
Tel: (04) 934 3343
Fax: (04) 934 3344
www.solmelia.com
Located in the business and diplomatic district, this glitzy affair managed the Spanish Sol and Melia chain of hotels has 308 rooms, restaurants, bar and pool. It even has its own heliport. **$$$**

Price Categories

A general guide for a standard double room, excluding taxes.
$$$$ = above US$150
$$$ = US$100–150
$$ = US$50–100
$ = under US$50

Sofitel Plaza Hanoi
1 Pho Thanh Nien
Tel: (04) 823 8888
Fax: (04) 823 9388
www.accorhotels-asia.com
Formerly the Meritus Westlake, this splendid hotel overlooks Hanoi's picturesque West Lake. The Summit Lounge on the 20th floor provides a wonderful view of Hanoi. **$$$**
De Syloia Hotel
17A Tran Hung Dao
Tel: (04) 824 5346
Fax: (04) 824 1083
www.desyloia.com
An international-quality hotel, with an excellent restaurant called the Cay Cau serving fine Vietnamese food and a fitness centre. **$$**
Hanoi Hilton Opera
1 Le Thanh Tong
Tel: (04) 933 0500
Fax: (04) 933 0530
www.hanoi.hilton.com
Superb location in an architecturally impressive building which aims to compliment the neighbouring French-built Opera House. Excellent range of facilities, including a swimming pool and spa. **$$$–$$$$**

Hoa Binh Hotel
27 Ly Thuong Kiet
Tel: (04) 825 3315
Fax: (04) 826 9818
e-mail: kshoabinh@hn.vnn.vn
Old, French-style hotel with 102 rooms. Small but elegant and centrally located. Known for its restaurant serving good Vietnamese food. **$$**

HO CHI MINH CITY

Caravelle Hotel
19 Lam Son Square, District 1
Tel: (08) 823 4999
Fax: (08) 824 3999
www.caravellehotel.com
Extensively renovated but still retains a strong French character. Rooftop affords great views of the city. Easily the best hotel in HCMC **$$$$**

Continental Hotel
132-134 Dong Khoi Street, District 1
Tel: (08) 829 9201
Fax: (08) 829 0936
www.continental-saigon.com
The setting for Graham Greene's *The Quiet American*. Refurbished tastefully, the place exudes old world charm and comfort. A personal favourite of many visitors to Vietnam. **$$–$$$**

Majestic Hotel
1 Dong Khoi Street, District 1
Tel: (08) 829 5514/7
Fax: (08) 829 5510
www.majestic-saigon.com
Ask for rooms with balconies overlooking the Saigon River. A full refurbishment in 1995 left this classy colonial hotel rather less stylish than before. **$$–$$$**

Rex Hotel
141 Nguyen Hue Boulevard, District 1
Tel: (08) 829 2185
Fax: (08) 829 3115
www.rexhotelvietnam.com
A classic, somewhat eccentric hotel with a popular rooftop garden restaurant. That this hotel is still a popular choice has less to do with its garish mix of Eastern and Western decorative styles than with its colourful history. **$$–$$$**

Saigon Prince Hotel
63 Nguyen Hue Boulevard, District 1
Tel: (08) 822 2999
Fax: (08) 824 1888
www.duxton.com/hotels
Well located in the heart of the city. This modern, spacious hotel complete with fountains and wide, curving staircases attracts mostly business executives and tour groups. Good Japanese, international and Chinese restaurants. **$$$–$$$$**

The Equatorial
242 Tran Binh Trong, District 5
Tel: (08) 839 0000
Fax: (08) 839 0011
www.equatorial.com
A modern hotel located midway between the Cholon area and Saigon. Has one of the best Chinese restaurants in the city, the Golden Phoenix. **$$$**

Bong Sen Hotel
117-123 Dong Khoi Street, District 1
Tel: (08) 829 1721
Fax: (08) 829 8076
www.hotelbongsen.com
85 air conditioned rooms located conveniently in the middle of the central shopping district and in close proximity to a number of excellent Vietnamese and French restaurants. **$$–$$$**

Oscar Saigon Hotel
68A Nguyen Hue Boulevard, District 1
Tel: (08) 829 2959
Fax: (08) 829 2732
www.oscarsaigon.com
Formerly known as the Century Saigon this comfortable modern hotel in French colonial-style is located in Saigon's central district. **$$–$$$**

Palace Hotel
56-66 Nguyen Hue Boulevard
Tel: (08) 824 4236
Fax: (08) 824 4230
www.palacesaigon.com
Amenities include two restaurants, bar, swimming pool. **$$**

Windsor Saigon Hotel
193 Tran Hung Dao Street, District 1
Tel: (08) 836 7848
Fax: (08) 836 7889
www.windsorsaigonhotel.com
Located less than a kilometre from downtown this boutique hotel has large rooms with balconies. Caters particularly to business people on long stays. Its restaurants and bakery are recommended. **$$**

Where to Eat

What to Eat

Vietnamese cuisine reflects long years of cultural exchange with China, Cambodia and France. Rice is the main staple, though bread – especially baguettes introduced by the French – is usually very good. Dishes are usually served at the same time rather than by course, and eaten with long-grain rice, *nuoc mam* (fish sauce), and a range of fresh herbs and vegetables.

Some of the more popular Vietnamese dishes include *Cha gio*: small 'spring rolls' of minced pork, prawn, crabmeat, mushrooms and vegetables wrapped in thin rice paper and then fried. *Cha gio* is rolled in a lettuce leaf with fresh mint and other herbs, then dipped in a sweet sauce. *Chao tom* is a northern delicacy: Mashed shrimp is baked on a stick of sugar cane, then eaten with lettuce, cucumber, coriander and mint, and dipped in fish sauce. Another dish eaten in a similar fashion is *cuon diep*, or shrimp, noodles, mint, coriander and pork wrapped in lettuce leaves.

Hue is famous for its vegetarian cuisine and for its *banh khoai*, or 'Hue pancake'. A batter of rice flour and corn is fried with egg to make a pancake, then wrapped around pork or shrimp, onion, bean sprouts and mushrooms. Another Hue speciality is *bun bo*, or fried beef and noodles served with coriander, onion, garlic, cucumber, chilli and tomato paste.

Soups are popular, and generally served with almost every meal. Perhaps the best known of all Vietnamese soup dishes, often eaten for breakfast or as a late night snack, is *pho*, a broth of rice noodles topped with beef or chicken, fresh herbs and onion.

Restaurant Listings

HANOI

Al Fresco's
23L Hai Ba Trung
Tel: (04) 826 7782
A variety of steaks, pizzas, pastas and fresh salads. Be wary when ordering, the portions are huge. **$$**

Brother's Café
26 Nguyen Thai Hoc Street
Tel: (04) 733 3866
Charming Vietnamese restaurant set in a colonial villa and serving authentic dishes buffet-style. Indoor and outdoor seating available. **$$**

Cay Cau
De Syloia Hotel, 17A Tran Hung Dao
Tel: (04) 933 1010
Excellent Vietnamese place popular among people in the know. Pomelo salad, crabs in tamarind and pork-stuffed egg plant are all winners. **$$**

Cha Ca La Vong
14 Cha Ca Street
Tel: (04) 825 3929
It only serves fried freshwater fish, a Hanoi speciality, and it's truly excellent. There are plenty of other *Cha Ca* restaurants around town but this is the best. **$$**

Gustave's
17 Trang Tien Street
Tel: (04) 825 0625
Flamboyantly renovated French villa with great food to match. Perfect for whiling away the night. **$$$**

Le Beaulieu
Sofitel Metropole,
15 Ngo Quyen
Tel: (04) 826 6919
A Vietnamese and mainly French menu. Each morning there is a large breakfast buffet with various freshly baked cakes and breads. **$$$**

Seasons of Hanoi
95B Quan Thanh
Tel: (04) 843 5444
Classic Vietnamese cuisine in a beautiful French-style villa with live traditional music. **$$**

Tandoor
24 Hang Be
Tel: (04) 824 2252
Located in the Old Quarter near the Hoan Kiem Lake. Excellent North Indian and vegetarian curries. **$$**

HO CHI MINH CITY

Asian Reflections
Caravelle Hotel, 19 Lam Son Square, District 1
Tel: (08) 823 4999
Cutting-edge Asian fusion cuisine – like Sichuan pepper beef salad and macadamia-crusted softshell crabs – plated Western-style. Stylish atmosphere and excellent service. **$$$**

Au Manoir De Khai
251 Dien Bien Phu Street, District 3
Tel: (08) 930 3394
High-class French cuisine in a renovated manor. Advance bookings are essential. **$$$**

Restaurant Price Guide

A general guide for dinner for two people excluding beverages:
$$$ = above US$20
$$ = US$10–20
$ = under US$10

Lemon Grass
4 Nguyen Thiep Street, District 1
Tel: (08) 822 0496
Excellent Vietnamese cuisine. The fish soup is recommended. You may be serenaded by guitarists playing traditional Vietnamese folk music. **$$–$$$**

Mandarine
11A Ngo Van Nam Street, District 1
Tel: (08) 822 9783
A fabulous selection of traditional Vietnamese cuisine in beautiful surroundings. **$$**

Q Bar
7 Lam Son Square
Tel: (08) 823 3479
An intimate bar with surreal decor and music that will make you forget where you are. Also has the best guacamole in the Eastern Hemisphere. The classiest bar in town. **$$**

Vietnam House
93-95 Dong Khoi, District 1
Tel: (08) 829 1623
A restaurant in an old colonial villa with live music on each floor. Your choice of a four-piece traditional group or a pianist. **$$**

Culture

Museums

HANOI

Army Museum (Vien Bao Tang Quan Doi), 28-A Dien Bien Phu. Tel: (04) 823 4264. Daily, 8.30–11.30am and 1.30–4pm.

Fine Arts Museum (Vien Bao Tang My Thuat), 66 Nguyen Thai Hoc. Tuesday–Sunday, 8am–noon and 1–4pm.

Geology Museum (Vien Bao Tang Dia Chat), 6 Pham Ngu Lao. Tel: (01) 826 6802. Monday–Saturday 8am–noon and 1.30–4.30pm.

History Museum (Vien Bao Tang Lich Su), 1 Pham Ngu Lao. Tel: (01) 825 3518. Friday–Wednesday, 8.15–11.45am and 1.30–4.30pm. Exhibits displayed here cover every era of Vietnam's fascinating and complex history.

Ho Chi Minh Mausoleum (Lang Chu Tich Ho Chi Minh), Ba Dinh Square, near Hung Vuong Street. Tel: (01) 845 5124. Daily except Monday and Friday, 8.30–11.30am. Closed from September to December.

Ho Chi Minh Museum (Vien Bao Tang Ho Chi Minh), 3 Ngoc Ha Street. Tel: (01) 846 3746. Tuesday–Sunday, 8–11.30am and 1.30–4pm.

Revolutionary Museum (Vien Bao Tang Cach Mang), 25 Tong Dan. Tel: (01) 825 4151. Daily, 8–11.30am and 1.30–4.30pm.

Temple of Literature (Van Mieu), Quoc Tu Giam Street, between Van Mieu and Ton Duc Thang Streets. Tel: (01) 845 2917. Daily, 7.30am–5.30pm.

HO CHI MINH CITY

Fine Arts Museum (Bao Tang My Thuat), 97-A Duc Chinh St, Dist. 1. Tel: (08) 821 0001. Tuesday–Sunday, 8–11.30am and 1.30–4.30pm.

History Museum (Bao Tang Lich Su). Located just inside the entrance gate to the zoo, Nguyen Binh Khiem Street. Tel: (08) 829 8146. Tuesday–Sunday, 8–11.30am and 1–4pm.

Ho Chi Minh Museum. Across the Khanh Hoi bridge at 1 Nguyen Tat Thanh St, Dist. 4. Tel: (08) 829 1060. Daily except Monday and Friday mornings, 7.30–11.30am and 1.30–4.30pm.

Military Museum (officially called the Museum of Ho Chi Minh's Campaign, Bao Tang Chien Dich Ho Chi Minh), 2-T Le Duan. Tel: (08) 822 4824. Daily, 8–10.30am and 1–4pm.

Reunification Palace (Hoi Truong Thong Nhat), Nam Ky Khoi Nghia Street at Le Duan; the entrance for visitors is at 106 Nguyen Du. Tel: (08) 829 0629. Daily, 7.30–11am and 1–4pm.

Revolutionary Museum (Bao Tang Cach Mang), 65 Ly Tu Trong. Tel: (08) 829 9741. Daily except Monday, 8am–4.30pm.

War Remnants Museum (Bao Tang Chung Tich Chien Tranh), 28 Vo Van Tan. Tel: (08) 829 0325. Daily, 7.30–11.45am and 1.30–4.45pm.

HUE

Imperial Museum (Vien Bao Tang Hue), 11 Le Loi St. Tel: (54) 822 489. Daily except Sunday, 7.30–11.30am and 2–4.30pm.

Military Museum (Vien Bao Tang Quan Su), 6 Le Loi St. Tel: (54) 822 152. Daily except Sunday, 7.30–11.30am and 2–4.30pm.

DANANG

Cham Museum (Vien Vo Cham, or Bao Tang Dieu Khac Cham), 2 Tieu La. Tel: (51) 821 951. Daily, 7am–5.30pm.

Festivals

Many traditional and religious festivals take place in Vietnam, particularly in the north in and around Hanoi during *Tet*. Festivities last three days (officially), preceded, particularly in Ho Chi Minh City and Hanoi, by a week-long flower market. Dates, unless otherwise stated, fall in the first lunar month.

Dong Ky Festival A firecracker competition festival, held on the 15th in Dong Ky village, Tien Son District. One of the largest and most spectacular festivals.

Mai Dong Festival Takes place from the 4th to 6th at the Mai Dong Temple in Hai Ba Trung District, Hanoi, is held in honour of Le Cham, the Trung Sisters' brave female general who fought against the Chinese in the first century.

Dong Da Festival Held on the 5th, in Hanoi's Dong Da District, commemorates King Trung Quang's victory at Dong Da and those who died in this battle against the Tsing in 1789.

An Duong Vuong Festival Occurs between the 6th and 16th, in the temple of the same name in Co Loa village near Hanoi. Held in memory of King Thuc An Duong Vuong, one of the founders of ancient Vietnam who built the Co Loa Citadel.

Le Phung Hieu Festival Held on the 7th, at the temple of the same name in Hoang Hoa district, Thanh Hoa Province.

Lim Festival On the 13th in the Lim village pagoda, Ha Bac Province. Features singing and a wide range of cultural and artistic activities.

Ha Loi Festival Held on the 15th at Ha Loi Temple in the Me Linh suburb of Hanoi. Commemorates the Trung Sisters.

Den Va Temple Festival Dedicated to Tan Vien, God of the Mountain, and held in the Bat Bat suburb of Hanoi on the 15th.

Ram Thang Gieng The most important Buddhist festival, takes place on the 15th.

Van Village Festival Celebrated in Hanoi's Viet Yen District from the 17th to the 20th.

Khu Lac and Di Nau Festival Occurs on the 7th and 26th in Tam Thanh District, Vinh Phu Province.

Lac Long Quan Festival From the 1st to 6th days of the third lunar month, at Binh Minh village, Ha Tay Province. Dedicated to Lac Long Quan, the quasi-legendary ancestor of the Vietnamese people. Features traditional music, elders dressed in traditional silk robes, fireworks displays and a stunning display of young ladies carrying altars laden with fruit and flowers through Binh Minh's narrow streets.

Tet: Vietnam's New Year

Tet Nguyen Dan is the most important festival on the Vietnamese calendar. It takes place late January or early February, on the day of the full moon between the winter solstice and the spring equinox, and lasts seven days. It is a time of hope, when relatives gather to celebrate new beginnings and to appease ancestral spirits.

Houses are given a good spring cleaning and decorated with flowers. Parades and fireworks fill the streets.

Age is reckoned by tet years, so everyone has their birthday during this period too. Excellent celebratory cakes are for sale, and families hold feasts.

During the Tet holidays, the whole of the country closes down, and transportation and hotels get booked up well in advance for the weeks before and afterwards. Don't plan spontaneous travel.

Huong Tich Festival Takes place throughout the spring in the spectacular Huong Son mountains west of Hanoi in Ha Tay Province. Can be visited at the same time as Lac Long Quan Festival.

The Buffalo Immolation Festival, Celebrated during spring in the Tay Nguyen Highlands.

Thay Pagoda Festival Held on the 7th day of the 3rd lunar month in Quoc Hai, Ha Tay Province, is dedicated to To Dao Hanh, a revered Buddhist monk and teacher. An excellent opportunity to see the traditional water puppet theatre in an historical and idyllic setting. Also features rowing contests and mountain climbing.

12 March The Den Festival takes place at the site of the ancient capital of Hoa Lu in Ha Nam Ninh Province. It commemorates King Dinh Bo Linh and General Le who fought against the Sung invaders.

16 March De Tham Festival in Hanoi's Yen The district.

8 April, the Dau Pagoda festival in Thuan Thanh.

Easter More in the south.

12 April Anniversary of Vietnam's first King, Hung Vuong.

15 May Buddha's birth, enlightenment and death, celebrated in pagodas, temples and homes throughout the country.

July/August On the first day of the 7th lunar month offerings of food and gifts are made in homes and temples for the wandering souls of the dead.

September/October Mid-Autumn Festival on the day of the full moon in the 8th lunar month. Celebrated with sticky rice mooncakes filled with lotus seeds, salted duck egg yolks, peanuts and melon seeds. Brightly coloured lanterns depicting all manner of things – dragons, boats, butterflies – are carried by children in evening processions.

The Kiep Bac Temple Festival Held in Hai Hung Province on the 20th day of the 8th lunar month to commemorate the national hero Tran Hung Dao who wiped out the invading Mongol forces in the 13th century.

25 December Christmas.

Shopping

What to Buy

There is a wide variety of traditional Vietnamese handicrafts to choose from, including embroidery, silk paintings, lacquerware, pottery, mother-of-pearl inlay, ceramics, precious wood, tortoise shell, jade, bamboo and wickerware, baskets, wool carpets, sculpture, wood, marble/bone carvings, jewellery, engraving, silk and brocade.

You may like to add a *non la*, the famous Vietnamese conical hat and an *ao dai*, the traditional costume worn by Vietnamese women, to your wardrobe. Green pith helmets, worn by soldiers during the war and by cyclo drivers and labourers today, are sold, as well as old-fashioned "Uncle Ho" sandals made from used tire treads. In Ho Chi Minh City, a popular item are helicopters, airplanes and cyclos made out of Coca-Cola and Tiger beer cans.

Heavy taxation has discouraged the sale of antiquities, which has become almost clandestine and very limited in the North and strictly controlled in the South. Only after enquiring of the proprietor will you discover all that may be available, as the best pieces are never displayed. Antique shops in the centre of Ho Chi Minh City and the old town of Hanoi sell Vietnamese wood or Laotian bronze Buddhas, old porcelain, objects in silver and ivory, small jade statuettes and objects used by the various cults. Prices are in US dollars and subject to bargaining.

Russian vodka, caviar and even French champagne may be found at reasonable prices. Clothing is comparatively cheap and tailors can quickly produce well made garments to the design of your choice.

HO CHI MINH CITY

Shops

Books/Newspapers

Bookazine, 28 Dong Khoi, Dist 1. Tel: (08) 829 7455. Excellent for large-format arts and culture books, and foreign magazines.

Fahasa Bookshop, 1st Floor, 40 Nguyen Hue. Tel: (08) 822 5796. Books in English, French, Vietnamese and Russian.

Lacquerware/Handicrafts

Artexport (state-run), 159 Dong Khoi. Objets d'art and antiquities.

Cultrimex (state-run), 94 Dong Khoi. Tel: (08) 829 2574, 829 2896. Handicrafts, paintings, lacquer work, reproductions of antiquities.

Cuu Long, 177 Dong Khoi. Ao dai and fabrics.

Phuong Nam Lacquerware, 219 Nguyen Trai Street, Dist 1. Tel: (08) 837 0434; Fax: (08) 837 0435. Good-quality lacquerware, wooden carvings, and handicrafts.

Sodasy, 115 Le Than Ton. Tel: (08) 829 7752. Shell and ivory articles.

Gift Shop, 30 Ngo Duc Ke, Dist 1. Tel: (08) 829 8784.

Made in Vietnam, 26B Le Thanh Ton, Dist 1. Tel: (08) 822 0841.

Fashion/Clothing/Tailors

Catinat Fashion, 2–4–6 Dong Khoi,

Ho Chi Minh's Market

The city's central market is **Ben Thanh Market**, at the intersection of Ham Nghi, Le Loi, Tran Hung Dao and Le Thanh Ton Streets. Its thronging stalls spill out from the main arcade on to the pavement, and just about everything is for sale here, from fruits, vegetables, rice and meats to electronics, clothes, household goods, and flowers. Not for the squeamish, there is a fascinating fish/meat section, where you may catch a glimpse of live frogs hanging by the leg and other delicacies. There are also some small food stalls selling soup and rice dishes.

Dist 1. Tel: (08) 829 1074.
Imported designer clothes.
Fadin, Fashion Design Institute, 41
Ben Choung Duong, Dist 1. Tel: (08)
829 7226.
Lac Long, 143 Le Than Ton.
Leather and skin goods.
Vietsilk, 19–21 Dong Khoi, Dist 1.
Tel: (08) 823 4860.
Zakka, 23 Dong Khoi, Dist 1. Tel:
(08) 829 8086.

Shopping Areas
Binh Tay Market, Cho Lon's main
marketplace located on Hau Giang
Blvd. The usual household goods
and food items are on sale here.
Le Thanh Ton Street. Several shops
sell embroidery and silk clothes in
Western styles. A shop across from
the Norfolk Hotel sells modern
glass, ceramics, linens and wood
items, all made in Vietnam. Near
the New World Hotel a shop sells
glass, ethnic fabrics and ceramics.
Saigon's main antique street is Le
Cong Kieu. Dong Khoi Street also
has a number of stores selling
everything from old furniture to
trinkets. Beware of fakes.
Dan Sinh Market, at the corner of
Yersin and Nguyen Thai Binh
streets. Once known as the
American market, this place now
only has a few stalls in the back
selling paraphernalia related to the
Vietnam War. Most of the other
stalls offer housewares, tools,
machinery, clothing and electronics.

HANOI

Shops
Crafts and Bookshops
Souvenirs of Vietnam, 30A Ly
Thuong Kiet. Vietnamese
handicrafts.
Cultrimex Gallery, 22B Ha Ba
Trung. Silk paintings, paintings and
antique reproductions.
Xunhasaba, 32 Hai Ba Trung.
Ministry of Culture-sponsored
society for the sale and export of
books, periodicals, reproductions
of objets d'art and handicrafts.
Foreign-language publications are
also available.
Souvenir Shop, 89 Dinh Thien Hoa.

Han Art, 43 Trang Tien Street.
Tel: (04) 824 0038. Ceramics,
lacquerware.
Hanoi Gallery, 61 Trang Tien Street.
International Bookshop, 61 Trang
Tien Street. Tel: (04) 824 8914.
Book Sach, 57 Trang Tien. Foreign-
language publications.
Vietnamese Bookshop, On the
corner of 19 Ngo Quyen and 40
Trang Tien. A few foreign-language
publications.
Hanoi Foreign Trade Company, 56
Trang Tien Street.
Souvenir Shop, 89 Dinh Thien Hoang.

Shopping Areas
Silk and embroidery
There are many shops on Hang Gai
and Hang Bong Streets to be found
in the Old Quarter.
Tailoring
The upmarket garment shops of
Hang Gai and Hang Bong Streets
will also make clothes with fabric
brought from elsewhere. Quality is
good, but bargain hard.
Musical instruments
Wooden percussion instruments,
stringed instruments and bamboo
xylophones are sold in several
shops in the Old Quarter on Hang
Non Street.
Antiques
Several shops on Le Duan Street,
near Lenin Park and Tran Tien
sell antiques.

Hanoi's Markets

These sell all manner of foods
and packaged goods. Some also
sell electronics, household goods
and clothing.
Cho Hang Da, at the corner of
Dau Duong Thanh and Hang Dieu.
Cho Hoa Binh, at the corner of
Tran Nhan Tang and Pho Hue.
Cho Hom, at the corner of
Tran Xuan Son and Pho Hue.
Cho Long Bien, near the Long
Bien Bridge.
Cho Mo, at the corner of Truong
Dinh and Minh Khai.
Cho Hang Be, 2 Da Ngu.
Cho Cua Nam, on Cua Nam.
Cho 19–12 (or Cho Ma), 41 Hai
Ba Trung.

villages, shorts are not a good idea – save them for the beach. Check the required attire before entering any house of worship.

For businessmen, a white shirt and tie are adequate for office calls – jackets are seldom required. For women a tailored dress or business suit is appropriate. In the evenings, only a few exclusive nightclubs and restaurants favour the traditional jacket and tie. Most hotels, restaurants, coffeehouses and discos accept casually elegant attire. However, jeans and sneakers are taboo at some restaurants and discos, so to avoid embarrassment, it is best to check the dress code of better establishments in advance.

Getting There

BY AIR

Malaysia is well connected by airlines to all continents, and if coming from Europe or North America, you will enter the country at the **Kuala Lumpur International Airport (KLIA)**, opened in 1998 as one of the most advanced airports in the world, situated 70 km (45 miles) south of Kuala Lumpur. A high-speed rail link passes through the so-called Multimedia Super Corridor to connect with KL's city centre.

If you are arriving from a nearby Asian country (Hong Kong, Thailand, Indonesia or Singapore), it is possible to fly to some other Malaysian cities either directly or by connecting flights through Kuala Lumpur. Penang, Langkawi and Tioman can be reached directly from Singapore. For details on domestic flights within Malaysia, contact **Malaysia Airlines** (www.malaysiaairlines.com).

Nomenclature

Malaysian refers to anyone who is a citizen of Malaysia.
Malayan refers to people from the peninsula.
Malay is the name for the ethnic Malay people who are mainly Muslim.

BY RAIL

An extensive railway network runs through Malaysia (for information on trains, see *Getting Around* section) from Singapore, with connections to Bangkok. The Thai-owned International Express leaves daily from Bangkok for Butterworth and trains from Hat Yai in the south of Thailand connect to trains on the Eastern Malaysian railway. The trip from Bangkok takes about two days, and you can travel in a first-class air-conditioned sleeper, a second-class non-air-conditioned sleeper, or in upright seats in third class. For reservations, contact the railway station in Bangkok (Hualamphong) or a local travel agent. Trains from Singapore to Kuala Lumpur and Kota Bahru run several times daily and take from 7 to 10 hours (Kuala Lumpur) or 12 to 15 hours (Kota Bahru) respectively.

BY ROAD

From Thailand, it is possible to get buses from Bangkok or Hat Yai that cross the border at Padang Besar and travel to Penang or Kuala Lumpur, or at Sungai Golok on the East Coast. From Singapore, there are buses which travel to peninsular Malaysia from the Ban San Street terminal, Singapore. For more information call: (65) 6292 8151.

Long-distance taxis also run from Queen Street in Singapore, although you will get a better bargain by taking the bus to Johor Bahru across the Malaysian causeway and taking a taxi from there.

Alternately, you can rent a car in either Thailand or Singapore and have complete freedom during your stay in Malaysia. The North-South highway makes travelling along Peninsula Malaysia's west coast a breeze – with trips from the Thai border to Singapore possible in about 10–12 hours. However, try to avoid border crossing on Friday afternoons or during public holidays as there can be bad congestion.

Practical Tips

Media

Newspapers & Magazines

The main daily newspapers are in Bahasa Malaysia and English. There are also Chinese and Tamil language newspapers. The *New Straits Times* is the voice of the government, but it is difficult to be otherwise when all media have to apply annually to renew their operating licence under the Printing and Presses Act. The other big English language national daily is *The Star*. Business papers include *The Edge* and *Business Times*. The *Malay Mail* is an afternoon tabloid with a more chatty, local slant. Sabah and Sarawak have their own papers, including *The Sabah Times*, *Sabah Daily News*, *Daily Express*, *People's Mirror*, *Sarawak Tribune* and *Borneo Post*.

Most of these papers have online editions; *The Star Online* is one of the most popular websites for Malaysian news. Foreign newspapers and magazines can be purchased in large cities.

Postal Services

Malaysia postal services are quick and reliable. There are post offices in all state capitals and in most cities and towns. All post offices, including the General Post Office in Kuala Lumpur, open from 8am–5pm (Mon–Sat).

Most large hotels provide postal services, and stamps and

Emergency Number

In an emergency, the charge-free number to call is **999** for ambulance, fire or police.

Tourist Information in Malaysia

Tourism Malaysia
(www.tourism.gov.my) has offices
throughout Malaysia. They vary in
the literature they offer, but they
usually have brochures on local
places of interest. Regional
offices can also be contacted for
details of reputed tour operators
and travel companies, most of
which are registered with them.
Kuala Lumpur Head Office
24–27th & 30th Floor, Menara
Dato' Onn, Putra World Trade
Centre, 45 Jalan Tun Ismail.
Tel: (03) 2693 5188,
e-mail: tourism@tourism.gov.my
**Malaysia Tourist Information
Centre** (MTC), 109 Jalan Ampang
KL. Tel: (03) 2164 3929,
e-mail: ticmtc@tourism.gov.my
East Coast Region
5th floor, Menara Yayasan Islam
Terrengganu, Jalan Sultan Omar,
Kuala Terengganu
Tel: (09) 622 1893
e-mail: mtpbkt@tourism.gov.my

Northern Region
10 Jalan Tun Syed Sheh
Barakbah, Penang
Tel: (04) 261 9067
e-mail: mtpbpen@tourism.gov.my
Southern Region
Suite 5-2, Johor Tourism,
Information Centre, 2 Jalan Ayer
Molek, Johor Bahru
Tel: (07) 222 3591
e-mail: mtpbjhb@tourism.gov.my
Sabah
Ground Floor, EON CMG Life
Building, 1, Jalan Sagunting, Kota
Kinabalu. Tel: (088) 248 698
e-mail: mtpbbki@tourism.gov.my
Sarawak
2nd Floor, Rugayah Building, Jalan
Song Thian Cheok, Kuching.
Tel: (082) 246 575
e-mail: mtpbkch@tourism.gov.my
   In addition, both Sabah and
Sarawak operate independent
tourism offices. For Sabah, check
www.sabahtourism.com and for
Sarawak, www.sarawaktourism.com

aerogrammes are often sold at the
small Indian sweet and tobacco
stalls on street corners.

Telecommunications

Coin operated public phones can be
found in most towns, often in front
of restaurants. Many also accept
credit cards and/or telephone
cards. Long-distance and
international calls can be made
from post offices, hotels and some
public phones.
   A 24-hour Kedai Telekom, at the
Central Telegraph Office, Bukit
Mahkamah, is available in the town
centre of Kuala Lumpur. For further
enquiries, call 102, Telekom's 24-
hour enquiry line. Cybercafés and
hotels in the main tourist areas
provide Internet access.

Medical Treatment

Medical supplies are widely and
readily available in Malaysia, and all
large towns have government
polyclinics as well as private clinics.

French- and German-speaking
doctors can be found by contacting
the relevant embassies. Travel and
health insurance, as well as
documents concerning allergies to
certain drugs should also be
carried. Should medical care be
required that is beyond the
capabilities of the hospitals in
Kuala Lumpur, world-class medical
care is available in Singapore, just
an hour's flight to the south.
   Below are also some hospitals in
the Kuala Lumpur area that have
24-hour outpatient emergency
services:
Assunta Hospital, Jalan Templer,

Petaling Jaya, Tel: (03) 792 3433.
Subang Medical Centre, 1 Jalan
SS12/1A, Subang Jaya, KL,
Tel: (03) 734 1212.
Tawakal Hospital, 202A, Jalan
Pahang, KL, Tel: (03) 423 3500.
City Medical Centre, 415-427,
Jalan Pudu, KL, Tel: (03) 222 0413.

Religious Services

Minarets, spires, domes and
steeples adorning the skyline of
Kuala Lumpur reflect a rich diversity
of faiths in Malaysia. Below is a
small selection of places of worship
in the Kuala Lumpur area. Hotels
and travel agents provide the times
of services and can help arrange
transport.
Kuala Lumpur Baptist Church, 70
Cangkat Raja Chulan, KL,
Tel: (03) 241 9154.
National Mosque (Masjid Negara),
Jalan Sultan Hishamuddin, KL.
Seventh Day Adventist Mission,
166 Jalan Bukit Bintang, KL,
Tel: (03) 242 7795.
Sikh Temple Maindaub, 75 Jalan
Pudu Lama, KL, Tel: (03) 238 7435.
Sri Maha Mariamman Temple
(Hindu), 163 Jalan Bandar, KL,
Tel: (03) 238 3467.
St Andrew's Presbyterian Church,
31 Jalan Raja Chulan, KL,
Tel: (03) 232 5687.
St Francis Xavier Church (Roman
Catholic), Jalan Gasing, Petaling
Jaya, Tel: (03) 757 7136.
St John's Cathedral (Roman
Catholic), Bukit Nanas, KL,
Tel: (03) 238 5089.
St Mary's Church (Anglican), Jalan
Raja, KL, Tel: (03) 292 8672.
Wesley Methodist Church, off
Jalan Hang Jebat, KL,
Tel: (03) 232 9982.

Embassies/Consulates in Kuala Lumpur

● **Australia**
6 Jalan Yap Kwan, Seng, KL
Tel: (03) 2146 5555
● **Canada**
7th Floor, MBF Plaza,
172 Jalan Ampang, 50450 KL
Tel: (03) 2161 2000
● **New Zealand**

193, Jalan Tun Razak, 50400 KL
Tel: (03) 2072 9917
● **United Kingdom**
186 Jalan Ampang, 50450 KL
Tel: (03) 2148 2122
● **United States**
376 Jalan Tun Razak, 50400 KL
Tel: (03) 2168 5000

Getting Around

On Arrival

Buses, public and private, taxis and even limousine services operate from major airports in Malaysia. Many airports have a taxi desk, where taxis can be booked and paid for and where the price is fixed. Where there is no such service, enquire at the information desk about how far the town is from the airport, and how much you should pay a taxi driver. Taxi fares from airports are in general much higher than around the town and if you are in a hurry to get to the airport, you may have to pay the taxi driver more to persuade him to take the expressways, because of the tolls.

Domestic Travel

BY AIR

Malaysia Airlines (www.malaysiaairlines.com) runs an extensive network of airways over the entire nation. In remote jungle areas, the Fokker 50s and Twin Otters operate services linking out-of-the-way places to national centres. Singapore Airlines, Royal Brunei, Cathay Pacific and Thai International have regular flights to Malaysian destinations other than Kuala Lumpur. Enquire at the appropriate offices. Below is a list of MAS offices in Malaysia for bookings and confirmations:

Alor Setar, Lot 180, Kompleks Alor Setar, Lebuhraya Darulaman, Kedah, Tel: (04) 731 1107, (04) 731 1186.

Ipoh, Lot G-01, Bangunan Seri Kinta, Jalan Sultan Idris Shah, Perak, Tel: (05) 253 0278.

Johor Bahru, Suite 1.1, Level 1, Menara Pelangi, Jalan Kuning, Taman Pelangi, Johor, Tel: (07) 331 0035.

Kota Bharu, Ground Floor, Komplek Yakin, Jalan Gajah Mati, Kelantan, Tel: (09) 748 3477.

Kota Kinabalu, 1st Floor, MAS Admin Building, off Jalan Petagas, Kota Kinabalu International Airport, Tel: (088) 239 310.

Kuala Lumpur, Bangunan MAS, Jalan Sultan Ismail, (24 hours) Tel: (03) 746 3000; Lot 157, 1st Floor, Complex Dayabumi, Jalan Sultan Hishamuddin.

Kuala Terengganu, No. 13, Jalan Sultan Omar, Terengganu, Tel: (09) 622 2266.

Kuantan, No. 7, Ground floor, Wisma Persatuan Bolasepak Pahang, Jalan Gambut, Pahang, Tel: (09) 515 6030.

Kuching, Lot 215, Jalan Song Thian Cheok, Sarawak, Tel: (082) 244 144.

Labuan, Lot No. 1, Wisma Kee Chia Jalan Bunga Kesuma Sabah, Tel: (087) 431 737.

Langkawi, GF5/GF44, Langkawi Fair Shopping Mall, Jalan Persiaran Putra, Kedah, Tel: (04) 966 8611.

Melaka, 1st floor, Hotel Shopping Arcade, City Bayview Hotel, Jalan Bendehara, Melaka, Tel: (06) 283 0654.

Miri, Lot 239, Beautiful Jade Centre, Sarawak, Tel: (085) 417 315.

Penang, Level 3, Krystal Point, Jalan Sultan Azlan Shah, Sungai Nibony, Penang, Tel: (04) 262 1405/6.

Sandakan, Mezzanine floor, Sabah Bldg., Jalan Pelabuhan, Sabah, Tel: (089) 273 907.

Sibu, 61 Jalan Tuanku Osman, Sarawak, Tel: (084) 321 055.

Tawau, First and Second Floor, TB 319 Block 38, Jalan Haji Sahabudin Fajar Complex, Sabah, Tel: (089) 765 533.

BY RAIL

Malaysian Railways, or Keretapi Tanah Melayu (KTM), runs right from the heart of Singapore's business centre, through the Malay peninsula and on into Thailand in the north, calling at major cities and towns including Kuala Lumpur. Another line, the East Coast line, branches off the main one at Gemas, plunges through the central forests and emerges eventually at Tumpat, near the border to Thailand.

Malaysian trains are generally comfortable, many equipped with televisions screening movie videos. Passengers can choose between air-conditioned first-class coaches or, on the night trains, first-class twin-berth cabins. In second class are fan-cooled sleepers and sleeperettes are in the third-class coaches. The passenger has also the choice of travelling on a normal train which stops at most stations, or the express train, which stops only at major towns.

Public Transport

TAXI

Taxis remain one of the most popular and cheap means of transport. You can hail them by the roadside, hire them from authorised taxi stands, or book them by phone, in which case, mileage is calculated from the stand or garage from which the vehicle is hired.

Although most taxis are fitted with meters, not all drivers use them. Make sure that your driver is willing to use his meter, or negotiate a charge at the beginning of the journey.

There is a surcharge for a telephone booking and traffic jams,

Railpass

For foreign tourists, KTM offers a railpass that entitles the holder to unlimited travel in any class and to any destination for a period of 10 or 30 days. For more information, call the KTM central information line. Tel: (03) 2267 1200, 2263 1267, Fax: (03) 2710 5716, e-mail: passenger@ktmb.com.my, www.ktmb.com.my.

trips between midnight and 6am will have a 50 percent surcharge and there could be a small additional charge for more than two passengers.

From most airports and railway stations, taxi fares are fixed and you should prepay at the taxi counter. For 24-hour taxi service in Kuala Lumpur, call:
Comfort Taxi Tel: (03) 8024 2727
New Supercab Tel: (03) 7875 7333
For taxi complaints, call (03) 255 4444.

BUS

There are three types of buses that operate in Malaysia: the non-air-conditioned buses that travel between the states, the non-air-conditioned buses that provide services within each state, and the air-conditioned express buses connecting major towns in Malaysia. Buses seldom adhere to the schedule but are frequent between 9am to 6pm. Buses within towns and cities usually charge fares according to distance covered, with the exception of the mini buses in Kuala Lumpur, which charge a standard fare of.

Travelling by bus within Kuala Lumpur and to the surrounding areas of Petaling Jaya, Subang Jaya and Klang is definitely not for the faint-hearted. Published or posted timetables are a mystery to most, and listings of the stops or final destinations of each route are equally elusive, save for the signs carried on the front of each individual vehicle. However, for those determined to savour this fascinating grass-roots mode of transport within the capital and its environs, the experience is likened to an exhilarating roller-coaster ride, thanks to the drivers' daredevil attempts to meet their quotas, irrespective of traffic laws and other road users.

Kuala Lumpur bus terminals:
Eastcoast Express: Putra Bus Station (opposite the World Trade Centre), Tel: (03) 442 9530.

Water Transport

Traditionally, transport in Malaysia, particularly in the west, was by water. In Pahang, on the Endau River, and of course, in Sarawak, water transport still has some importance, but in general, roads have taken over as the main means of transport.

On rivers in peninsular Malaysia, you may find boats for hire, but often the best way is to find out which boats are going where and hitch a ride. Boat rental can sometimes be expensive, especially, for example, if you want a ride downriver. The boatman will be reluctant, because he has to motor all the way upriver again afterwards. He might prefer to sell the entire boat to you!

In Sarawak, there is a lot of traffic on the rivers inland throughout most of the year as roads are still few and far between and mostly in poor condition. On the Rejang River, regular boats run between Sibu and Kapit, and if the waters are high enough, all the way to Belaga. Boats to smaller rivers and to remote longhouses can be fearfully expensive, and it is best to go down to the jetty and see where all those women with

Eastcoast: Pekeliling Bus Station, Tel: (03) 442 1256.
North and Southbound: Pudu Raya Bus Station, Tel: (03) 230 0145.

Private Transport

CAR RENTAL

Having your own transport gives you the freedom to explore places off the beaten track at your leisure. Peninsular Malaysia has an excellent network of trunk roads and a dual-carriageway on the west coast. Driving is also enjoyable in Sabah and Sarawk, but you need a sturdy vehicle or even a four-wheel drive, and plenty of time. Visitors need an international driving licence.

baskets are heading for and change your plans accordingly.

Other regular ferry and boat services include boats to the islands of Pangkor, Penang and Langkawi. Boats to Pangkor stop running at 7pm, but ferries to Penang run 24 hours, and boats to Langkawi till 6pm.

Boats out to islands on the east coast are slightly less regular, especially in the monsoon season when several services may stop altogether.

There are services to the Perhentian Islands, Kepas, Redang and Tenggol in the north, and many boats run out to the islands off Mersing. Mersing boats can be a little confusing as there is a wide choice.

Boats to Tioman range from fishing boats that charge RM25 per person one way, or catamarans and ferries that cost RM30 and take 2 hours, to the hydrofoil which takes 75 minutes and costs around RM25.

Some of the other islands also have ferries (e.g. Rawa and Sibu) or you can hire a fishing boat to get there. The price of the boat is the same whether you are one person or 12 (maximum).

Malaysian drivers can be speed maniacs and bullies – the bigger the vehicle, the more so. Give way. In towns, motorcyclists can shoot out of nowhere or hog the road.

The principal car rental firms are listed here. Most have branches in the main towns throughout Malaysia including those in Sabah and Sarawak.

Cars are usually for rent on an unlimited mileage basis. Weekly rates are also available. Four-wheel drive is advisable in Sabah, Sarawak and the central regions of the Malay peninsula. The Automobile Association of Malasia (AAM) is the national motoring organisation and has offices in most states – it has a prompt breakdown service, tel: (03) 2142 5777.

Avis Rent A Car, 40, Jalan Sultan Ismail, Kuala Lumpur, Tel: (03) 2142 3500 (toll free: 1-800 881 054), fax: (03) 2142 9650, KLIA: (03) 8787 4087.

Hertz Rent A Car, Lot 214A, Kompleks Antarabangsa, Jalan Sultan Ismail, Tel: (03) 2148 6433, Fax: (03) 2148 8481, KLIA: (03) 8787 4572.

National Car Rental, Shop 9, Ground floor, President House, Jalan Sultan Ismail, KL, Tel: (03) 2148 0522, Fax: (03) 2148 2823, KLIA: (03) 8787 3890.

Pacific Rent A Car, Tel: (03) 2145 4119, (Freephone: 1-800 886 155), Fax: (03) 2145 1125, KLIA: (03) 8787 4393.

Security & Crime

Malaysia is an extremely safe place to visit. Lone female travellers will encounter few problems, and violent crime against either sex is very rare. Malaysia does not suffer from the theft problems of Indonesia and Thailand, but you should still exercise reasonable caution with your luggage and possessions. Topless bathing is not a good idea in Malaysia. Though not illegal, it will embarrass Malaysian families and sensibilities. And, as anywhere, it may attract unwanted attention from men.

Warning: Trafficking in illegal drugs can result in the death penalty, and many tourists have had holidays hastily curtailed by prison; a few have also been executed.

Where to Stay

Choosing a Hotel

The glut of hotels means that high-quality accommodation has become remarkably affordable. This has unfortunately pushed some medium-priced accommodation out of the market, but there is always plenty of budget accommodation.

Always enquire about packages, which include a buffet or local breakfast with the room, and if you stay more than one night, you can try bargaining for better rates.

Most five-star properties also have reduced rates if you're staying on a weekend (Fri–Sun).

Hotels are supposed to display net rates (including the 10 percent service and 5 percent government tax).

Price Guide

A general guide for a standard double room, excluding taxes.
$$$$ = above US$100
$$$ = US$50–100
$$ = US$30–50
$ = under US$30

Hotel Listing

KUALA LUMPUR

J W Marriott
183 Jalan Bukit Bintang
Tel: (03) 2715 9000
Fax: (03) 2715 7013
www.marriott.com
Centrally located luxury hotel with fabulous spa, and well-known Shook restaurant with four kitchens – Japanese, Italian, Chinese and grills. Also has Marriott Café on the adjacent Bukit Bintang Walk and a well-known tapas bar. **$$$$**

Mandarin Oriental
Kuala Lumpur City Centre
Tel: (03) 2380 8888
Fax: (03) 2380 8833
www.mandarinoriental.com
Set within the office/shopping complex featuring the world's tallest twin buildings, this hotel has 643 luxurious rooms and executive apartments, six restaurants featuring sumptuous buffets, a grill and bar, and a Cantonese restaurant specialising in seafood. **$$$$**

Regent of Kuala Lumpur
160 Jalan Bukit Bintang
Tel: (03) 2141 8000
Fax: (03) 2142 1441
www.regenthotels.com
KL's most elegant hotel sits on the fringes of bustling Bukit Bintang, and is well-known for its service and opulence. Classical music welcomes you in the lovely lounge; the gym has Roman baths; and the 469 rooms are tastefully furnished. **$$$$**

Concorde Hotel
Jalan Sultan Ismail
Tel: (03) 2144 2200
Fax: (03) 2144 1628
www.concorde.net
Central, busy hotel close to nightlife and trendy eateries. It has 673 rooms, and a popular coffee shop and lounge attracting spill-over weekend crowds from the nearby Hard Rock Café. **$$$**

Crown Princess
Jalan Tun Razak
Tel: (03) 2162 5522
Fax: (03) 2162 4687
www.fhihotels.com
At the far end of Jalan Ampang, this was probably the original hotel-in-a-shopping-and-business-complex and targets business travellers. It has 528 rooms and an award-winning Indian restaurant with great ambience. **$$$**

Federal Hotel
35 Jalan Bukit Bintang
Tel: (03) 2148 9166
Fax: (03) 2148 2877
www.fhihotels.com
Hotel shares the same age as Malaysia with a colourful history, situated right on Bukit Bintang. It has 450 rooms, a revolving lounge,

decent Chinese restaurant, full-window café that is great for people-watching, supper club showcasing golden oldies stars, and an 18-lane bowling alley. **$$$**

Pan Pacific Kuala Lumpur
Jalan Putra
Tel: (03) 4042 5555
Fax: (03) 4043 8717
www.panpac.com
Opposite the Mall and next to the Putra World Trade Centre with all-glass elevators on the exterior providing good views of this part of the city. It has 571 rooms, and is busy during conventions. **$$$**

Heritage Station Hotel
Bangunan Stesen Keretapi
Jalan Sultan Hishamuddin
Tel: (03) 2273 5588
Fax: (03) 2273 2842
Sitting among the graceful cupolas of the Kuala Lumpur Railway Station, this hotel has been extensively renovated. Although the rooms are smaller now, some of the old-style charm is retained in the furnishings and furniture, including its restaurants. **$$**

Hotel Capitol
Jalan Bukit Bintang
Tel: (03) 2143 7000
Fax: (03) 2143 0000
www.capitol.com.my
Part of the Federal group, this 240-room hotel is smack in the middle of Bukit Bintang, with no car park and a faceless lobby, but it has a one-stop service to answer all guests' needs; good restaurant and a café with gourmet sandwiches and coffee. **$$**

The Travellers Station
Kuala Lumpur Railway Station
Tel: (03) 2273 5588 (ext 3070)
e-mail: station1@tm.net.my
Decent backpackers' accommodation among the station's beautiful minarets, with hot showers, kitchen, laundry, Internet facilities, air-conditioned dormitories and rooms, and useful "diaries" with latest input by travellers. **$**

Where to Eat

What to Eat

All of Malaysia's medium-class hotels have decent eateries, the higher-class ones have good restaurants, while hotels at the very top of the range will probably have at least one Western outlet – but these are not listed here unless they are outstanding.

Hotels also usually offer high-tea at the weekend, and their coffee houses would have the usual buffet breakfast, lunch and sometimes dinner, to cater to value-for-money demand. Western fast food chains such as McDonald's, KFC and A&W are everywhere for those who cannot possibly stomach another scorcher of a curry, as are coffee-house chains like Coffee Bean, Starbucks and Gloria Jeans. There are also fairly decent burger stalls, run by Malay boys.

Otherwise, try the local fare, which is not only different according to where you are, but subdivide into regional varieties, too. The best often comes as hawker food, sold at street stalls or in coffeeshops; sometimes you can get authentic preparations in restaurants, but you miss out on the atmosphere of the roadside stalls. Restaurants charge a 10 percent government tax and 5 percent service tax.

Restaurant Listing

KUALA LUMPUR

Bombay Palace
388 Jalan Tun Razak
Tel: (03) 2145 4241/7220
Fine Indian food in a beautiful setting; with large variety of spicy and non-spicy meat and vegetable dishes, including North Indian breads. **$$**

Ciao
Jalan Tun Razak
Tel: (03) 9285 4827
Authentic Italian pasta and pizza in a candlelit bungalow; has some good wines. **$$$**

Esquire Kitchen
Level 1 Sungei Wang Plaza
Jalan Bukit Bintang
Tel: (03) 2148 4506
A variety of Chinese delicacies; well known for its *woh tieh* or fried dumplings. **$**

Fortune Palace
Melia Kuala Lumpur, Jalan Imbi
Tel: (03) 2142 8333
Cantonese and Szechuan specialities, with *dim sum* served both for breakfast and lunch. **$$**

Old China Café
11 Jalan Balai Polis
Tel: (03) 232 5915
Best time-trip café in KL, where the historical ambiance, old photos and memorabilia and marble-topped tables provide the perfect location for just as memorable *nonya* cuisine. Specialities include *laksa* (noodles in spicy gravy) and fish head in tamarind sauce. Try the delicious sago dessert called *gula melaka*. **$$**

Restaurant Price Guide

A general guide for dinner for two people, excluding beverages.
$$$ = above US$40
$$ = US$20–40
$ = under US$20

Rama V
5 Jalan U Thant
Tel: 03-2143 2663
Elegant Thai restaurant in the embassy area is a welcome oasis of lotus-filled ponds. Salads are wonderful, particularly the spicy catfish salad and the mango salad with glass noodles. **$$$**

Restoran Rasa Utara
Bukit Bintang Plaza
Tel: (03) 2148 8369
This chain serves Malay specialities, including satay, and spicy *sambal* and *rendang*; fully air-conditioned. **$$**

Restoran Seri Melayu
1 Jalan Conlay
Tel: (03) 2145 1833
A tourist-targeted outfit complete with Minangkabau roof and nightly cultural performances, but the food is decent; buffet available. **$$**

Scalini's
19 Jalan Sultan Ismail
Tel: 03-2145 3211
Where celebrities eat when in KL. Long-time excellent Italian restaurant where the food is authentic and served with style. The antipasto is memorable as is the beef carpaccio sprinkled with truffles. One of KL's best wine lists. **$$$**

Shook
Basement of Starhill shopping mall
Bukit Bintang
Tel: (03) 2716 8535
Part of the JW Marriott Hotel, this chic inclusion into KL's eating scene has 4 kitchens: Chinese, Japanese, Italian and Grills. It's spacious and contemporary and you can choose food from all the kitchens. **$$$**

The Mango Tree
4 Jalan Maarof, Bangsar Utama
Tel: (03) 2284 6268
Pioneer of contemporary cuisine in KL. Try the scamorza cheese on pitta bread, or squid-ink pasta with prawns. **$$$**

The Taj
Crown Princess Hotel
Jalan Tun Razak
Tel: (03) 2162 5522
Award-winning restaurant with an excellent menu, including vindaloo, tandoori and Goanese dishes in an authentic Indian setting and often with live music. **$$$**

Restaurant Price Guide

A general guide for dinner for two people, excluding beverages.
$$$ = above US$40
$$ = US$20–40
$ = under US$20

Culture

Museums

Malaysia has a host of museums. Most intriguing and most talked about is the Sarawak Museum in Kuching, founded in 1888 by the second white Rajah, Sir Charles Brooke, and the great evolutionist Alfred Russell Wallace. Their foresight resulted in the finest collection of Borneo artistry, and the museum is visited annually by more than 10,000 people.

Other museums worth visiting include Kuala Lumpur's Musium Negara (National Museum), with its life-sized displays of court and *kampung* life, the Malacca Museum, crowded with Menangkabau treasures and colonial mementos, the Perak State Museum in Taiping and the Abu Bakar Museum at the Grand Palace in Johor Bahru.

Most are open 9am–5pm daily, except for Fridays when they are closed between noon–2.30pm. Admission is free or at a nominal fee. Tours are rare, and information is usually in English and Bahasa Malaysia. Permission to view archives not on display can be obtained by consulting the curator. Call the Museum Information Office, tel: (03) 282 6255.

Art Galleries

Paintings on Malaysian art gallery walls mirror the traditional way of life, and the conflict with the new. Much can be gleaned about how young Malaysian artists envision the future. Batik painting is much favoured, combining an old art with contemporary scenes. But other media are equally popular, and range from watercolours of *kampung* scenes to abstract oil paintings to performance art.

The National Art Gallery is at Jalan Sultan Hishamuddin (opposite the Kuala Lumpur Railway Station). The Gallery is housed in the former Majestic Hotel built in 1932, and is now conserved under the National Heritage Trust. A collection of works by local and foreign artists is displayed. It is open daily 10am–6pm (closed on Fridays 12.45–2.45pm), and admission is free. Tel: (03) 2274 0157.

Besides the main public art galleries, there are many small galleries in towns, cities and artists' villages, where you can buy a painting from the artist himself. For more information, call the Ministry of Culture, Arts and Tourism, Tel: (03) 293 1515.

Festivals

It's difficult to say which is the most exciting spectacle – a blowpipe's bull's eye in the Borneo interior; a top that spins for 50 minutes under a makeshift canopy on Malaysia's east coast; an imperial howl at Penang's Chinese opera; or an Indian dancer with bells on her toes. In Malaysia, not only do all these occur, but several may be going on at the same time. The country has a public holiday nearly every month, not counting the market feasts, royal birthdays and religious processions that sprinkle calendar pages like confetti.

The Muslim calendar consists of 354 days in a year. The Chinese and Hindu calendars, unlike the Gregorian calendar, use the lunar month as their basic unit of calculation. Hence dates vary widely from year to year. These festivals and celebrations with variable dates probably include some of Malaysia's more exciting events. For immediate events, read the daily newspapers and *Kuala Lumpur This Month*, distributed free at leading hotels or look up www.tourism.gov.my.

Shopping

General

Shopping malls are found in every city and comprise a supermarket, department store (the big chains sell branded goods) and lots of little shops, including boutiques, shoe-stores, and stores selling watches, electrical goods, computers, mobile phones, music shops, bookshops and/or stationery/magazine stores, sometimes with money changers and tour agencies, cinemas and video-arcades. Some malls specialise in certain items. They usually have eateries, too, including hawker fare-type food courts, Western fast food chains, or restaurants.

Kuala Lumpur

From branded goods to rustic handicrafts, foodstuffs to software, Kuala Lumpur's shops have it all. The main shopping area is **Bukit Bintang** around Jalan Bukit Bintang and Jalan Sultan Ismail. Here you'll find **Bukit Bintang Plaza** (BB Plaza), which is joined to **Sungei Wang Plaza**, well known for its electrical items and photographic equipment. The more upmarket **Lot 10** is across the road from Sungei Wang Plaza with mid- to high-priced items and branded goods in the top floor; there's a good bookshop, too. Down the road is the even more upmarket **Starhill Centre**, with its international shops. Next door at **KL Plaza** is the American Tower Records, Kuala Lumpur's largest music store. Along Jalan Imbi, **Imbi Plaza** is the place for computer goods, including software and peripherals.

Central Market is probably the best place for souvenirs, with its two levels offering Malaysiana, Asian hand-crafted goods and souvenirs, and artwork. Kuala Lumpur's glitziest shopping mall to date is the modernistic Suria KLCC at the base of the Petronas Twin Towers, which houses all the big chains as well as interesting boutique shops, international cuisine and cosy cafés as well as cinemas.

Sogo Kuala Lumpur on Jalan Raja Laut is one of the largest department stores in Southeast Asia with eight floors, a waterfall on the top floor where the restaurants are, and good sales.

Down the road, **Pertama Complex** sells cheaper goods, but is good for shoes. **The Mall** on Jalan Putra opposite the Putra World Trade Centre is still popular for *haute couture* and specialist shops; there is a stuffy hawker centre on the top floor and souvenir stalls.

Jalan Tuanku Abdul Rahman has small interesting shops selling Asianware such as Chinese embroidery and antiques. The **Globe Silk Store** along this road has affordable clothes and textiles. Jalan Tuanku Abdul Rahman is closed to traffic every Saturday 5–10pm and transformed into a *pasar malam* (night market) with bargain goods hawked in stalls.

Jewellery, Indian saris and comfy cotton *kurta*-pyjamas are found behind this road in Masjid India. The famous and crowded **Petaling Street** *pasar malam* comes to life 5–11pm every evening, with a variety of stalls offering textiles, clothes, leather goods, jewellery, and "designer watches".

Melaka

Jonkers Street, once *the* place to shop in Melaka, has been a victim of money-driven urbanisation in recent years. Traditional craftsmen have been evicted and several historic shophouses have been demolished or else subject to sham restoration projects where only the facades are kept while the interiors been modified beyond recognition. Still, antique collectors and bargain-hunters will find what they want if they search hard enough. Authentic artefacts and relics, some over 300

Antiques and Curios in Kuching

Shopping is a Kuching speciality. Antiques, Iban textiles, handicrafts, and quality collectables as well as pretty and interesting handcrafted souvenirs are readily available in what is perhaps the best antique market in Malaysia.

Walking down the **Main Bazaar** can take all day for a shopping enthusiast. Old trading houses and shophouses have been converted and restored into galleries and shops selling a range of goods.

Look out for **Fabriko**, with Edric Ong's fine range of silk woven *pua* blankets, and scarves with authentic Iban motifs using natural dyes. **Nelson's Gallery** offers an eclectic collection – even if you don't buy, a meeting with this local character is a must. Margaret Tan's **Galeri M** in the Hilton Lobby has a fine collection of antique *pua*, jewellery and numerous collectables. Lucas Goh's **Atelier** opposite the Chinese museum is also filled with fine textiles and collectables, while **Arts of Asia**, in the Main Bazaar, has beautifully crafted wooden bowls, statues, and woodcarvings among its treasures. Richard Yong's **Sarawak House** has fine top-end pieces.

In addition there are several air-conditioned malls with lots of shops selling food, adventure gear and fashion items.

Don't miss Kuching's **Sunday market** which starts on Saturday afternoon. Held at Jalan Satok, the market is filled with Bidayuh vegetable sellers, Chinese and Malay stalls selling all manner of handicrafts, jungle products, wild honey, pets, snacks and plants.

years old, can be found along with a host of other more recent collectables.

Amid shops selling traditional crafts are trendy modern and creative handicraft shops such as the **Orang Utan House** at No. 59, run by an artist whose humorous T-shirts and artwork make great souvenirs. **Wah Aik Shoemaker**, formerly at No. 92, has unfortunately been demolished and moved to No. 103 Jalan Kubu, outside the main conservation area. This shop is famous for its tiny shoes made for Chinese women with bound feet, an ancient Chinese tradition of beauty that has long since died out.

Handicraft stalls are at **Taman Merdeka**, and there is a *pasar malam* on Sunday at **Jalan Parameswara**.

The city's biggest shopping mall is the **Mahkota Parade** at Jalan Merdeka, which also has an Asian antique and handicraft centre.

Penang

Georgetown's maze of little shops around **Jalan Penang** is great for antiques and curios, such as antique clocks, old bronze and brassware, chinaware, Dutch ceiling lamps, old phonographs and Chinese embroideries and porcelain and batik. **Saw Joo Aun** at 139 Jalan Pintai Tali has a large range of antique furniture.

Elsewhere in Penang, **Little India** on Lebuh King and Lebuh Queen has brightly coloured saris and *kurta*, brassware and jewellery. Chulia Street has good second-hand bookshops.

Chowrasta Market specialises in all kinds of cotton, silk and other materials, as well as dried local foods such as nutmeg and preserved fruits.

More bargain-price Chinese souvenirs are at the Kek Lok Si Temple in **Ayer Itam**. **Batu Ferringhi** and **Teluk Bahang** have brightly coloured, hand-painted batik sarongs and T-shirt souvenirs; the night market at the former sells fake but decent quality designer clothes and watches.

Night Markets

Open-air *pasar malam* (night markets) are good to soak in the local atmosphere and find bargain-price items, including clothes (which you try on in the open), shoes, trinkets, CDs and VCDs (often pirated) and household items. You can usually buy fresh produce, including fruit, and delicious local street food and titbits. The traders are itinerant, so check locations in the local press or at your hotel.

Modern shopping malls are at **KOMTAR**, **Yaohan** and **Gama** on Jalan Penang, the **Midlands Shopping Mall** on Jalan Kelawei, the suburban **Sunshine Square** in Bayan Baru and **Bukit Jambul Complex**, which also has an ice-skating rink.

Johor Bahru

Like KL, Johor Bahru is home to giant shopping malls, the biggest of which is the 440-unit **Holiday Plaza** on Jalan Dato Suleiman. Another popular spot is the Plaza Pelangi in Taman Pelangi.

The new Johor **Bahru Duty Free Complex** on Jalan Ibrahim Sultan (Stulang Laut) which comprises multiple facilities, sits on a 160-metre (540-ft) waterfront, and includes 180 of the usual kind of shops over four floors.

Bargain-hunters head for **Kompleks Lien Hoe**, just off Jalan Tebrau, which has a bazaar on the ground floor.

JARP (Johor Area Rehabilitation Organisation) on Jalan Sungai Chat has a showroom and workshop where handicapped people produce cane furniture, soft toys, rattan baskets as well as bind books. Commercialised handicrafts are at **Mawar House** on the same road.

There is a *pasar malam* (night market) on Jalan Tebrau every Monday.

Terengganu

Jalan Bandar is the place to head for, with the Central Market selling batik and local handicraft.

Teratai Arts and Craft, at No. 151, is a lovely gallery/shop owned by renowned artist Chang Fee Ming. It showcases his depictions of local life, as well as curios from all over Asia, including coconut shell craft and textiles.

The **Batik Gallery** next to the Chinese temple has contemporary hand-printed batik cotton material and souvenirs as well as interesting clothing designs beyond the usual *kaftan* and shapeless shirts.

Kelantan

Like Terengganu, Kota Bharu's **Central Market** has copious amounts of batik and foodstuffs. The ultimate handicraft heaven is the road to PCB (Pantai Cahaya Bulan), along which certain *kampung* are renowned for their particular handicraft – grab a Tourism Malaysia brochure.

Kota Kinabalu

Kota Kinabalu is more orientated towards adventure and relaxation than shopping. Several air-conditioned plazas have an array of shops selling locally made clothes and some international brands.

Some handicraft shops can be found in the **Wisma Karamunsing** and the **Wisma Merdeka** where Borneo Books has the best range of books on the country. **Borneo Handicraft** has plenty of handicrafts but purists will find that most come from Bali.

The **Filipino Market** offers an interesting excursion into the more colourful side of Kota Kinabalu – pearls (some genuine), Filipino handicrafts, basketware and shell crafts abound. But beware of pickpockets; there have been reports of bag-snatching and worse.

Nightlife

Pubs, discos and karaoke dens are how Malaysians party at night. The best nightlife is in the capital. Elsewhere, the action concentrates in hotel lounges and discos. Other than in Kuala Lumpur, people tend not to dress up, but shorts and sandals are definite no-nos.

Nightclubs/Discos

Kuala Lumpur

Nightlife has tended to congregate in specific areas. Clubs and discos may be the trendsetters, but they have a shorter shelf-life and pubs stick around longer, particularly the neighbourhood ones. Generally, club crowds swell after 11pm or even midnight, and there is a cover charge on Friday and Saturday, which includes one drink from a limited menu. In most places, jeans, shorts, collarless T-shirts and sandals are not allowed, and the yuppies dress to kill.

Live bands are popular and usually play three sets from 10pm onwards. Almost all the larger hotels have bars featuring live music. This is usually broad-appeal, middle-of-the-road music, so hotel lounges are not listed here unless

Bangsar – the Place to Party

The most "happening" place in Kuala Lumpur is a suburb south of the city centre called Bangsar, where the young and not-so-young but totally trendy hang out. Here, back-to-back are bars, coffee bars, restaurants and art galleries, whose names you don't bother remembering because the sky-high rents ensure they don't last anyway. This is where the

they have a reputation for something different.

Pub- or club-hopping has long been happening in the Jalan Sultan Ismail/Jalan Ampang area. The Rennaisance Hotel's basement **Roxy** plays techno and features dancers. Across the road is the **Hard Rock Café** at Concorde Hotel, with great local and international live acts and a small dance floor. The hot dance clubs along this stretch include **Emporium**, **Beach**, **Nuvo**, **Twelve SI** and the **Grand Modestos**.

The Backroom behind Shangri-La plays techno and house at the front section, and jungle/rave at the back, and has a young following. At KL Hilton, the older, more sophisticated crowd grooves to live 1980s sounds at the **TM2 Fun Bar & Nite Club**. The Bukit Bintang area has the open-air relaxed, café-type **Blues Café** at the bottom of Lot 10, which sometimes has good live acts. **Sydney Two Thousand** at Jalan Bukit Bintang is a converted movie theatre that reverberates with non-stop techno. Head out to the Bukit Damansara suburb for the country's top jazz act at a basement place called **All That Jazz at Grubz**, where local and international personalities perform with the resident band.

Penang

This is not really a town with a sizzling nightlife. Most of the action tends to centre on the beach hotels, such as the trendy **Modesto's** at Paradise Sandy Bay or **Beers** at Parkroyal Hotel. In town,

expatriates hang out and, like bees to the honey pot, the so-called *sarong* party girls, whom they pick up (or vice-versa). There's always a shortage of parking and lots of partying here. At one end is a huge all-night hawker centre with Malay and Indian fare, to which the bleary-eyed and not-so-sober retire when the party ends.

20 Leith Street, housed in a beautifully renovated colonial mansion, has a beer garden in front and a cosy bar that spins out some great music. Elsewhere in Georgetown's backpacker alley, there are little Chinese watering holes. Bear in mind, however, that some of these are of dubious nature.

Pulau Langkawi

Nightlife concentrates in Pantai Cenang and Tengah, at the little restaurants such as **Beach Garden**, **Champor-Champor** and the beachside, coconut-tree strewn **Charlie Bar's** at the end. There is a disco at **Holiday Villa**, while for good jazz and a great atmosphere, visit **Barn Thai**.

Cherating

The action focuses on Kampung Cherating, and usually starts at **Pop Inn** at the northern end, where a live band plays from Thursday to the weekend, moves on to the dimly lit **La Pippin** down the road, and usually ends up in the wee hours at **Nan's Beach Bar**, behind Coconut Inn. The **Moon's Deadly Nightshade** is a tiny hillside bar-restaurant in a rough *attap*-roofed open setting with great ambience.

Kuching

Kuching is a relaxed town where the friendly inhabitants like to enjoy themselves. A popular stop for visitors is the **De Tavern** opposite the Hilton. **Hornbill's Cafe and Corner Pub** is also a popular meeting place with both locals and visitors on Jalan Ban Hock. Pubs, discos and karaoke bars abound, from the more upmarket venues in the big hotels like the Hilton to small, dimly lit places that hide between bigger buildings.

Kota Kinabalu

In Kota Kinabalu try **The Cottage** on Jalan Bukit Pandang, a popular gathering place for both locals and visitors, or the lively pub at the **Pan Pacific Hotel**.

Getting Acquainted

The Place

Situation The small state of Brunei is along the northwest coast of Borneo, bordering the South China Sea and Sarawak.
Area 5,770 sq km (2,228 sq miles), one of the smallest countries in the world.
Terrain Around 70 per cent of Brunei is rainforest.
Capital Bandar Seri Begawan.
Population 336,000, of whom around 62 percent are Malays and 15 percent Chinese. The rest are Indians and indigenous tribes. There are also round 250,000 expats in Brunei.
Language Malay, but most people also speak English.
Religion Muslim.
Time Zone The same as Singapore and Malaysia, 8 hours ahead of Greenwich Mean Time, so New York is 13 hours, Los Angeles 16 hours and London 8 hours behind, Australia 2 hours ahead.

Business Hours

The overlap of Muslim custom and modern business makes opening hours a bit complicated.
Government offices open 7.45am–12.15pm and 1.30–4.30pm Monday–Thursday, and Saturday. Closed on Friday and Sunday. During the Muslim fasting month of *Ramadan*, open 8am to 2pm.
Private offices follow 8am–5pm business hours weekdays.
Shops open 8am–6pm Monday–Saturday; some close at 9pm.
Banks 9am–3pm Monday to Friday, 9–11am on Saturday.

Currency Brunei dollar (B$), tied to the Singapore dollar, which is accepted in many outlets.
Weights and Measures Metric.
Electricity 220–240V, using three square-pin plugs.
International Dialing Code 673.

The People

The majority of Bruneians are Malay, with similar customs and beliefs as the inhabitants of Malaysia. Brunei is strictly Muslim, so the state is more or less dry of alcohol, and pork is banned. As even offering booze to Bruneians is against the law, non-Islamic restaurants display signs that they are not for Muslims. Nightlife is virtually non-existent, and unmarried Brunei couples are forbidden to hold hands in public.

But although strictly Muslim, Brunei is hospitable to visitors and tolerates other religions. In deference to the country's beliefs, however, visitors should adhere to the following codes of conduct:

● Remove shoes before entering a mosque or private home.
● Never walk in front of someone at prayer nor touch the *Koran* in a mosque.
● Do not pound the right fist into the left palm.
● Avoid pointing or beckoning someone with your index finger. Use a clenched fist with your thumb sticking out instead.
● To call someone towards you, wave your entire hand with the palm facing down.
● Members of the opposite sex do not shake hands in Brunei, while men prefer a light handshake rather than the vigorous shake that is common in the West.

Climate

The climate is hot, humid and sunny all year round. The rainy season is in November and December. April to July is usually the driest period. Temperatures can range from as high as 32°C (90°F) in the day to 22°C (71°F) at night.

Public Holidays

● **1 January** New Year's Day
● **January/February** Chinese New Year
● **23 February** National Day
● **31 May** Anniversary of the Royal Brunei Armed Forces
● **15 July** Sultan's birthday
● **25 December** Christmas Day

Various Muslim festivals, such as Ramadan, are celebrated as public holidays. They are subject to the lunar calender and thus change from year to year.

Government

Brunei is a monarchy, ruled by the Sultan. Democratic elections do not exist, however – the last was in the 1960s – and the Sultan's brothers are also ministers. The judicial system, based roughly on the British judiciary, is presided over by the Supreme Court and Magistrate's Court, with breaches of Islamic law tried by special courts *(shariah)*.

Economy

Although around three-quarters of the country's food has to be imported, Brunei is one of the richest nations in the world. Oil is its livelihood, with Brunei Shell Petroleum its largest employer and exporter. The Sultan of Brunei is stupendously wealthy, and all Bruneians have a high standard of living, with good wages, free healthcare, schooling and pensions and no income tax. Although plans are afoot for when the oil supply dries up – most notably rice plantations, forests and beef production – the prospect of a Brunei without oil is still a long way off. That means prices are high for the budget-conscious traveller.

Planning the Trip

Visas & Passports

Citizens of Belgium, Canada, Denmark, France, Indonesia, Italy, Japan, Liechtenstein, Luxembourg, Maldives, Netherlands, New Zealand, Norway, Oman, Philippines, Republic of Korea, Spain, Sweden, Switzerland and Thailand do not need a visa for a stay of up to 14 days.

British, German, Singaporean and Malaysian passport holders can stay for 30 days without visas. Australians with confirmed tickets to a third country can apply for a transit visa valid for 72 hours on arrival. They can obtain a 14-day visa on arrival, but it is preferable to arrange one before travelling, and compulsory for visits exceeding 14 days.

All visitors must have onward/ return tickets and sufficient funds to support themselves while in Brunei.

Holders of other passports must have a valid visa. These are obtainable at Brunei embassies overseas. If there is no embassy in your country, try the nearest British diplomatic mission.

Customs

Duty-free allowances for Brunei (for those 17 or over) are 200 cigarettes, 50 cigars or 250 grams of tobacco, and 60ml of perfume. Foreigners are allowed to bring in 1 litre of wine or spirits for their own use. Narcotics, weapons and pornography are strictly forbidden. Drug trafficking carries the death penalty.

Health

Brunei is a safe country from a health and hygiene point of view. Standards of healthcare are good, but visitors are advised to drink bottled water and to take out private medical insurance.

Money Matters

The Brunei dollar is on a par with the Singapore dollar. It comes in denominations of 1, 5, 10, 50, 100, 500, 1,000 and 10,000 dollar notes and 1, 5, 10, 20 and 50 cent coins. Credit cards are widely accepted.

What to Wear

Light cotton or summer clothes are ideal. Women should cover their head, knees and arms when entering a mosque, and generally refrain from wearing shorts, mini-skirts or sleeveless dresses. For men, bathing trunks, shorts and tank top T-shirts are frowned upon when worn away from the beach or pool. Men may be require suits and ties at some formal occasions.

Getting There

BY AIR

Brunei International Airport in Bandar Seri Begawan is well served

Women Travellers

Brunei is a very safe country to travel around, even for the lone female visitor. Though Muslim, Bruneian women are less conservative than their counterparts elsewhere in Southeast Asia, and because there is such a substantial expatriate population, the men here are tolerant of Western ways. Pay heed to Muslim sensibilities, though, by dressing modestly in public places*.

by regional Asian airlines. Royal Brunei Airlines flies to over 30 destinations. There is a B$12 airport tax (B$5 for flights to Singapore and Malaysia) payable on departure. Infants below two years of age are exempted.

BY SEA

Ferries travel daily between Bandar Seri Begawan and Labuan, a tax haven island off the southwest coast of Sabah. A speedboat goes to Lawas, the northernmost port in Sarawak, from where you go by bus or taxi to Kota Kinabalu. Fast ferries to Labuan and Limbang are boarded in the municipal pier in Bandar Seri Begawan or at Muara port.

Tourist Information Abroad

Tourist information on Brunei is limited. There are no tourist offices abroad, but you can obtain brochures and general leaflets from Brunei's diplomatic offices in your home country:
● **Canada**
395 Laurier Avenue East, Ottawa, Ontario K1N 6R4.
Tel: 613-234 5656.
● **United Kingdom**
19/20 Belgrave Square, London SW1X 8PG.
Tel: (020) 7581 0521.
● **United States**
3520 International Court NW,

Washington DC 20008.
Tel: 202-237 1838.
   Useful publications available from them on request include: *Brunei Darussalam in Profile* (facts and figures on the country), *Brunei Darussalam in Profile* and *Selamat Datang*.
   If you intend an extended stay in the country, however, your best bet is to wait until you arrive and get hold of a copy of *Brunei Darussalem, A Guide*, an excellent guide published by Brunei Shell (see *Tourist Information in Brunei*, over the page).

Practical Tips

Media

Newspapers
Foreign magazines and yesterday's newspapers are sold in BSB. English-language publications available are the *Daily News Digest*, the independent daily *Borneo Bulletin* and the fortnightly *Brunei Darussalam Newsletter*.
Television and radio
TV is a diet of Brunei and Malaysian programmes only. One of Brunei's two radio channels broadcasts in English from 6.30am to 8.30am and 2pm to 8–10pm. Broadcasts are interspersed with the Muslim call to prayers five times daily.

Foreign Embassies

● **United Kingdom**
Hong Kong Bank Building, Jalan Sultan, Bandar Seri Begawan. Tel: (02) 226 001.
● **United States**
3rd floor, Teck Guan Plaza, Jalan Sultan. Bandar Seri Begawan. Tel: (02) 229670.

Tourist Information in Brunei

The Brunei Tourist Information Bureau has an office at the airport that is open during normal business hours. *Explore Brunei* is the goverment's guide, with a good map of Bandar Seri Begawan.

● Brochures and information are also obtainable from:
The Tourism Development Division, Ministry of Industry & Primary Resources, Jalan Mentiri Besar, Bandar Seri Begawan 3910, Brunei Darussalam.

Tel: (02) 382 822.
Fax: (02) 382 824.
www.visitbrunei.com

● If you are staying for a while, the best source of information is *Brunei Darussalam, A Guide*. Published by Brunei Shell, it is written for expats based in Brunei and has good suggestions for places to visit and day trips. Though sold in bookshops, it can be difficult to find, but you can buy a copy from Brunei Shell in BSB, opposite the Hong Kong Bank.

Telecommunications

Domestic and international calls can be made from phone booths at the Telecom office next to the post office in Bandar Seri Begawan, on the corner of Jalan Sultan and Jalan Elizabeth Dua. There are a few public phones from which international calls can be made, and phone cards for these are available in denominations of B$10, 20, 50 and 100. You can send telegrams and faxes from most of the Telecom offices or from hotels. Rates are very high.
International access codes:
AT&T: 800 1111; MCI: 800 011; Sprint: 800 015.

Postal Services

Post offices are plentiful in all areas of Brunei. The main post office in Bandar Seri Begawan opens 8am–4.30pm daily except Friday (8–11am and 2–4.30pm) and Sundays, when they are all closed.

Medical Treatment

Medical standards are high in Brunei and, unlike in the rest of Southeast Asia, there is no risk of malaria. RIPAS Hospital and Jerudong Park Medical Centre are comparable to the best in Asia, and there is a nationwide network of smaller hospitals and clinics.

Getting Around

From the Airport

Brunei International Airport is about 12 km (8 miles) from the centre of Bandar Seri Begawan. Normal travel time into the city is 15–20 minutes. Taxis cost B$25–35. Hotel transport is normally available if you provide the hotel with your flight number and arrival time.

Public Transport

The Brunei Bus Service charges a B$1 flat rate for any distance in one route. It starts at 6am and ends at 9pm. The buses run at intervals of 15–20 minutes.

TAXIS

Metered taxis cost B$3 for the first kilometre. Fares range from B$10 for a short trip in the city centre to more than B$100 for a journey from Bandar Seri Begawan to Kuala Belait.

Private Transport
CAR RENTAL

Car hire agencies at Brunei International Airport and the major hotels charge B$100 per day for an economy-sized sedan. Cars with drivers cost B$360 a day (10 hours). Petrol is cheap in Brunei.

Water Transport

Between the Bandar Seri Begawan waterfront to Kampong Ayer, the standard fare for a boat trip is 50 cents. For charter journeys, the price is negotiable, ranging from B$15–20 per hour.

Shopping

Culture

What to Buy

Brunei specialities include textiles, baskets, brocade, silver and brass. For a one-stop shop for such souvenirs, Brunei Arts and Handicrafts Training Centre is a two-minute drive east of downtown Bandar Seri Begawan. Prices tend to be higher than elsewhere in Southeast Asia. Import tax on luxury goods has been abolished.

Where to Buy

Experience the open air local market alongside the Kianggeh River or the night market opposite it. The following is a list of recommended department stores and supermarkets.

Hua Ho has two branches in Gadong and one at Sengkurong.

First Emporium, Mushammad Yussof Complex, B.S.B.

Gadong Centrepoint, Jln Gadong, B.S.B.

Liang Toon, Latiffudin Complex, Jln Tunku Link, B.S.B.

Yayasan Suktaan Haji Hassanal, Bolkiah Complex, B.S.B.

Kota Mutiara Dept Store, Darussalam Bldg, B.S.B.

Millimewah Dept Store, Darussalam Bldg, B.S.B.

Seria, Seria Plaza, Jln. Sultan Omar Ali, Seria.

Museums

Brunei Museum 6km from the centre of BSB, houses a collection of 15th-century Bruneian artefacts, with an interesting section on oil. Open 9am–5pm daily, except Monday (when it is closed) and Friday when it opens 9.30–11am and 2.30–5pm. Buses run from the central station to the museum.

Malay Technology Museum, next door, sits on the riverbank and centres round the technologies and livelihood of the water villages of Brunei. Open 9am–5pm daily, except Tuesday (when it is closed) and Friday when it opens 9–11.30am and 2.30–5pm.

Brunei History Centre traces the history of the Sultan and his family. Open Monday to Thursday and Saturday 8am–12.15pm and 1.30–4.30pm. Admission is free.

Getting Acquainted

The Place

Situation Tip of the Malaysian peninsula on the Strait of Malacca.
Area 682 sq kilometres (263 sq mi).
Population Nearly 4 million, of whom 76.8 percent are Chinese, 13.9 percent Malays, 7.9 percent Indians and the rest other ethnic groups.
Languages Malay, English, Tamil and Mandarin are official languages.
Religions Buddhism is the main religion, with Taoist elements. The Malay population is Muslim, and Indians Hindu, Muslim or Sikh. All Eurasians and significant numbers of Chinese and Indians are Christian.
Time zone 8 hours ahead of Greenwich Mean Time (GMT).
Currency Singapore dollars ($), divided into 100 cents.
Weights and measures Metric.
Electricity 220–240 volts, using several plug configurations, including 3-prong square, 2-prong flat, and 2-prong round.
International dialing code 65 (no area codes).

The People

The customs, religions and languages of nearly every nation in the world have converged in Singapore at some time in history, although Buddhism and Daoism are the most commonly practised religions. Adjectives beginning with

Singlish

It may sound like a machine-gun rattle, but it's actually English. Singaporeans blend words, disregard syntax and add "*lah*" to about everything.

"multi" are commonplace on the Singapore scene, and a cosmopolitan tolerance is part of the city's character.

With everyday etiquette relaxed and straightforward, visitors behaving courteously stand little chance of unintentionally giving offense. Some ceremonies and special occasions, however, recall inherited traditions, and a familiarity with certain customs will set everyone at ease.

Climate

The average daily temperature is 27°C (81°F), often rising to around 30°C (86°F), and cooling only to around 23°C (73°F) at night. Humidity is high, averaging daily at 80 percent.

The northeast monsoon blows from November to January, and the southwest from May to September, and wind speeds are light all year.

Spectacular thunderstorms occur frequently between the monsoons, in April to May and October to November. The average rainfall is 2,352mm (93 in) with the heaviest rains falling between November to January, and the least falling in July.

Economy

Singapore is one of the world's busiest container ports with some 117,00 ships cruising in its Straits per year bringing with them around 768,500 tonnes of goods. As Singapore lacks natural resources, finance and business services (28 percent), manufacturing (24 percent), commerce (18 percent), transport and communications (10 percent) and construction (8 percent) are the backbone of its thriving economy, which consistently has an inflation rate of around 1.4 percent. Major trading partners include the US, Malaysia, European Union, Hong Kong and Japan.

Per capita GNP is US$37,988. Despite the seeming affluence – visible in the number of BMWs' and Mercedes' on the road and high penetration rate of mobile phones – Singapore's economy has been

affected by the US economic slowdown. In 2001, the unemployment rate hit a 15-year high of 4.7 percent.

It has a strong tourism industry with over 7 million visitors per year. The government's aim is to improve the already efficient infrastructure and become the business hub of Asia Pacific, with first-class products and services.

Business Hours

Offices 9am–5pm
Banks 10am–3pm weekdays, 9.30–11am Saturday. Some also open 11am–4pm Sunday.
Shops About 10am–8pm (most open on Sundays). Department stores usually open until 9pm.

Government

Singapore has a single-chamber parliamentary government, with general elections held every five years. The People's Action Party (PAP), in power since 1965, is led by Prime Minister Goh Chok Tong, who was elected in 1990. President S.R. Nathan is Head of State.

Public Holidays

● **1 January** New Year's Day
● **January/February*** Chinese New Year (two days)
● **March/April*** Hari Raya Puasa
● **March/April*** Good Friday
● **1 May** Labour Day
● **May/June*** Hari Raya Haji
● **May*** Vesak Day
● **9 August** National Day
● **October/November*** Deepavali
● **25 December** Christmas Day
On public holidays many restaurants and shops are closed. Bear in mind too that over Ramadan and the Chinese New Year accommodation and transport are usually booked.

* Variable depending on the Chinese, Muslim, Hindu or Christian calendars. Check with the tourist office for exact dates.

Planning the Trip

Visas & Passports

As long as you have a passport valid for six months, onward travel reservations and adequate finance, only citizens of Afghanistan, Algeria, Cambodia, India, Iraq, Jordan, Kuwait, Laos, Lebanon, Libya, People's Republic of China, Syria, Tunisia, Vietnam and Yemen are required to produce a visa. Holders of Russian Federation or People's Republic of China, Afghanistan, Vietnam, Laos and Cambodia passports may transit for 36 hours if they hold the relevant documents. Enquiries should be made at your nearest Singapore embassy for current details on these matters, which are regularly subject to change.

You will normally be given a 30-day tourist visa if arriving by air, 14 days by sea and land, so remember to check the date and renew if necessary at the Immigration Office, 10 Kallang Road, tel: 6391 6100; www.sir.gov.sg.

Customs

If you arrive from anywhere but Malaysia (from where there are no duty restrictions), you are allowed to import a litre of spirits, wine and beer duty-free. No duty-free cigarettes are allowed into Singapore, although they may be purchased on the way out.

Singapore is a duty-free haven, with many goods sold free of tax. But bear in mind that your own Customs will levy tax if you take home goods over a certain value, so check duty-free allowances with them before you travel.

Health

Singapore is as sparklingly clean as billed. Safe drinking water and strict government control of all food outlets make this a hygienic place to visit, but should the need arise, medical facilities are excellent. There are no reciprocal healthcare arrangements between Singapore and other countries, however, so you need to take out medical insurance before you set off.

Vaccination against yellow fever is necessary if you are arriving from a country where the disease is endemic.

Money Matters

The Singapore dollar is divided into 100 cents. Notes are in $1, $2, $5, $10, $20, $50, $100, $500 and $1,000 denominations, and there are $1 and 1, 5, 10, 20 and 50 cent coins. There are no restrictions on the amount of money you can bring in or out of Singapore.

Traveller's cheques are probably the best form of money to take, in US dollars or sterling. Banks and licensed money changers offer better exchange rates than hotels and you are never far from one or the other. Some shops will even accept traveller's cheques as cash. Major credit cards are widely accepted, and can be used to obtain cash at banks.

If you wish to deal with banks for your foreign currency transactions, it is advisable to do so on weekdays. Some banks do not handle such transactions on Saturdays, while others conduct them in small amounts only, based on Friday's rate.

What to Wear/Bring

Light summer clothes that are easy to move in are the most practical choice for a full day out in town. Men should wear a white shirt and tie, women a smart business suit, for office calls.

In the evening, only a few plush nightclubs and exclusive restaurants favour the traditional jacket and tie. Most hotels, restaurants, coffee houses and discos accept casually elegant attire. However, jeans, T-shirts, sneakers and shorts are taboo at some restaurants and discos. To avoid embarrassment, it is best to call to check an establishment's dress code in advance.

You really can travel light in Singapore, as shops are excellent and shopping is perhaps the national sport. Photographic film and developing are very cheap.

Tourist Information Offices Abroad

The Singapore Tourist Board produces a wealth of brochures, maps, travel details (including timetables) and other information, and has office in most countries. Alternatively, you can browse their website:
www.visitsingapore.com

● **Australia**
Level 11, AWA Building, 47 York Street, Sydney, NSW 2000
Tel: (02) 9290 2888
Fax: (02) 9290 2555
● **Canada**
Standard Life Centre, 121 King Street West, Suite 1000, Toronto, Ontario M5H 3T9

Tel: (416) 363 8898
Fax: (416) 363 5752
● **New Zealand**
3rd floor, 43 High Street, Auckland
Tel: (09) 358 1191
Fax: (09) 358 1196
● **United Kingdom**
1st floor, Carrington House, 126–30 Regent Street, London W1R 5PE
Tel: (020) 7437 0033
Fax: (020) 7734 2191
● **United States**
12th floor, 590 Fifth Avenue, New York, NY 10036
Tel: (212) 302 4861
Fax: (212) 302 4801

Getting There

BY AIR

Singapore's **Changi Airport** has been voted the world's best airport an extraordinary 14 consecutive years by Britain's *Business Traveller* magazine. In November 1990, the Airport's second terminal opened, enabling Changi Airport to handle over 24.5 million passengers smoothly and efficiently. The two terminals are linked by the Sky Train, an automated miniature rapid transit system with a track of 600 meters (2,000 ft); the first of its kind outside the USA and UK.

This airport is so efficient that one can be in the taxi – after clearing immigration, retrieving bags and passing through customs – in 15 minutes after landing.

The national carrier, **Singapore Airlines** (SIA), flies to 67 cities in 40 countries. In all, 58 airlines operate out of Changi, with 3,000 flights a week to 138 cities in 50 countries.

BY SEA

Arriving slowly by sea, as everyone did in days gone by, is a pleasant experience; sailing in past 600 or so other vessels lying at anchor, watching the skyline clarify into looming skyscrapers. Singapore is the world's busiest port in terms of tonnage. Most visitors arrive at one of the three terminals of the **Singapore Cruise Centre**, HarbourFront Centre, which can accommodate up to 1,000 passengers at a time.

BY RAIL

Down the west coast of Peninsular Malaysia by train and then over the Straits of Singapore on the causeway is a leisurely way to arrive. Daily train departures from Bangkok get you to Butterworth the following day, where you change trains. After arriving in Kuala Lumpur and a later departure, you arrive at the station at Keppel Road, Singapore, in the early morning. The journey from

Maps

There are several excellent free maps available around Singapore that feature detailed sections of parts of the city of interest to the visitor. Most bookshops also stock larger maps of Singapore and Malaysia.

Kuala Lumpur takes about 6 hours on the express train. The mail train takes 10 hours for half the price. For details call the **Malayan Railway Station**, tel: 6222 5165.

Eastern & Oriental Express: Introduced in 1993, the Orient Express is the ultimate $30 million recreation of a bygone age of elegant Asian rail travel. Decked out in the E&O livery of cream and racing green, it carries a maximum of 130 passengers on the two-night trip from Singapore to Kuala Lumpur, through the Cameron Highlands, southern Thailand up to Bangkok (or vice versa). The 42-hour, 1,943-km (1,205-mile) route was planned to enable its passengers to enjoy the best of Malaysia and Thailand's scenery during daylight hours. Side trips include Penang. Expensive!

For reservations call tel: 6392 3500 or check www.orient-express.com.

OVERLAND

There are good highways down the west and east coasts of Peninsular Malaysia crossing the causeway into Singapore. It's a fascinating drive, through oil palm and rubber plantations, past *kampongs* (villages) and dusty little towns, rather like Singapore used to be many years ago. Nowadays the contrast is immediate as you arrive in the clean, green and well regulated republic.

There are private air-conditioned buses running from Malaysia (Butterworth, Kuala Lumpur, Kuantan, Malacca, Mersing and Penang) to Singapore.

Practical Tips

Media

Newspapers and Magazines

The *Straits Times* and *Business Times* are good English-language dailies, with the tabloid *New Paper* appearing in the afternoons. The *International Herald Tribune* is available on the day of publication. One of the best sources of information on what's on is *8 Days*, a weekly magazine widely available. American, British, Australian, European and Asian newspapers and magazines are available at newsstands hotel kiosks everywhere, and bookstores such as MPH, Times, Kinokuniya and Borders. Borders, at the corner of Scotts and Orchard Road, is the largest and best bookstore in Singapore, with an extensive selection of international books and media. Tower Records at Pacific Plaza and Tower Books at Boat Quay have a good range, too.

Embassies

Please call to confirm opening hours before visiting.
● **Australia**
25 Napier Road.
Tel: 6836 4100.
● **Canada**
80 Anson Road, #14-00 IBM Towers.
Tel: 6325 3200.
● **New Zealand**
391A Orchard Road, #15-00, Ngee Ann City Tower A.
Tel: 6235 9966.
● **United Kingdom**
100 Tanglin Road.
Tel: 6473 9333.
● **United States**
27 Napier Road.
Tel: 6476 9100.

Television and Radio
There are eight programme channels, the ones in English being Channel 5, Channel i, Central and NewsAsia. Several radio stations feature English shows. One FM (90.5FM) features music and chat shows; Perfect 10 (98.7 FM) plays contemporary hits; FM92.4 (92.4FM) classical music; and Class 95 (95FM) classic hits. BBC World Service is on 88.9FM.

Postal Services

Singapore's postal system is advanced and fast. An aerogramme or airmail postcard to anywhere but the moon costs just 50 cents. Apart from postal services Singapore's post offices provide other services such as parcel delivery, traveller's cheques, local and foreign money orders, philatelic sales, posting box-mail collection, surface airlifted mail service, international bank drafts as well as a variety of postal products.

Telecommunications

Singapore is completely up to date and efficient in all kinds of telecommunications. The public telephone book has a wealth of information on what services are available. Most hotels and offices have fax machines, and almost every hotel room has an IDD phone, with 001 being the international code. For collect or person to person calls dial 104. For IDD country codes, dial 166.

There are three types of public pay phones: coin-operated phones

Useful Numbers

Fire/Ambulance 995
Police 999
Non-Emergency Ambulance Service 1777
Flight Information 6542 4422
Meteorological Office 6542 7788
Postal enquiries 1605
International Operator 104
Local Directory Enquiries 100
Time Announcing Service 1711

Post Offices

The main branches are at:
● Change Alley, 16 Collyer Quay, #02-02, Hitachi Tower.
Tel: 6538 6899.
Open Mon–Fri 8am–9pm; Sat 8am–4pm; closed Sun and public holidays.
● 1 Killiney Road.
Tel: 6734 7899.
Open Mon–Sat 9am–9pm; Sun and public holidays 9am–4.30pm.
● The post offices at Changi Airport, Terminals 1 and 2 are open daily 8am–9.30pm.
● Most other branches are open 8.30am–5pm on weekdays (Wed until 8pm) and 8.30am–1pm on Sat.

Most hotels provide basic mail service for letters and parcels. Call 1605 for information about postal rates and other services.

for local calls; card phones operated by phonecards enabling local, STD and IDD calls to be made; credit card pay phones for local, STD and IDD calls, found mostly at Changi Airport, major Singapore Telecom Service Outlets and Orchard Mall.

US International access codes: AT&T: 8000 111 111; MCI: 8000 112 112; Sprint: 8000 177 177.

Phone cards are available in $3, $5, $10, $20 and $50 denominations and can be used for both local and overseas calls. They can be purchased at newsstands, kiosks and street vendors.

Tourist Information

The **Singapore Tourism Board** (STB) has a wealth of free brochures, and staff are very helpful and knowledgeable. Its main centre is located at:
Tourism Court, 1 Orchard Spring Lane. Tel: 6736 6622.
Open: Mon–Fri 8.30am–5pm; Sat 8.30am–1pm.
www.visitsingapore.com

Medical Treatment

Standards of healthcare are excellent and most staff speak good English. **Singapore General Hospital** is on Outram Road. (tel: 6222 3322). Ask at your hotel for local doctors and dentists, or you could consult the Singapore Buying Guide (equivalent to the UK's Yellow Pages). Private clinics are dotted round the city, and you should keep all receipts for insurance claims.

Pharmacies, which stock most medicines, are open Monday to Saturday 9.30am–7pm.

Tipping

Tipping is not common practice in Singapore. Restaurants add a service charge to the bill. But you may wish to give a small gratuity to anyone who gives good service.

Religious Services

In multi-racial, multi-religious Singapore, most major religions have their adherents and hours of worship may be ascertained from the various temples, mosques etc. The Sunday services in English at St. Andrew's Cathedral are at 7am, 8am, 11am and 5pm. Services at the Catholic Cathedral of the Good Shepherd are at 8am, 10am and 6pm.

Fines

Singapore is an extremely safe place, and violent crime and theft are rare. But to keep these high standards, the country imposes fines on just about every misdemeanour: from smoking in public places and dropping litter, to crossing a road other than at a pedestrian crossing to, believe it or not, failing to flush a toilet!

Getting Around

Orientation

Singapore is an easy city to get around. The hardy walker can easily cover most areas of interest such as the Singapore River area, Chinatown, Civic District, Arab Street, Little India and the Orchard Road area on foot. These and all the outlying places of attractions can be reached easily with public transport (MRT and buses) or by taxi.

From the Airport

Changi Airport is linked to the city centre by the East Coast Parkway (20 minutes' travelling time) and to the rest of Singapore by the Pan-Island Expressway and Tampines Expressway.

There are five types of transport from the airport – private car, taxi, airport shuttle, public bus or MRT. At both Terminals 1 and 2, the **taxi** rank is situated on the same level as the Arrival Hall. A surcharge of $3/$5 applies in addition to the fare shown on the taxi meter. A taxi to the city centre will cost under S$20, excluding the S$3 or S$5 surcharge.

The comfortable airport shuttle called **Maxicab** operates between the airport and major hotels, with flexible alighting points in the Central Business District. Tickets

are S$7 for adults and S$5 for children and are available at the shuttle counters located at both terminals.

In Terminal 1, inclined travellators in the Arrival Hall lead to the Passenger Crescent, where a **private car** pick-up point is located. In Terminal 2 the car pick-up point is on the same level as the Arrival Hall.

In the basement of both terminals are bus depots with easy **public bus** connections to the city.

The **MRT** link to Changi Airport is situated underground between Terminal 2 and the future Terminal 3. Trains leave every 12 minutes and a ride to the city centre – City Hall station – takes about 27 minutes and costs S$1.40.

Public Transport

BY BUS & MRT

Singapore's public transport system is fast, efficient, comprehensive, spotlessly maintained and cheap. An especially helpful source for all information about the use of buses and the MRT is the **Transitlink Guide** which is available at most bookstores and newsstands. This booklet gives complete details of all bus and MRT routes and contains a section on public transport services to major tourist spots. Or call one of the following:
Singapore Bus Service (SBS)
Tel: 1800-287 2727
Trans-Island Bus Services (TIBS)
Tel: 1800-482 5433
Transit Link, Tel: 1800-767 4333
If you are going to be moving around a lot by public transport, it is convenient to buy a Transit Link ez-link card, which is a stored value

card for use on the MRT and buses. The ez-link card is available from all Transit Link offices at MRT stations and bus interchanges for S$15, of which S$5 is a non-refundable deposit. To use this card, tap it on the electronic readers located at MRT turnstiles or the entrances of buses. The electronic readers will automatically deduct the maximum fare. When exiting from MRT turnstiles and buses, tap the card again against the electronic reader and the unused portion of the fare is credited back to your card. You can top up the value of your card when it runs low.

BY TAXI

Taxis are plentiful, although you may have trouble hailing one in the street during rush hour and when it rains. Be aware that a string of surcharges apply: 50 percent extra from midnight to 6am; for trips leaving the business district; during peak hours; for advance bookings; Electronic Road Pricing (ERP) fees; and trips from the airport. Most drivers speak or understand some English. To book a taxi, contact:
Comfort, Tel: 6552 1111
CityCab, Tel: 6552 2222
TIBS, Tel: 6555 8888

Private Transport

In a bid to tackle congestion and keep down pollution, the government severely restricts city traffic. Don't bother to drive as car rentals are prohibitively expensive and the Electronic Road Pricing (ERP) system too difficult to understand if you're only going to be in the country for a few days.

Tours of the City

Various tours are available, the most popular of which is a four-hour trip taking in Orchard Road, Chinatown and Little India. There are also eight-hour island sightseeing tours, or you could choose something more

specialised, such as Singapore by night or a Raffles tour. Registered tourist guides (tel: 1800-736 2000) can give you a personal visit round the sites.
Tour operators include:
Holiday Tours, Tel: 6738 2622

RMG Tours,
Tel: 6220 1661
Singapore Explorer,
Tel: 6339 6833
Singapore Sightseeing,
Tel: 6336 9011
www.singaporetours.com.sg

Where to Stay

Choosing a Hotel

In terms of accommodation, amenities and service standards, Singapore's upmarket hotels easily compare with the best in the world. Deluxe, first-class and business-orientated hotels all have conference and business facilities, in-room computer ports, cable television and in-room IDD phones. If you arrive without prior hotel reservations, the Singapore Hotel Association counters at Singapore Changi Airport's Terminals 1 & 2 arrival halls can help with bookings. The counters are open from 7.30am to 11.30pm daily. Or simply call the hotel of your choice direct.

When making reservations directly – even from the airport – it is wise to ask for discounts or special rates. Rates are subject to 10 percent service charge, 4 percent GST (Goods and Service Tax) and 1 percent cess (tax).

Hotel Listing

Grand Hyatt
10 Scotts Road
Tel: 6738 1234
www.singapore.hyatt.com
A stone's throw from Orchard Road and its MRT station. Minimalist, almost stark decor, comfortable rooms and excellent service are its defining hallmarks. Restaurants serving Chinese, Italian, stylish mezza9 restaurant with elegant bar, coffee house, bar/club. Its free-form pool with lush gardens is a haven in this busy neck of the woods. **$$$$**

Raffles Hotel
1 Beach Road
Tel: 6337 1886
www.raffleshotel.com

The city's most famous and most expensive hotel, beautifully restored to its former grandeur with upmarket shopping annex, hotel museum and Victorian-style theatre. A total of 13 restaurants and bars offering continental and American-style deli foods, innovative Asian and local cuisines and lots of old-world atmosphere. **$$$$**

Ritz-Carlton Millenia
7 Raffles Avenue
Tel: 6337 8888
www.ritzcarlton.com
Striking modern hotel, with US$5 million dollar art collection and Singapore's biggest guest rooms (and stunning bathrooms with views to match). Located beside the Suntec conference centre. Restaurants serving New Asia cuisine, fine Cantonese, and a stylish café. The bar with a riveting glass sculpture as its talking point is perfect for after-dinner drinks. **$$$$**

Price Guide

A general guide for a standard double room, excluding taxes.
$$$$ = above US$150
$$$ = US$100–150
$$ = US$50–100
$ = under US$50

The Fullerton
1 Fullerton Square
Tel: 6733 8388
www.fullertonhotel.com
The city's former General Post Office, this restored landmark sits in the heart of the Civic District, along the Singapore River. Business travellers will appreciate its proximity to the financial district and its contemporary Art Deco interior filled with Philippe Starck fittings. Cafe, exquisite Chinese restaurant, trendy bar and exclusive fine-dining restaurant with stunning views. One Fullerton across the road entices with more waterfront dining options. **$$$$**

Carlton
76 Bras Basah Road
Tel: 6338 8333
www.carlton.com.sg

Close to museum district and the Chjimes entertainment area. Restaurants serving local, Western and Chinese food, 24-hour café. **$$$**

Crown Prince
270 Orchard Road
Tel: 6732 1111
www.crownprince.com.sg
Smack in the middle of Orchard Road and surrounded by shopping malls. Restaurants serving local, Continental, Japanese and Chinese food, 24-hour ice-cream parlour/restaurant. **$$$**

Marriott
320 Orchard Road
Tel: 6735 5800
www.marriott.com
Pagoda-roofed hotel at the corner of Scotts and Orchard Roads. Opposite the MRT station and perfect for shopping and nightlife. Popular café-restaurant with outdoor seating, distinguished Chinese restaurant serving *dim sum*. Famous Tangs department store is just next door. **$$$**

Mandarin Singapore
333 Orchard Road
Tel: 6737 4411
www.mandarin-singapore.com
Serious shoppers would do well to stay here as all the major malls and boutiques (and two MRT stations) are within walking distance. Continental cuisines served in Singapore's highest revolving restaurant; International and Chinese food available in speciality restaurants; lounge, 24-hour Chatterbox coffee house is noted for its local speciality of Hainanese chicken rice. **$$$**

Pan Pacific
7 Raffles Boulevard
Tel: 6336 8111
www.singapore.panpac.com
John Portman-designed hotel with grand atrium. Well located beside Suntec City, the island's biggest convention centre. Cantonese restaurant with grand views (from 37th floor), traditional-style Japanese restaurant, outdoor buffet dining, Italian and North Indian restaurant, bakery, coffee shop, lounge bar. **$$$**

Allson
101 Victoria Street
Tel: 6336 0811
www.allsonhotels.com.my/allson
Close to the museum district and
good value for money. Restaurants
serving local, continental, Chinese
and Thai food. **$$**

Hotel Rendezvous
9 Bras Basah Road
Tel: 6336 0220
www.rendezvoushotels.com
Four-star hotel next door to the
Singapore Art Museum and close to
the Civic District. Its Rendezvous
Restaurant is sure to delight diners
with its famous spicy *Nasi Padang*
(Indonesian-style rice and curries)
The spacious Palong Lobby Bar is
the ideal spot to relax after
sightseeing or a long business day.
$$

Phoenix
277 Orchard Road
Tel: 6737 8666
www.hotelphoenixsingapore.com
Excellent value for its fantastic
location on Orchard Road. Next
door is the Somerset MRT station.
All rooms have a personal
multimedia computer with email
and Internet access. Coffee house,
lobby lounge, pastry shop. **$$**

YMCA International House
1 Orchard Road
Tel: 6336 6000
www.ymca.org.sg
Situated in the colonial Civic District
close to Dhoby Ghaut MRT station –
a good location for shopping too.
There are conference facilities, a
coffee house, rooftop swimming
pool, fitness centre, squash and
badminton courts. **$**

Where to Eat

What to Eat

Singaporeans love to eat and their
preoccupation with culinary matters
means that finding good food here –
at the right price – presents no
problem. Whether you fancy *haute
cuisine*, ethnic foods, vegetarian or
spicy local dishes, you are sure to
find many great choices.

All hawker centres and food
courts – which have an astounding
variety of foods – are subject to
regular government health and
safety inspections, so you can be
well assured of hygienic standards
and fair selling practices.

Local favourites at these centres
include Hainanese chicken rice,
prawn noodles, fish ball noodles,
satay, fish rice porridge, barbecued
chicken wings and a wide range of
barbecued seafood including
lobster, prawns and fish.

The restaurant dining scene is
equally exciting, with fine-dining
French restaurants, simple bistro-
style food and Italian fare, East-
meets-West "fusion" cuisine as well
as a slew of Asian restaurants.

Several areas are host to a
variety of eateries. Among these
locations are **Ngee Ann City**
(Orchard Road), with at least three
floors of restaurants; **Boat Quay**,
Clarke Quay, **Empress Place**
Waterfront and **Riverside Point** with
rows of restaurants (all four are
strung along the Singapore River);
Ann Siang and Club streets (with a
number of nice dining spots); the
all-weather **Far East Square**,
Robertson Walk (off River Valley
Road); **Marina Bay** at One Fullerton
building; and of course, the ever-
popular **Holland Village**.

Restaurant Listings

Annalakshmi
Excelsior Hotel, 5 Coleman Street
Tel: 6339 9993
Wonderful setting for exquisite
vegetarian cuisine. Waiting staff are
actually dancers with a cultural
institute. Décor items in restaurant
are for sale. Lavish lunch and
dinner buffets. **$**

Blue Ginger
97 Tanjong Pagar Road
Tel: 6222 3928
A stylish modern restaurant in a
converted shophouse offering time-
honoured Peranakan cuisine. Very
good food but small portions; try
the fresh mackerel simmered in
spicy tamarind, the beef *rendang*
and the deep-fried eggplant. **$$**

Cherry Garden
5 Raffles Avenue
The Oriental Singapore
Tel: 6331 0538
Imaginative Hunan, Sichuan and
Cantonese dishes served in a
Chinese-style spring courtyard with
timber ceiling. Signature dishes are
marked with a red fan such as the
camphor-smoked duck, lotus leaf-
wrapped chicken and stir-fried
chicken with red pepper and garlic.
Steamed fillet of black cod with
bean crumbs is delicious as is the
mango pudding dessert. **$$$**

Coriander Leaf
The Gallery Hotel, 76 Robertson Quay
Tel: 6732 3354
Housed in a hip avant-garde hotel,
this equally cutting-edge restaurant,
helmed by chef Samia Ahad, dishes
out innovative Mediterranean,
Middle Eastern and Asian fare. If
sufficiently enamoured of the food –
most people are – sign up for the
restaurant's cooking classes.
$$–$$$

Da Paolo e Judie
81 Neil Road
Tel: 6225 8306
Seafood takes precedence in this
sleek and sexy Da Paolo outlet,
housed in a pre-war shophouse.
Their two-storey trattoria, at 80 Club
Street (tel: 6224 7081) is equally
as stylish and well-run. Sames goes
for Da Paolo's Terazza on 44 Jalan
Merah Saga (Holland Village). All

the Da Paolo's branches excel in their antipasti, pasta dishes (taglioni verdi, linguine vongole) and skilfully prepared seafood and meats. **$$$–$$$$**

Duo
38 Club Street
Tel: 6224 4428
As the name suggests, this establishment is perfect for a tête-à-tête. Stylishly decorated featuring 'compartments' for two and a larger dining room, this restaurant has won kudos for its modern French cuisine with clever Asian accents. Attentive staff serve beautifully prepared plates from the kitchen with signature dishes that include oven-roasted duck with sweet potato and cumin mash, and lemongrass and blueberry crème brulee with coconut sorbet. **$$$**

Restaurant Price Guide

A general guide for dinner for two people, excluding beverages.
$$$$ = above US$80
$$$ = US$50–80
$$ = US$30–50
$ = under US$30

East Coast Seafood Centre
1110 East Coast Parkway
A collection of informal, family-type restaurants that fill up on weekends. A good place to gorge on seafood prepared Singapore-style. Cheap unless ordering Sri Lankan crabs. The restaurants here include: **Red House** (tel: 6442 3112); **Jumbo** (tel: 6442 3435); **Lucky View** (tel: 6242 1011); and **New Kheng Luck** (tel: 6241 0291). **$$**

Fatty's Wing Seong
#01-31 Burlington Square
Tel: 6338 1087
Reliably good Cantonese dishes in modest surroundings at reasonable prices. The locals and savvy backpackers swarm here. **$**

Golden Peony
Conrad Centennial Hotel
Temasek Boulevard
Tel: 6334 8888
Refined Cantonese cuisine in intimate and plush surroundings. Delicate dim sum is available at lunchtime. Round off the meal with some silky noodles with crab-meat in a rich broth, and fragrant Chinese tea served in individual lidded cups. At dinner time, classic dishes include minced pigeon served in lettuce cups, and tang-ho leaves cooked with century and salted eggs. **$$$**

Les Amis
#02-16 Shaw Centre, 1 Scotts Road
Tel: 6733 2225
Very chic award-winning restaurant with great wine cellar. Modern French cuisine is exquisitely prepared with attention to freshness and simple, but pure flavours. **$$$$**

Rendezvous Restaurant
Hotel Rendezvous
9 Bras Basah Road
Tel: 6336 0220
Its history stretches six decades but the steamy corner coffee shop is now a comfortable air-conditoned restaurant located in Hotel Rendezvous. Still enduring are its fiery *nasi padang* favourites from fish to vegetable curries and *sambal* (spicy) seafood dishes. **$$**

Saint Pierre
#01-01 Central Mall
3 Magazine Road
Tel: 6438 0887
Named New Restaurant of the Year in 2002, good taste reigns in this cosy eatery – from its shamelessly sleek décor to exquisite modern French cuisine with Japanese accents. **$$$**

The Rice Table
#02-09 International Building
360 Orchard Road
Tel: 6835 3783; also at
43 Cuppage Road
Tel: 6735 9117
One of the very few eateries in town serving the Dutch-Indonesian *rijsttafel*; the individual dishes making up the meal are also available à la carte. **$$**

The Tandoor
Holiday Inn Park View
Tel: 6733 8333
Romantic ambience in a golden glow with soft music playing as diners enjoy their meal. The crab *lababdar* gets rave reviews as does the tandoori chicken and grilled king prawns. **$$$**

Culture

The Ministry of Information and the Arts (MITA) has embarked on a programme of making Singapore Southeast Asia's centre of the arts. This was boosted with the recent opening of the excellent The Esplanade – Theatres on the Bay. Check www.esplanade.com for the most current programme.

Buying Tickets

Tickets for all events can either be obtained directly at the various ticket offices or at the ticketing outlets of SISTIC and Ticketcharge.
SISTIC Ticket outlets: Alliance Francaise, Bhaskar's Arts, Bishan Junction 8, Chinese Opera Teahouse, DBS Arts Centre, Downtown East, Singapore Indoor Stadium, Specialists' Shopping Centre, Cold Storage Jelita, Parco Bugis Junction, Parkway Parade, Millenia Walk, Tampines Mall, Victoria Concert Hall, Suntec City Mall, Scotts Shopping Centre, Singapore Conference Hall, Raffles City Shopping Centre, Wisma Atria. Hotline: 6348 5555, fax: 6440 6784, or www.sistic.com.sg
Ticketcharge outlets:
Centrepoint, Century Square, Chijmes, Funan – The IT Mall, Forum – The Shopping Mall, Jurong Point, NTUC Downtown East, Marina Square, Great World City, Tanglin Mall, West Mall, YMS – Waterloo Street. Hotline: 6296 2929, fax: 6296 9897, www.ticketcharge.com.sg.

Art Galleries

Art-2 Gallery
#01-03 MITA Building
140 Hill Street
Tel: 6339 9371
www.art2.com.sg

Art Focus
#05-07 Centrepoint
176 Orchard Road
Tel: 6733 8337

Art Seasons Gallery
5 Gemmill Lane
Tel: 6221 1800
International contemporary art
pieces reside in this new three-
storey gallery.

Plum Blossoms
#01-02 MITA Building
140 Hill Street
Tel: 6339 9768
Collection includes museum-quality
Asian art, Chinese porcelain and
textiles and Vietnamese art.

Notices The Gallery
#01-08 Four Seasons Hotel
Shopping Arcade
190 Orchard Boulevard
Tel: 6734 2070

Singapore Tyler Print Institute
41 Robertson Quay
Tel: 6336 3663
New S$16 million gallery and
teaching facility for artists housed
in a restored warehouse.

Soobin
#01-10 MITA Building
140 Hill Street
Tel: 6837 2777
Specialising in Southeast Asian and
Chinese Art.

The Substation Art Gallery
45 Armenian Street
Tel: 6337 7535
Exhibits experimental, original and
traditional art forms.

Shopping

Where to Buy

ANTIQUES

Exotic treasures from all over the
region can be found in Singapore.
Antique desks, chairs, tables,
vases, statues, mirrors and opium
beds from various regions of China
are just some of the items
available. Many of these pieces are
restored to their original beauty and
reputable dealers can usually
provide certificates of
authentication. Reproduction
furniture also makes an attractive
buy and this is found throughout
Singapore at very reasonable
prices; check **Dempsey Road** and
around **Holland Village**.

Antiques of the Orient
#02-40, Tanglin Shopping Centre,
Tel: 6734 9351.

Kwok Gallery
#03-01, Far East Shopping Centre,
Tel: 6235 2516.

Ming Village
32 Pandan Road,
Tel: 6265 7711.

Ming-Ching Antique House
70 Mohammed Sultan Road,
Tel: 6235 6509.

One Price Store
3 Emerald Hill Road,
Tel: 6734 1680.

The John Erdos Collection
83 Kim Yam Road,
Tel: 6735 3307.

ARTS AND CRAFTS

Lims Arts and Living
#02-01, Holland Village Shopping
Centre, Tel: 6467 1300.

Ming Village
(porcelain) 32 Pandan Road,
Tel: 6265 7711.

Renee Hoy Fine Arts
#01-44, Tanglin Shopping Centre,
Tel: 6235 1596.

CAMERAS

Singapore is one of the best places
in Southeast Asia for the duty-free
purchase of leading camera brands.
Peninsular Plaza and the Peninsular
Hotel's shopping arcade, both on
Coleman Street, are the local and
professional's favourite places for
buying cameras and camera
equipment. They have a dozen well-
stocked shops between them.

Albert Photo
#01-16, Orchard Tower,
Tel: 6235 2815.

Alley Photo
#03-39/40 Centrepoint,
Tel: 6235 6666;
#03-10 Raffles City Shopping
Centre, Tel: 6338 7755.

Cathay Photo Store
Peninsular Paza, Tel: 6338 0451;
Marina Square, Tel: 6339 6188.

CARPETS

The selection of Oriental carpets
extends from tribal rugs to exquisite
silk on silk carpets with glorious
colours and intricate designs. The
carpets may come from China,
India, Pakistan, Iran or Turkey, each
with its distinctive style.

Amir & Sons
#03-01/07, Lucky Plaza,
Tel: 6734 9112.

Hassan's Carpet
#03-01/06, Tanglin Shopping
Centre, Tel: 6737 5626.

Mohammad Akhtar Carpets
#02-27, Tanglin Shopping Centre,
Tel: 6737 0027.

Qureshi's Carpets
#05-12, Centrepoint,
Tel: 6235 1523.

CHINESE MEDICINE

A visit to an emporium selling
tradtional Chinese medicinal herbs
is worthwhile – even if you're not ill!

Eu Yan Sang
269 South Bridge Road,
Tel: 6223 6333.
Thye Shan Medical Hall
201 New Bridge Road,
Tel: 6223 1326.

COMPUTERS

Funan Centre, 109 North Bridge Road and **Sim Lim Square**, 1 Rochor Canal Road, are two shopping centres packed with numerous computer stores.

GOLD AND JEWELLERY

Bvlgari
#01-08, Hilton Hotel Shopping Gallery, Tel: 6737 1652.
Je t'aime
Ngee Ann City, Tower B #02-12C/D,
Tel: 6734 2275.
Larry Jewellery
#01-38, Raffles City,
Tel: 6336 9648;
#01-10 Paragon, Tel: 6732 3222.
Little India Goldsmiths
Blk 664 Buffalo Road,
Tel: 6294 5000.
Poh Heng
27-28 North Canal Road,
Tel: 6533 3333;
#01-17 People's Park Complex,
Tel: 6535 9127.
Swarovski Crystal
#01-20 Raffles Hotel Arcade,
Tel: 6338 0171.
Tiffany
#01-05, Raffles Hotel,
Tel: 6334 0168;
Unit 5/6, Ngee Ann City Tower B,
Tel: 6735 8823.
Lee Hwa
#B1-30, Wisma Atria,
Tel: 6736 0266.
Tian Po
#01-43/46 Centrepoint,
Tel: 6235 1889.

SILK

Asher Fabrics
119 Arab Street, Tel: 6293 6892.
China Silk House
#02-11/13, Tanglin Shopping

Department Stores

Daimaru
#04-10, Liang Court,
Tel: 6339 1111.
Isetan
Wisma Atria Shopping Centre,
Tel: 6733 7777.
Shaw Centre, Tel: 6733 1111.
John Little
Specialists Shopping Centre,
Tel: 6737 2222.
Metro
Paragon, Tel: 6835 3322.
Marina Square, Tel: 6333 3322.
Mustafa Centre
145 Syed Alwi Road,
Tel: 6295 5855.
OG Departmental Store
224/228 Orchard Road,
Tel: 6737 4488.
Robinson's
#05-05, Centrepoint,
Tel: 6733 0888;
also at Raffles City Shopping

Centre, Tel: 6235 5020;
#02-01, Centrepoint,
Tel: 6733 0555;
#03-18, Takashima Shopping
Centre, Tel: 6235 3528;
#01-03, Scotts Shopping Centre,
Tel: 6235 4696;
#03-226, Marina Square,
Tel: 6339 8698;
#01-26, Raffles Hotel Shopping
Arcade, Tel: 6336 6663.
Jim Thompson
#01-07 Raffles Hotel Shopping
Arcade, Tel: 6336 5322;
Tower A, 2nd Floor, Takashimaya
Shopping Centre, Tel: 6735 3935.
Malaya Silk Store
#01-01/02, Orchard Shopping
Centre, Tel: 6235 2467.

WATCHES

All Watches
#B1-128, Lucky Plaza,
Tel: 6732 7673.
City Chain Stores
#02-130 Marina Square,
Tel: 6339 3878;
#01-03 Centrepoint Shopping
Centre, Tel: 6235 3370;
#01-31 Raffles City Shopping

Centre, Tel: 6216 8388.
Marks & Spencer
Levels 1 & 2 Centrepoint,
Tel: 6734 1800;
also within Robinsons at Raffles
City Shopping Centre,
Tel: 6339 9013;
B1 & B2 Wheelock Place,
Tel: 6733 8122;
#03-22 Paragon,
Tel: 6732 9732.
Takashimaya
391 Orchard Road, Ngee Ann City,
Tel: 6738 1111.
Tangs
320 Orchard Road,
Tel: 6737 5500.
Yue Hwa
70 Eu Tong Sen Street,
Tel: 6538 4222.
Renovated building now full of
authentic Chinese traditional
products. Open daily 11am–10pm.

Centre, Tel: 6339 4277.
Dickson
#01-05 Centrepoint Shopping
Centre, Tel: 6734 5822;
#01-001 Suntec City,
Tel: 6336 4871.
The Hour Glass
#01-36A, Lucky Plaza,
Tel: 6733 1262;
#01-02, Ngee Ann City,
Tel: 6734 2420;
#01-01 Peninsula Plaza,
Tel: 6337 8309;
#01-09/11 Scotts Shopping
Centre, Tel: 6235 7198.
Rolex
#01-01, Tong Building, 302 Orchard
Road, Tel: 6737 9033.
Sincere Fine Watches
#01-22, Lucky Plaza,
Tel: 6737 4593;
#01-12, Ngee Ann City Tower B,
Tel: 6733 0618;
#01-013 Suntec City Mall,
Tel: 6337 5150.
Watches of Switzerland
#01-09, Scotts Shopping Centre,
Tel: 6737 3708.

Getting Acquainted

The Place

Situation Over a distance of around 5,000 km (3,100 mi), the 17,508 Indonesian islands (6,000 of which are inhabited) are dotted from the Asian mainland down into the Pacific Ocean.

Area Though the total area (sea and land) is about 2.5 times greater than Australia, the land area is just 2 million sq km (770,000 sq miles), a bit larger than Queensland. Java is approximately 130,000 sq km (50,000 sq miles).

Population 220 million, rising by nearly 2 percent per year. Java is the most densely populated island, with almost 115 million inhabitants, twice the population density of the UK. Over 60 percent of Indonesians live on Java and Bali, although they account for only 8 percent of the nation's landmass.

Languages The national language is Bahasa Indonesian, similar to Malay, but most Indonesians also speak one of over 580 local languages and dialects.

Religion 87% Muslim, with small numbers of Hindus, Buddhists and Christians.

Time zones Indonesia's considerable spread covers three time zones. Java, Sumatra and West and Central Kalimantan are on Western Indonesia Standard Time, 7 hours ahead of GMT. Bali, Lombok, East and South Kalimantan, Sulawesi, Nusa Tenggara and West Timor are on Central Indonesian Standard Time, 8 hours ahead of GMT (the same time zone as Singapore and Hong Kong). Maluku and West Papua (Irian Jaya) are on Eastern Indonesia Standard Time, at GMT plus 9 hours.

Currency *Rupiah* (rp).
Weights and Measures Metric.
Electricity Mainly 220V using rounded two-pin plugs, but in some places 110V. Electricity is expensive and small hotels operate on 25-watt bulbs, so light can be quite dim at night! Power cuts are frequent in rural areas.
International Dialling Code 62.

Climate

All of the archipelago's islands lie within the tropical zone, and the surrounding seas have a homogenising effect on temperatures and humidity. Consequently, local factors like topography, altitude and rainfall produce more variation in climate than latitude or season. Mean temperatures at sea level vary by only a few degrees throughout the region (25–28°C, or 77–82°F). In the mountains, however, the temperature decreases about 1°C (2°F) for every 200 metres (650 ft) of altitude, which makes for a cool, pleasant climate in upland towns like Java's Bandung and Sumatra's Bukittinggi.

Much of the archipelago also lies within the equatorial ever-wet zone, where no month passes without several inches of rainfall. The northeast monsoon means that many islands receive drenching precipitation between November and April. Moreover, the tropical sun and the oceans combine to produce continuously high humidity everywhere. Due to local wind patterns, a few places like Bogor in West Java receive as much as 400 cm (157 in) of rain annually.

The southeast monsoon tends to counteract this generally high humidity by blowing hot, dry air up from over the Australian landmass between May and October. Although much depends upon local topography, on most islands this produces a dry season of markedly reduced precipitation, and as one moves south and eastward in the archipelago, the influence of this desiccating dry monsoon increases.

Business Hours

Government offices 8am–3pm weekdays, except Friday when they close at 11.30am. On Saturdays, they are often open until around 2pm.
Business offices weekdays 8–9am until 4 or 5pm. Some companies work Saturday mornings as well. **Banks** 8am–3pm on weekdays, and sometimes on Saturday mornings. Foreign banks are closed on Saturdays.

Public Holidays

Many public holidays are based on different lunar dates and change yearly.

January 1	New Year's Day
January/February	Lunar New Year (Tahun Baru Imlek)
March/April	Nyepi (Hindu New Year, day after new moon)
	Good Friday (Friday preceding Easter)
April/May	Ascension of Jesus (40 days after Easter)
May (full moon)	Waisak (Birth, enlightenment and death of Buddha)
August 17	National Independence Day
December 25	Christmas Day
Variable dates	Hijriyah (Islamic New Year)
	Ma'ulud (Birthday of the Prophet Muhammad)
	Isra Mi'raj (Ascension of the Prophet Muhammad)
	Idul Fitri (End of the Muslim fasting month)
	Idul Adha (Muslim day of sacrifice)

Planning the Trip

Visas & Passports

All travellers to Indonesia must be in possession of a passport valid for at least six months after arrival and with proof (tickets) of onward passage. Many nationalities do not require a visa prior to arrival; for those that do, tourist visas can be easily obtained from any Indonesian embassy or consulate.

Health

Yellow fever vaccinations are required if you arrive within six days of leaving or passing through an infected area. Check with your physician regarding vaccinations for other ailments such as typhoid, cholera and hepatitis A and B.

Check if you will be travelling in a malaria-infected area (not all of Indonesia is). Minimise contact with mosquitoes with repellent; and as mosquitoes are most active around dawn and dusk, wear long-sleeved shirts and long pants at those times. Sleep under a mosquito net in infected areas. All bites and cuts can easily become infected in the tropics; treat them immediately.

Dengue fever, carried by daytime mosquitoes, is far more prevalent in Indonesia than malaria is. There is no prophylactic; take the precautions described above if travelling in an infected area.

Healthcare is variable in Indonesia. Although some cities such as Jakarta have western-standard hospitals, the poor level of sanitation and health provisions in less populated areas means that it is essential to arrange health insurance before you travel.

Particular care should be taken with water. Most Indonesian tap water is undrinkable and could make you extremely ill. Bottled water is widely available.

Street food may be highly risky, and you should avoid salads and make sure you peel fruit.

Money Matters

Indonesia's national currency, the *rupiah*, comes in bank note denominations of 100,000, 50,000; 20,000; 10,000; 5,000; 1,000; 500 and 100. Coins come in 1,000, 500, 100, 50 and 25 rupiahs.

Changing money: Bring only new notes (no coins), as practically no one will change dirty or torn bank notes. The best exchange rate is usually obtained at money-changers, found at the airports of all major cities. Hotels usually offer a lower rate, and banks often offer even worse rates.

It is advisable to change most currencies in the cities. Rupiah may be freely converted to foreign currencies when leaving.

If you are travelling around Indonesia, it is wisest to bring US dollars and American Express traveller's cheques. Banks in many smaller towns are not necessarily conversant with all foreign bank notes and some do not even accept traveller's cheques.

Larger shops, hotels and restaurants accept credit cards, and you can get cash advances in banks in the main cities. But in remoter areas you are unlikely to be able to use your plastic.

What to Wear/Bring

Light, loose clothing is most practical in Indonesia's tropical climate. Etiquette requires that you reserve shorts and scanty tops for the beach only, as Muslim Indonesians expect a high standard of modesty.

Sunblock, sunglasses and a sun hat are essential, and a light raincoat or waterproof is advisable as no month passes by without some rain.

Although you can get hold of most things in Indonesia if you run out, you may have difficulty finding tampons and shaving foam, so bring a good supply. And you may wish to pack a torch as power cuts are frequent and less expensive hotels use low-wattage lighting to save on electricity bills, so bring a torch or nightlight if you like things brighter.

Getting There

BY AIR

International flights, with a few exceptions, arrive either at **Sukarno-Hatta International Airport**, 20 km (13 miles) west of Jakarta, or **Ngurah Rai Airport**, near Denpasar on Bali.

A highway links Sukarno–Hatta airport with Jakarta. Buses operate at regular intervals to Gambir, itself the location of a railway station and only a few minutes by road from the city.

A majority of visitors arrive in Jakarta from Singapore. Garuda and Singapore Airlines have multiple daily flights between the two destinations. Other flights from within the region include daily flights from Kuala Lumpur in Malaysia on Garuda and MAS. Flights from Hong Kong are served by Garuda and Cathay Pacific. Thai International and Royal Brunei fly from their home capitals to Bali. There are flights from Japan on Garuda and from Taiwan on Garuda and EVA Air. In Australia, Qantas and Garuda fly from Perth, Sydney, Melbourne, Cairns and Adelaide.

BY SEA

Luxury cruise lines offer fly/cruise arrangements that allow you to fly to Bali and other ports, then catch a ship on the way home, or vice versa. Contact a travel agent to see who is presently offering Indonesia as part of their itinerary.

If travelling with footloose budget travellers, you can hop on a ferry leaving **Tanah Merah Ferry Terminal** in Singapore for **Tanjung Pinang,** where you can catch one of PELNI's (Indonesia's national shipping line) several passenger ships serving Indonesia's main ports. Contact **Bintan Resort Ferries** (tel: (65) 6542 4369) for timetables and tickets.

Packages are also available from tour agencies that include the boat ride from Singapore, the transfer from Tanjung Pinang to the PELNI ship by sampan, and accommodation on board according to the class booked. Food and drinks can be purchased on board but may be costly. It is an unforgettable two-day trip across the Java Sea. It is advisable to leave Singapore two days before the ship departs and spend time on Tanjung Pinang. Cabins must be booked one to two weeks in advance. Deck class can be obtained at short notice.

Practical Tips

Media

Newspapers and magazines

There are two daily newspapers in English: *The Jakarta Post* and the *Indonesian Observer*. In addition, most international newspapers – English-language and others – are available in hotel newsstands. Business magazines published in English include *Indonesia Business Weekly*, *Economic Business Review Indonesia*, *Indonesian Quarterly*, and *Products & Industry*.

Several publications with listings of city events and restaurants are available, including *Jakarta Now* and *What's On*. These are usually available in hotels and other tourist-related locations.

Television

Television is available everywhere, even in the most remote locations. Larger hotels have cable TV, so in addition to Indonesian channels, they receive CNN, HBO, MTV and the like. They tend to be tuned to the two main Indonesian channels, however, operated by Televisi Republik Indonesia.

Useful Numbers

● **Bali Tourist Assistance** (0361) 228 996/231 443 (operated by the tourist office, open 24 hours a day)
● **Ambulance** 118
● **Fire** 113
● **Police** 110
● **International directory enquiries** 102
● **International operator** 101
● **Local operator** 100

Trouble Spots

Although Indonesia has usually been a safe country for travellers, the recent political unrest means you should exercise caution.

Contact your own ministry of foreign affairs to keep yourself informed of the current situation and avoid travel to trouble spots such as Kalimantan (Borneo), Maluku, some parts of West Papua (Irian Jaya), West Timor and other strife-prone areas.

Postal Services

Post is slow from Indonesia. If you're sending a letter or parcel, it's usually worth paying for registered post, which is faster. Staff usually expect to see the contents of parcels before you seal them. Post offices are generally open 8am–2pm Monday to Thursday 8am–noon Friday; main branches in larger cities may not close until 8pm and may operate on Saturday mornings 8–1pm.

Telecommunications

Telephone services are rapidly being modernised and overhauled, particularly in urban areas. As the phone system is brought into the 21st century, however, telephone numbers are often changed, especially in Jakarta and other urban areas.

If a number listed in this guide doesn't work, most probably it has been upgraded – and changed. (From 1994 to 1999, five million telephone lines were installed – an ambitious project considering that only 900,000 lines were put in between 1968 and 1988.)

Moreover, most hotels have several different telephone lines, obtained at different times – in Jakarta, some of them are six digits, others seven. Thus, comparisons of listings never seem to match one another. The telephone and fax numbers in this book are as accurate as possible,

Medical Emergencies

● **Health Information Hotline**
0900 1200 MWF
Tel: (021) 754 5486/5488
ext 1424
● **Ambulance (SOS Medika)**
Tel: (021) 750 6001

but they may have changed – or will change one day.

Hotels offer international direct dial services, with the usual surcharges. Public telephones often accept telephone cards (these phones seem to work better than coin phones, but can't usually be used to make international calls). International calls can be made at a number of Telkom (the state telecoms company) offices (dial 001 or 008, followed by your country's code, the area code minus the initial 0 and the number). Faxes and telexes can also be sent from Telkom offices.

Medical Treatment

Pharmacies (apotik)
For most minor ailments you should have no problem finding medicines. A full range of drugs is available from pharmacies (which also sell prescription-only medicine over the counter). Some hotels have a drugstore and grocery shops supply drugs in remoter areas.

Most pharmacies are open daily 8am to 6pm, and some also stay open late at night, on Sundays and holidays. In Denpasar they open out of hours on a rota system, which should be pinned in the window of every pharmacy.

Hospitals
Every village in Bali now has a small government clinic called *Puskesmas*, but for major problems, visit one of the hotel clinics or a public hospital in Denpasar. Jakarta has the best hospitals in the country. Although some expatriates living in Indonesia prefer to be flown out to Singapore for medical treatment, the following hospitals and clinics are popular and have English-speaking staff.
SOS Medika (AEA Int'l Clinic)
Jl Puri Sakti 10, Cipete, Jakarta,
Tel: (021) 750 6001.
Medical Scheme
Setiabudi Bldg 11
Jl HR Rasuna Said, Jakarta,
Tel: (021) 525 5367,
Fax: (021) 520 2524.

Security & Crime

Violent crime is a rarity in Indonesia,but pickpocketing and petty theft can be a problem. You are most at risk in crowded places, like tourist spots, buses and trains, and particularly stations. Thieves work skilfully in gangs, and visitors often don't realise they have been robbed at the time. So keep essential valuables like your money and passport in a money belt and

Foreign Embassies

Java
Most foreign embassies are based in Jakarta:
● **Australia**
Jl H.R. Rasuna Said, Kav C,
Tel: (021) 2550 5555.
● **Canada**
1st–5th floor, Wisma Metropolitan I, Jl Jenderal Sudirman, Kav 29,
Tel: (021) 525 0790.
● **United States**
Jl Medan Merdeka Selatan 5,
Jakarta Pusat,
Tel: (021) 344 2211.

never leave luggage unattended. It is often wise to lock your hotel door at night too, and not leave valuables with staff.

It is unusual for a young woman to travel alone in Indonesia, and solo females may have to put up with being pestered by gregarious Indonesian men. However, you will be quite safe as long as you dress and behave modestly.

Tipping

Although tipping is not standard in Indonesia, as elsewhere in Southeast Asia, small gratuities for good service are always welcome. Hotel porters and guides who have shown you round a tourist site will be looking for a few hundred rupiahs, and it is usual to round taxi fares up to the next 500 rp.

Tourist Offices and Useful Websites

The Indonesian Directorate General of Tourism is based in Jakarta. There are many regional offices of varying helpfulness. In tourist spots like Bali and Yogyakarta, they provide excellent information, but in remoter areas literature can be minimal and staff may not even speak English.
Java (Head Office)
Indonesian Directorate General of Tourism, Jl Merdeka Barat 17–19, Jakarta, Tel: (021) 383 8231/4, Fax: (021) 386 0828.

Bali
Denpasar Government Tourist Office, Jl Surapati 7, Denpasar, Tel: (0361) 223602.

Useful Websites
www.indonesia-tourisminfo.com
www.visitindonesia.com
www.indonesia.com
www.asiatravel.com/indonesia
www.tourismindonesia.com
www.indo.com
www.bali-paradise.com
www.balihotels.com

Getting Around

Domestic Air Travel

The domestic airline industry is in a constant state of flux, but even during economic distress, remote airports are extending their runways to accommodate larger aircraft, and airports are being upgraded.

New domestic carriers like Perlita Air, Air Wagon International and Lion Airlines are popping onto the scene, giving Merpati Nusantara, the frequently unreliable national domestic carrier, a run for its money. Therefore, it's better to arrange all domestic flights once you are in Indonesia. The other main airlines are Garuda, Bouraq and Mandala.

Note that in remote areas, flights are not linked to a computerised reservation system, so it's best to purchase tickets in the town itself rather than pre-book them from a larger city.

Reconfirm all domestic flights to make sure they are on schedule. Be sure to get a computer printout with a confirmation number on it. Seats are not always assigned in advance.

Sea Travel

PELNI (Pelayaran Nasional Indonesia), the state-owned shipping company, serves about 30 ports, with each ferry accommodating 1,000–1,500 passengers in four classes. They are basic and often dangerously overloaded.

PELNI tickets can be purchased at their local offices or at travel agencies. Or check www.pelni.co.id for more information. In bad weather, the seas can be quite rough, particularly between Sumatra and Java, between Bali and Lombok, and around Komodo.

Hassles and Harassment

One of the dubious "joys" of staying in Indonesia is the attention you are likely to receive from locals – this is more curiosity than harassment so treat it lightheartedly.

Bali and Java are so acclimatised to tourists that you're less likely to experience this hassle. But in remoter islands, everywhere you go you'll be greeted by "Hello, Meester" (whatever your sex). Indonesians also tend to stare at foreigners, and youngsters will often swarm round. You may find yourself followed by someone who takes curiosity that little bit further.

Local Transport

BY BUS

Buses are the mainstay of local transport on the Indonesian islands. Their quality varies from island to island, from the luxury air-conditioned services on Java and Bali which travel on well maintained roads, to ramshackle tins on wheels rattling on earth roads and spilling over with passengers on some of the tiny islands.

Generally, there are three classes. Top are luxury, air-conditioned buses with TV and toilets. Often they travel during the night when roads are less congested. Available on Bali, Java and Sumatra, these can be booked through travel agents.

Bottom grade (and extremely cheap), transporting locals from village to village, are *ekonomi* – for the robust traveller only. These stop everywhere, are packed and hot and sticky, and you may be sharing your ride with an odd goat or pig. Ask at local bus stations for the next service.

In between, the express buses cover longer distances. Some are little better than *ekonomi*, others are air-conditioned and can be booked ahead at bus stations.

BY PUBLIC MINIBUS (BEMO)

This is the way locals get round cities and travel from town back home to out-of-the-way villages. Most minibuses offer a standard route, however, picking up passengers anywhere on the way. Most carry about 12 people, and are a cheap way of getting from A to B. Expect a lot of luggage too and a fair amount of livestock.

From Jakarta's Airport

The **Sukarno-Hatta International Airport** is 18 km (11 miles) from the city centre, or 45 minutes to 2 hours away – depending on traffic. Terminal 1 is for domestic travel; Terminal 2 handles all international flights, along with all Garuda flights – both domestic and international.

The airport is modern with facilities such as fast-food joints, hotel, and an efficient coupon-based taxi service. Taxi fares to Jakarta town are usually about US$10–15. Purchase a coupon from the taxi counter for door-to-door service. This is the best hassle-free option, ensuring English-speaking personnel, fixed prices and an air-conditioned ride.

You could also hop aboard one of the many DAMRI airport buses which run from 3am–10pm, servicing strategic stops in the city. The air-con buses run every half hour between the city and the airport for a US$5 fare. Travellers heading for the Jalan Jaksa/Kebon Sirih area should alight at Gambir train station.

For information on airport departures and arrivals, call (021) 550-5307/8.

Travelling Around Bali

Balinese roads are a parade ground, used for escorting village deities to the sea, for funeral cremation processions, for filing to the local temple in Sunday best, or for performances of a trans-island *barong* dance.

They are also now very crowded, the volume of traffic having increased dramatically over the past two decades.

In the end, the best way to see Bali is on foot, although one must have sufficient time to hike around the different parts of the island. Away from the busy main roads, the island takes on an entirely different complexion.

Taxis

There is a taxi service from the airport, with fixed prices. Taxis and mini-buses are for hire at every hotel, just with a driver, or with an English-speaking driver/guide. Often there is little difference (other than the price) between renting a car and going on a professionally guided tour, as many drivers speak good English. It is courteous to give the driver some money for his meals if you make a stop to eat. And if you are pleased with his services, a small tip is appropriate.

Rental cars

Driving in Bali is dangerous: the roads are narrow and poorly maintained, and dogs and chickens frequently stray onto them. If a collision occurs, you are responsible for all costs.

Self-drive car hire is available on producing a valid Indonesian or international driving licence, or tourist driving permit from the police station in Renon. Bookings can be made at your hotel or at any of the companies listed below. Mini-vans are a better option. Whichever you choose, do practise defensive driving.

Avis: Jl. Uluwatu No. 84, Jimbaran, Tel: (0361) 701 770.
Norman's: Holiday's Art Shop, Jl. Danau Tamblingan, Sanur, Tel: (0361) 288 328, 288 830.
Nusa Dua Rent-a-Car: Jl. Pantai Mengiat No. 23, (nearby Hotel Bualu), Nusa Dua, Tel: (0361) 771 905.
Toyota: Ngurah Rai Airport, Tel: (0361) 753 744; Jl. Raya Tuban No. 99X, Tel: 751 282. Jl. Bypass Ngurah Rai, Jimbaran, Tel: 701 747.

Public mini-buses/buses

The local system of pick-ups and mini-buses (collectively known as *bemos*) and intra-island buses is efficient and inexpensive. In addition, almost every bemo on the road in Bali may be hired by the trip or by the day; you just tell the driver where you want to go and then agree on a price.

These are four bus/bemo terminals in Denpasar serving points to the south, west, north and east of the city. Rather than taking a taxi from the airport, walk about 1.5 km to the road and catch a local bemo to Kutaor Denpasar. All inter-city buses leave from Suci Terminal on Jl Hasannudin, and the bus companies have their offices here.

Ask at your hotel or the local tourist office about the standard rates, or watch what other passengers are paying, as minibus drivers can inflate rates for unwitting tourists.

Tourist minibuses shuttle between the major tourist areas in Sumatra and Bali. These are smaller (taking seven or eight people) and positively luxurious compared with standard bemos, with more room and air conditioning. Your hotel can book one for pick up at the door.

BY TRAIN

There is an adequate train service in Java, a more limited one in Sumatra, but it's virtually non-existent elsewhere.

In Java, the railway extends from the west (which connects with a ferry to Sumatra) and to the east (this connects with a ferry to Bali).

In Sumatra, there are three rail systems, none of which is linked to the others. In northern Sumatra, a line runs from Medan north to Banda Aceh and south to Rantauprapat. In West Sumatra, a line from Padang runs north to Bukittinggi and Payakumbuh and south to Solok and Lunt. In South Sumatra, the line begins at Tanjung Karang and runs north to Parabumulih, east to Palembang and west to Lubulkinggau.

BY MOTORCYCLE/CAR

These are readily available for rent. Motorcycles are very cheap and a great way to potter round. Hiring a car with driver is recommended.

Negotiate better rates if you are booking a vehicle for a week or longer but note that you are responsible for the driver's food and lodging, and for the petrol.

Where to Stay

Choosing a Hotel

In Jakarta and large cities in Java as well as Bali, hotels range from one to five star. Top-class hotels are luxurious and come with every possible amenity. In fact Bali's resorts are often highly rated in worldwide hotel surveys. Bali's claim to hotel fame is also legendary: it has three super deluxe Aman resorts and two Four Seasons. In more remote places, however, expect only the most basic. With the decline in tourism and a weak rupiah, plenty of bargains are to be found outside of the high season. Note: never accept the first price quoted; ask for a discount or package rates.

Price Guide

A general guide for a standard double room, excluding taxes.
$$$$ = above US$150
$$$ = US$100–150
$$ = US$50–100
$ = under US$50

JAKARTA

Grand Hyatt Jakarta
Jl. Jend M.H. Thamrin
Tel: (021) 390 1234
www.hyatt.com
Considered to be the best in Jakarta, this sophisticated hotel sits above the Plaza Indonesia mall. Excellent service. **$$$$**

Regent
Jl. Rasuna Said
Tel: (021) 252 3456
www.regenthotels.com
Situated in the Merdeka Monument area, this upscale hotel has all the facilities one expects from a Regent

property. Very popular with business people. **$$$$**

Shangri-La
Jl. Jend. Sudirman Kav. 1
Tel: (021) 570 7440
www.shangri-la.com
This 32-storey luxury hotel is centrally located. An excellent Chinese restaurant serves *dim sum* on Sundays, while the popular B.A.T.S. bar is on the first level. **$$$$**

The Dharmawangsa
Jl. Brawijaya Raya, No. 26
Tel: (021) 725 8181
www.dharmawangsa.com
Intimate boutique-style hotel with only 100 rooms, a third of which are suites. A haven of understated luxury, with expensive artworks throughout. The dramatic Sriwijaya restaurant combines Western flair and presentation with local ingredients and traditional Indonesian flavours. **$$$$**

Crowne Plaza Jakarta
Jl. Gatot Subroto
Tel: (021) 526 8833
www.crowneplaza.com
A five-star hotel with the excellent Spanish restaurant, Plaza de Espuma. Includes a 24-hour café and 24-hour business centre. **$$$**

Gran Meliá Jakarta
Jl. Rasuna Said
Tel: (021) 527 3747
www.granmelia.co.id
One of the city's newer five-star hotels and part of the Spanish-run Melia Sol chain. An elegant 428-room hotel with beautiful landscaped gardens. Known for its good Sunday brunch. **$$$**

Arcadia
Jl. Wahid Hasyim No. 114
Tel: (021) 230 0050
e-mail: arcadia@indosat.net.id
This small and interesting hotel of art-deco design is well located and has a good range of services. **$$**

Atlet Century Park
Jl. Pintu 1
Tel: (021) 571 2041
www.centuryhotels.com
Originally built as the athlete's village for the Senayan Sports Complex, and situated in the southwest of the city near the Central Business District. **$$**

Sofyan Cikini
Jl. Cikini Raya 79
Tel: (021) 314 0695
Fax: (021) 310 0432
www.sofyanhotel.com
A small, comfortable hotel that's a taxi ride away from the city centre. The staff is friendly and there is a good range of services. **$$**

Djody
Jl. Jaksa 35
Tel: (021) 390 5976
Situated close to the Medan Merdeka (Freedom Square) and the Gambir train station, this hotel has several small restaurants within walking distance. The rooms are very basic, with fan or air-con but no hot water. **$**

BALI

Sanur

Bali Hyatt
Jl. Danau Tamblingan
Tel: (0361) 281 234
www.hyatt.com
A big hotel with almost 400 rooms, including suites overlooking the sea. It is remarkably breezy and public areas are spacious. Pluses are the clay tennis courts, fabulous gardens and a luxury spa. **$$$**

Besakih Beach Resort
Jl. Danau Tamblingan No. 45
Tel: (0361) 288 423
e-mail: besakih@indosat.net.id
The rooms are set along a meandering garden path that winds gracefully to the sea. **$$**

Segara Village
Jl. Segara Ayu
Tel: (0361) 288 407
www.segaravillage.com
More than 100 private bungalows, a few patterned after traditional rice granaries, arranged in tiny "villages" bordering the sea. There are three swimming pools, and for families, there is a children's recreation room. **$$**

Kuta and Legian

Hard Rock Beach Hotel
Jl. Kuta Beach, Kuta
Tel: (0361) 761 869
www.hardrockhotels.com
The hotel has more than 400

rooms and suites along the beach and has Bali's largest free-form pool, a children's club, and retail outlets. Dining options include Hard Rock Café of course. A great place for families. **$$$**

Legian Beach Hotel
Jl. Melasti, Legian
Tel: (0361) 751 711
www.legianbeachbali.com
217 rooms in a large complex wrapped in a relaxed atmosphere near the beach. **$$**

Poppies Cottages I
Gang Poppies I, Kuta
Tel: (0361) 751 059
www.poppies.net
A selection of well-designed cottages in a beautiful garden that is only 300 metres (328 yards) from the beach. Very popular, so reservations are essential. **$$**

Santika Beach Hotel
Jl. Kartika Plaza, Tuban
Tel: (0361) 751 267
www.santikabali.com
An exquisite 170-room hotel situated on the beach with villa-style rooms and three swimming pools. **$$**

Seminyak

Oberoi Bali
Jl. Laksmana, Petitenget
Tel: (0361) 730 361
www.oberoihotels.com
Located right on the beach, these luxurious rooms and villas have either a sea or garden view and are equipped with satellite TV and stereo systems. A few villas include a private pool. The hotel's coral-rock verandas and villas are adaptations of classic Balinese palace designs. **$$$$**

The Legian
Jl. Kayu Aya, Petitenget
Tel: (0361) 730 622
www.ghmhotels.com
An upscale resort with luxury suites along a wide sandy beach. Architecture combines Balinese design with modern minimalist touches. Pluses are a fine dining restaurant and a spa. Free shuttle to Kuta daily. **$$$$**

Resor Seminyak
Jl. Leksmana, Petitenget
Tel: (0361) 730 814
www.bali-paradise.com/resorseminyak

Moderate hotel facing the beach, with both rooms and cottages. Far from the madding crowds of Kuta. There is a spa, pool and beachside dining. **$$**

Jimbaran

Four Seasons Resort
Jimbaran
Tel: (0361) 701 010
www.fourseasons.com
Built on a terraced hillside amid landscaped gardens, this award-winning resort has a spectacular view of the bay and Gunung Agung. An all-villa resort, each with its own plunge pools. **$$$$**

Bali Inter-Continental
Jl. Uluwatu, Jimbaran
Tel: (0361) 701 888
www.interconti.com
The resort has more than 400 rooms set on 14 hectares (35 acres) of landscaped Balinese gardens and pools on a beautiful beach. An ideal viewing spot for Bali's sunsets. **$$$**

Ritz-Carlton
Jl. Karang Mas Sejahtera, Jimbaran
Tel: (0361) 702 222
www.ritz-carlton-bali.com
This four-storey resort has club rooms and villas and sits perched on a bluff overlooking white-sand beaches and the ocean. There are two pools and a spa. **$$$**

Nusa Dua

Grand Hyatt Bali
P.O. Box 53, Nusa Dua
Tel: (0361) 771 234
www.hyatt.com
One of the most spectacular resorts in Asia. There are four Balinese-style villages with five swimming pools. Huge range of facilities. **$$$$**

Meliá Bali
P.O. Box 88, Nusa Dua
Tel: (0361) 771 510
www.solmelia.com
The newly-renovated rooms are set in lush landscaped gardens. There are also club villas. Facilities include a gym and watersports options and five restaurants. **$$$**

Sheraton Laguna
P.O. Box 77 Kuta, Nusa Dua
Tel: (0361) 771 327
www.sheraton.com

Rooms come with butler service and are set amidst cascading waterfalls and swimming lagoons. A much nicer option than its sister property next door. **$$$**

Ubud

Amandari
Sayan
Tel: (0361) 975 333
www.amanresorts.com
Luxurious isolation within the resort's 30 villas that overlook Sungai Ayung. The main swimming pool (filtered with salt, not chlorine) is modelled after a Balinese rice paddy. Out of this world. **$$$$**

Komaneka Resort
Jl. Monkey Forest
Tel: (0361) 976 090
www.komaneka.com
Very central location but set back from main road so very quiet. Charming bungalows, gardens, pool, restaurant, spa, art gallery and boutique. **$$-$$$**

Campuhan Hotel
Jl. Raya Campuhan
Tel: (0361) 975 368/9
www.tjampuhan.com
The former home of German artist Walter Spies, a major influence among Balinese painters, now comprises 64 bungalows with spectacular views. There is a large spring-fed swimming pool. A 10-minute walk to the centre of Ubud. **$$**

Ulun Ubud
Jl. Sanggingan
Tel: (0361) 975 024, 975-762
www.ulunubud.com
A gem of a hotel with 23 rooms carved out of the hillside. The grounds are filled with art pieces. One of the lower-level pools has stunning views of the paddy fields. It may be some distance from the Ubud town centre but the hotel provides transport. **$$**

Villa Indah
Kedewatan, 4 km (3 miles) from Ubud town
Tel/Fax: (0361) 975 490
Six suites with kitchen and private staff. Your meals are prepared-to-order and served on a wrap-around terrace. Soak in the peaceful view over Sungai Sayan valley. **$**

Where to Eat

What to Eat

The staple for the majority of Indonesians is rice. Coconut milk and hot chillies are popular ingredients in the local cuisine, and dishes can range from very spicy meat, fish and vegetables to those which can be quite sweet. The most popular dishes are *nasi goreng* (fried rice), *satay* (grilled beef or chicken on skewers) and *gado gado* (boiled vegetables in peanut sauce).

Jakarta's eateries offer something for everyone: from fine dining (usually in hotels) to Western-style fast-food joints in shopping malls, and very simple local fare from *warung* (roadside food stalls). Bali too offers a wide mix of cuisines with prices to suit all budgets. The best restaurants are found in the major tourist centres of Ubud, Kuta/Legian/Seminyak, Sanur and to a lesser extent Nusa Dua.

Restaurant Listings

JAKARTA

Café Batavia
Jl. Pintu Besar Utara 14
Tel: (021) 691 5531
A stylish restaurant housed in a 19th-century Dutch heritage building. Good Indonesian and international dishes. **$$$**
Dragon City
Lippo Plaza Podium, Jl. Sudirman
Tel: (021) 522 1933
This popular business-lunch meeting point serves Szechuan seafood delicacies. **$$**
Hazara
Jl. Wahid Hasyim No. 112
Tel: (021) 315 0424
Good North Indian food amid curios

and antiques in an interesting setting. **$$**
Oasis
Jl. Raden Saleh No. 47
Tel: (021) 327 818
A landmark restaurant reminiscent of old-world colonial elegance. The speciality is *rijstafel*, served by waitresses in traditional dress, each carrying a separate dish. **$$$**
Sari Bundo
Jl. H. Juanda 27
Tel: (021) 358 343
One of the best places to try spicy-hot Padang food where several dishes are laid out. **$**
Sriwijaya
The Dharmawangsa
Jl. Brawijaya No. 26
Tel: (021) 725 8181
Very elegant restaurant located in the upmarket Dharmawangsa hotel. The menu features a blend of European and Indonesian dishes like spiced coconut soup and coriander roasted lamb. **$$$**

Restaurant Price Guide

A general guide for dinner for two people, excluding beverages.
$$$ = above US$25
$$ = US$10–25
$ = under US$10

BALI

Sanur
Café Batu Jimbar
Jl. Danau Tamblingan
Tel: (0361) 287 374
Popular with local expats and the business lunch crowd. **$$**
Kul Kul Restaurant
Near the Hyatt
Tel: (0361) 288 038
Has an elegant bar and serves good Western, Indonesian and Chinese. **$$**

Kuta and Legian
Made's Warung
Jl. Pantai, Kuta
Tel: (0361) 755 297
Great food and music go down well with a young and hip crowd. Try the spare ribs, Thai salads and home-made ice cream and yogurt. **$$**

Warung Kopi
Jl. Legian Tengah No. 427
Tel: (0361) 753 602
Decent Indian food, *falafels* and curries and desserts. **$$**

Seminyak
Gateway of India
Jl. Abimanyu (formerly Jl. Dyanapura) No. 10, Legian
Tel: (0361) 732 940
Authentic Indian fare with wonderful *tandoori* dishes. **$**
Kafe Warisan
Jl. Kerobokan Banjar Taman No. 68
Tel: (0361) 731 1175
French and Algerian restaurateurs dish up fresh, light and tasty fare that leans towards French cuisine: pasta, salmon, salads and steaks. **$$$**
La Lucciola
Jl. Laksmana, Petitenget
Tel: (0361) 261 047
The best Mediterranean food served in a big, two-level thatched structure that overlooks the sea. Great for sunset cocktails. **$$**

Nusa Dua and Jimbaran
There are not many options outside of hotel eateries. In **Nusa Dua**, the **Galeria Nusa Dua** shopping complex has a decent selection of restaurants. In **Jimbaran**, beachside dining under the stars is a favourite indulgence. Scores of *warung*-style restaurants offer barbecued seafood. Particularly good is **Ayu Wandira** (tel: (0361) 701-950) where the seafood platter is heaped with chunks of grilled snapper, squid, prawns and a half lobster.

Ubud
Batan Waru Kafé
Jl. Dewi Sita
Tel: (0361) 977 528
Delicious Indonesian and Western cuisine in big portions are served here. Excellent value for money and highly recommended. **$**
Café Wayan
Monkey Forest Road
Tel: (0361) 975 447
Ibu Wayan serves tasty local dishes and also Western specialities in an outdoor garden setting. A longtime favourite with Bali visitors. **$$**

Shopping

What to Buy

JAKARTA

Handicrafts

Pasar Raya at Blok M is the best one-stop shop for the full gamut of Indonesian products. Good, but smaller, are **Sarinah** on Jl. Thamrin and **Keris Gallery** in Menteng. These stores stock everything from baskets, cane chairs, and leather sandals to placemats, paintings, carvings, clothes, toys, and batik.

At the **Jakarta Handicraft Centre**, Jl. Pekalongan No. 12A, there is a large collection of high-quality handicrafts. As most of the merchandise is manufactured for export, the wood will have been treated for climatic changes.

Many of the antique and art shops along **Jl. Kebon Sirih Timur Dalam**, **Jl. Majapahit** and **Jl. Paletehan (Kebayoran)** also sell handicrafts.

Antiques

Although some copies are difficult to detect, there's a better chance of getting a genuine article at reputable dealers who offer refunds.

Gallery 50B: Jl. Ciputat Raya No. 50B. Tel: (021) 749-2850. This place provides a free hotel pickup service for serious buyers.
Cony Art: Jl. Melawai Raya No. 189E (near Blok M). Tel: (021) 720-2844. There are two floors of antique ceramic collections, mainly from Sulawesi.
Johan Art Curio: Jl. Salim No. 59A. Tel: (021) 336 023. It has one of the largest collections of old Chinese porcelains and statues.

Other shops are scattered throughout the city, but especially on **Jl. Kebon Sirih Timur Dalam**, where there are several tiny shops. **Bali**, **Bima**, **Djody** and **Nasrun** are all stocked with old furniture, weavings, masks, puppets and porcelains. Djody is especially well-respected.

The so-called "antique" market on **Jl. Surabaya**, near Embassy Row (Jl. Diponegoro), consists of numerous stalls selling porcelain, puppets, tiles, brass and silver bric-a-brac. Most of it is new but has been made to look old. **Ciputat Village**, at Jl. Ciputat Raya, is a little outside of town, but it's well worth a visit for those interested in larger pieces, such as furniture.

YOGYAKARTA

Silver

Kota Gede, to the southeast of Yogya, is the centre of the silver industry. There are two major workshops, **M.D. Silver** and **Tom's Silver**, and a number of small shops where one can watching the filigree-making process.

Leather Goods

There are many shops on **Jl. Malioboro** selling leather goods and one of the better ones is Toko Setia. For slightly better quality, try **Kusuma**, just off Malioboro, or **Moeljosoehardjo's**, near Taman Sari.

Antiques

If antiques are your passion, head for the many shops that line **Jl. Malioboro**. Also check out the streets to the south and west of the Keraton, and the handful of small shops near the Ambarrukmo Palace Hotel and most of the batik galleries. Among the choice picks are carved and gilded chests for herbal medicines or a pair of *loro blunyo* (seated wedding figures) – traditionally kept in the ceremonial chamber of aristocratic Javanese homes. Elaborately carved Dutch and Chinese teakwood furniture is also interesting, along with covered wedding beds, gilded panels, wicker chairs, massive chests and vanity tables with delicate carvings.

Art

For fine art objects, visit **Affandi** on Jl. Laksda Adisucipto, a large studio-cum-gallery overlooking the river, or the **Indonesia Arts Institute** (ISI) on Jl. Parangtritis to view works by up-and-coming Indonesian artists: paintings, sculptures and handicrafts. ISI is regarded as one of the top art academies in the country.

Puppets

The process of making *wayang kulit* puppets starts with buffalo hide, even if the thin, translucent *kulit* used is not tanned and could more accurately be described as parchment. Try **Ledgar** and **Swasthigita** or **Aris Handicraft** from the shop at Jl. Kauman No. 14.

SURAKARTA (SOLO)

Batik

Solo is known as Batik City and the three largest producers , all with showrooms, are based here: **Batik Keris**, **Batik Semar** and **Batik Danar Hadi**. Danar Hadi has many better quality *kain* and batik shirts. Semar aims at the mass market, with printed batik dresses and shirts. Keris is in between. For the best in Solonese tulis work, visit **Ibu Bei Siswosugiarto** (Sidomulyo is her label) in the south of town. Have a look also at the thousands of pieces for sale in **Pasar Klewer**, and wander the side streets nearby, behind the Grand Mosque, where there are quality producers.
Batik Danar Hadi, Jl. Dr. Rajiman.
Batik Keris, Jl. Yos. Sudarso 37.
Batik Semar (factory showroom), Jl. Pasar Nongko 132. (branch), Jl. R.M. Said 148.
Sidomulyo (Ibu Bei Siswosugiarto), Jl. Dawung Wetan R.T. 53/54.

Antiques

For an idea of what's available in the local antiques market, visit **Pasar Triwindu** market on Jl. Diponegoro: antique brass oil lamps, round marble-top tables with matching chairs, and Chinese wedding beds. Then visit the established shops on Slamet Riyadi and Urip Sumarharjo, where there are all sorts of treasures. These shops are reputable, but do chose carefully and bargain hard. Look in **Eka Hartono** (Jl. Dawung Tengah No. 11/38) or **Mertojo** "Sing Pellet" (Jl. Kepatihan No. 31).

Wayang puppets

The acknowledged centre for *wayang kulit* production in Java is the village of **Manyaran**, about 35 km (21 miles) to the south and west of Solo. Here, the village head organises the village craftsmen and sells their wares at quite reasonable and fixed prices.

Gamelan

To buy a complete *gamelan* orchestra, a single instrument or just to observe these bronze metallophones being cast and forged as they have been for thousands of years – using hand-operated bellows, teakwood charcoal and simple tools – visit the gamelan assembly of **Pak Tentrem Sarwanto**. His family has been suppliers of instruments to the court for generations. Located in the southeast of town: Jl. Ngepung RT 2/RK I, Semanggi.

BALI

Bali is a great place to shop. Hundreds of boutiques and roadside stalls have set up all over the island, and thousands of artisans, craftsmen, seamstresses and painters are busy supplying the tourist trade.

Woodcarvings

You are sure to find good woodcarvings in the shops along the main roads in **Mas** (Ida Bagus Tilem's Gallery and Museum is well known). Also try the villages of **Pujung** (past Tegalalang north of Ubud), **Batuan** and **Jati**. All types of indigenous wood, ranging from the butter-coloured jackwood to inexpensive bespeckled coconut, are sculpted here in bold designs that set the standards for carvers

elsewhere in the archipelago. Wood imported from other islands – buff hibiscus, Javanese teak and black Sulawesian ebony – are also hewn into delicate forms by Balinese craftsmen. Hunt for antique woodcarvings that once adorned gilded temple pavilions or royal palaces, in shops in **Kuta**, **Sanur** and on the main street of **Klungkung**.

Paintings

The artist's centre is **Ubud**, including the villages of **Pengosekan, Penestanan, Sanggingan, Peliatan, Mas** and **Batuan**. The famous **Neka Museum** and the **Puri Lukisan Museum**, both in Ubud, will give an idea of the range of styles and artistry achieved by the best painters. Then visit some of the other galleries in the area: **Gallery Munut, Oka Kartini Art Gallery, Gallery Agung** and the gallery of the **Pengosekan Community of Artists**. Examples from every school of painting in Bali are found here, as well as canvasses of young artists portraying festivals and dancers.

For quality works of art, seek out the gallery-homes of well known artists in Ubud such as **Antonio Blanco, Hans Snel, Wayan Rendi, Arie Smit** and the late, great **I Gusti Nyoman Lempad**. In other villages, seek out **Mokoh** and **I Made Budi** (Batuan).

For traditional astrological calendars and *iderider* – long strips of cotton that are suspended from the eaves of shrines during temple ceremonies – paintings in the so called *wayang* style, visit **Kamasan**, just south of Klungkung. This style has been around for many centuries and some of the paintings are antique. Examples are found in **Klungkung** and in many antique shops.

Stone Carvings

For traditional sandstone carvings, stop at the workshops in **Batubulan**. And **Wayan Cemul**, an Ubud stone carver with an international following, has a house full of his own creations. Also try **Ida Bagus Tilem Carver**, in Ubud.

Textiles

For batik clothing, try the many boutiques in **Kuta Beach**. Brocades that gleam like gold lame, and also the simpler, hand-loomed *sarung* cloths, are sold in every village. **Gianyar** is the home of the hand-loom industry, but the villages of **Blayu, Sideman, Mengwi, Batuan, Gelgel, Tengganan** and **Ubud** all produce their own style of weavings.

Gold and Silver

The centres for metal working are **Celuk** and **Kamasan**, where all such ornaments are on sale at reasonable prices. **Kuta** is another centre for export gold and silver wares. For traditional Balinese jewellery, visit the shops on Jl. Sulawesi and Jl. Kartini in Denpasar.

Antiques

Be careful when buying antiques: there's no guarantee of the actual age of the items: intricately carved doors, ornate wedding beds, ceremonial daggers, colonial-style lamps, masks and textiles. Chinese ceramics and sculptures from many parts of Indonesia and China are also available to the discriminating buyer. The antique shops adjacent to the Kerta Gosa in Klungkung house collections of rare Chinese porcelain pieces, with old Kamasan *wayang*-style paintings, antique jewellery and Balinese weavings. Prices are reasonable. On the main streets of Singaraja are a few of the best antique shops in Bali.

Ceramics

Jenggala Keramik in Jimbaran is a good source for tea sets, dinnerware and vases. In Sanur, **Pesamuan Studio** has outlets at One World Gallery on Jalan Hanoman in Ubud, Warung Made II on Jalan Raya Seminyak, and at its factory at Jalan Pungutan No. 25, Sanur.